Explaining Decisions in the European Union

Explaining outcomes of decision-making at the European level has occupied scholars since the late 1950s, yet analysts continue to disagree on the most important factors in the process. Arne Niemann examines the interplay of the supranational, governmental and non-governmental actors involved in EU integration, along with the influence of domestic, supranational and international structures. This book restates and develops neofunctionalism – the most widely discussed and criticised integration theory as an approach for explaining decisions in the European Union and assesses the usefulness of the revised neofunctionalist framework on three case studies: the emergence and development of the PHARE programme, the reform of the Common Commercial Policy, and the communitarisation of visa, asylum and immigration policy. Niemann argues that this classic theory can be modified in such a way as to draw on a wider theoretical repertoire and that a number of micro-level concepts can sensibly be accommodated within his revised neofunctionalist framework.

ARNE NIEMANN is lecturer in European Integration Studies and International Relations at the University of Amsterdam. He has published articles in the *Journal of European Public Policy* and *International Negotiation* and is the editor of *Herausforderungen an die deutsche und europäische Außenpolitik: Analysen und Politikempfehlungen* (2005).

Explaining Decisions in the European Union

Arne Niemann

CAMBRIDGE
UNIVERSITY PRESS

CAMBRIDGE UNIVERSITY PRESS
Cambridge, New York, Melbourne, Madrid, Cape Town, Singapore, São Paulo

Cambridge University Press
The Edinburgh Building, Cambridge CB2 2RU, UK

Published in the United States of America by Cambridge University Press,
New York

www.cambridge.org
Information on this title: www.cambridge.org/9780521864053

First published 2006

Printed in the United Kingdom at the University Press, Cambridge

A catalogue record for this book is available from the British Library

ISBN-13 978-0-521-86405-3 hardback
ISBN-10 0-521-86405-4 hardback

Cambridge University Press has no responsibility for the persistence or accuracy
of URLs for external or third-party internet websites referred to in this book, and
does not guarantee that any content on such websites is, or will remain, accurate
or appropriate.

To my parents: Rita and Rudi

Contents

Tables

Acknowledgements

This book has come about in two stages. The first step was the completion of my PhD at the University of Cambridge – including a period as Visiting Researcher at the European University Institute in Florence and a placement at the Council Secretariat in Brussels. After a two-year stint in the private sector, I resumed my academic career at the University of Dresden where I completed this manuscript before taking up the lectureship at the University of Amsterdam.

I would like to thank numerous people, who commented on different parts and aspects of this study. Particularly, David Allen, Predrag Aramovic, Alexandra Bensch, Martin Dahl, Geoffrey Edwards, Adrienne Héritier, Demos Ioannou, Jan Ole Kiso, Patrick Leblond, Walter Mattli, Sonia Mazey, Fernando Perreau de Pinninck, Thomas Risse, Jeremy Richardson, Philippe Schmitter, Julie Smith, Charlotte Warakaulle and two anonymous reviewers have all given valuable feedback at various stages of this project. Special thanks go to Geoffrey Edwards, my PhD supervisor, for his patience in reading many drafts of my work, the very constructive criticisms he provided, his continuous encouragement and great humour!

This book has also benefited from a number of seminars and conference presentations over the years, including the Seminar Series on Comparative Case Studies at the European University Institute, the European Affairs Research Seminars at the Centre of International Studies in Cambridge, the 2nd UACES Research Conference in Loughborough, the 22nd British International Studies Association Conference in Leeds, the 46th International Studies Association Conference in Hawaii and the 9th European Union Studies Association Conference in Austin.

As my analysis is, to a considerable degree, concerned with what is implicit, rather than explicit, about EU decision-making, a substantial part of the information had to be gathered from interviews. I wish to thank the over 120 officials at the various EU institutions, Permanent Representations, national ministries, NGOs and other organisations in Brussels, London, Bonn, Berlin and Geneva, who took the time to share their knowledge and views with me. I am very grateful to my former colleagues at the Council Secretariat who, during a four-months *stage*, gave me the opportunity to attend a large number of Council committee and working group meetings, which allowed me to gain precious insights as a participant observer.

I would also like to express my gratitude to the British Council, the Kurt Hahn Trust, the Cambridge European Trust and Pembroke College for their generous financial support at different stages of the project. Many thanks also to Sarah Ganter and Stephan Petzold for their competent research assistance, and my colleagues at the chair of international politics in Dresden, and particularly Monika Medick-Krakau, for providing an open ear at all times. I would also like to thank John Haslam of Cambridge University Press for his valuable advice.

Finally, I want to thank my friends and family, and above all my parents, Rita and Rudi, who have been a great source of support and encouragement throughout the entire process!

Abbreviations

ACP	Africa–Caribbean–Pacific
BDA	Federation of German Employers' Associations (Bundesvereinigung der Deutschen Arbeitgeberverbände)
BDI	Federation of German Industry (Bundesverband der Deutschen Industrie)
CAP	Common Agricultural Policies
CCP	Common Commercial Policy
CDU	Christian Democratic Union
CEEC	Central and Eastern European Countries
CFSP	Common Foreign and Security Policy
COREPER	Committee of Permanent Representatives
DG	Directorate-General
EBRD	European Bank of Reconstruction and Development
EC	European Community
ECJ	European Court of Justice
ECR	European Court Reports
ECSC	European Coal and Steel Community
ECU	European Currency Unit
EEC	European Economic Community
EFTA	European Free Trade Association
EIB	European Investment Bank
EMS	European Monetary System
EMU	Economic and Monetary Union
EP	European Parliament
EPC	European Political Cooperation
ERM	Exchange Rate Mechanism
ERT	European Roundtable of Industrialists
ERTA	Case 22/70 *Commission v. Council*
ESDP	European Security and Defence Policy
ETUC	European Trade Union Federation
EURATOM	European Atomic Energy Community

FDI	Foreign Direct Investment
FEACO	Federation Européenne d'Association de Conseil d'Organisation
G7	Group of Seven
G24	Group of Twenty-Four
GATS	General Agreement on Trade in Services
GATT	General Agreement on Tariffs and Trade
IAEA	International Atomic Energy Agency
IGC	Intergovernmental Conference
ILO	International Labour Organization
IMF	International Monetary Fund
IPRs	Intellectual property rights
ITA	Information Technology Agreement
JHA	Justice and Home Affairs
MECU	Million ECU (European Currency Unit)
MEP	Member of European Parliament
NATO	North Atlantic Treaty Organisation
NGO	Non-governmental organisation
NIS	New Independent States
OECD	Organization for Economic Co-operation and Development
OJ	Official Journal
PHARE	Poland and Hungary: Aid for Restructuring of the Economies
QMV	Qualified majority voting
SEA	Single European Act
SEM	Single European Market
TACIS	Technical assistance for the Commonwealth of Independent States
TEC	Treaty Establishing the European Community
TEU	Treaty on European Union
TPEG	Twinning Programme Engineering Group
TREVI	Terrorism, Radicalism, Extremism and Political Violence
TRIMS	Trade-Related Investment Measures
TRIPS	Trade-Related Intellectual Property Rights
UNICE	Union des Confédérations de l'Industrie et des Employeurs d'Europe
UR	Uruguay Round
WIPO	World Intellectual Property Organization
WTO	World Trade Organization

Introduction

This book seeks to explain outcomes of EU decision-making. It aims at identifying the factors most relevant for such explanation. For this purpose, the study analyses the interplay of the various supranational, governmental and non-governmental actors involved in decision-making along with supranational, domestic and international structures influencing the process. In the last decade many researchers have shifted their attention to questions such as the nature of the EU political system, the social and political consequences of the integration process and the normative dimension of European integration. However, the issue of explaining outcomes of EU decision-making, which has occupied scholars since the 1950s, is still a very important one. The ongoing salience of this question partly stems from the continuing disagreement among analysts as regards the most relevant factors accounting for the dynamics and standstills of the European integration process and certain segments of it. In addition, this question is of particular interest since the integration process is moving into areas which are commonly referred to as 'high politics', spheres that some researchers had factored out of their theories.

Political processes cannot be viewed in a theoretical vacuum since our analysis is always based on certain assumptions and concerns. Hence, empirical findings are always inspired by some theoretical perspective, perhaps without the researcher being aware of it. Theoretical frameworks structure our observations and are useful in terms of choosing variables and collecting data for conducting empirical research.[1] In the past decade European integration theory has become a growth industry among scholars focusing on the European Union. Yet, the object of investigation and the research question considerably limit the choice of theory. Most approaches devised for the study of the European Union or regional integration more generally are not applicable for my purpose.[2]

---

[1] See e.g. King *et al.* (1994: ch. 1).

[2] The next paragraph draws on Wiener and Diez (2004: 241). I largely share the authors' categorisation. However, a clear-cut classification along the functions of 'explanatory/ understanding', 'analytical/descriptive' and 'critical/normative' and along the areas of

For example, some of the more recent theorising does not share my focus on seeking to *explain* outcomes. Instead, they aim at *describing* or at *providing a normative or critical perspective*, like federalist, gender/critical perspectives or part of legal theorising and discourse analysis.[3] In addition, along the triad of *polity*, *politics* and *policy*, my analysis primarily focuses on the former two, polity and politics. The area of *polity* mainly involves the explication of certain institutional changes. The *politics* dimension deals with the impact of certain (groups of) actors on outcomes and the style of how decisions are reached. The *policy* (i.e. content of a policy) dimension of my study is relevant only in so far as policy changes influence the strength and scope of the EU polity and certain political actors and processes. My focus on polity and politics renders policy network analysis and the explanatory variants of discourse analysis, which are more geared towards the policy dimension, less plausible as a theoretical choice. New institutionalism (in its rational choice, historical and sociological variants) does share an interest in the politics dimension, but less so as regards polity, and thus does not seem an ideal choice either. Governance theory, which is sometimes viewed as a catch-all theory, arguably also does not have its core competencies at explaining outcomes along the polity/politics dimension. Only few theories, such as neofunctionalism, (liberal) intergovernmentalism and, to a lesser extent, fusion theory, operate at the nexus of explaining, on the one hand, and the interface of polity and politics, on the other hand.[4]

In this study, neofunctionalism has been chosen as a point of departure. This is only partly due to the restricted choice of theoretical endeavours that tend to have their core competencies in my research problem area. My prior research has indicated the general usefulness of neofunctionalist insights concerning this type of inquiry.[5] Moreover, it suggests that several of the criticisms that were levelled against the theory were either exaggerated or unjustified, that the theory has been misread by a number of authors, and that it is possible to draw on a wider neofunctionalist theoretical repertoire than the one commonly

---

'polity', 'policy' and 'politics' is not always possible. These categorisations are thus merely meant to reflect tendencies.

[3] On federalist theory see e.g. Pinder (1986); on gender perspectives see e.g. Mazey (2000); on 'critical' discourse analysis see e.g. Derrida (1992).

[4] On policy network analysis see e.g. Peterson and Bomberg (1999); on the explanatory variant of discourse analysis see e.g. Diez (1999); on new institutionalism of the various types see e.g. Aspinwall and Schneider (2001a, 2001b); on governance theory see e.g. Jachtenfuchs (2001); on the fusion approach see e.g. Wessels (1997); on liberal intergovernmentalism see e.g. Moravcsik (1993, 1998). Various important neofunctionalist works will be introduced below.

[5] See Niemann (1996, 1998, 2000) for earlier stages of my research on this question.

perceived. In addition, my previous work indicates that neofunctionalism is best understood as a dynamic theory[6] – due to its inherent propensity for self-reflection as well as the time sensitivity of several neofunctionalist assumptions made almost five decades ago – and that many of the more recent micro-level concepts can sensibly be accommodated within the larger neofunctionalist framework[7]. The apparent possibility of developing and modifying neofunctionalism in a meaningful way was in stark contrast to the general lack of enthusiasm in the scholarly community to use, revive or revise neofunctionalist theory.[8] This discrepancy puzzled and encouraged me to undertake a more comprehensive investigation into the state and validity of neofunctionalism and the possibility of revising it. Apart from specifying and modifying neofunctionalist theory, this book also aims at testing the revised neofunctionalist hypotheses set out in Chapter 1.

The revised neofunctionalist framework has been tested on three case studies: first, the Poland and Hungary: Aid for Restructuring of the Economies (PHARE) programme which originated from the G7 summit in July 1989, when heads of government decided to give the mandate for the Western aid effort to the Commission. This task has subsequently led to the development of the Community's own aid initiative, the PHARE programme, which subsequently turned into an important part of the EU's pre-accession strategy for integrating the Central and Eastern European Countries (CEEC) into the Union. The second case study is concerned with Treaty revision in the area of the Common Commercial Policy (CCP). The main focus lies at the 1996/97 IGC negotiations on the reform of the external trade policy and is complemented by an analysis of negotiations concerning the IGC 2000 as well as the Convention and IGC 2003/04. The final case study traces the negotiations concerning the communitarisation of visa, asylum and immigration policy at the Intergovernmental Conferences leading to the Treaties of Amsterdam and Nice and the Constitutional Treaty. This case again primarily concentrates on the IGC 1996/97 but also takes the last two Treaty revisions duly into account.

My case studies have been chosen on empirical, theoretical and methodological grounds. Empirically, the above make for interesting cases.

---

[6] On this point, see also Rosamond (2005: esp. 247ff).

[7] See Niemann (1998).

[8] Only recently has there been renewed interest in neofunctionalist theorising. See e.g. JEPP Special Issue (2005), which paid tribute to Ernst Haas, who had passed away in 2003. Towards the end of his career Haas (2001, 2004) himself again reflected upon neofunctionalist theory. Only few authors today seem to work in the neofunctionalist tradition (see Stone Sweet and Sandholtz 1997; Caporaso and Stone Sweet 2001), and apart from Schmitter (2004) there are no recent explicit attempts to revise the theory.

We will look at: first, one of the highest foreign policy responsibilities ever granted to the Community; second, temporary stagnation – if not regression – in one of the oldest and most integrated areas of Community policy which eventually led to progress in the last Treaty revision exercise; and finally, the field which has been described as the decisive battlefield in the struggle between the pre-eminence of the nation-state and supranational integration in Europe and which has arguably become the most dynamic area of European integration.[9] In theoretical (and methodological) terms, the above cases provide a variance between routine policy-making and history-making decisions as well as between external relations and the internal dimension of the Community. This is valuable because the theoretical scope of models is more thoroughly challenged and ascertained on diverse settings.[10] The most important consideration for my case selection was methodological. From a methodological perspective, my cases have been selected in order to ensure variation on the dependent variable. As will be further elaborated in Chapter 1, this is important in order to avoid selection bias and to establish some degree of positive causality between hypothesised pressures and decision-making outcomes.

Outline of the Book

The book is structured as follows: Chapter 1 specifies my theoretical framework and research design and thus provides the basis for subsequent empirical analysis. Chapters 2, 3 and 4 contain my case studies on the PHARE programme, the reform of the Common Commercial Policy and the communitarisation of visa, asylum and immigration policy, respectively. In Chapter 5, I draw some conclusions from my findings in the preceding chapters.

Chapter 1 starts by stating the core assumptions and main concepts of the original neofunctionalist approach before dealing with the criticisms levelled against it. Taking early neofunctionalism as a starting point, the second part of this chapter specifies the revised neofunctionalist framework which departs from the original approach in several ways: a more explicitly 'soft' constructivist ontology is formulated (and combined with the 'soft' rational-choice ontology of Haas's neofunctionalism) along with a more equal ontological status between structure and agents. Integration is no longer viewed as an automatic and exclusively dynamic process, but rather occurs under certain conditions and is

---

[9] See e.g. Monar (1998a: 137ff).
[10] Caporaso (1995: 457–60) emphasises this point in his discussion of falsification and delimitation of theory.

better characterised as a dialectic process, i.e. the product of both dynamics and countervailing forces. In addition, instead of a grand theory, the revised approach is understood as a wide-ranging, but partial, theory. Moreover, the 'end of ideology' and 'unabated economic growth' assumptions, which were particularly time sensitive, are buried. And while elites are still attributed a primary role for decision outcomes, the wider publics are assumed to impact on the evolution of the European integration process, too.

In addition, I hold that the explanatory variables need to be further developed and specified: perhaps most obviously, countervailing forces, mainly in the form of domestic constraints and diversities as well as sovereignty-consciousness, are hypothesised for. Also, exogenous spillover is included in order to account for the tensions and contradictions originating outside the European integration process itself. Furthermore, other more established neofunctionalist concepts are further extended and refined. Functional spillover is broadened in scope to go beyond merely economic linkages and is freed from its deterministic ontology. Functional 'pressure from within' – which captures pressures for increased co-operation within the same, rather than another, sector – is made more explicit and upgraded as an explanatory tool. So is cultivated spillover – the concept that originally denoted the role of the Commission/High Authority – which is also widened to include the integrative roles played by the Council Presidency, the European Parliament, the European Court of Justice and epistemic communities. The concept of political spillover, which broadly speaking conceptualises the role of non-governmental elites, is also stretched. Interest groups are taken to be influenced not only by endogenous–functional, but also by exogenous and domestic structures, and advocacy coalitions are incorporated within political spillover. The concept of social spillover is split off from political spillover, in order to better explain (reflexive) learning and socialisation processes. The concepts of communicative and norm-regulated action are incorporated into social spillover to describe and explain socialisation more adequately. It is suggested that learning and socialisation should no longer be seen as constant but as being subject to conditions.

The final part of Chapter 1 details my research design and methodology. As a basis for subsequent discussion, I first state my epistemological position which can be located somewhere between the positivist and post-positivist extremes, acknowledging the importance of interpretative and contextual features in establishing causal inferences and middle-range generalisations. My dependent variable is the outcome of instances of decision-making/negotiations, and my key causal (independent) variables are the various pressures mentioned in the previous paragraph. I start off from a multiple causality assumption, arguing that the same outcome can be caused by different combinations of factors. My analysis can be described as qualitative. In order to arrive at valid causal inferences, allowing for some degree of positive causality, a number of methods are employed, including comparative analysis, tracing of causal mechanisms and processes, as well as triangulation across multiple data sources. I argue that the danger of case selection bias has been minimised by choosing cases according to a range of values concerning the dependent variable, without paying attention to the values of the key causal variables (the identification of which was subject to my inquiry). The operationalisation of key causal variables is advanced by specifying indicators on which hypotheses are observed and measured.

Chapter 2 traces the most important aspects regarding the emergence and development of the PHARE programme. The question underlying this chapter (and the two following ones) is how my theoretical assumptions and hypotheses square with empirical 'reality'. Hence, the hypothesised pressures are tested against my empirical findings concerning the PHARE programme. I argue that exogenous and cultivated (i.e. formal supranational institutional) spillover pressures based on virtually non-existent countervailing forces can convincingly explain the origins of PHARE. Functional and cultivated spillover pressures account for the development of the programme into an important instrument within the Community's pre-accession strategy. Cultivated spillover also largely explains the expansion of PHARE funds for cofinancing infrastructures, which was possible even in face of more moderate to substantial countervailing forces. The concept also provides an important conceptual linkage for the accommodation of epistemic communities which have been very influential in establishing nuclear safety as an important part within the PHARE programme. Moreover, I suggest that social spillover (i.e. socialisation and learning processes) provided an important lubricant for the development of PHARE.

My analysis in Chapter 2 challenges the empirical and theoretical findings of Haggard and Moravcsik, who asserted that the Commission had played a marginal role in initiating and shaping EC aid for the CEEC. Moreover, I claim that the PHARE programme has proven to be far broader and much more viable than they anticipated. It developed into the single largest source of know-how transfer to the CEEC, showed considerable flexibility in adapting to the changing phases of economic and political transition in the East and obtained a central position in the Union's reinforced pre-accession strategy. In that sense it could be argued that the Community managed to minimise what

Christopher Hill – in his conceptualisation of Europe's international role – coined the capability–expectations gap. Although the demands and expectations in the Community to co-ordinate and provide effective aid were substantial, the Community took on this role, acted swiftly and proactively, provided significant funds, repeatedly adjusted the programme in face of changing circumstances and tied it to its wider objective by incorporating PHARE into its strategy of accession.

Chapter 3 examines the attempts to reform the Union's external trade policy to bring services, intellectual property and investment within the scope of this policy. Whereas the IGC 1996–97 largely failed to realise this undertaking, the last two Treaty revisions were gradually more successful in that respect. I argue that the failure to modernise Article 113 at the Amsterdam IGC can be explained here as the result of overall weak dynamics combined with strong countervailing pressures. Exogenous pressures, especially stemming from the changing trade agenda that increasingly included the newer trade issues, constituted the strongest dynamics. However, these were not convincing enough to a minority of reluctant Member States. Functional arguments stemming from the internal market were less pressing and had been rejected by the Court in its opinion 1/94. In addition, I discuss the role of organised interests and suggest that they never really caught on to the idea of widening the scope of external trade policy. As for the socialisation of governmental elites, I propose several factors which offset such processes. Moreover, the central institutions (and the Council Presidency), traditional agents of integration, barely fostered the issue, and at times even hindered an extension of the CCP. On the side of countervailing factors, there was above all the issue of sovereignty-consciousness, complemented by domestic constraints due to increasing politicisation of the new trade issues and a diffuse anti-integrationist climate.

Thereafter, I consider the IGC 2000 negotiations on the Common Commercial Policy. I propose that these were characterised by stronger overall dynamics. Exogenous pressures were as strong as at Amsterdam, if not stronger. Functional pressures stemming from the internal market, and particularly from enlargement, had also become quite substantial. Some aspects of cultivated spillover (e.g. assertion on the part of the Commission and the EP) had grown slightly, too. On the other hand, social and political spillover pressures remained at about the same modest level as during the IGC 1996–97. I argue that, in combination, these dynamics can explain the furtherance of Community competence and an extension of qualified majority voting. These pressures were countered by a number of countervailing forces that were of similar strength as during the Amsterdam IGC. While suspicion in the Commission – an important factor at the IGC 1996–97 – had decreased, the politicisation of some issues in the domestic context had grown.

In the final part of Chapter 3 I examine the last Treaty revision, the outcome of which was more progressive resulting in a clear-cut exclusive Community competence (with only minor exceptions) on the issues of services, intellectual property and investment. I argue that spillover pressures had gathered further strength at the Convention, after the partial reform of the CCP during the Intergovernmental Conference 2000. Exogenous spillover, creating pressure from a changing world economy and an evolving world trade agenda, as well as functional spillover pressures, particularly through enlargement, provided important structural pressures. One of the central claims of this sub-chapter is that these two structural pressures could unfold their strengths much more easily because of social spillover. Convincing arguments built on the exogenous and functional spillover rationales could register with actors due to important processes of socialisation, deliberation and arguing. Social spillover can also largely explain the bonding strength of the Convention text, which came about due to learning processes and participants' (including Member States' representatives') concurrence with the results. I maintain that these dynamics were further reinforced by (limited) political and, more importantly, considerable cultivated spillover. In contrast to the past two CCP Treaty revisions, cultivated spillover pressures played an enhanced role. These were important in terms of activating and initiating functional and exogenous spillover arguments, supporting and pushing the Convention idea in the first place and by asserting, more generally, their institutional (integrative) interests. On the whole, countervailing forces were (substantially) weaker than at the Amsterdam and Nice Intergovernmental Conferences. This facilitated the stronger ignition and dissemination of integrational dynamics.

Chapter 4 deals with the communitarisation of visa, asylum and immigration policy. Again my hypothesised assumptions and pressures are discussed in the light of empirical findings. The Amsterdam provisions in this issue area brought about considerable progress in the direction of further integration. I argue that during the 1996–97 IGC fairly substantial countervailing pressures, particularly due to domestic constraints and sovereignty-consciousness, were overcome by strong dynamics. Of the two structural pressures, functional and exogenous, the former appears to have been predominant in the considerations of decision-makers. The functional pressure related to the objective of the free movement of persons was assisted by pressures that arose from the dissatisfaction with the non-achievement of attaining 'effective co-operation' in this field. Exogenous developments, i.e. mainly migration streams, have constituted important complementary, though secondary, pressures for a communitarisation of the subject matters discussed here. In addition, the relevance and impact of social spillover is considered. Somewhat paradoxically, the minimal development of socialisation processes and the parallel occurrence of flawed co-operation among Member States, induced only very few agents to conclude that the new system needed time to develop. Most concluded that the cumbersome, intergovernmental decision-making procedures were responsible for the lack of progress. Political spillover in terms of non-governmental elites had a limited impact on the communitarisation of visa, asylum and immigration policy. As far as cultivated spillover is concerned, this analysis suggests that the roles played by the central institutions, and above all by the Commission and the various Presidencies, substantially promoted the process of communitarisation.

Next, the issue of visa, asylum and immigration policy decision rule reform is discussed with regard to the IGC 2000 negotiations. I assert that the dynamics at work both in the run-up to, and during, the Intergovernmental Conference were less substantial than during the IGC 1996/97. While exogenous spillover provided a similar rationale as three years prior, functional spillover pressures had changed. Particularly, the internal market rationale had diminished. These decreasing functional pressures were, only to some extent, compensated by additional functional pressures stemming from enlargement. More grave, I argue, was the fact that these still substantial structural forces were not adequately acted out by agents in terms of cultivated spillover. The Commission, the French Presidency and also the European Parliament were either unable or unwilling to push for integrative outcomes, to reason out the logics for further communitarisation or to upgrade common Community interests. This was further compounded by the lack of social and political spillover pressures, especially in terms of governmental elites. Their absence removed an important basis for connecting actors with the structural (functional and exogenous) spillover rationales. In addition, the role of countervailing forces is considered. My findings suggest that diminished spillover dynamics were met by strong countervailing forces of sovereignty-consciousness, domestic constraints and diversity.

The final section of Chapter 4 considers the relevance of the revised neofunctionalist framework for explaining the progressive results of the last Treaty revision on visa, asylum and immigration policy. On the one hand, I suggest that the dynamics of integration had gathered further strength. Structural (functional and to a extent lesser, exogenous) spillover rationales had grown. Perhaps even more importantly, agents that can typically be expected to act upon these structural pressures, such as the Commission and the European Parliament, were much more able to assert themselves. And perhaps most significantly, social spillover pressures, especially in terms of governmental elites in the Convention provided the much needed lubricant between structures and agents and constituted an important platform for the unfoldment of structural pressures. Convincing arguments built on functional and exogenous spillover rationales could register with actors due to important processes of enmeshment, socialisation, deliberation and arguing. On the other hand, countervailing pressures were diminished in comparison with the Amsterdam and Nice IGCs. As a result, a stronger ignition and dissemination of integrational dynamics was possible. Finally, my analysis considers how the interplay between dynamics and countervailing pressures may also explain the more specific aspects of the final outcome concerning decision rules.

Chapter 5 reflects upon my analysis in the preceding chapters and offers conclusions on a number of empirical, theoretical and methodological aspects. First, my findings on each of the revised neofunctionalist pressures are summarised and assessed in terms of the presumptions of the revised framework. The various pressures are also linked to the wider theoretical context. Moreover, attention is drawn to empirical findings on the different pressures (or related aspects) that can be gathered in the wider literature. In addition, some conditions for delimiting the various pressures that can be extrapolated from my analysis of Chapters 2, 3 and 4 are suggested. These proposed conditions are to be understood as tentative rather than probed or tested. Furthermore, the interrelationship between the various pressures is (re-)considered and the ability of the revised neofunctionalist framework to account for more specific aspects of decision outcomes is discussed.

The second main section of Chapter 5 deepens my analysis on comparison and causality. For this purpose the values attributed to my hypothesised pressures and outcomes across (sub-)cases are summarised in a table. In addition to the tracing of causal mechanisms and processes in the preceding analysis, more systematic use is made of the comparative method. Two variations of comparative analysis are used: (i) the identification and isolation of causal processes that lead to different outcomes (especially examining whether hypothesised pressures co-vary with outcomes); and (ii) examining cases where the dependent variable takes on the same value (in order to identify causal variables of lesser relevance). My analysis particularly confirms the causal relevance of cultivated, functional and social (and, to a lesser extent, exogenous) spillover pressures, which corroborates my findings gained from process tracing. Political spillover, although somewhat challenged, has not been conclusively disconfirmed, suggesting that this pressure is conducive (rather than necessary or sufficient) for the occurrence of spillover. My analysis substantiates the multiple causality assumption and suggests that the combination of comparative analysis and process tracing is a useful one in order to strengthen the conclusiveness of causal relationships.

Third, the revised neofunctionalist framework is integrated more systematically into the wider theoretical cosmos and related more closely to important disciplinary debates. I argue that several of the more recent theoretical approaches bear considerable resemblance to neofunctionalism and that neofunctionalist insights have also informed other theoretical approaches in a number of ways, although only few authors have given explicit credit to neofunctionalism. Commenting on the classical intergovernmentalist–neofunctionalist debate, I suggest that this is still an important one, albeit not as central as it used to be. I claim that while other approaches such as supranational governance and liberal intergovernmentalism remain trapped in this dichotomy, the revised neofunctionalist framework manages to bridge the old divide in several ways, while also going beyond this debate. Thereafter, the revised framework is discussed with regard to the rationalist–reflectivist divide. I consider how constructivists and rationalists may benefit from the revised neofunctionalist framework. I argue that scholars, who are more driven by empirical puzzles than the ontological purity of the argument, may find my work insightful and that these researchers may also agree that this book contributes to promoting dialogue between the two 'camps'. Subsequently, I discuss the potential contribution of this study to the so-called 'constitutional debate' and to the evolving debate on epistemology in the field of EU integration studies. This section terminates with some brief thoughts on the nature and challenges of theorising integration.

The final section discusses several potential shortcomings of this book. Questions such as the operationalisation of hypothesised pressures, falsifiability, the diminished parsimony and reduced predictive pretence of the revised neofunctionalist framework are addressed. I conclude with the claim that the revised framework has provided a robust theoretical framework for analysis of the inception and development of the PHARE programme and Treaty revision negotiations on the reform of external trade policy as well as the communitarisation of visa, asylum and immigration policy. Finally, the existing scope for further research is briefly pointed out.

1   Theoretical Framework and Research Design

Neofunctionalism as a Starting Point

Neofunctionalism is the most refined, ambitious and criticised theory of regional integration. It was developed mainly by Ernst Haas and Leon Lindberg in the 1950s and 1960s in response to the establishment of the European Coal and Steel Community (ECSC) and the European Community (EC). Its intellectual roots can be found in functionalist, federalist and communications theories as well as in the early 'group theorists' of American political science. Haas and Lindberg, the two most influential and prolific neofunctionalist writers, mainly combined functionalist and federalist thinking by tying functionalist methods to federalist goals. Neofunctionalism shares with functionalism a focus on technocratic decision-making, incremental change and learning processes. However, although the theory has been dubbed neofunctionalism, this is in some ways a case of 'mistaken identity',[1] since it departed significantly from Mitrany's functionalism.[2] Whereas functionalists held that the form, scope and purpose of an organisation would be determined by the task that it was designed to fulfil, neofunctionalists attached considerable importance to the autonomous influence of supranational institutions. While functionalists did not limit integration to any territorial area, neofunctionalists gave integration a regional focus.[3] Moreover, unlike Mitrany, the neofunctionalists did not attach much importance to the change in popular attitudes, but focused instead on the change of elite attitudes.

Another important precursor to neofunctionalist theory was Jean Monnet. Apart from his federal aspirations, he influenced neofunctionalism in other ways. The concept of functional spillover, which will be elaborated below, was already recognised as a key factor by

---

[1] The case for a 'mistaken identity' has been argued by Groom (1978: 15).
[2] Cf. Mitrany (1966, 1975).
[3] Mitrany directly opposed the creation of territorially based state structures at the European level. Cf. Taylor (1990: 132, 127–8).

Monnet before it was given its academic formulation. The foundations of neofunctionalism suggest that it was not only a conceptual framework, but also a plan for action. The writings of Haas and Lindberg reflect considerable sympathy with the project of European unification. Hence, although Haas pointed out that the purpose of his theory was to describe, explain and predict,[4] it was also meant to prescribe.[5]

An analysis on the basis of neofunctionalism is no easy task. The theory has come to mean different things to different people. There are a number of reasons for this. First, it is difficult to say what exactly qualifies as neofunctionalist thought due to the theory's increasing *ad hoc* reformulations in the late 1960s and early 1970s. The original accounts of Ernst Haas and Leon Lindberg were revised and modified by a number of writers, such as Philippe Schmitter, Stuart Scheingold and Joseph Nye, and also by Haas and Lindberg themselves. Second, the debate on neofunctionalism has been confused by the fact that authors have been put into the neofunctionalist camp whose views vary in some significant aspects. A closely related, if not identical, point is that of internal disagreements within the neofunctionalist school of thought. Neofunctionalist scholars differed on the dependent variable problem (the question of the end state of integration), whether, and to what extent, loyalties shifted to the new centre,[6] and whether depoliticisation or politicisation constituted a precondition for the spillover process.[7] Third, the uncertainty about the substance and boundaries of neofunctionalist thought also gave rise to much semantic confusion. Terms such as 'spillover' and '*engrenage*', for example, have been taken to mean different phenomena. In addition, similar or identical ideas have been disguised by different terminologies. A fourth problem constitutes the sometimes very selective and narrow interpretations of neofunctionalism in the European integration literature.[8]

The above issues need to be clarified in order to pave the way for a sensible theoretical discussion and empirical testing of neofunctionalism.

[4] The purpose and theoretical status of his theory has been summarised in Haas (1970: 627–8).

[5] This view has been expressed by a number of authors, including Tranholm-Mikkelsen (1991: 4).

[6] On the latter two issues, compare, for example, Haas (1958: 16, 311) with Lindberg (1963: 6). See also the subsequent discussion on the definition of integration.

[7] Compare, for instance, Haas (1961) who believed that issue areas need to be depoliticised and characterised by pragmatic interest politics in order to spill over, with Schmitter (1969: 166). The latter pointed out that politicisation was a necessary driving force for the progression of the integration process.

[8] Perhaps the most striking example of such a kind of selective and misleading reading of the neofunctionalist approach is the work of Alan Milward (1992: 11–12). On selective and narrow interpretations of neofunctionalism cf. also Niemann (2000: 13–23).

This chapter seeks to define terms and hypotheses clearly and to avoid semantic confusion by pointing to alternative or misleading labels in the academic literature. In order to set out the groundwork for the subsequent case studies we will return to the early neofunctionalist accounts of Ernst Haas and Leon Lindberg as a starting point.[9] The remainder of this section will explicate the neofunctionalist understanding and definition of integration, synthesise the main neofunctionalist maxims, specify the main neofunctionalist dynamics centred around the concept of spillover and spell out the most important problems of the original neofunctionalist theory. This will provide the basis for specifying the revised neofunctionalist framework.

Definition of Integration

Neofunctionalism offers no single authoritative definition of integration. Instead, neofunctionalists revised their definition of integration over time. Both Haas and Lindberg conceived of integration as a process and not a state. They also perceived integration to involve the creation of central institutions. Moreover, they both stressed some degree of change in expectations and activities on the part of political actors. Whilst Lindberg restricted his study to the European Economic Community (EEC), Haas based his analysis on the ECSC, but extended his conclusions to both the EEC and the European Atomic Energy Community (EURATOM). Haas defined integration as:

the process whereby political actors in several distinct national settings are persuaded to shift their loyalties, expectations and political activities toward a new centre, whose institutions possess or demand jurisdiction over the preexisting national states. The end result of a process of political integration is a new political community, superimposed over the pre-existing ones.[10]

Lindberg's definition of integration differs in some respects from Haas'. By integration Lindberg meant:

(1) The process whereby nations forgo the desire and ability to conduct foreign and domestic policies independently of each other, seeking instead to make joint decisions or to delegate the decision-making process to new central organs: and (2) the process whereby political actors in several distinct settings are persuaded to shift their expectations and political activities to a new centre.[11]

It is worth pointing out that, unlike Haas, Lindberg did not imply any end point for the integration process, thereby acknowledging that the

---

[9] Mainly Haas (1958) and Lindberg (1963).   [10] Haas (1958: 16).
[11] Lindberg (1963: 6).

breadth and depth of integration could be in constant flux. Lindberg also suggested that political actors merely shift their expectations and not their loyalties to a new centre. In sum, Lindberg took a more cautious approach than Haas in his conception and definition of integration.[12]

Underlying Assumptions

The essence of neofunctionalist theory of integration can be derived from a number of basic tenets, some of which have been hinted at in the neofunctionalist understanding and definition of integration. First, in line with the mainstream of US political science of the time, early neofunctionalists aimed at general theory-building. Hence, neofunctionalism, as it was originally conceived, understood itself as a 'grand' or general theory of integration.[13] Second, as already alluded to above, integration is understood as a process. Here neofunctionalists fundamentally differ from intergovernmentalists, who tend to look at isolated events. While intergovernmentalists look at a single 'photo-graph', neofunctionalists examine a whole 'film'.[14] Implicit in the notion of integration as a process is the assumption that processes evolve over time and take on their own dynamic. Third, neofunctionalism is a 'pluralist' theory. In contrast to traditional realist theories, it contests both that states are single unified actors and that states are the only relevant actors in international relations. Instead, neofunctionalists assume the prevalence of pluralist politics with multiple and diverse actors which are not restricted to the domestic political realm but can make contact and build coalitions across national frontiers and national bureaucracies.[15] Fourth, neofunctionalists saw the Community primarily as 'a creature of elites'. While Haas mainly concentrated on the role of nongovernmental elites, Lindberg largely focused on governmental elites.[16] Little significance was attached to the role of public opinion. The preferred conclusion was that there was a 'permissive consensus' in favour of European integration.[17] Fifth, although Haas

---

[12] Contrary to the conventional reading and misinterpretation of neofunctionalism, Haas actually held that such a shift in loyalties need not be absolute or permanent, allowing for multiple loyalties (Haas 1958: 14). In addition, soon after devising his original definition of integration, Haas downplayed the previously amalgamated end-point (Haas 1960), and also abandoned shifting *loyalties* as a defining characteristic of integration. Instead, he emphasised the transfer of *authority* and *legitimacy* (Haas 1970: 627–8, 633).

[13] Cf. Haas (1961: 366ff) as well as Haas and Schmitter (1964: esp. 706–07, 720, 726).

[14] This contrast between the two approaches has been made most strikingly by Pierson (1996: 127).

[15] See e.g. Haas (1964a: 68ff).   [16] Haas (1958: chs. 5 and 6); Lindberg (1963: ch. 4).

[17] Lindberg and Scheingold (1970: 41).

formulated no explicit economic analysis, it can be argued that one important underlying neofunctionalist assumption was that European economic growth would continue unabated.[18] Linked to this was the similarly naive neofunctionalist 'end of ideology' assumption, which held that as societies became richer, they would become more concerned with the pursuit of wealth rather than with nationalist, socialist or religious ideals.

Neofunctionalism is mainly a theory about the dynamics of European integration. The dynamics which drive the integration process forward are encapsulated in the last five neofunctionalist maxims. First, neofunctionalists assume rational and largely self-interested[19] actors, who (nevertheless) have the capacity to learn and change their preferences. Interest-driven national and supranational elites, recognising the limitations of national solutions, provide a key impetus to the integration process. The shift of expectations, activities and perhaps loyalties towards the new centre is also seen as one which is primarily motivated by actors' interests. However, interests are not perceived as being constant but subject to change during the integration process, since actors can learn from the benefits of communitarisation and from their experiences in co-operative decision-making.[20] Neofunctionalists contest the intergovernmentalist assumption of national interest aggregation via some hermetic national process. Instead, Haas argued that membership in the Community alters the way that interest groups, and henceforth governments, perceive the national interest.[21] Second, once established, institutions can take on a life of their own and are difficult to control by those who created them. Concerned with increasing their own powers, supranational institutions become agents of integration, which can influence the perceptions of elites', and therefore governments' (national), interest. Third, and related to the previous point, later reformulations emphasised that regional integration relies on the primacy of incremental decision-making over grand designs, and is often the result of unintended consequences, as most political actors are incapable of long-range purposive behaviour since they 'stumble' from one decision into the next as a result of earlier decisions. Decisions on integration are normally taken with very imperfect knowledge of their consequences and frequently under the pressure of deadlines.[22] Fourth, contrary to conventional realist belief, neofunctionalists pointed out that not all games played between actors (in the Community setting) are zero-sum games. Interaction is often better characterised by positive-sum

[18] Cf. Holland (1980).   [19] Cf. e.g. Haas (1970: 627).   [20] See e.g. Haas (1958: 291).
[21] Cf. Haas (1958: 9–10).   [22] Haas (1970: 627).

games and a supranational style of decision-making which Haas defined as 'a cumulative pattern of accommodation in which the participants refrain from unconditionally vetoing proposals and instead seek to attain agreement by means of compromises upgrading common interests'.[23] Finally, Haas followed the assumption made by some economists, such as Pierre Uri, who was the chief economist of the ECSC in the 1950s, that interdependence between economies as well as between sectors provokes and fosters (ever) further integration.[24] Mainly based on this assumption, Haas originally thought that the spillover process would be an automatic one. It also led him to assume the emergence of a political community of Europe, which he predicted to occur before the end of the transitional period.[25]

Explaining Integration and the Concept of Spillover

Based on these assumptions early neofunctionalists explained the integration process in Europe. The neofunctionalist conception of change is encapsulated in the idea of 'spillover'. The term was applied by early neofunctionalists in two distinctive manners. First, it was used as shorthand for the occurrence of (further) integration. Second, the term 'spillover' described a driving force and inherent logic of functional-economic integration.[26] Haas talked about an 'expansive logic of sector integration'.[27] After the integration of one sector, technical pressures push states to integrate other sectors. The idea is that some sectors within industrial economies are so interdependent that it is impossible to isolate them from the rest. Thus, the regional integration of one sector would only work if followed by the integration of other sectors, as the functional integration of one task inevitably leads to problems which can only be solved by integrating yet more tasks. Haas held that sector integration 'begets its own impetus toward extension of the entire economy ....'.[28] For example, integration in the coal and steel sectors was regarded as viable only if other related sectors followed suit, such as transport policy, which was important in order to ensure a smooth movement of necessary raw materials. In the literature the term

---

[23] Haas (1964a: 66).
[24] See Haas (1958: 372f). The integration process was assumed to begin with those sectors that were considered the least controversial.
[25] Haas (1958: 311).
[26] As described in the next section ('The revised neofunctionalist framework'), later on the term spillover was used to explain all the different neofunctionalist dynamics.
[27] Haas (1958: 383).   [28] Haas (1958: 297).

functional spillover later came to denote the functional-economic rationale for further integration.[29]

Haas and Lindberg put considerable emphasis on the role of economic
and political elites supporting the integration process. National elites
were assumed to realise that problems of substantial interest cannot be
satisfactorily solved at the domestic level, not least because of the above-
mentioned functional-economic logic. This would lead to a gradual
learning process whereby elites shift their expectations, political activities
and – according to Haas – even loyalties to a new European centre. As a
result national elites would promote further integration, thus adding a
political stimulus to the process. Haas in particular focused on the
pressures exerted by non-governmental elites.[30] Those pressures include
the altered perceptions of political parties, trade associations, trade
unions or interest groups. This implies that integration in a particular
sector leads the interest groups concerned to move part of their activity to
the regional level. Such groups may gradually shift their focus and
expectations to the European level. As they become more aware of the
benefits of integration, they will promote further integration.[31]

Lindberg particularly stressed the role of governmental elites and
socialisation processes. He pointed to the fact that the rapid increase of
working groups and sub-committees on the European level had led to a
complex system of bureaucratic interpenetration that brought thousands
of national officials in frequent contact with each other and with
Commission officials. Lindberg emphasised the likelihood of socialisation processes occurring amongst national civil servants within the
Council framework as a result of these interaction patterns.[32] In addition, neofunctionalists saw Community decision-making not in terms of
classic intergovernmental strategic bargaining but as a 'supranational'
problem-solving process, 'a cumulative pattern of accommodation in
which the participants refrain from unconditionally vetoing proposals
and instead seek to attain agreement by means of compromises
upgrading common interests'.[33] It was also implied that socialisation
processes would induce consensus formation amongst member governments and would eventually lead to more integrative outcomes.[34]
This process was later termed *engrenage*.[35] Neofunctionalists also argued

---

[29] Cf. Tranholm-Mikkelsen (1991: 4–5). The terminologies of functional, political and
cultivated spillover were not part of the first-generation neofunctionalist vocabulary.
[30] E.g. Haas (1958: 312–13).   [31] Haas (1958: chs. 8 and 9).
[32] Lindberg (1963: ch. 4).   [33] Haas (1958: 66).
[34] Cf. Lindberg (1963); Lindberg and Scheingold (1970: 119).
[35] See Taylor (1983: 9–10). It should be noted that the term *engrenage* has been given
different meanings by different authors which has led to considerable semantic
confusion: Pinder (1991a: 26, 32) calls *engrenage* what Lindberg meant by 'informal

that socialisation processes and particularly the increased habit of national elites to look for European solutions in solving their problems would help to generate a shift of expectations and perhaps loyalties towards the new centre on the part of national elites. The integrative pressures exerted by national (governmental and non-governmental) elites were later termed *political spillover* in the literature.[36]

In addition, neofunctionalists attributed further integrationist pressures to the role of supranational institutions as likely agents of integration. Haas emphasised the role of the High Authority and the Commission in the facilitation of agreement on integrative outcomes. As opposed to lowest common denominator bargaining, which he saw as inherent in intergovernmental decisions, the supranational systems were characterised by 'splitting the difference' and more significantly a bargaining process of 'upgrading common interests'. Parties agree that they should have a common stand in order not to jeopardise those areas in which consensus prevails. The participants in such negotiations tend to swap concessions in related fields. The swapping takes place on the basis of an institutionalised mediator such as the Commission. Governments do not feel as if they have been bullied. Common interests are upgraded in the sense that each feels that by conceding something it has gained something else. In addition, Haas saw the Commission as the main actor cultivating the functional-economic integration logic. In line with his assumption of rational actors, Haas also suggested that the Commission would gradually expand its mandate as the scope and level of integration increased, providing the process with yet more impetus.[37] Lindberg emphasised the Commission's cultivation of ties with national elites. He pointed out that the Commission is in a privileged position of centrality and authority, enabling it to direct not only the dynamics of relations among states but also the relations of groups within pluralist states. According to Lindberg, the Commission's cultivation of contacts with national civil servants and national interest groups would gradually lead to the Commission's 'informal co-optation' of member states' national elites to help realise its European objectives.[38] The role attributed to the Commission (or supranational institutions more generally) was later termed *cultivated spillover*.[39]

---

co-optation' (see later on in this sub-section). William Wallace (1990a: 17) stretches the term to include the reorientation of economic interests among mass publics. Finally, Nye (1971: 51–2) and Robert Russell (1975: 61–2) attached a wholly different meaning to the term. Their notion of *engrenage* can be seen as a variation of functional spillover.
[36] Tranholm-Mikkelsen (1991: 5).   [37] Cf. Haas (1961: 369ff); Haas (1964a: 75ff).
[38] Lindberg (1963: 71).   [39] Cf. Tranholm-Mikkelsen (1991: 6).

Criticisms

Neofunctionalism is probably the most heavily criticised integration theory. After the passing of its heyday in the mid-1960s, neofunctionalism began to be critiqued by intergovernmentalist scholars,[40] and also increasingly within the neofunctionalist camp itself, not least by its self-critical founding father, who also abandoned the theory in the mid-1970s.[41] Even after the theory was pronounced obsolescent by Haas and Lindberg, who subsequently 'retired' from neofunctionalism, critiques of their works flourished in the 1980s[42] and never went out of fashion ever since.[43] It is important to note, however, that a number of criticisms levelled against neofunctionalism misrepresent its claims, distort its arguments or interpret the theory selectively and narrowly.

Therefore, some of the critiques of neofunctionalist theory are not, or not entirely, justified. For example, scholars have misrepresented the theory for its alleged failure to account for unintended consequences[44] or its supposed deficiency to recognise that loyalties and identities tend to be of a multiple nature.[45] Its critics have also exaggerated neofunctionalism's predictive pretensions and especially Haas' pronouncement of a political Community as a likely outcome of the integration process before the end of the twelve-year transitional period referred to in the Treaty of Rome,[46] although neofunctionalists had already avoided talking about a possible end-state from the early 1960s.[47] In addition, neofunctionalism was, somewhat unfairly, accused of having limited explanatory power on issues beyond its research focus and analytical spectrum, such as questions related to the nature of interest representation and intermediation in the European Union[48] or the inception of the integration process in Europe.[49] However, this latter type of criticism does have a certain validity given the early neofunctionalist claim for developing a grand theory of integration, an issue that will be taken up in a moment. A more extensive account of contestable critiques *vis-à-vis* neofunctionalist theory has been provided elsewhere.[50]

---

[40] E.g. Hoffmann (1995 [1964]: 84ff).   [41] Haas (1976: 175ff).
[42] Holland (1980); Webb (1983); Taylor (1983).
[43] See e.g. Moravcsik (1991: 47–48; 1993: 475ff); Milward (1992: 11–12); Risse-Kappen (1996: 56ff).
[44] McNamara (1993: 309).
[45] For a misinterpretation of neofunctionalism on this point, see Marcussen and Risse (1997). Contrary to Marcussen and Risse, Haas acknowledged the existence of multiple identities already in Haas (1958: 5, 9, 14).
[46] Haas (1958: 311).   [47] Cf. Haas (1960, 1964b); Lindberg (1963: 6).
[48] On this point see Hix (1994: 6).   [49] See Milward (1992: esp. ch. 1).
[50] Niemann (2000: 13–23); also cf. Rosamond (2005) who suggests that Haas has been misread on several points.

There are a number of criticisms levelled against (early) neofunction-alism which provide more fundamental and significant challenges to the theory. First, neofunctionalism has been criticised for its grand theoretical pretensions. It has been rightly argued that neofunctionalism does not and cannot provide a general theory of integration. The theory possesses certain analytical tools to deal with a certain kind of question, i.e. those related to explaining integration. And even this particular issue it can arguably only cope with in an unsatisfactory manner, as it mainly concentrates on the dynamics of the integration process.

Second, both intergovernmentalist[51] and interdependence theorists[52] have criticised neofunctionalism for viewing spillover as automatic or for accepting an economic determinism. In *The Uniting of Europe* Haas indeed considered the spillover process as more or less automatic.[53] Later on neofunctionalists began to make certain qualifications to the occurrence of spillover. Some of them constituted sensible delimitations of neofunctionalist concepts, such as the requirement that the task assigned to institutions was inherently expansive, i.e. contained func-tional connections with other issue areas.[54] Other specifications pointed in the right direction, but were rather *ad hoc*, not sufficiently elaborated and not adequately linked with the main body of theory, like Haas' notion of the 'dramatic political actor'[55] or Lindberg's claim that spil-lover cannot be expected to take place in the absence of a will to proceed on the part of the Member States.[56] Hence, overall neofunctionalism lacks a comprehensive, refined and integrated specification of the con-ditions under which spillover may occur.

Third, neofunctionalism has been taken up on its alleged actor-centredness.[57] It is not true that neofunctionalism had no structural elements. For example, the functional-economic rationale based on the interdependence of sectors, which has also been referred to as 'func-tional spillover', is essentially a structural pressure. However, one may argue that neofunctionalism placed too much emphasis on actors, and that agents and structural explanations need to be linked with one another more adequately. While the insufficient integration of agents and structures may be true of many theories, this aspect nevertheless also provides scope for (further) revision. Fourth, it has been argued that neofunctionalists underestimated the impact of sovereignty-consciousness and nationalism on the integration process.[58] In the

---

[51] E.g. Moravcsik (1993: 475ff).
[52] Keohane and Nye (1975); Keohane and Nye (1977).
[53] Haas (1958: ch. 8).   [54] Lindberg (1963: 10).   [55] Haas (1968: preface).
[56] Lindberg (1963: 11).   [57] Jørgensen and Christiansen (1999: 4).
[58] Hoffmann (1995 [1964]: esp. 75–84).

history of European integration the importance of these tendencies can be illustrated by the disruptiveness of French EC policies under Charles de Gaulle and British policies under Margaret Thatcher.

Fifth, it has been argued that the concept of spillover was connected to the implicit neofunctionalist assumption that economic growth would continue unabated in the capitalist world, and that all Member States would benefit more or less equally from that growth.[59] In the 1950s and 1960s, at the time when neofunctionalism dominated the academic debate, such an assumption was widespread amongst economists, not least because western free-market economies were enjoying a period of unprecedented growth and duration. This all changed in the 1970s, as growth rates fell and unemployment rose. It has been suggested that this adverse economic climate was partly responsible for fostering the stagnation of the integration process and for the shift of the institutional balance in the European Community in favour of intergovernmentalism, as under such circumstances Member States 'have appeared both uncertain and defensive and frequently unwilling to take the Community option'.[60]

Sixth, as pointed out by a number of observers,[61] neofunctionalism failed to take the external environment adequately into account. It has been rightly argued that the European Community is only a part of the world economy, and the international system would deny the possibility of insulating Europe from its effects. Hoffmann saw external factors as a disintegrative force. He contended that the external environment would tend to provoke diverse responses from the Member States, which in turn would create divisions and prove disintegrative.[62] His criticism overlaps with Webb's and Holland's on the changing (international) economic climate. Other writers have emphasised the integrative impact of the world setting. Schmitter, for example, has pointed to European monetary policy co-operation, which started to develop after US President Nixon's decision to take the dollar off the gold standard in 1971.[63] Haas himself considered neofunctionalism's neglect of the wider world context as a serious shortcoming.[64] He eventually came to the drastic conclusion that the entire research focus on regional integration needed to be switched to the wider issues of interdependence.[65]

---

[59] This critique has been made by Holland (1980) and Webb (1983). The unabated economic growth assumption in neofunctionalist reasoning is evident for example in Haas (1964a: 68).
[60] Webb (1983: 21).   [61] E.g. Hoffmann (1995) [1964]; Webb (1983); George (1991).
[62] Hoffmann (1995 [1964]: 84).   [63] Cf. Schmitter (1996a: 13).
[64] E.g. Haas (1968: preface).   [65] Haas (1976: 208).

Finally, neofunctionalism has been justifiably criticised for its inadequate account of domestic political processes and structures. It has been argued that neofunctionalism underestimated the role of national leadership, wrongly assumed that decision-makers were 'economic incrementalists', overemphasised the role of interest groups in influencing policy and assumed too much homogeneity in the pressures that would be brought to bear on different governments.[66] Moreover, as pointed out by Moravcsik, neofunctionalism fails to explain government choices on the basis of models of pressure from predictable, distributional coalitions.[67] Lindberg himself admitted this failure. Together with Scheingold, he pointed out that neofunctionalism describes domestic processes, but says little about basic causes of variation in national demands for integration. However, no way was offered to remedy this shortcoming.[68] The above challenges will be further addressed in the revised neofunctionalist framework.

In response to the numerous criticisms as well as the integration process itself, the neofunctionalists undertook a number of reformulations of the theory. Whereas some of their modifications provide useful insights for my revised framework, others are of only limited usefulness.[69] As a result, neofunctionalism became increasingly reactive and the indeterminacy of many of its conclusions led observers to point out that the theory offers no clear direction for revision.[70] Hence, since the 1970s most scholars dismissed neofunctionalism for theorising the European integration process. However, a few scholars have implicitly – or sometimes even explicitly – recognised the value of neofunctionalist theory, suggesting that the approach contains useful building blocks for contemporary theorising.[71] And others maintained that it may be worth resurrecting the theory in light of the Community's resurgence in the late 1980s.[72] However, few have actively sought to refine the theory in the face of the challenges that were levelled against it.[73]

---

[66] Cf. Hansen (1973); George (1991).   [67] Moravcsik (1993: 477).

[68] Lindberg and Scheingold (1970: 284).

[69] For example concepts such as 'spill-around' and 'muddle-about' were devised, which were of a rather *ad hoc* nature and were also insufficiently linked with the main neofunctionalist body of theory. See Schmitter (1971: 240–2).

[70] E.g. Moravcsik (1993: 476).

[71] E.g. Keohane and Hoffmann (1991); Marks, *et al.* (1996); Pierson (1996).

[72] E.g. Taylor (1989: 23–4); Tranholm-Mikkelsen (1991).

[73] While few authors today seem to work in the neofunctionalist tradition (Stone Sweet and Sandholtz 1997; Caporaso and Stone Sweet 2001), even fewer have made explicit attempts to revise the theory. But see Schmitter (2004).

The Revised Neofunctionalist Framework

Basic Ontology

At the time of their writing, early neofunctionalists did not describe their key ontological assumptions in any systematic manner. However, the neofunctionalist ontology can be derived from their writings. When doing so, one discovers elements that can be solidly located in the rational-choice tradition with rational, intentional and self-interested actors,[74] while other aspects are more reminiscent of constructivist thought with actors capable of learning and changing their preferences as a result of such processes.[75] For a more coherent theoretical understanding and a more meaningful application of neofunctionalist theory, a more extensive specification of the neofunctionalist ontology would seem in order. Haas has largely provided this in a *post hoc* fashion for the original neo-functionalist theory.[76] In his account, he describes the neofunctionalist ontology as 'soft' rational-choice. My revised neofunctionalist framework does not significantly depart from this stance, but slightly broadens the ontological scope towards a wider and more inclusive ontology by encroaching onto constructivism to a larger extent than early neo-functionalism. The revised framework also seeks to further specify and modify the relationship between structure and agency.

This account does not strive for ontological purity. While eschewing arch-rationalist and hardcore reflectivist ontological extremes, my approach takes on board the (empirical) insight that agents tend to be subject to different social logics and rationalities and that they combine several modes of action in their behaviour. The recent literature suggests that the rational-choice logic of consequentialism and the more constructivist logics of appropriateness and arguing coexist in the real world.[77] There are different interpretations concerning the relationships between these logics. My ontological position is that these logics are activated under different conditions and in different environments, but

[74] On the rational-choice assumptions within neofunctionalism, see especially Burley and Mattli (1993: 54–5).

[75] See e.g. Haas (1958: 291–2); Lindberg and Scheingold (1970: 119). I agree with Rosamond (2005: 242, 250) who suggests that Haas's neofunctionalism was shot through with interests in cognitions, perception and the sociological dimension of institutionalised interaction, and that the deployment of constructivist vocabulary benefits (revised) neofunctionalist theory. See also Haas (2001, 2004) who made the relationship between neofunctionalism and constructivism a prominent theme in his final contributions to European integration.

[76] Cf. Haas (2001: 22–4).

[77] On these logics, cf. March and Olsen (1998: esp. 952–3); and Checkel (1999: 546). Risse (2000: 1–9) added the logic of arguing to the other two logics.

that the relationship between the rational-choice logic and the two more constructivist ones tends to be a developmental one: agents are more likely to enter into new relationships following an instrumental rationale, but tend to develop certain norms and identities and may change their preferences as a result of their experience and interaction.[78]

However, the ontology of the revised neofunctionalist approach can be further specified by delimiting the frame within which these logics take place. Some of the hardcore rational-choice[79] maxims are loosened in my framework (even regarding the consequentialist mode of action), while two core rational-choice assumptions are recognised: first, agents are rational, i.e. they choose that option which they believe best fulfils their purposes. Preferences do not result from random choice but reflect deliberate behaviour. Second, actors are basically egoistic. They base their behaviour on consequential calculations of self-interests and try to enhance their utility through strategic exchanges. Hence, an instrumental–utilitarian conception of rationality does have a place in the revised neofunctionalist framework. However, some other rational-choice tenets cannot be taken on board. Assumptions of preferences as consistent, stable and exogenously given are relaxed. Moreover, rational-choice presumptions of intentions as causes determining outcomes and suppositions of formally predictable outcome patterns are dropped. In addition and partly following from the above, the unequivocally materialist philosophy of science – according to which behaviour is the simple response to the forces of physics that act on material objects from the outside – that characterises many rational-choice accounts is not shared. On the other hand, the reflectivist or postmodernist[80] extreme is also dismissed. According to this ontological stance, it makes no sense to assume the independent existence of an external reality, as reality cannot be known outside human language. There is no way of deciding whether statements correspond to reality except by means of other statements. Hence, reality, under such ontology, is turned into linguistic conventions.

In contrast, my ontological position is situated in between these two poles. While acknowledging that there is a real (material) world out there, which offers resistance when we act upon it, behaviour is only to

---

[78] That the occurrence of a certain mode of behaviour depends on specific circumstances has been noted before: see Risse (2000: 19, 20), Checkel (2001a: 563ff), Niemann (2004: 385ff). The developmental nature between different logics has been suggested as one possible relationship by March and Olsen (1998: 953).

[79] On rational-choice theory and its various assumptions, see for example: Brennan (1997: esp. 91–104); Green and Shapiro (1994: 14–17).

[80] E.g. Rosenau (1992); Alexander (1995).

some extent shaped by physical reality. Instead, agents' capacity for learning and reflection has an impact on the way in which they attach meaning to the material world. Agents cognitively frame or construct the world according to their knowledge, norms, experience and understandings. Hence, actors' interests and identities are moulded and constituted by both cognitive and material structures. Their preferences are shaped by social interaction and the evolving structures, norms and rules of the domestic and the EU polity (i.e. membership matters) rather than exogenously given. Collective actions are not merely the aggregation of individual preferences, but individual actors' objectives are influenced by and derived from the social group with which an agent interacts and identifies. And because agents are assumed to have the capacity to learn, their preferences are subject to change rather than stable, given evolving social structures and varying actor constellations in the real world. The nature of being is thus viewed as transformative. This perspective is regarded as a complement (and not a substitute) to the soft rationalist position outlined above.

Finally, what is the ontological status of structure and agency in the revised neofunctionalist framework? Early neofunctionalism viewed agents as predominant and paid relatively little attention to structure.[81] The revised neofunctionalist account regards the properties of both structure and agency as very significant to explaining social and political processes and, for that matter, European integration. It dismisses both structural determinism and agency-centred voluntarism. Instead, my framework embraces the concept of structuration which emphasises the interdependence of structures and agents.[82] Structure and agency mutually constitute each other. Structure has a dual nature. It enters simultaneously into the constitution of the agent and social practices, and exists in the generating moments of this constitution. Agency, however, is not reduced to a servant of structure. Agents have created structural properties in the first place and can potentially change any aspect of structure. They act upon both structures and their own preconceived interests. Structures in the revised neofunctionalist framework are, for example, the EU and international system of states, the EU institutional order, domestic constellations/institutional balances and functional-economic interdependencies and necessities. Relevant actors are manifold, ranging from governmental elites to private and

---

[81] However, structure was arguably more important in (early) neofunctionalism than acknowledged by Haas (2001: 29), given the emphasis on functional-economic interdependencies.

[82] Cf. Giddens (1984: ch. 1).

supranational actors. Revised neofunctionalism assigns agency and structure an equal ontological status.

Additional Underlying Assumptions

In response to the justified challenges to the original neofunctionalist account, along with my own prior empirical findings, but also following logically from the above discussion regarding ontology and owing to the additional changes specified later on in this chapter, some of the neofunctionalist tenets have to be reassessed. Many of the original assumptions remain unchanged: (1) integration is still understood and characterised as a process, (2) which is influenced by multiple and diverse actors (and structures). States are not unified actors and certainly not the only actors. (3) Preferences are not perceived as constant but tend to change during the integration process since actors undergo learning processes. (4) Once established, institutions can take on a life of their own and are difficult to control by those who created them. (5) There is scope for unintended consequences because decisions are often taken with uncertainty, imperfect knowledge or under time pressure which restricts the possibility of *long-term* purposive action. (6) Functional interdependencies between issue areas spur the propensity for further or more intensified co-operation/integration.

Yet, other early neofunctionalist assumptions have to be relaxed or dropped. First, the 'grand' theory presumption has been refuted by empirical research and can no longer be maintained. Revised neofunctionalism can only provide a 'partial theory',[83] which accounts only for a certain part of the EU animal, namely explaining outcomes/integration. While constituting a partial theory, revised neofunctionalism is still viewed as a 'wider' approach (in the realm of explaining), given the comprehensiveness and modifications of the revised framework specified in this chapter.

Second, the automaticity of the spillover maxim[84] has been dismissed, both in the literature and in my own prior research. The appeal for a surrender of the original neofunctionalist teleology, which had already been advocated by some neofunctionalists in their later writings, is upheld and put into practice here. This revision of neofunctionalism accepts the difficulties of predicting political developments; political science has perhaps too often tried to imitate the natural sciences only to

---

[83] Cf. Tranholm-Mikkelsen (1991: 18); Matlary (1994).

[84] This assumption led Haas to go as far as to predict that political actors would shift their loyalties to the European level by the end of the transitional period. See Haas (1958: 16).

be found wanting. Nonetheless, if we loosen the theory's predictive strait-jacket to treat the different kinds of spillover merely as tools for describing and explaining certain dynamics of European integration, we continue both to achieve a rich understanding of the process and to provide ourselves with a basis for making 'informed judgements' rather than 'hard prediction'.[85] In addition, original neofunctionalism lacks a comprehensive, refined and integrated delimitation of the concept of spillover, i.e. a specification of the conditions under which the integration process progresses and spillover occurs.[86] This book seeks to provide insights into this question. However, rather than engage in probing or testing conditions, this work has the more modest aim of (tentatively) identifying or hypothesising those conditions and mechanisms which are likely to impact on spillover (and particularly socialisation and learning) processes.

Third, in view of the criticisms that have been expressed and following (logically) from my subsequent revisions concerning the integration of countervailing forces into the revised neofunctionalist framework, the 'end of ideology' and 'continuation of unabated economic growth' assumptions have been dropped: the former by accounting for the impact of sovereignty-consciousness and nationalism on actors' dispositions, the latter through formulating 'negative integrative climate' as a countervailing pressure which is linked to economic recession.

Fourth, for early neofunctionalists, Community politics was basically dominated by (governmental and non-governmental) elites, with little or no role foreseen for the public in the integration process. Fifty years on, this supposition is no longer supportable, with a directly elected European Parliament, the prominent debate about the Union's democratic deficit and the increasing role of national referenda.[87] While the revised neofunctionalist account still attributes a primary role to elites, the public has, to some extent, been integrated into the revised framework. Electoral and, more generally, public pressure is one important aspect of the countervailing force of 'domestic constraints' and

---

[85] See George (1991: 250). As Stone Sweet and Sandholtz (1997: 301) rightly stated, 'there is substantial room for supranational governance without the ultimate shift in identification'.

[86] Keohane and Hoffmann (1991: 19–20) also drew attention to the importance of delimiting the concept of spillover, without, however, contributing to the substance of this question.

[87] However, Schmitter's (1969) writings on politicisation suggested that with the progression of the integration project, the audience interested in the process would widen. Yet, that the 'permissive consensus' would turn into a 'constraining dissensus' (cf. Hooghe and Marks 2005: 5) was not expected.

the public also plays a role in the spillback force 'negative integrative climate'.[88]

Fifth, and already sufficiently explained above, whereas early neofunctionalism can be characterised by a 'soft' rational-choice ontology, the revised framework accepts this ontology, but also embraces ('soft') constructivism, which is regarded as a complement rather than a substitute. It also parts from original neofunctionalism's actor-centredness; instead, it attributes structure and agency equal ontological status and draws on the concept of structuration. Finally, while the initial neofunctionalist account emphasised the dynamics of integration, this modified framework seeks to balance the dynamics – in favour of which a stronger presumption is still made – with countervailing pressures.

The Dynamics of Integration: the Concept of Spillover

The above assumptions provide the basis for the main revised neofunctionalist hypotheses. The first part of these hypotheses is concerned with the dynamics of the integration process which centre around the concept of spillover. The problem with this term is that its meaning gradually broadened and came to denote any type of neofunctionalist explanation for political change to cover the multitude of different mechanisms and patterns of causation that seemed to have been involved in the expansion of tasks. The distinctions that underlie it and the agents that activate these mechanisms became thoroughly blurred. 'As a result, the term spillover has no fixed meaning, and confusion rather than sharp analysis has resulted.'[89]

Some scholars have tried to rectify this confusion by making (useful) distinctions between the different phenomena that have been labelled 'spillover'. Generally, three types of spillover have been identified: functional, political and cultivated spillover.[90] The assumptions which lie behind these spillovers can be found in the writings of Haas and Lindberg. The terminologies of functional, political and cultivated

---

[88] See my analysis below (in this chapter) on countervailing forces and their integration of the role of the public.

[89] Lindberg and Scheingold (1970: 156).

[90] This distinction and these terminologies have been introduced by Tranholm-Mikkelsen (1991: 4ff). George (1991: ch. 2) also distinguished between functional and political spillover, but did not formally recognise 'cultivated spillover' as a form of spillover. However, he does refer to the 'Commission leadership' which he identifies as a third neofunctional pressure for integration. The term cultivated spillover was first used by Nye (1970: 804). He gave the term a slightly different meaning, referring to it as 'deliberate linkages created or overstated by political actors'. However, throughout this book cultivated spillover is understood as defined by Tranholm-Mikkelsen (i.e. integrative role of the Commission, or more broadly the role of the central institutions).

spillover, however, are not part of the first-generation neofunctionalist vocabulary. The revised neofunctionalist account will make use of these distinctions as a starting point for further modifications and additions. The subsequent revisions, to some extent, reflect and accommodate my own ideas and conceptions (partly on the basis of prior research), and are, to some degree, deduced from my basic ontology and underlying assumptions. The injected changes also partly stem from later or sub-sidiary neofunctionalist thought – drawing on the full repertoire of neofunctionalist ideas. My revision also integrates contributions from scholars who do not conceive themselves as working in the neo-functionalist tradition.[91]

Functional Spillover

'Functional' spillover originated in Haas' writings on functional-economic interdependencies inducing an expansive logic of sector integration. The functional spillover dynamic builds on these original neofunctionalist insights, which have already been described above. However, the revised neofunctionalist conception of functional spillover is broader. It takes Lindberg's notion of spillover as a starting point for further specification. For Lindberg (functional) spillover 'refers to a situation in which the original goal can be assured only by taking further actions, which in turn create a further condition and need for more action, and so forth'.[92] This wider definition allows us to depart from Haas' narrow focus on *economic* linkage between *policy areas*. Instead, it enables us to encompass all types of *endogenous-functional* inter-dependencies, i.e. all tensions and contradictions arising from within, or which are closely related to, the European integration project, and its policies, politics and polity, which induce policy-makers to take addi-tional integrative steps in order to achieve their original objectives.

This broader conception not only enables us to account for pressures (resulting from the dissatisfaction of collective goal attainment in one area) to induce (further) integrational steps in *other* sectors or policy areas, but also for pressures to generate increased co-operation in the *same* field. To distinguish between these two phenomena, the former will be referred to as (functional) 'spillover pressure', and the latter as (functional) 'pressure from within'. This differentiation is not to be confused with the distinction between expanding the 'breadth' (of issues to be resolved on the European level) and increasing the 'depth'

---

[91] Ideas and contributions which are not my own are, of course, clearly indicated.
[92] Lindberg (1963: 10).

of (supranational) co-operation.[93] While the distinction between 'spillover pressures' and 'pressures from within' elucidates the causal origin of change, the 'breadth/depth' differentiation refers to the outcome of pressure. Both 'spillover pressures' and 'pressures from within' can result in an expanded breadth *and* an increased depth of integration. Functional 'pressure from within' is not a new feature in the (neofunctionalist) literature. It has been implied by the term 'task expansion'.[94] Yet, this phenomenon has been treated as a very subsidiary hypothesis, overshadowed by functional (sector-to-sector) 'spillover pressure', and has been largely ignored and almost forgotten in neofunctionalist and other theorising. It is hypothesised here that a considerable portion of functional pressure is in fact 'from within' and that this conception deserves more attention as an analytical tool, as will be substantiated in the subsequent empirical analysis.

Functional pressures constitute a structural component of the revised neofunctionalist framework. These pressures have a propensity for causing further integration, as rational and intentional actors tend to be persuaded by the functional tensions and contradictions. However, in line with my above-described ontology, functional structures do not 'determine' actors' behaviour in any mechanical or predictable fashion. Endogenous-functional structures contain an important element of human agreement. Agents have to perceive functional structures as plausible and somewhat compelling. They need to conceive of them as (strong) pressures in order to act upon them. (Endogenous-functional) structures and (national, supranational and other) actors are interdependent. Functional structures enter into the constitution of actors (i.e. influence their preferences) and also, to some extent, exist from the generating moments of this constitution, as actors tend to reproduce structures under the impact of their interests that have been moulded by structures. However, actors are not structural idiots. They have created structures in the first place and can potentially change them at any time. And, in doing so, there is a (considerable) degree of non-structural autonomy. Functional spillover in the revised neofunctionalist framework thus reflects a 'soft' functionalism and departs from the deterministic/mechanical ontology of some functionalist accounts.[95]

---

[93] For a definition of breadth and depth of integration see first part of my methodology section.

[94] See Groom (1978: 23). The term 'task expansion' has been dismissed here, because its semantic connotation refers to a certain result (i.e. an expansion of scope) rather than to the origin of endogenous-functional pressure.

[95] Cf. Hempel (1959); Lowi (1963: 570–83).

Exogenous Spillover

'Exogenous' spillover further extends the concept of spillover to incorporate those factors that originate outside the integration process itself, i.e. that are exogenous to it. It is an attempt to take account of the fact that changes in, and pressures from, the external political and economic environment affect the behaviour of national and supranational actors and also influence EU and domestic structures. It is thereby recognised that the Community and its development need to be viewed in the global context. To some extent, the early neofunctionalists discussed an integration process that was insulated from the outside world. Of course, it impinged on the process, not least in the form of trade policy or the CAP, but the emphasis was on the endogenous dynamics of the process.[96] The inadequate emphasis put on exogenous factors has been a major criticism levelled against neofunctionalism.[97]

It is maintained here that this important variable can be sensibly incorporated into revised neofunctionalism without distorting or overstretching the framework. My reading of Haas, which is shared by other scholars,[98] suggests that his emphasis on sector-to-sector linkages between economies also goes beyond the narrow realm of the six members of the ECSC, although he focused on the interdependencies between the economies participating in the integration project. Haas not only implied global interdependence, but also pointed to the relevance of some exogenous factors, without however attributing them the necessary significance.[99] Schmitter made an attempt to bring in exogenous events. His externalisation hypothesis, which will be further elaborated below, makes a valuable connection between the Community and its external environment.[100] Moreover, it should not be forgotten that Haas put forward his theoretical account when the European integration project was still in the infant stages of its development. As the integration process has evolved considerably since the publication of *The Uniting of Europe*, it only seems fair and logical to adjust neofunctionalism accordingly. If one takes account of change, the theoretical tools designed four decades ago cannot be left unaltered. Finally, exogenous spillover ought to form part of a revised neofunctionalist framework, as the theory is mainly one which deals with the *dynamics* of integration. Exogenous factors – although they can constitute an

---

[96] Cf. Schmitter (1996a: 13).   [97] E.g. Hoffmann (1964, 1995).

[98] Stone Sweet and Sandholtz (1997: 300) also interpreted Haas' thinking as encompassing '*global* interdependence' (italics added).

[99] In addition, Haas (1968: xxviii) himself proposed that the theory should be amended to account for exogenous pressures.

[100] See Schmitter (1969: 165); also cf. Niemann (1998: 431–5).

obstacle to further integration – generally encourage or provoke further integrative steps.[101]

There are several logics behind hypothesising exogenous factors as a *dynamic* of integration. First, some exogenous events and developments are viewed as threats or shocks. It has been pointed out in the literature that perceived threats are conducive to the integration of regional blocks. This has been illustrated, for example, in terms of the Cold War origins of the European Communities.[102] The rationale behind the integrative impact of external shocks and threats is that in such instances close co-operation partners (or Member States of an integration project) tend to rally together and find common solutions. One particular but frequent type of threat is competition between states and/or regions. Perceived competition with other international players tends to encourage EU Member States to pool their strengths and resources through further co-operation/integration with the intention of advancing the Union's competitive position. Examples of the integrative impact of external (mainly US and Japanese economic) competition in the history of European integration include agreement on the 1992 programme or the development of industrial and high technology policies.[103]

A second logic of external spillover is grounded in the nature of many international problems and their perception. Regional integration is often viewed as a more effective buffer against disadvantageous or uncertain external developments. This is related to the perception that many problems go beyond the governance potential of individual Member States. Phenomena and processes such as globalisation, migration, environmental destruction or international terrorism require a common approach (e.g. of integration partners) in order to tackle them with some success.[104] This exogenous aspect is linked to, and further explained by, an endogenous one. European democratic nation-states depend on the delivery of economic, social and other well-being to their people. Increasingly, due to regional interdependencies and more global problems, they lose their power to deliver these goods. To circumvent the decrease in influence over their territory, national governments tend to co-operate more closely on the European level.[105]

---

[101] E.g. Hill (1993); but also cf. George (1991) and Tranholm-Mikkelsen (1991).
[102] Milward and Sørensen (1993); Neuss (2000).
[103] On external causes of the Single European Act and the 1992 programme, see Sandholtz and Zysman (1989). On the explanatory factors of technology policies see Peterson (1991, 1992).
[104] Cf. George and Bache (2000: 39).
[105] The latter point has drawn on Wessels (1997: 286ff).

Third, Schmitter has pointed out that once a regional integration project has got under way and developed common policies 'participants will find themselves compelled – regardless of their original intentions – to adopt common policies *vis-à-vis* non-participant third parties. Members will be forced to hammer out a collective external position (and in the process are likely to rely increasingly on the new central institutions to do it)'.[106] Schmitter points to the incentive of forging common positions and policies to increase the collective bargaining power of the Community *vis-à-vis* the outside world as well as involuntary motives such as the demands of the extra-Community environment reacting to (successful) developments within the regional integration project. Hence, there is an endogenous logic linking internal and external events.

It has already been alluded to in the preceding analysis that exogenous factors are often closely linked to, and not always separable from, endogenous ones. Perhaps even more importantly, actors' preferences cannot be treated as given. The external environment/system, just like EU membership, to some extent, constitutes decision-makers' preferences. This is difficult to trace in empirical analysis. One indicator for the significance of such, often 'invisible', influences of the wider international context is the impact of internationally prevailing policy paradigms and discourses. For example, the gradual acceptance of (originally Anglo-Saxon) neoliberal economic ideas by West European elites has certainly facilitated agreement on the Single European Market and the liberalisation of many policy sectors.[107] Finally, it should be pointed out that, like endogenous-functional spillover, exogenous spillover is essentially a structural pressure.[108]

Political Spillover

Neofunctionalists also pointed to the integrative pressures exerted by national elites, who realise that problems of substantial interest cannot be satisfactorily solved at the domestic level. This would lead to a gradual learning process whereby elites shift their expectations, political activities and loyalties to a new European centre. As a result national elites, including interest groups and civil servants, would promote further integration, thus adding a political stimulus to the process. Subsequently, this pressure became known as 'political' spillover.[109]

---

[106] Schmitter (1969: 165).   [107] See e.g. Green Cowles (1995: 521).

[108] However, it is not entirely a structural pressure because third countries and their elites can exert pressure directly on EU decision-makers (cf. chapter II, section on exogenous spillover).

[109] Tranholm-Mikkelsen (1991: 5). Subsequently, a number of authors such as George (1991: 23) took up this terminology.

It is argued here that this factor is excessively broad and tries to subsume too much in one variable, thus compromising analytical clarity.[110] As a result, I will subsequently distinguish between (1) the development of organised interests at European level, mainly (but not exclusively) relating to non-governmental elites which change their perceptions largely because of incentive-based learning. This pressure will retain the label 'political' spillover because it involves the build-up of *political* impetus and activism in favour of further integration within Member States and (2) processes of elite enmeshment, socialisation and learning, including, but going beyond, incentive-based learning among primarily (but not exclusively) governmental elites. Given the prominence of socialisation and greater emphasis on the social conditioning of rationality here, this pressure reflecting the nature of this dynamic will be termed 'social' spillover.

Haas particularly emphasised the potential integrative pressures exerted by organised interests. Two hypotheses can be derived from neofunctionalist thought concerning the role of non-governmental elites. The first was that groups would gradually focus more of their attention, lobbying and organisation onto the European level with the growing competence of supranational institutions and the increased number of policy sectors governed (at least partially) by the European level. Second, it was argued that interest groups would gradually promote further integration, as they became aware of the benefits of European level co-operation in their policy area. Early neofunctionalists underpinned this tendency of interest groups to demand further integration in other sectors with the functional logic, i.e. that integration in one sector would only be effective if followed by integration in other areas, due to functional interdependencies. Hence, non-governmental elites would become carriers of functional spillover. The primary driving force for groups to support further integration was mainly held to be their own (material) self-interest. This was to alter both their (more short/medium-term) expectations as well as their (more long-term) loyalties. That the neofunctionalist account of learning may be insufficiently specified will be further elaborated below.

The revised neofunctionalist framework still regards endogenous European-level dynamics – i.e. functional spillover pressures, pull-factors from European integration and the EU institutional development – as

---

[110] Arguably, this was the case as the previous political spillover variable tried to combine processes such as politicisation with bureaucratisation/depoliticisation. The former is to be found in what will subsequently remain to be called 'political' spillover, and the latter was presumed under assumptions of what will be called 'social' spillover.

significant factors influencing interest groups.[111] However, I argue that this is only part of the story. In line with the widened scope of the revised model, other structures such as exogenous pressures or domestic constrains are hypothesised to influence the behaviour of non-governmental elites. For example, rationales largely exogenous to the integration process itself, such as the nature of many (global/international) problems which exceed the governance potential of individual Member States, also contribute to (non-governmental) elites seeking European-level solutions.

Haas, in *The Uniting of Europe* and most of his subsequent works, particularly focused his analysis on the integrative pressures exerted by trade associations and trade unions.[112] A slight extension of his thought to include the various other types of societal groups, including all (economic) interest groups and NGOs, to encompass non-governmental elites more generally, seems plausible as the plurality of relevant societal actors has increased since the time of Haas' writing. Second-generation neofunctionalists already referred to a broader range of non-governmental elites.[113] The notion of political spillover in terms of non-governmental elites will be further stretched here to incorporate the concept of advocacy coalitions. This extension is undertaken because it largely reflects neofunctionalist premises[114] and would have probably been included by neofunctionalists at the time if this phenomenon and this conception had gained the same prominence (in European policy-making) back then as they have today.

Advocacy coalitions consist of actors from a variety of private and also governmental organisations who share a set of policy beliefs and seek to realise them by influencing multiple governmental institutions over time.[115] Advocacy coalitions are glued together by common beliefs rather than by common interests, as opposed to 'material' interest groups for which material self-interest is of fundamental importance.[116]

---

[111] Important aspects in that respect, which were implicit rather than explicit in (early) neofunctionalism, are the benefit which many societal (especially business) groups see in one set rather than six, 15 or 25 sets of rules and the advantages of larger markets and economies of scales, more generally.

[112] Haas (1958: chs. 4 and 11) also paid significant attention to the role of political parties.

[113] E.g. Schmitter (1971: 257, 263).

[114] Both neofunctionalism and the concept of advocacy coalition share, for example, an emphasis on learning, on multiple and diverse actors, and on processes rather than single events.

[115] On the advocacy coalition framework, see e.g. Sabatier (1988, 1998); Sabatier and Jenkins-Smith (1993).

[116] Sabatier and Jenkins-Smith (1993: 233). Advocacy coalitions can be distinguished from the wider concept of policy-networks in that the former aggregates actors within a subsystem into a manageable number of belief-based coalitions, whereas network

While neofunctionalists concentrated primarily on material interest groups, advocacy coalitions are actually more likely to shift their attention, expectations and perhaps loyalties to the European level, since they are less prone to enter into coalitions of convenience than are 'material' interest groups, because their beliefs are less fluid than those of material interest groups' representatives.[117] In the neofunctionalist spirit it can thus be hypothesised that as the European level of governance gradually increases in importance over time, advocacy coalitions develop the perception that their beliefs and interests need to be articulated (or are perhaps even better served) on the European level. Once advocacy coalitions' beliefs are well served in the European arena, they are not likely to abandon their interest in European solutions, since their interests (beliefs) usually only change through external events, such as changes in socio-economic conditions, changes in public opinion or changes in the political system of governance.[118]

Social Spillover[119]

Lindberg particularly emphasised the role of governmental elites and *engrenage*.[120] Even though it did not contain a neatly structured body within the neofunctionalist literature, four hypotheses can be ascertained from the neofunctionalist writings on social spillover: (1) socialisation[121] processes occur amongst national civil servants within the Council framework, often involving Commission officials; (2) Community decision-making cannot be captured in terms of classic

analysts view individuals as largely autonomous and thus deal with a complex set of actors (cf. Heclo 1978). They can also be distinguished from epistemic communities. The latter are united around causal beliefs and through their shared expertise, whereas advocacy coalitions tend more to be held together by 'core' beliefs which are relatively stable over time. As core beliefs are stable, so are advocacy coalition compositions. Epistemic communities, on the other hand, are relatively volatile. Whereas the propensity of shorter life-spans precluded epistemic communities being incorporated within the concept of political spillover (see below), advocacy coalitions seem to fulfil this criterion. Hence, they could take on a similar European vocation as non-governmental elites in the way hypothesised by neofunctionalism.

[117] See Sabatier and Jenkins-Smith (1993: 255).
[118] Sabatier and Jenkins-Smith (1993: 224).
[119] I would like to thank Janina Dill and Nicolas Lamp for suggesting the term. Cf. Dill and Lamp (2004).
[120] Cf. Lindberg (1963: ch. 4). 'Engrenage' has been defined on pp. 18–19, note 35 of this chapter.
[121] Here socialisation is to mean the 'induction of new members [...] into the ways of behaviour that are preferred in a society' (Barnes, Carter and Skidmore 1980: 35). Complementarily, it is understood as 'the process by which actors internalise norms which then influence how they see themselves and what they perceive as their interests' (Risse and Wiener 1999: 778).

intergovernmental strategic bargaining but is better characterised as a 'supranational' problem-solving process; (3) processes of enmeshment and socialisation tend to ease decision-making deadlocks and induce consensus formation and progress among member governments; (4) learning processes help generate a shift of expectations and perhaps loyalties towards the emerging European polity on the part of national elites. My theoretical and empirical analysis will focus on the first three aspects of *engrenage*, while the fourth one will be addressed in the conclusion.

From the early writings of Lindberg until the mid-1990s, there was little interest in socialisation processes in the European Community, and there were only a few explicit studies on *engrenage*, dating back to the early and mid-1970s. While most works did not substantiate the findings of Lindberg and Scheingold,[122] Scheinman and Feld came to the conclusion that 'even partial assimilation is likely to advance the European cause; [...] the depth of change over time, not the speed of change, should be a criterion of success'.[123] As socialisation is indeed hypothesised as a long-term process, and given the potential bearing of this variable on policy-style and decision-making in the European Union, much more systematic investigation into its role and impact needs to be undertaken, a task which has been partially advanced by some scholars in recent years.[124] One insight of the more recent literature on this issue, which parallels and in a way confirms neofunctionalist thought, will be highlighted here. A number of authors have suggested that institutions at the European level – often broadly defined to include norms – shape agents' behaviour, preferences and identities. This insight was always implicit, and has been made more explicit through the ontology of the revised framework above.[125]

I argue that the (early) neofunctionalist ideas of socialisation and learning provide a useful starting point for further investigation. However, at the same time neofunctionalist thought is, to some extent and in some instances, unclear, imprecise and incomplete, and thus needs to be further specified in order to warrant a useful development and application of social spillover as an explanatory variable. It can be suggested, for example, not only that the duration, quantity and intensity of interaction have a bearing on the evolution of socialisation and learning processes (as primarily hypothesised by neofunctionalists), but that the

---

[122] Cf. e.g. Feld and Wildgen (1975).   [123] Scheinman and Feld (1972: 135).
[124] See e.g. Lewis (1998b); Beyers and Dierickx (1998); Trondal (2000).
[125] Neofunctionalists' implicit assumptions to that effect have been acknowledged by Sandholtz (1993: 3). As for the more recent literature underlining this insight, see e.g. Matlary (1997); Lewis (1998a); Christiansen, Jorgensen and Wiener (2001).

quality of interaction also constitutes a significant factor.[126] In addition, although neofunctionalists seem to imply reflexive forms of learning, these appear secondary to interest- or incentive-based learning (with actors changing their expectations due to functional incentives/imperatives).[127] Yet, arguably, deeply rooted genuine learning cannot be sufficiently explained through incentives/interests of egoistic actors.[128] More 'complex' learning goes beyond adaptation – the redefinition of means or strategies to reach basically unaltered and unquestioned goals. Instead, it constitutes changed behaviour as a result of challenged and scrutinised assumptions, values and objectives.[129] Arguably, to account for this type of learning we have to look for 'endogenous' preference formation, i.e. taking place during/through the interaction. Furthermore, if we want to understand and explain social behaviour and learning, we need to take communication and language into greater consideration. It is through speech that actors make sense of the world and attribute meaning to their actions. Hence – in order to account for the *quality* of interaction, to provide a more fundamental basis for *reflexive* learning and to integrate the role of *communication* more thoroughly – the notion of communicative action will be incorporated into the revised neofunctionalist framework. This way, the concept of social spillover is rendered more precise, robust and plausible.

The concept of communicative action, as devised by Habermas, refers to the interaction of people whose actions are co-ordinated not via egocentric calculations of success but through acts of reaching understanding.[130] In communicative action, participants are not primarily oriented to achieving their own individual success; they pursue their individual objectives under the condition that they can coordinate or harmonise their plans of action on the basis of shared definitions of the situation.[131] Agents engaging in communicative action seek to reach understanding about valid behaviour. Habermas distinguishes between three validity claims that can be challenged in discourse: first, that a statement is true, i.e. conforms to the facts; second, that a speech act is right with respect to the existing normative context; and third, that the

---

[126] See Checkel (2001c: 225).   [127] Cf. Haas (1958: 291, 312–13).
[128] Cf. Checkel (2001c: 242).
[129] I have based my distinction between deeply rooted, reflexive or complex learning, on the one hand, and adaptation or incentive-based learning, on the other hand, on Nye (1987: 380) who used the terms 'complex' and 'simple' learning. I also thank Janina Dill and Nicolas Lamp for drawing my attention to this aspect. Cf. Dill and Lamp (2004).
[130] Habermas's theory of communicative action was devised and developed in the following works: Habermas (1981a, b, 1986, 1995).
[131] Habermas (1981a: 385–6).

manifest intention of the speaker is truthful, i.e. that s/he means what s/he says. Communicative behaviour, which aims at reasoned understanding, counterfactually assumes the existence of an 'ideal speech situation', in which nothing but the better argument counts and actors attempt to convince each other (and are open to persuasion) with regard to the three types of validity claims. If a listener doubts a validity claim, the speaker must explain himself and come up with reasons which are debatable in a rational discourse. By arguing in relation to standards of truth, rightness and sincerity, agents have a basis for judging what constitute reasonable choices of action, through which they can reach agreement.[132] Where communicative rationality prevails, actors' pursuit of their interests is conditioned by their perception of valid behaviour according to these three standards. Stated differently, when engaging in communicative action, agents do not seek to maximise their interests, but to challenge and substantiate the validity claims that are inherent in their interest. Interests may also change in the process of communicative interaction, as actors challenge each other's causal and principled beliefs.[133]

While agents bargain in strategic interaction, they *discuss, deliberate, reason, argue* and *persuade* in communicative interaction. Actors engaging in communicative behaviour have the potential to undergo more profound learning processes. Rather than merely adapting the means to achieve basically unchanged goals, as in strategic interaction, they redefine their very priorities and preferences in validity-seeking processes aimed at reaching mutual understanding. Epistemic communities, i.e. networks of knowledge-based experts, may also contribute to deeply rooted or complex learning, as they challenge cause-and-effect relationships and engage in truth-seeking processes.[134] They contribute to consensual knowledge and may – through the generation of new

---

[132] Cf. Habermas (1981a: 149).

[133] According to Habermas, the possibility for communicative action is dependent on a number of factors. First, actors have to share a common lifeworld, i.e. collectively share the same patterns of interpretation of the world. Second, actors should recognise each other as equals and need to have equal access to the discourse. Third, communicative action is dependent on actors' ability to empathise, i.e. see things with the eyes of the discourse partner (Habermas 1981b: ch. vi).

[134] While the concept complements my notion of social spillover, it has also been accommodated within the concept of cultivated spillover (see next section). It may be worth mentioning here that epistemic communities themselves are unlikely to become long-term agents of European integration. Their behaviour (and support for Community measures) is based on common knowledge and similar causal beliefs, which are rather volatile (Haas 1992: 3ff). Continued epistemic community support for an EU policy can easily be fragmented through the emergence of different scientific research results and subsequent internal conflict (cf. Peterson 1992).

ideas – alter actors' preferences. They may be engaged in communicative interaction, but the social legitimation of scientists (i.e. epistemic actors) and their claim to represent not only normative but also causal claims could inject an element of hierarchy (i.e. power) into the interaction with non-members of the community and thus lapse, to some extent, from communicative action. Somewhere between hard bargaining and communicative action lies what has been referred to as 'rhetorical action', the strategic use of norm-based arguments.[135] Actors whose self-interested preferences are in line with certain prevailing norms or values can use these argumentatively to add cheap legitimacy to their position and delegitimise the position of their opponents. Whereas communicative actors attempt to reach reasoned understanding, rhetorical actors seek to strengthen their own position strategically and are not prepared to be persuaded by the better argument.

Once Community/collaborative norms (i.e. 'collective expectations for the proper behaviour')[136] have become internalised by actors, another mode of action becomes increasingly relevant for social spillover in the revised neofunctionalist model: normatively regulated behaviour. This action mode further specifies the concept of social spillover. Normatively regulated action refers to members of a social group who orient their action towards common values or norms which they have thoroughly internalised.[137] The individual actor complies with a norm when, in a given situation, the conditions are present to which the norm has application. All members of a group for whom a given norm has validity may expect of one another that, in a certain situation, they will carry out the actions proscribed. Norms are taken for granted. They are not enacted out of choice, but out of habit. Norms make an impact because 'the individual intentionality that each person has is derived from the collective intentionality that they share'.[138]

In the revised neofunctionalist framework, communicative action is granted greater potential for deep-rooted learning than rhetorical action, and especially hard-bargaining. And socialised actors are more likely to engage in norm-regulated and communicative action than agents who have not undergone these common processes. However, consistent with my ontological position, agents combine all these (complementary) modes of action in their behaviour. What is of paramount importance then, and what is lacking in many works on socialisation, is the

---

[135] Schimmelfennig (2001: 62ff).
[136] Katzenstein (1996: 5).   [137] Habermas (1981a; 127).
[138] See Searle (1995: 25). Concepts like bargaining, communicative action and normatively regulated action should be seen as ideal types which do not often appear in their pure form.

specification of the conditions conducive to the different modes of behaviour, and in particular to socialisation and learning. In contrast to early neofunctionalism, which assumed constant learning and socialisation, the revised framework departs from this presumption and is concerned with delimiting the scope of social spillover.

While social spillover is mainly about the social interaction of agents, this pressure also links actors to broader structures. For example, endogenous-functional, exogenous, domestic and EU institutional structures become part of decision-makers' norms and values throughout processes of socialisation and learning. In addition, actors who engage in communicative action, in their quest to arrive at the most 'valid' solution to the problems at hand, tend to be more open-minded, i.e. beyond the narrow confines of their preconceived interests, and are thus more inclined to also consider arguments derived from the (wider) structural environment. Put differently, during communicative interaction agents are likely to uncover structural factors, which are subsequently incorporated in their deliberations. Social spillover thus (also) works as an interface between structure and agency.

Cultivated Spillover

Haas and Lindberg also referred to another pressure, the integrative impact of the High Authority and the Commission.[139] They particularly pointed to attempts by these institutions to cultivate relations with interest groups and national civil servants so as to gain their support for realising integrative objectives, and to cultivate pressures vis-à-vis governments, particularly by pointing to functional interdependencies or by upgrading common interests (e.g. through facilitating logrolling or package deals). This dynamic has, therefore, appropriately been termed 'cultivated' spillover.[140] Of the various spillover pressures, neofunctionalists put least emphasis on cultivated spillover. Haas held that with the dissipating initial élan of the Commission, the quality of supranational bargaining was only altered subtly, and far from fatal to the integration process. Although he thought that this produced decelerating effects, on the whole Haas attributed only secondary importance to the role of the Commission.[141] In the subsequent analysis it will be suggested that this pressure should be upgraded within the revised neofunctionalist framework.

[139] E.g. Haas (1961: esp. 368); Lindberg (1963: 71).
[140] Tranholm-Mikkelsen (1991: 6). The term has subsequently been taken by a number of authors such as George and Bache (2000: 12) and Rosamond (2000: 61).
[141] Cf. Haas (1964a: 78, 1968: xxvii).

The concept of cultivated spillover will be further extended here to signify the intrinsic propensity of supranational institutions to advance the European integration process more generally. Such extension can be deduced from the (early and revised) neofunctionalist tenets. Restating and substantiating the conceptual basis of cultivated spillover, we seek to enhance its plausibility for the revised framework: first, neofunctionalists emphasised the probability of unintended consequences, as most political actors are incapable of long-range purposive behaviour since they tend to 'stumble' from one decision into the next as a result of earlier decisions. Decisions on integration are normally taken with very imperfect knowledge of their consequences and frequently under the pressure of deadlines.[142] Secondly and mainly following from this, institutions, once established, can take on a life of their own and are difficult to control by those who created them. Third, concerned with increasing their own powers, supranational institutions become agents of integration, because they tend to benefit from the progression of this process. Finally, institutional structures (of which supranational institutions are part) have an impact on how actors perceive their interests and identities.

Cultivated spillover in the revised neofunctionalist framework also seeks to reflect the Community's institutional development over the past four decades, which could perhaps not be foreseen by neofunctionalists at the time. Given the changes of the European Union's institutional set-up and the broader specification of this dynamic above, it seems logical to incorporate institutions such as the European Parliament (EP), the European Court of Justice (ECJ) or the Council Presidency into the concept of cultivated spillover. My subsequent analysis will further substantiate these extensions concerning the scope of cultivated spillover.

With the Luxembourg Compromise, which forced the Commission to take a back seat, and the arrival of European Political Cooperation (EPC), Technical Councils and European Councils, the Council Presidency began to develop into an alternative architect of compromise.[143] Governments taking on the six-month role face a number of pressures, such as increased media attention as well as peer group evaluation, to abstain from pursuing their national interest and to assume the role of a neutral mediator.[144] During their Presidency, national officials also tend to undergo a sometimes rapid learning process about the various

---

[142] Haas (1970: 627); Haas and Schmitter (1964).   [143] Edwards and Wallace (1977).
[144] Wallace (1985a). The Presidency is assisted in various aspects of its responsibilities by the Council Secretariat. While the latter formally only had a secretarial function, it has been suggested that the Council Secretariat has developed its own pro-integration agenda (Beach 2005). However, the Council Secretariat will not be examined in depth in this book. On its role cf. Christiansen (2002); Beach (2005).

national dimensions which induces a more 'European thinking' and often results in 'European compromises'.[145] A number of case studies confirm the acceptance by member governments to take on the role of honest and promotional broker, and to try to push the negotiating parties beyond the lowest common denominator.[146] Haas pointed out that the use of an institutionalised mediator usually leads to upgrading the common interest of the parties involved in multilateral negotiations. In the context of the ECSC and the EEC, he saw this role fulfilled by the High Authority and the European Commission. However, the mediating services did not necessarily have to come from those supranational institutions, but could simply be provided by 'a single person or board of experts with an autonomous range of powers'.[147] The Council Presidency's role as an institutionalised mediator is thus consistent with the broader concept of cultivated spillover.

Although the early neofunctionalists did not dwell on their potential impact, the integrative roles of the European Court of Justice[148] and the European Parliament are easily reconcilable with neofunctionalist theory. Apart from its emphasis on assertive supranational agency neofunctionalism's original assumption of an evolution towards political union would seem to allow for, if not imply, a certain development of both institutions in that direction. The European Parliament has fought, and in many respects won, a battle to become, from being an unelected institution with minor powers under the Treaty of Rome, an institution which since the Treaty of Amsterdam is on an equal footing with the Council in the larger part of normal secondary legislation.[149] It has very clearly become another centre of close interest group attention[150] and plays a critical, even if not wholly successful, role in the legitimisation of the European Union. As part of that process, it has traditionally pushed for further integration, partly in order to expand its own powers.[151]

---

[145] See Wurzel (1996: 272, 288). The learning processes pointed out by Wurzel and its function as a socialising mechanism suggest the possibility of accommodating the Presidency's mediating role within the concept of social spillover. However, there are even closer affiliations with the concept of cultivated spillover, as further elaborated below.

[146] See e.g. Regelsberger and Wessels (1984); Kirchner (1992).   [147] Haas (1961: 368).

[148] With the exception of Scheingold (1965). As pointed out by Weiler (1994) this ignorance of the role played by the ECJ and the legal dimension in European integration has, until recently, been common to all political science studies. Sparked off by a debate between neofunctionalism and intergovernmentalism (see, e.g. Burley and Mattli 1993; Garrett 1995; Mattli and Slaughter 1995; and Wincott 1995), scholars have become generally concerned with integrating the legal dimension into the political science side of European Studies (cf. Shaw 1996; Armstrong and Shaw 1998).

[149] Cf. Maurer (2003b: 230).   [150] Bouwen (2004).

[151] See e.g. Westlake (1994a; 1994b: 243–4).

For its part, the European Court of Justice has been able to assert the primacy of Community law and transform the Treaty of Rome into something like a constitution, a process described as 'normative supranationalism'.[152] Burley and Mattli have shown that neofunctionalism provides a useful framework for an explanation of legal integration and the role of the Court.[153] They have pointed out that the Court of Justice raised the awareness of subnational actors concerning the opportunities offered to them by the Community legal system. The Court helped create these opportunities by giving pro-Community constituencies a direct stake in Community law through the doctrine of direct effect. The European Court of Justice also had a self-interested stake in the process: it sought to promote its own prestige and power by raising the visibility, effectiveness and scope of EC law. Four additional aspects of the Court-driven legal integration can be pinpointed as conforming with, as well as substantiating, neofunctionalist theory. First, the Court has been singled out as an important agent of recognising and giving way to functional pressures.[154] Second, the Court is upgrading common interest. While the Commission is doing so by acting as an institutionalised mediator, the ECJ is justifying its decisions in light of the common interests of members as enshrined in the general objectives of the original EEC Treaty. The *modus operandi* is the 'teleological' method of interpretation, by which the Court managed to rationalise many important decisions, such as those on direct effect.[155] Third, the need for a 'functional' or 'technical' domain to circumvent a direct clash of political interests constitutes an important insight of neofunctionalist theory. Law tends to function as such a mask for politics in much the way that neofunctionalists originally forecast for economics.[156] Finally, it has been noted that judges tend to develop '*une certain ideé de l'Europe*', resembling the neofunctionalist argument concerning socialisation. The generally pro-European outlook of the judges may to some extent account for the frequent choice of the teleological method.[157]

---

[152] Weiler (1981, 1991).

[153] See Burley and Mattli (1993); Mattli and Slaughter (1995, 1998). This view is confirmed by de Burca (2005) who asserts, however, that neofunctionalism, also in the way applied to legal integration by Burley and Mattli, failed to offer an explanatory account of how the law influences *political* integration.

[154] Burley and Mattli (1993: 43, 65).   [155] Burley and Mattli (1993: 68–9).

[156] Burley and Mattli (1993: 44).

[157] See Rasmussen (1988: 28). The neofunctionalist conceptualisation of the ECJ has been subject to criticism. Mattli and Slaughter (1998) when revising their original neofunctionalist approach to the Court noted that their initial account is open to the charge of subjugating the role of the ECJ to a systemic (functional-teleological) determinism. This kind of criticism has been addressed above by not returning to a

While the European Commission will remain the most important focal point of our analysis regarding cultivated spillover, aspects of the Commission's activity – such as its (often superior) expertise and institutional cohesion – which were less explicit in the writings of Haas and Lindberg, will be examined in order to further corroborate its role as a potentially effective agent of European integration. One important aspect which also deserves more concentration is the strategic position of the Commission. It is centrally located within a web of policy networks and relationships, which often results in the Commission functioning as a bourse where problems and interests are traded and through which support for its policies is secured. One particular group of actors – which goes beyond the neofunctionalist preoccupation with the involvement of interest groups or national civil servants – deserves particular attention given the potentially powerful lever it constitutes when used/ instrumentalised by the Commission, i.e. epistemic communities, which will subsequently be accommodated within the concept of cultivated spillover.

Epistemic community has been defined as 'a network of professionals with recognised expertise and competence in a particular domain and an authoritative claim to policy-relevant knowledge within that domain or issue area'.[158] Communities of knowledge-based experts may influence decision-making by 'articulating the cause-and-effect relationships of complex problems, helping states identify their interests, framing issues for collective debate, proposing specific policies, and identifying salient points for negotiation'.[159] The Commission, given its privileged position of centrality and authority, its capacity for directing the dynamics of relations with different (epistemic and other) networks, and through its cultivation of and participation in epistemic communities, can use them for its own ends, for example by obtaining the backing of an epistemic community for its policy proposals. The scientific or specialist analysis and policy recommendations provided by a community of knowledge-based experts, if pointing in the desired direction, constitute a potent

---

deterministic account of spillover and by conferring structures and agents an equal ontological status. Armstrong (1998) has criticised the neofunctionalist approach for leaving the legitimacy of the legal order which emerges unexplored. When taken as a 'partial' theory, as accepted above, this 'omission' poses no problem to the revised framework.

[158] Haas (1992: 3).

[159] Haas (1992: 2). Epistemic communities can have a considerable influence on EU policy-making, as illustrated, for example, by Cameron (1995: 37ff), Mazey and Richardson (1997a), Verdun (1999: 308ff), Zito (2001: 585ff), van Waarden (2002: 913ff) and Kaelberer (2003: 365ff).

lever for the Commission or other supranational institutions for the cultivation of common European, i.e. integrative, solutions.[160]

Countervailing Forces

Another innovation in the original neofunctionalist account is the introduction of 'countervailing' forces. Neofunctionalism is mainly a theory of the *dynamics* of integration, but does not tell us much about the other side of the equation. Although disintegrative pressures are somewhat implicit in neofunctionalism, and the lack of explicit hypothesising for them in the original body of theory was deplored by neofunctionalists in the late 1960s,[161] countervailing pressures have never been adequately incorporated into the theory.[162] However, it is maintained here that one can only ascertain the relative strength of the dynamics of integration if one also accounts for spillback forces.[163] In the absence of strong countervailing pressures even weak integrative forces may drive the integration process forward. In such a case the strength of the dynamics may easily be overestimated. When demonstrating that outcomes, which went beyond the lowest common denominator, came about even inspite of strong countervailing forces, the case for the concept of spillover is considerably strengthened. Hence, by incorporating such forces into the theory, it is also possible to ascertain more surely the causal significance of the (revised) neofunctionalist pressures. In addition, informed guesses about the integration process cannot be made without taking countervailing pressures on board. Countervailing forces may either be stagnating (directed towards *status quo*/standstill) or opposing (directed towards spillback/reversal of integration) in nature. For reasons of simplicity and methodology[164]

---

[160] For example, Mazey and Richardson (1994, 1997a) have noted that in the field of environmental law and other sectors, where the Commission had no specific Treaty mandate to initiate policies, it has gradually attained a *de facto* policy role which it partly acquired through the assistance and support of epistemic communities.

[161] Haas (1968: preface) appears to regret his 'end of ideology' assumption, which was unable to account for the impact of nationalism on the integration process. Haas sought to rectify this by introducing the concept of 'dramatic–political' actors who – as happened with de Gaulle – may disrupt the incremental process of integration. However, this modification can be criticised for being rather *ad hoc* (cf. Webb 1983; George 1991).

[162] Tranholm-Mikkelsen (1991: 16–19) points to the importance of countervailing pressures, but he does not appear to seek to incorporate them into neofunctionalism.

[163] The terms 'countervailing' and 'spillback' forces will be used synonymously throughout this study.

[164] Limiting the number of variables is advisable in comparative research which looks at only a few cases, as otherwise the researcher would not have enough observations per variable and the outcome would be indeterminate (Lijphart 1971: 678).

'countervailing forces' are grouped together here and conceptualised as one single hypothesis. The following main countervailing forces – which partly overlap – can be hypothesised.

Sovereignty-consciousness   Sovereignty-consciousness – which in its most extreme form can be described as nationalism – encapsulates actors' lacking disposition to delegate sovereignty to the supranational level, or more specifically to yield competences to EU institutions. Sovereignty consciousness tends to be linked to (national) traditions, identities and ideologies and may be cultivated through political culture and symbolisms.[165] The incorporation of this countervailing force into the revised neofunctionalist theory thus allows us to drop the original neofunctionalist 'end of ideology assumption'. Sovereignty conscious-ness has repeatedly impeded the development of the Community, as, for example, during de Gaulle's and Thatcher's terms of office. Other less prominent actors such as bureaucrats, especially when working in ministries or policy areas belonging to the last bastions of the nation-state, can be sovereignty-conscious agents. Sovereignty-consciousness tends to rise with waning trust in the objects of delegation, i.e. EU institutions.

Domestic Constraints and Diversities   Domestic constraints may significantly circumscribe governments' autonomy to act.[166] Govern-ments may be constrained directly by agents, such as by lobby groups, opposition parties, the media/public pressure, or more indirectly by structural limitations, such as a country's economy, its demography, its legal tradition or its administrative structure. Governments' restricted autonomy to act may prove disintegrative, especially when countries face very diverging domestic constraints. This may disrupt emerging integrative outcomes, as domestic constraints of governments may lead to national vetoes or prevent policies from moving beyond the lowest common denominator. In the case of strong domestic constraints in different Member States, considerable overlap in the (domestic constraint-based) positions might be necessary in order to arrive at substantial common accords due to the restricted scope for changing positions on the part of governments. Bureaucratic politics also partly comes under this rubric, when constraints created at this level are not so much ideological in nature (cf. sovereignty-consciousness), but when

---

[165] Sovereignty-consciousness has, to some extent, been made explicit in the following studies: Callovi (1992); Meunier and Nicolaïdis (1999: 485).

[166] In the (more theoretical) literature the importance of domestic constraints has been argued convincingly by Moravcsik (1993: 483–94) and Hoffmann (1964: esp. 89, 93).

bureaucrats limit governmental autonomy of action in order to protect their personal interests or to channel the interests of their 'constituencies'.

Diversity[167] can be viewed either as a sub-issue, or the structural component, of domestic constraints or as a countervailing pressure on its own. The economic, political, legal, demographic, sociological, administrative or cultural diversity of Member States may counter common integrative endeavours. The sheer differences between Member States can prove to be a disintegrative force because common positions or policies may require some Member States to diverge substantially from existing structures, customs and policies which tend to have evolved over substantial periods of time and are linked to certain grown traditions. Hence, diversity may potentially entail considerable costs of adjustment for some actors. Diversity may also develop and have conflictual implications (among member governments) as a result of material benefits/costs and prospects of gaining or losing decision-making power through particular policy decisions. Diversity among Member States is reinforced through the gradual enlargement of the European Union. The accommodation of 'domestic constraints and diversities' as a countervailing pressure in the revised neofunctionalist framework improves on one principal deficiency of the original framework: namely, the ability to explain variation in national choices for integration.

Negative integrative climate Integrative climate is a broad variable that depicts general attitudes towards European integration and the European Union. Since the early 1990s, national governments and the sub-national actors have increasingly stressed the importance of subsidiarity, public appeal for the Community has decreased and the Brussels bureaucracy has been seen more and more as high-handed and aloof.[168] Although it can barely be traced, and may overall be of less relevance than the other two countervailing forces, the negative integrative climate is believed to have a diffuse detrimental impact on decision-makers. As an unfavourable integrationist climate is also often related to economic recession,[169] the inclusion of this countervailing pressure allows us to drop the erroneous neofunctionalist assumption that growth would continue unabated in Western Europe. The 'negative integrative climate' and also 'domestic constraints' both contain an

---

[167] On the issue of diversity in the integration literature, see e.g. Wallace (1985b); Héritier (1999: esp. 4–8).
[168] See Papademetriou (1996: 63).   [169] Holland (1980).

element which was ignored throughout neofunctionalist theorising, i.e. the role that the wider (national) publics may play in the integration process.

Conclusion

As already alluded to earlier, the various pressures formulated above are interlinked in many ways and cannot always completely be separated from each other. In particular, the spillover pressures are intertwined in multiple and complex ways. For example, the two structural pressures of functional and exogenous spillover require agency – particularly those actors specified with the political, social and cultivated spillover pressures – to make an impact. Conversely, pro-integrative preference formation and learning processes implying European solutions – of national, supranational or transnational agents spelt out in political, social and cultivated spillover – call for some (endogenous-functional or exogenous) structural input and medium to develop. In addition, the two structural spillover pressures are interconnected, as exogenous dynamics (such as international competition) can give rise to or help create functional-endogenous logics (e.g. those stemming from the single market). The more actor-centred spillovers are also interwoven. For instance, supranational actors often cultivate relations with interest groups and thus foster political spillover pressures. Hence, the presence of a certain spillover pressure may activate other dynamics, as a result of which spillover pressures can be seen as mutually reinforcing. The linkages among countervailing forces are also significant as the above account of domestic constraints and diversity suggests.

Particularly interesting is the relationship between the two key types of pressures. By bringing countervailing forces into the revised framework it follows, almost logically, that integration should be viewed or hypothesised as a *dialectical* process.[170] This dialectical process is made up of spillover pressures constituting the dynamics of integration, on the one hand, and countervailing forces, on the other hand. The strength, variation and interplay of pressures on both sides of the equation thus determine the outcome of a particular decision-making issue or process.

---

[170] Tranholm-Mikkelsen (1991: 18–19) has suggested viewing integration as a dialectical process, determined by the twin forces of the 'logic of integration' and the 'logic of disintegration'. Although this is where he saw the limitations of neofunctionalism, he does not seem to make this suggestion with a view to reforming the theory. It is argued here that seeing integration as a dialectical process would be a valuable addition and extension of neofunctionalism.

More specific insights about the relationship between spillover and countervailing pressures are expected from the subsequent empirical analysis. A few words on the much employed notion of 'national interest': following from my ontological position and specification of pressures, there is no such thing as a unitary national interest. And, of course, the interests of national decision-makers are not merely influenced by domestic constraints and diversities, or the countervailing side of the equation, but also by endogenous-functional and exogenous structures, and supranational and transnational actors. In short, the interest perceptions of national (and other) decision-makers involved in EU decision-making are decisively shaped by the various spillover and countervailing pressures hypothesised above.

This dialectical account of neofunctionalism, once and for all, unmistakably sets the theory free from its determinism as well as the end-state fallacy that characterised some early neofunctionalist writings and that was intergrated into the theory later on. The revised neofunctionalist framework stays rather silent on the specific outcome of the integration process.[171] Instead of theorising about the progression of the integration project as a whole, this revised account seeks to provide a model for explaining particular decision-making instances or processes. However, it is supposed here that the process will further continue, in terms of both breadth and depth of integration, as spillback forces will – at least from time to time – not be strong enough to counterbalance the integrational dynamics. In addition, over time diversity among the Member States is likely to diminish and socialisation as well as learning processes are hypothesised to advance – with the European Union increasingly factoring in actors' construction of preferences, norms and identities – although these developments may be offset, to a certain extent, by successive enlargements and (as of now unforeseen) countervailing developments. Hence, overall certain (probably additive) developments (such as learning processes or the evolution of supranational institutions) feed back into future decision cycles and are likely to provide continued integrative impetus.[172] Tables 1.1 and 1.2 summarise the most important changes that have been made for the revised neofunctionalist framework, compared with original neofunctionalist theorising.

---

[171] For some precise thoughts on possible outcomes of the integration process see Schmitter (1996b: 137–8).

[172] On the notion of decision cycles and 'additivity' in neofunctionalist thought, see especially Schmitter (1971: 238ff and 2004: 57, 59, 60–1).

Table 1.1. *Principal changes in underlying assumptions from the original to the revised neofunctionalist framework*

Original neofunctionalist assumption	Revised neofunctionalist assumption
No systematic formulation of a basic ontology. A mainly 'soft' rational-choice ontology with some reflexive elements	No striving for ontological purity. Agents combine several action modes in their behaviour. A 'soft' rational-choice is complemented by a 'soft' constructivist ontology
(More) emphasis on agents	Structuration: equal ontological status of structure and agents
Integration/spillover an automatic process	Integration occurs under certain conditions (broadly when spillover pressures are stronger than countervailing forces). Conditions require further specification
Integration as a dynamic process	Integration as a dialectical process
Understands itself as a grand theory	A wide-ranging but partial theory
End-state: 'political community' of Europe. Later on the end-state was left open. Often misinterpreted as federal supra-state	No predicted end-state; further deepening in terms of breadth and depth of integration likely. End-state fallacy clarified
Community a creature of elites; permissive consensus	Primary role still attributed to elites, but wider publics assumed to have an impact
End of ideology (especially nationalism)	End of ideology assumption dropped
Growth in Europe continues unabated	Unabated growth assumption dropped

Research design and methodology

Epistemology

My epistemological position can be located somewhere between the positivist and interpretist extremes, probably leaning somewhat towards positivism. My work aims at causal relationships and seeks to produce generalisable findings. The previous section has generated hypotheses which are to be tested, aspiring validation or falsification. However, I reject the extreme positivist view that all social phenomena can necessarily be objectively observed, clearly measured and directly compared. Instead, interpretative understanding is viewed here as an inherent, even though not exclusive, part of, and step towards, causal explanation. On the other hand, I dismiss the relativist position which argues that context is everything, and that eventually no matters can be compared because they are embedded in unique contexts, thereby not

Table 1.2. *Main changes concerning the hypothesised pressures from early neofunctionalism to the revised neofunctionalist framework*

Change pressure	Specification	Extension
Functional spillover	• (Functional) 'pressures from within' brought out more explicitly and upgraded in importance. • Departure from deterministic ontology ('soft' functionalism)	• Scope broadened from economic linkages to include all endogenous – functional tensions and contradictions
Exogenous spillover		• Exogenous spillover itself a new (mainly structural) pressure
Political spillover	• Interest groups not only influenced by functional, but also by exogenous and domestic structures	• Advocacy coalitions are integrated into the concept
Social spillover	• Emphasis on the *quality* of interaction, *reflexive* learning and the role of *communication.* • Learning and socialisation not constant but subject to conditions	• Concept of communicative and norm-regulated action is incorporated
Cultivated spillover	• Was underestimated by neofunctionalists as a dynamic; now upgraded	• (1) Council Presidency, (2) ECJ, (3) EP and (4) Epistemic communities incorporated
Countervailing forces		• Countervailing forces themselves a new element

allowing for the generation of legitimate generalisations. I thus acknowledge the importance of interpretative and contextual features in establishing causal relationships and (middle-range) generalisation.[173]

---

[173] For similar epistemological stances see Smelser (1995: 3); Weber (1949: 88).

Research Objectives: Causal Inferences

The aim of this book is to make causal inferences. However, in order to make these, both description (the collection of facts) and descriptive inferences (the process of using the facts we know to learn about the facts we do not know) are necessary. To make descriptive inferences in this study requires seeking to understand the degree to which certain hypothesised pressures in the decision-making process reflect either typical phenomena (systemic features) or exceptions. Description and descriptive inference set the stage for causal inferences – learning about causal effects from the data observed. Causal effects are the difference in outcomes when hypothesised dynamics vary in strength.[174]

This study starts from a multiple causality assumption, according to which the same outcome can be caused by combinations of different factors.[175] Dessler has defined cause as any factor conducive or necessary (though itself insufficient) for a conjuncture of conditions that is sufficient for the specified outcome. A cause is thus any factor that is an insufficient but conducive or necessary part of a sufficient but unnecessary condition. It is an unnecessary condition because a combination of other conditions can have the same effect.[176] This conception can capture phenomena produced by multiple causal sequences. In line with my ontological and epistemological position, causal relations are not viewed as deterministic, as they are in the natural sciences where causes inextricably connect entities and determine outcomes. Instead, in the social–political world, causes are conditioned and constituted by actors' interests, norms and identities and thus (merely) provide agents with direction and objectives for action, rather than 'determine' their behaviour.[177]

Causal inferences are used to test my revised neofunctionalist hypotheses and to ascertain the degree to which certain hypothesised systematic pressures have caused progress on the formation of common positions, the development of policies and agreement on Treaty changes. Finally, apart from seeking to explain, this study also aspires to provide a basis for informed judgements about the European integration process. However, as stated earlier, there is no aspiration to make hard predictions.

---

[174] For a definition of these terms see King, *et al.* (1994: 8, 26, 81–2).

[175] Cf. King *et al.* (1994: 87–9); Ragin (1987); Mill (1950).

[176] Dessler (1991: 347). Strictly speaking Dessler only talked about cause as a *necessary* factor (though itself insufficient) for a conjuncture of conditions that is sufficient for the specified outcome. In my view this notion of causality can be slightly modified by adding that it can be a *necessary or conducive* factor (though itself insufficient) for a conjuncture of conditions that is sufficient for the specified outcome.

[177] For non-deterministic accounts of causality see e.g. Giddens (1984: 345); Adler (1997: 329); and Finnemore (1996: 28).

Specification of Variables

The Dependent Variable My dependent variable can be described as the outcome of negotiations, the outcome of instances of decision-making or simply as the decisions reached. My dependent variable is not confined to a single instance of decision-making but can comprise a series of decisions or the development of a policy. As for the IGC cases, the dependent variable may take on values, such as:

1. no change ('non-decision');
2a. changes in the *breadth* (*scope*)[178] of mutual commitment: the expansion of issues or policies to be resolved on the supranational level, i.e. the extension of EU/EC tasks into new issue areas. More generally, the breadth of integration (also) refers to the allocation of competences between the Community and the Member States, or the number of issues/policies in a given polity for which the European Union/European Community has the power to legislate.
2b. changes in the *depth* (*level*) of mutual commitment (in a sector already partly governed supranationally): this entails a strengthened authority of Community institutions and increased elements of supranational decision rules. Mutual commitment may intensify, for example, through the Commission gaining a right of initiative (or expanding it to an exclusive right of initiative), an expansion of QMV, giving a role to the European Parliament (or enhancing its role through the introduction of co-decision), bestowing a (more substantial) role on the ECJ and the introduction or extension of binding legal methods, etc.

In the PHARE case, the dependent variable could also be measured in terms of the breadth/depth distinction. The breadth (scope) can be ascertained, for instance, according to the success or failure of achieving a Community involvement in this area and the extent to which the content of the policy is governed on the European level. The depth or level of a mutual commitment (and changes therein) can be established, for example, by the degree to which the Community method is used to reach decisions, the ability of Community institutions to assert themselves and influence policy-making, and the extent

---

[178] The terms 'breadth' and 'depth' are arguably better suited than 'scope' and 'level', given that the latter terminologies have been attributed different (and sometimes contradictory) meanings by different authors. Compare, for example, Schmitter (1969: 163) who first introduced them (and whose understanding of these terms has been largely followed) with Lindberg and Scheingold (1970) and Börzel (2005).

to which decisions are contrary to member governments' initial preferences.

Key Causal Variables   I hypothesise that the dependent variable is caused by six explanatory variables. These key causal variables are the six pressures of the revised neofunctionalist framework described in detail above: (1) functional spillover, (2) exogenous spillover, (3) political spillover, (4) social spillover, (5) cultivated spillover and (6) countervailing forces.

Control Variables and Intervening Variables   'Control' variables are those independent variables which are not part of one's hypothesised key explanatory variables. [179] 'Intervening' variables are those standing in a causal sequence between the cause (independent variable) and the final effect (dependent variable). Both 'control' and 'intervening' variables constitute a problem in the field of (EU) decision-making because they tend to be manifold, they need to be controlled as far as possible, but they are difficult to hold constant. Given these similarities, and since they are often difficult to distinguish from one another in empirical research, control variables and intervening variables will be dealt with together here, without further attempts to differentiate between these categories.

Without aiming at an exhaustive list, important control/intervening variables for EU decision-making include extreme values of the following factors: 'degree of uncertainty', 'completeness of information', 'speed of events' and 'size of the agenda'. Failure to hold the above variables constant biases one's estimate or perception of the effect of one's independent variables. However, it is impossible to control for all (or even most) intervening variables when selecting case studies, as a variation of such factors may only become obvious at a later stage. Yet, what can be done is to flag control/intervening variables when they occur, so that in the conclusion one is able to take the direction of any bias into account. For example, very fast-moving events or those which entail very high degrees of uncertainty and very incomplete information are likely to increase the influence of supranational institutions in the decision-making process, as national decision-makers tend to grant them more authority in such cases.[180] And very large agendas provide disproportionate scope for upgrading interests and reaching agreement.[181]

---

[179] Hence independent variables, also referred to as explanatory variables, are divided into key causal variables and control variables.
[180] Cf. Moravcsik (1995).   [181] Héritier (1999: esp. 16).

Two additional control/intervening variables will be highlighted: first, 'intergovernmental versus supranational decision-making' (the degree to which the Community method applics for reaching decisions[182]), and second, 'persistence versus termination of a policy in the event of non-decision'.[183] As far as these variables are concerned, there is variation in my cases, which, in the former case, was actively sought to probe the theory in diverse settings. One task of this book is to ascertain the conditions under which my hypothesised pressures are likely to be (in)effective. Paying attention to control/intervening variables should help us to delimit the revised neofunctionalist framework.

Analytic Induction

In this study, theory and qualitative investigation will *not* be linked through what has been called *post factum* interpretation,[184] where theoretical reflection is carried out subsequent to the empirical research. My research approach, which in broad terms can be characterised as qualitative, is more consciously driven by theoretical concerns. Similar to the method of *analytic induction*,[185] my hypotheses were developed (inductively) at an early stage of my research and any major misfit between empirical analysis and theoretical formulation has led to a revision of existing hypotheses. Changes in the theoretical framework resulting from my empirical analysis of a certain case have always been (re)applied to all cases. As pointed out by Silverman the comparative method is very suitable for pursuing analytic induction.[186]

The Comparative Method

The goal of my comparative analysis is to identify the differences responsible for contradictory outcomes. Instead of studying the similarities between relatively dissimilar objects, the investigator studies the causally decisive differences between relatively similar objects.[187] By making partial use of Mill's methods of 'difference' and 'concomitant variation', one can examine whether hypothesised pressures co-vary

---

[182] However, as for the decision mode, QMV versus unanimity, this has been held constant. I have only chosen cases decided under unanimity, either by heads of state and government in the two IGC cases or the Council/Coreper as regards the PHARE programme. Although in the PHARE Management Committee decisions are made by QMV, it deals mainly with the day-to-day running of the PHARE programme, while the broader strategic questions have been dealt with in the Council framework under unanimity.

[183] Cf. Scharpf (1988: 250ff).   [184] Gans (1962).   [185] Lindesmith (1968).

[186] Silverman (1993: 162).   [187] Cf. Ragin (1987: 47).

with outcomes. Changing levels of progressiveness in terms of outcome would corroborate those dynamics changing as hypothesised, and challenge those remaining constant or changing in the direction opposite to the one hypothesised. In other words, higher values on the decision outcome (or on the overall dynamics) would confirm those dynamics that also display higher scores, and challenge the causal relevance of those decreasing or remaining constant.[188]

A number of authors have argued in favour of the utility of adopting a multi-method approach in order to enhance both generalisation and the establishment of causal relationships.[189] In this case, apart from using the comparative methods of 'difference' and 'concomitant variation', one may, to some degree, additionally use Mill's method of 'agreement'.[190] Here, one looks at all cases where the dependent variable takes on the same value. In this way, no positive causality can be established, but irrelevant variables can be identified.[191] For example, one can look at all cases where the outcome happened to be one of stalemate. Those variables which were still (repeatedly) present, according to this logic, cannot have been that important and may overall carry only a small degree of causal significance.

Collection and Organisation of Data – Process Tracing and Triangulation Across Multiple Data Sources

It has been recommended that, in view of the often overwhelming quantity of data, researchers need to be selective and focused in their data collection and treatment of a case. Researchers' theoretical interests should define which aspects of a case they single out for description and explanation.[192] Hence, my theoretical hypotheses have been used as a guide in the collection and organisation of data. The method chosen here for this purpose is usually called 'process tracing' or the tracing of 'causal mechanisms'.[193] Process tracing is usually understood as a method for the analysis of causal mechanisms, which carefully traces events, processes and actors' beliefs and expectations. On a more general level, it is viewed as a method that establishes a link between cause and effect beyond the level of correlation by appealing to knowledge of the real structures that produce observed phenomena.[194] More specifically, process tracing is seen as a method for analysing the relationship between actors' cognitions and their behaviour. In order to make

---

[188] Mill (1950).   [189] Cf. e.g. Martin (1992: esp. 10–12).   [190] Mill (1950).
[191] Cf. Collier (1995: 464).   [192] Cf. George (1979: 175ff); King, et al. (1994: 48).
[193] See George (1979: 113); George and McKeown (1985: 34–41).   [194] Dessler (1991).

causal inferences, process tracing is viewed here as a method which is complementary to a comparative analysis.[195]

Process tracing has been put into practice through four different techniques. First, I used *secondary literature, official documentation* and *major media*. Second, I conducted more than 120 non-attributable (and four attributable) *structured and semi-structured interviews* with national civil servants at the Permanent Representations and national ministries, officials from the Commission, the European Parliament and the Council Secretariat as well as representatives of organised interests. Third, during a four-month placement at the Council Secretariat I had access to *confidential documentation* (including outcomes of meetings' proceedings, correspondence between delegations and informal evaluations). Finally, during my placement at the Council Secretariat, I was able to witness over twenty committee and working group meetings (including Coreper and the Central Europe Working Group) as *a participant observer*. Triangulation across multiple data sources reduces reliance on any particular type of data, serves to verify the accounts mentioned in one particular source and enhances the confidence in the overall validity of our inferences.

'Many Variables' and 'Small-n' Problem

In the area of EU decision-making researchers are facing the problem of having to cope with many variables, whereas one can usually only analyse a small number of cases. In order to make valid causal inferences and avoid indeterminate research results, it has been held that more observations are needed than independent variables.[196] In order to solve this problem I have used a variety of methods. First, variables have been merged, for example, through grouping the role of the Presidency, the EP, the ECJ and epistemic communities within cultivated spillover together with the role of the Commission. By combining variables that express an essentially similar underlying characteristic into a single variable one can increase the average number of observations per cell.[197] Second, I have excluded variables like 'QMV versus unanimity' from my key causal variables, as more key causal variables mean less leverage for estimating any of the individual causal effects.[198] Third, rather than merely focusing on ultimate outcomes, process tracing increases the number of theoretically relevant observations.[199] Finally and closely connected, I have

---

[195] On the complementarity and linkage of these methods, see e.g. Little (1991: 31–2).
[196] Fearon (1991: 192).   [197] Lijphart (1971: 678).   [198] See Little (1991: 174–5).
[199] Cf. Little (1991: 228).

sought to increase the number of observations by dividing case studies into various instances and periods, as a result of which all three case studies contain at least three concrete observations each.

Case Selection

As a number of authors have remarked, random case selection has serious limitations in small-n research.[200] However, abandoning randomness opens the door to many sources of bias. Lijphart warns that the comparative method should not lapse into what Galtung calls 'the traditional quotation/illustration methodology', where cases are picked that are in accordance with one's hypotheses.[201] More specifically, this is the danger of selecting observations intentionally on the basis of both the explanatory and dependent variables, as these variables can be chosen such that they vary together in ways that are known to be consistent with the researcher's theory. In order to avoid selection bias, researchers have primarily been recommended to choose cases ensuring variation of independent variables, without regard to the values of the dependent variable. Alternatively, when this option is not possible or practicable, the selection of cases according to a range of values of the dependent variable – without paying attention to the values of the explanatory variables – has been proposed as another valid option.[202]

I have opted for the latter one, not out of choice but by default. The former option is not plausible here and would have (even) increased the danger of selection bias. While the outcomes of EU decision-making are usually fairly easily accessible, ascertaining the strengths of causal factors requires much more analysis. Hence, it would have been impossible in this research project to select cases on the basis of my key causal variables, without prior knowledge of the respective outcomes. This in turn would have opened the door to (accusation of) selection bias, since I could have easily chosen them in accordance with my favourite hypothesis or main argument.

There is another strong argument for this method of case selection. I chose cases which differ considerably in terms of the values of the dependent variable because thus more can be learned about the causal importance of my hypothesised pressures for explaining outcomes. Without variation of the dependent variable one can only learn which hypothesised pressures may *not* be causally relevant.[203] In order to

---

[200] E.g. Collier (1995: 463); King *et al.* (1994: 124–5).
[201] For quote see Galtung (1967: 505); on the overall argument see: Lijphart (1971: 686).
[202] Cf. King *et al.* (1994: 128–38); Collier (1995: 462).
[203] Mill (1950). Also see my section on the comparative method above.

maintain the possibility of ascertaining a degree of positive causality, it is essential to select cases with varying outcomes, based on the assumption/insight that variation of the dependent variable is the result of differing values regarding the hypothesised key causal variables. This way, attempts can be made to isolate the causal variable(s) that lead to different outcomes.[204]

The outcomes of the cases I have chosen vary significantly. On the progressive side of the spectrum are nearly all observations on the PHARE programme, its initiation, refocus and development which reflect a gradual expansion of breadth and, to a lesser extent, depth of integration, largely mirroring the design/interests of the central institutions. Another 'high-scoring' outcome is the communitarisation of visa, asylum and immigration policy at the 1996–97 IGC, both in terms of breadth (scope) and depth (level) of mutual commitment. The last Treaty revisions concerning the issues of visa, asylum and migration policy and the Common Commercial Policy also represent progressive results, mainly as regards the depth/level of integration.[205] The CCP extension at the Nice IGC can be viewed as a medium (to low) score on the dependent variable, and the outcome on visa, asylum and immigration policy at the IGC 2000 can be characterised as low (to medium). Finally, and closest to a 'non-decision', was the IGC 1996–97 reform of Article 113/133, which resulted in very modest changes.

Cases have been selected from the area of external policy as well as internal affairs and from policy-making/day-to-day decision-making as well as history-making negotiations. It has been pointed out that in terms of theory-building it is logical to test hypotheses about European integration on different issue areas.[206] In addition, Caporaso has noted that if a theory holds across highly diverse settings, this is more impressive than confirmation under similar conditions. The presumption is that under diversity, theories are more severely challenged and more likely to be falsified.[207]

---

[204] King (1994: 129–30, 141–2). Moreover, without variance on the dependent variable, selection bias is likely since the chosen sample may well over-represent cases for which independent variables other than the main explanatory variable play an important role in accounting for a given score on the dependent variable (Collier 1995: 464).

[205] My analysis of the last Treaty revision negotiations concerning Title IV and the CCP stretches from pre-negotiations (including the Convention) to the signing of the Constitutional Treaty. The ratification process – which continues at the time of writing – does not form part of this study. However, it would be interesting to assess if the current difficulties along this process (after the referendums in France and the Netherlands) may be explained through this framework, particularly by drawing on countervailing forces.

[206] Matlary (1994).   [207] Caporaso (1995: 458).

Operationalisation of Key Causal Variables

Translating hypotheses into a form that can be tested empirically mainly involves the specification of indicators or referents on which causal variables can be observed and measured. This is complemented here, at times, by stating the different methods and techniques used to attain inferences in order to render my operationalisation more concrete and plausible. In view of my epistemological and ontological position and especially given the complexity of the issues analysed, strict positivist standards regarding observation and measurement are not (always) adhered to.

Indicators for *functional spillover*, i.e. the pressures for further action in order to assure an original goal, include the following: first, the basis for functional pressure is that there is in fact an original goal. The salience of this goal also, to a large extent, determines the strength of the functional requirement. Second, another basis is the existence of a functional interdependence between issue A (original objective) and issue B (where further action may potentially be required). Actions in the area of B must affect issue A. Third, is further action in a particular issue area necessary to achieve the initial objective, or are there alternative solutions (i.e. in other areas)? If the original goal cannot be (adequately) reached by other means, the functional connection is likely to be a strong one.

In terms of *exogenous spillover*, the specification of clear-cut indicators is (even) more difficult. For the development or arrival of an (economic) threat or adverse competition to the regional block from outside, economic indicators such as trade balances (especially related to strategically important products and services) can be drawn upon. In the face of an exogenous challenge, the consequences of dissonance or speaking with different voices can, to some extent, be revealed, for example, by logical deduction or by comparison with past experiences under similar circumstances. As for the nature and increasing internationality of problems in face of limited capacities of individual Member States, the strength of exogenous spillover pressures can be approximated by comparing the scope of the problem with the governance potential of single nation-states. An indicator of the latter would be past capabilities (e.g. in terms of absorbing third-country nationals until the mid-1980s) conditioned by more recent developments (e.g. political and economic climate) compared with the (growing) scope of a problem (e.g. free movement of persons in the Community and the rise of total number of asylum seekers in the European Union in the early 1990s).

However, although the above indicators give a preliminary idea of the general logic regarding these structural (i.e. functional and exogenous) spillover pressures, there is no (entirely) objective estimation concerning these referents, which are, at least to a certain degree, cognitively and socially constructed. Therefore, eventually it largely boils down to the perceptions of decision-makers (how strong is the logic or pressure *perceived* as regards functional interdependencies, international competition/threats, the consequences of uncoordinated/individual action or the manageability of increasingly broad problems?). In other words, functional and exogenous spillover pressures are ultimately (only) as strong as they are perceived to be (and enacted) by policy-makers. In order to go deeper and ascertain, as far as possible, these perceptions additional indicators and techniques are necessary: first, and perhaps most importantly, interviews, verified by cross-interview and triangulation across other sources, can reveal the true perceptions and action rationales of decision-makers. Second, the persuasive value and general influence of functional, exogenous or other structural arguments tends to be reflected through their (frequent) appearance in the policy discourse, i.e. in national position papers, memoranda, policy papers etc. Manifestation in the policy discourse need not necessarily be a reflection of decision-makers' true perception, but when functional or exogenous arguments gain currency in the policy arena they nevertheless have an impact on outcomes.

Indicators for *cultivated spillover* include firstly supranational institutions' actual cultivation of relations with (national and other) decision-makers to get support for their endeavours. The level of activity can usually be ascertained through the study of major media, unofficial/ confidential documentation and, most importantly, interviews. Second, another indicator is the level of functional and exogenous spillover cultivation on the part of supranational institutions. This can be determined from the degree to which these logics have been employed, for example, in Commission or Presidency communications and argumentations. The third (and most important) indicator focuses on the output, rather than the input dimension of cultivated spillover. Important here is the extent to which attitudes, interests or positions on the part of decision-makers have changed towards the line taken by supranational institutions. Having identified such change, it still has to be ascertained if it was induced by supranational institutions. This brings us back to the first two indicators, but the causal connection between indicators 1 and 2 with indicator 3 would have to be substantiated through process tracing (see next paragraph). Another referent combining elements of the first three would be the admittance on the part of national decision-makers and, alternatively, independent insiders involved in the negotiations (such as Council Secretariat officials) that national preferences and positions changed towards those favoured by supranational institutions because of the involvement and reasoning of the latter. This should be corroborated across several, and different types of, sources.

In addition, one can resort to counterfactual reasoning[208] and ask whether a certain progressive outcome would have occurred even if the Commission (or EP/Presidency) had not been involved. A preferred way here is to examine and compare real cases. Thus, cases differing substantially on the values taken by the dependent variables have been compared to see how far the difference between decision and non-decision was due to different competencies/involvement of the Commission or other institutions (other things being equal as far as possible).[209] However, a correlation between an effective Commission and integrational outcomes does not constitute causation.[210] Neither does the correlation between an assertive Commission and preference changes on the part of Member States towards the line taken by the Commission. Hence, in addition, it is necessary to trace the mechanisms which connect cause (e.g. Commission involvement) and effect (e.g. upgrading of common interests).

As for *social spillover*, the operationalisation of this key causal variable may appear (particularly) problematic from an extreme positivist viewpoint, as observation and measurement of this factor are exceptionally difficult. While we have to rely to a greater extent (compared with the other hypothesised pressures) on context, understanding and interpretation, we can try to establish some signposts for empirical research. First, the object of investigation has been narrowed down. While it is conceivable to investigate social spillover broadly in terms of different interaction patterns of (especially national governmental) elites involved in decision-making processes, this study has focused on (national) civil servants in a limited number of forums (mainly the Central Europe Working Group in the PHARE case study and chiefly the IGC Representatives group in the other two case studies). Second, the level of enmeshment among national officials, for example, through their involvement in a certain working group, or in the Council framework more generally, can be ascertained. The frequency of formal and informal contact, as well as the duration of interaction can serve as pointers here. Third, the degree of socialisation can also be estimated. This (ideally) involves a comparison of actors and norms at different

---

[208] E.g. Fearon (1991: esp. 171ff).
[209] To hold other things equal was possible on some occasions, for example, when Presidencies changed, while most other key causal variables remained constant. Cf. e.g. Chapter 2 (section on cultivated spillover).
[210] Little (1991).

times, in order to be able to distinguish whether frequent and prolonged interaction in Council working groups, IGC representative groups and other forums led to generally good relations, the development of an *esprit de corps* and the internalisation of certain (co-operative) norms.

Fourth, as far as the quality, as opposed to the quantity, of interaction, is concerned, there are several indicators for communicative action as a mode of behaviour or policy style.[211] For example, arguments in communicative action mode are not based on hierarchy or authority. Pointing to status or rank to make an argument does not qualify as discourse. In addition, argumentative consistency is a good marker of communicative action. Actors that change their arguments depending on the audience probably engage in rhetorical behaviour. Moreover, characterisations of the interaction process in terms of reasoning and arguing by interviewees who have not been prodded along with structured interviews proposing different characterisations of the policy process can substantiate communicative action.[212]

Fifth, there is the question whether (more profound) learning processes have occurred. Through interviews and cross-interviews, verified by other sources, it can, to some extent, be inferred whether actors have adapted their strategies or really changed their interests. In addition, the assertion that persuasion and genuine learning have really taken place gains further substance when what has been learned is used or applied. More concretely, when decision-makers start to use arguments (in a non-strategic manner) by which they have been convinced, they are likely to have been truly persuaded and undergone reflexive learning processes. Sixth, it has to be investigated (for example through interviews), if in this process decision-makers' propensity for co-operation was fostered.[213] Finally, there is the question whether social spillover changes national positions and preferences. Here, it makes sense to focus on decisions where countries shifted their positions. There may be many different reasons why national positions change. For example, they may be bought off and be faced with the threat of exclusion. In order to establish a degree of positive causality of some certainty, one has to exhaust all other alternative explanations. Due to the limited

[211] Concepts like bargaining or communicative action should be seen as ideal types which do not often appear in their pure form. Hence, the empirical question to be asked is not whether actors behave in a strategic (i.e. bargaining), or communicative mode, but which mode captures most of the action in a given situation (Cf. Risse 2000: 18, 2004: 387).

[212] This paragraph has drawn on Risse (2000: 18) and Niemann (2004: 387–8) where also additional indicators for communicative behaviour can be found.

[213] Again, ideally, one should have taken the same people at different times, in order to control for idiosyncrasies. This was possible only in very few cases.

scope of this study, I could not undertake a proper operationalisation of this aspect of social spillover. Also, as for the (long-term) changes in actors' identities and loyalties, an adequate operationalisation was not feasible. This aspect will be revisited in the conclusion. Social spillover will be analysed most comprehensively in Chapter 3 (on the PHARE programme), where also some of the more general aspects surrounding this concept will be dealt with. Hence, that chapter, to some extent, paves the way for further, albeit less detailed, examination of social spillover in the other two empirical chapters.

The concept of *political spillover* can be operationalised in similar ways as other key causal variables. Indicators have been: (1) the degree of support for supranational solutions on the part of organised interests; (2) the level to which their support can be attributed to the endogenous and exogenous integrational logics pointed out above; (3) the strength of the correlation between supportive attitudes of non-governmental elites and the depth of integration of a particular issue area; (4) the extent to which the position of Member States (national governmental policy-makers) shifted towards that of organised interests (especially in face of existing countervailing forces); (5) the type of learning (i.e. incentive-based or reflexive) may be ascertained from whether (only) actors' *strategies* or their *underlying interests* changed (cf. point five of social spillover); (6) the (potential) intensification of learning processes and co-operative attitudes over time can, to some degree, be indicated by the level of support for European solutions at different points in time.

A few words on the operationalisation of my hypothesised *counter-vailing forces*: first, sovereignty-consciousness, of course, is a rather diffuse notion. However, structured and semi-structured interviews (and cross-interviews) have gone some way towards revealing the attitudes of decision-makers *vis-à-vis* issues such as delegation of powers to supranational institutions and deepening of the integration process. Second, there are several indicators for domestic constraints, including (a) popular opposition near national (or important regional) elections; (b) resistance from important factions of government or the national political system more generally. Diversity, viewed either as part of domestic constraints or as a factor on its own, can be 'measured' or rather estimated by the differences between the political and legal practices as well as the economic and sociological/demographic structures across Member States, as reflected in, and perceived by, the academic and policy-making literature. Specific indicators for each of these dimensions of diversity vary according to the issue investigated. Finally, Eurobarometer data have been used as indicators for approximating the integrative climate of a certain period.

2   The Emergence and Development of the PHARE Programme

The PHARE Programme

Initiated originally to assist Poland and Hungary, and later other countries in Central and Eastern Europe, PHARE (Poland and Hungary: Aid for Restructuring of the Economies) has undergone considerable change over the years and became the most important pre-accession instrument financed by the Union to support the applicant countries of that region in their preparation to join the European Union. The PHARE programme became operational in January 1990. Before that, in December 1989, the Council of Ministers had adopted – on the basis of Article 235 EC[1] – the PHARE regulation which forms the legal foundation of the programme.[2] The origins of the PHARE programme, however, go back even further. It originated in the Community's responsibility for the co-ordination of G24[3] aid to Poland and Hungary. This mandate, which the European Commission obtained at the G7 summit in Paris in July 1989, was until then 'the highest foreign policy accolade the Commission has ever had bestowed on it'.[4] Never before had the Commission been responsible for the aid co-ordination of its Member States and third countries.

From 1989 to 1997 the programme's aim was mainly to provide support for the process of transition towards a market economy and towards democratic institutions in the Central and Eastern European countries (CEEC). It focused on technical assistance at government and ministry level in the areas of public finance, agriculture, the environment

---

[1] Article 235 EC (now Article 308 TEC) has generally served as a legal basis for Community measures to the CEEC (MacLeod et al. 1996). It combines unanimity in the Council with consultation of the EP.

[2] Council (1989).

[3] The Group of Twenty-Four which was set up in the aftermath of the July 1989 Paris summit comprised the twelve EEC countries, the EFTA countries (Norway, Sweden, Finland, Austria and Switzerland), the United States, Canada, Australia, New Zealand, Japan and Turkey.

[4] Ehlermann (1989: 23).

and privatisation. As for the latter, advancement of small-firm development, apart from banking sector reforms, was a prime objective and assistance under PHARE aimed at overcoming the reluctance of the financial sector to support small firms, through the use of micro-credit schemes. Aid for regional development also became a priority, assisted by the use of cross-border co-operation programmes. One very important reorientation during that time was the expansion in support for infrastructure investment. The PHARE programme (also during this period) could not easily be separated from the overall background of the European Union's relations with the CEEC. PHARE became the financing instrument of the 'Europe Agreements' and obtained a central position in the strategy for accession by 1995. Assistance during that phase was managed by the Commission, under the aegis of Directorate-General 1A for External Political Relations (later by DG Enlargement), in co-operation with the beneficiary countries. Aid is mostly given in the form of grants rather than loans. Assistance under the PHARE programme has been and continues to be conditional on the partner country's demonstration of a firm commitment to political and economic reforms.[5] The programme currently (June 2006) covers ten countries: the eight new Central and Eastern European Member States: the Czech Republic, Estonia, Hungary, Latvia, Lithuania, Poland, Slovakia and Slovenia, as well as Bulgaria and Romania. Until 2000, three countries of the Western Balkans (Albania, Bosnia-Herzegovina and the Former Yugoslav Republic of Macedonia) were also temporarily beneficiaries of PHARE.[6]

The programme's complete pre-accession focus was put in place only in 1997 in response to the Luxembourg European Council's launching of the present enlargement process. PHARE funds came to focus wholly on the pre-accession priorities as emphasised in each country's Accession Partnership. From 1998 to 2000 assistance concentrated primarily on institution-building and investment support for infrastructure rebuilding, mainly in the areas of transport, agriculture and environment. In 2000 additional pre-accession instruments were introduced alongside PHARE: the Instrument for Structural Policies for Pre-Accession (ISPA) and the Special Accession Programme for Agriculture and Rural Development (SAPARD). The aim was for PHARE to become the precursor to the Structural Funds post-enlargement, for ISPA the Cohesion Funds, and for SAPARD the guidance section of the

---

[5] Smith (1998: 253ff, 1999).

[6] However, as of 2001 the CARDS programme (community assistance for reconstruction, development and stability in the Balkans) has provided financial assistance to the countries of the Western Balkans.

CAP, with total resources of the three instruments double the level of pre-2000 PHARE funding. The PHARE programme now focuses on promoting beneficiaries convergence with the *acquis communautaire*, strengthening their public administrations and institutions, and the promotion of economic and social cohesion. The year 2003 was the last programming year for pre-accession aid in those eight CEEC which joined the Union in 2004. Final disbursements for the new Member States from Central and Eastern Europe run until 2006, while increased aid is given to Bulgaria and Romania.[7]

This case study was the first one conducted within the scope of this book. Apart from methodological considerations (see Chapter 1), it was chosen at the time because the emergence and evolution of this Community competence had largely escaped theoretical explanation[8], and thus made an interesting case study, especially since external relations as a policy area for the purpose of testing (revised) neofunctionalism had, until then, essentially been ignored. My empirical analysis particularly concentrates on the period 1989–97.[9] Occasionally, the analysis will draw on developments that are related to the TACIS programme, the Community's aid programme providing grant-financed technical assistance to twelve countries of Eastern Europe and Central Asia, which was established after PHARE in 1991.[10]

Hypothesised Pressures

Exogenous Spillover

Giving the Mandate of Aid Co-ordination to the Commission   At the Arch Summit in Paris in July 1989 the heads of government of the seven most industrialised countries were faced with the task of deciding upon the co-ordination of Western assistance for Poland and Hungary. The decision to give the co-ordination mandate to the European Commission was largely brought about by two sets of exogenous pressures. First, as Schmitter[11] has pointed out, pressure can arise from the obligations

---

[7] The most up-to-date information on the PHARE programme is available on the Commission website under the following link: http://ec.europa.eu/comm/ enlargement/ pas/phare/ index.htm

[8] With the exception of Haggard and Moravcsik's (1993: 247ff) broad study on the political economy of assistance to Eastern Europe.

[9] Post-1997 data have also been considered to make sure that these later developments do not contradict my findings. Preliminary results have been published in Niemann (1998).

[10] Current beneficiaries are: Armenia, Azerbaijan, Belarus, Georgia, Kazakhstan, Kyrgyzstan, Moldova, Russia, Tajikistan, Turkmenistan, Ukraine and Uzbekistan.

[11] Schmitter (1969: 165).

of the very existence and possible success of a regional organisation, caused by the reactions, expectations and demands of outsiders. In this case the successful development of the Community in the late 1980s, along with the Commission's fruitful involvement in ACP development and in EC–CEEC trade agreements, led to a series of demands and expectations by the outside world that obliged the Community to respond to the events of 1989 and finally give responsibility to the Commission for the co-ordination of Western help. Most prominently, Lech Walesa continuously warned about the urgency of assistance in support of the reform process, and also asked the Commission President to ensure Poland got the right practical help.[12] Moreover, General Jaruzelski suggested to the Commission President that EC credit lines should be opened to enable Poland to import food from Western Europe. Jaruzelski also exerted pressure on the French Presidency and made suggestions for economic help within the EC framework.[13] Polish and Hungarian demands, expectations and attitudes were not the only ones that seemed to have played a role. As Petersen argues, due to the Community's success in the late 1980s, the United States came to view the European Community as an increasingly important entity.[14] From an American perspective the Community had gradually come to be regarded as a source for the supply of leadership, especially in times when there was increasing demand for such leadership.[15]

The second set of motives stems from the necessity to organise assistance given the geographic proximity and the speed of the events in Central and Eastern Europe, as well as the strength of the democratic movements and the uncertainties surrounding their success. The sudden changes in Central and Eastern Europe obliged Western leaders to come up with economic assistance in one form or another. By July 1989 both Hungary and Poland had instituted economic and political reforms, with Poland holding its first free elections since the Second World War, and Hungary announcing constitutional reforms which would pave the way for free elections. European defence and security considerations naturally came to the fore with part of the Warsaw Pact ridding itself of communism and turning towards the West after the iron curtain had divided the continent for four decades. Therefore, financial support for the success of the reform process was seen as vital by a number of European politicians, including Mrs Thatcher.[16] Moreover, the prospect of mass immigration required a response from the

---

[12] *Financial Times*, 18.05.1989.   [13] *Financial Times*, 08.07.1989.
[14] Petersen (1993: 25–6).   [15] Interviews, Brussels, June 1996.
[16] *The Independent*, 09.06.1989.

Community as much out of self-interest as for stability in the CEEC. As Pelkmans and Murphy put it, 'the EC could not remain indifferent to these events'.[17] Additional factors reinforced the rationale to come up with a Community response and for handing responsibility over to the Commission. As one commentator put it, 'certainly the Member States were obliged to think in an integrated way. The speed of the events and the enormity of the challenge were such that the classic progression of deliberations in EPC followed by action in the Community was no longer realistic'.[18] Hence, all in all the decision to give the mandate to the Commission can be explained by the concept of exogenous spillover, as the motives which inspired this decision were spurred by external factors and seem to have left European leaders little choice but to hammer out a common policy and to rely on the Commission to do it.[19]

Auxiliary Factors and Lack of Countervailing Forces   Pressures stemming from exogenous spillover provide the basis though not an entirely convincing explanation for the decision taken by the heads of government at the G7 summit in Paris. More light is shed on this matter by turning to three additional factors, which, in their interaction with externalisation pressures, offer a more complete picture. First, the choices were limited. Various nation-states were unwilling or unable to do it, the EBRD did not yet exist, the OECD was out of the question due to its small budget and the World Bank was considered by some to be on the wrong side of the Atlantic, while others pointed to its inexperience of dealing with such a potentially political as well as sizeable issue.[20]

Second, although the Commission lacked sufficient qualified staff, contacts, information and statistical data,[21] it was in many ways ideally placed to fulfil the role it was assigned in Paris.[22] The Commission had gained experience in development policy particularly with respect to the ACP countries under the Yaoundé, Arusha and Lomé Conventions, and the Mediterranean countries under the Maghreb and Mashreq protocols.[23] Moreover, the Commission had already been involved in dealings with the CEEC through the negotiations of the 'first generation' trade agreements, for example, with Hungary in June 1988 and Czechoslovakia in December 1988.[24] In addition, it can be argued that the

---

[17] Pelkmans and Murphy (1991: 130); also cf. Haggard and Moravcsik (1993: 440).
[18] Nuttall (1992: 280).
[19] Cf. Smith (1999) who also highlighted the importance of external pressures concerning this outcome.
[20] Interviews, Brussels, 1996.   [21] Pelkmans and Murphy (1991: 130).
[22] Andriessen (1989: 8).   [23] Grilli (1993).   [24] de la Serre (1991: 310).

Commission had gained experience in higher political matters through its gradually increasing involvement in EPC which was recognised in the 1981 London Report and given a legal basis in the Single European Act (SEA).[25] The fact that the role of the Commission had progressed to a considerable extent on those three levels provided the basis for spillover. Even more importantly, an assertive Commission under the leadership of Delors reinforced the exogenous spillover pressures by lobbying for the mandate to go to the Commission. Cultivated spillover as an important influence on the outcome of the Arch summit will be discussed in greater detail below.

Finally, exogenous spillover (aided by cultivated spillover pressures) was allowed to unfold due to virtually non-existing countervailing pressures – especially regarding the nature of domestic constraints and national diversities. Positions of key G7 governments gradually converged, which provided a fertile soil for spillover pressures. Their preferences were conditioned by exogenous (extra-European/EU), endogenous (related to EU integration) and domestic factors. Germany, although keen on supporting Poland and Hungary, was much in favour of a common Community response as a major national effort had apparently met some difficulties in the Bonn coalition.[26] France feared that the changes in Eastern Europe could lead to a redirection of Germany's interests towards the East. It is uncertain to what extent such considerations were at play in mid-1989. They certainly were later, when France concentrated its efforts on curtailing Germany, most evidently by pushing for further deepening through EMU. Overall, France much preferred a common European solution, rather than a German bilateral single-handed effort.[27] It became clear very early on that the United States did not want to take on responsibility for such a task. US co-ordination of aid to Eastern Europe would have been unacceptable to the Soviet Union.[28] Moreover, as a former advisor of Commissioner Andriessen told the author, the United States was reluctant to take a prominent role, as it was already constrained by a growing budget deficit.[29] However, the United States, along with Germany, promoted attempts to find a quick solution to the situation in Central and Eastern Europe. The US motivations may have been two-fold. First, there was some pressure from the Polish lobby in the United States. Second, agreement on EC responsibility was facilitated by the improved relations between Washington and Brussels.[30]

---

[25] Nuttall (1988, 1992).   [26] Ehlermann (1989: 24).   [27] Kramer (1993: 222).
[28] Pelkmans and Murphy (1991: 130).   [29] Interview, Brussels, 1996.
[30] Ehlermann (1989: 23–4); Krause (1991: 292–6).

Viewed from a different angle, the convergence of domestic preferences and constraints meant that one important source of countervailing forces did not manifest itself at the Paris summit. Moreover, there were no serious sovereignty concerns on the part of the EU nation-states, and the late 1980s were perhaps the height of a period of pro-integrative climate.[31] Hence, countervailing forces were minimal in this (sub-)case.

Functional Spillover

Explaining Change at the Essen and Cannes European Councils   In the history of PHARE there have been a number of changes in the focus of the programme. For example, in the early period food aid was an important element. Later technical assistance in areas such as agriculture, energy and environment became paramount. One of the most significant changes of the PHARE programme occurred after the heads of state and government had agreed at the Copenhagen European Council that those associated countries in Central and Eastern Europe that wanted to, could become members of the European Union, as soon as they could satisfy the economic and political conditions required.[32] This probability of an Eastern enlargement in the distant future set in motion functional pressures which led to a systematic change of the PHARE programme. This was the result of the dissatisfaction with the attainment of a collective goal (assisting the CEEC), due to the desire to achieve another related policy goal (making the CEEC fit for possible accession), under the existing scope and priorities of the programme. This led to the adoption of a comprehensive pre-accession strategy at the Essen European Council.

At Essen, the heads of government decided to raise the limit of the PHARE budget that could be used to co-finance infrastructure investment from 15 to 25 per cent. This 'reflects the importance of improving infrastructure as a major element in preparation for accession. This is because of the need to improve the physical links between the partner countries and the European Community'.[33] The increasing demand for funds in this area, as a result of the plans for accession, was coupled with the lack of capital in the CEEC, and the fact that EIB loans were only allowed to cover up to 75 per cent of the total cost, as decided at the

---

[31] Cf. Eurobarometer No. 31–34 (1989/1990), where between 62 and 69 per cent of interviewees said that the European Union is a good thing, compared with 48 per cent during 2003–04 (cf. Eurobarometers 59–61).
[32] Commission (1993b: 11).   [33] Commission (1995b: 11).

Edinburgh European Council.[34] Those functional pressures made an increase of PHARE funds for infrastructure projects indispensable, if the stated objectives were to be achieved.

Perhaps even more importantly, at the Cannes European Council, the fifteen heads of government finally decided, after no agreement had been reached on this issue at Essen, to increase considerably the overall PHARE budget. For the five-year span from 1995–99, 6.7 billion ECU were committed to the PHARE programme, about 2.5 billion more than had been spent on PHARE between 1990 and 1994, with an annual average of about 40 per cent over the 1994 PHARE budget.[35] 'This increase was decided with a clear view to the enormous challenges we are facing for the integration of the associated countries into the Union. The old budgetary allocations were considered as too low for this, not only by us but also by most Member States'.[36]

Functional pressures always need actors who perceive them and translate those rationales into particular policies. The functional pressures that have been pointed out above were first recognised by the Commission. In its two communications to the Council, the Commission identified the changes that were necessary for a progression towards the integration of the associated countries into the Community.[37] In addition, the German Presidency agreed that there was a need for a comprehensive and coherent pre-accession strategy and made this one of the primary objectives of its presidency.[38] It was sympathetic to the proposals made by the Commission and tried throughout various stages of the negotiations to go as far as possible. It also pointed out to the more reluctant Member States that they had already agreed on accession, and 'that it does not make sense to agree on it without making a concerted effort to ensure the feasibility of that goal'.[39] Moreover, the German Presidency worked out a compromise that allowed for agreement on a strategy that did not specify any figures for the future PHARE budget, thus avoiding a deadlock at Essen.[40]

Countervailing Forces at Essen and Cannes At the Essen European Council in 1994 there were only weak countervailing pressures at work. The countries with strong consulting firms, such as the United Kingdom, tended to be against an increase of PHARE funds to be used to co-finance infrastructure. Co-financing diminished the share

---

[34] Cf. Council (1994a: 23).   [35] Commission (1995a).
[36] Commission interview, Brussels, June 1996.
[37] Commission (1994a); Commission (1994b).
[38] *Agence Europe*, 10.11.1994.   [39] Interview, Brussels, June 1996.
[40] *Agence Europe*, 19.11.1994.

of PHARE money going into technical assistance for which their companies were (often successfully) bidding. However, the principle of introducing PHARE funds for co-financing infrastructure projects had already been introduced at the Copenhagen European Council in June 1993 (see my analysis on cultivated spillover below), and the battle over the use of PHARE credits for infrastructures had been lost at that point.[41]

The issue of increasing the PHARE budget was slightly more controversial. Some Mediterranean Member States, and above all Spain, made the substantial increase in the budget allocation for the PHARE programme conditional on a generous budget line for Mediterranean third countries under a global package of external financing. As there were enough funds available to satisfy all parties, the issue could eventually be resolved at the Cannes European Council, even without requiring significant compromises.[42]

The Aim of Enlargement as a Functional Pressure More Generally   As enlargement increasingly developed into an endogenous policy objective within the European Union, further functional pressures were set in motion as a result of this. CEEC accession became an internal goal, which required (or could only be fulfilled through) adequate pre-accession instruments since for the first time the European Union had made a strong political commitment concerning countries which yet had to fulfil the membership criteria.[43] Hence, the firmer this commitment became, the stronger grew the functional connection between enlargement and the PHARE programme. For example, PHARE's pre-accession focus was further strengthened in response to the Luxembourg European Council's launching of the enlargement process. The programme's logic shifted increasingly from being 'demand driven' – i.e. focusing to a large extent on the demands of the CEEC partners' demands as regards economic transition – to being 'accession-driven'.[44] Thus, PHARE funds were concentrated on the pre-accession concerns highlighted in the Road Maps and the Accession Partnerships that establish the overall priorities countries must address to prepare for accession and the resources available to assist them to do so.

Moreover, the political agreement reached on Agenda 2000 at the Berlin European Council in 1999, which included the financial framework for 2000–06 with a view to enlargement, more than doubled the pre-accession assistance to the candidate countries. This has been

[41] Interview, Brussels, 1996.   [42] Interview, Brussels, 1996; cf. *Agence Europe*, 28.06.95.
[43] Cf. e.g. Bailey and de Propris (2004: 89).   [44] Commission (2002a: 10).

largely attributed to the remaining accession problems and tasks, for example, concerning the strengthening of public administrations and institutions as well as regarding the promotion of convergence with the Union's *acquis communautaire*.[45] In addition, a key focus in early 2002 was the establishment of Action Plans by the CEEC in response to specific problems in the adoption of the *acquis* identified in, and in response to, the Commission's Strategy Reports 2001 and 2002.[46] Hence, the development of the PHARE programme became increasingly shaped by functional spillover pressures stemming from the internal goal of enlargement.

Political Spillover

Although spillover may occur without the participation of non-governmental elites, Haas emphasised the importance of their active involvement for the expansion of tasks.[47] He held that integration in a particular sector leads the interest groups concerned to move part of their activity to the regional level. Such groups may gradually shift their focus and expectations to the European level. As they have become more aware of the benefits of integration, they will promote further integration.

In this case study, neofunctionalist assumptions have provided less insight for the analysis of political spillover. The investigation into the role of organised interests with regard to the PHARE programme did not correspond to the neofunctionalist perception of interest group behaviour. First, there was little organised interest from the European level. As the most prominent actor here, the 'Federation Européenne d'Association de Conseil d'Organisation' (FEACO), the European umbrella organisation of management consultancies, was a rather weak player. FEACO's attempts to enhance the influence of consultants in the design of individual projects were strongly resisted by the Commission.[48]

Second, most lobbying has occurred at the level of tendering which has been important in terms of implementation but has had no impact on the overall design of the PHARE programme, which is subject to investigation in this chapter. Particularly regarding the period 1989–97, long before the implementation stage, the partner countries' annual or medium-term reform priorities and the funds allocated to specific sectors had already been discussed and determined in a dialogue between

---

[45] Interview, Brussels 2004.   [46] Cf. Commission (2002c: 7).   [47] Haas (1958: 297).
[48] Commission interview, Brussels, June 1996.

the CEEC and the Commission. The result of this dialogue was the creation of country specific indicative programmes which were voted on in the PHARE management committee. In order to establish the influence of organised interest on the shape of the PHARE programme we have to turn to their lobbying efforts on the level of prioritisation, *vis-à-vis* both the Commission as well as the member governments.

Third, according to neofunctionalist theory, interest groups gradually shift their expectations to the European level. Not only would this lead to their reformation on the supranational level, but they would also try to influence their respective governments to defend their interest, and possibly encourage them to allocate new tasks to the Community system.[49] Contrary to these neofunctionalist hypotheses, national governments were not very frequent targets of lobbying activity. Even when such lobbying occurred, Member States were either unable or unwilling to carry their influence to the decision-making level. In the PHARE programme up to the mid to late 1990s, Member States have had two possibilities of shaping the programme. First, they had a chance to state their opinion on the annual orientation papers which lead to the creation of annual indicative programmes and determine the prioritisation of sectors. However, their actual influence was very limited here, not least because PHARE was 'demand-driven' in nature, which meant that the beneficiary countries (mainly) decided on what money is spent. This principle was widely respected by the Commission and the Member States.[50] Second, Member States participate in framing PHARE regarding prioritisation through their decisions at a higher political level in the Commission or the European Council. The one exceptional case in which (consultancy) firms got noticeably involved was the controversial increase of infrastructure at the European summit meetings at Copenhagen in June 1993 and at Essen in December 1994. And here the pressure exerted by British and French consultancies on their governments was described as 'moderate at best'.[51]

Finally, on the whole, the PHARE programme has not provoked much attention from organised interests. One Commission official went as far as to claim for the first period of the programme that 'outside the consultancy industry, PHARE is not really an issue at all'.[52] In contrast to the findings that highlighted the relevance of neofunctionalist insights to explaining interest group pressure in favour of the 1992 project,[53] strong and influential players such as European business elites were

---

[49] Haas (1958: ch. 9).   [50] de Swann (1994); Interview, Brussels, 1996.
[51] Interview, Brussels, June 1996; cf. pp. 97–98 of this study.   [52] Interview, Brussels, 1996.
[53] E.g. Sandholtz and Zysman (1989: 116ff); Green Cowles (1995: 501ff).

absent here, owing to the fact that their interests were not really at stake. Moreover, interest groups were put off by the complexity of the PHARE decision-making system, which made it difficult for them to identify the right access points for their lobbying efforts.[54]

Social Spillover

Four underlying hypotheses can be ascertained from the neofunction-alist writings on social spillover: first, socialisation processes occur amongst national civil servants within the Council framework often involving Commission officials. Second, Community decision-making cannot be captured in terms of classic intergovernmental strategic bargaining but is better characterised as a 'supranational' problem-solving process. Third, processes of enmeshment and socialisation tend to ease decision-making deadlocks and induce consensus formation and progress among member governments. Fourth, learning processes help generate a shift of expectations and perhaps loyalties towards the emerging European polity on the part of national elites. The subsequent analysis will examine the first three hypotheses, while the last one will be addressed in Chapter 5.

While it is conceivable to investigate social spillover broadly in terms of different interaction patterns of (especially national) elites involved in decision-making processes, this study focuses on socialisation, *engrenage* and learning in terms of certain working groups and committees in the Council framework (or in the other two cases: the Representatives Group in the IGC framework). Given the difficulty of studying socialisation processes empirically, the investigation into social spillover within this chapter will at times go beyond merely analysing the empirical data that could be gathered concerning officials dealing with the PHARE programme. I will sometimes also draw on a wider range of interviews conducted with officials involved in EU trade policy and other fields. This has been complimented by participant observation (during a placement in the Council Secretariat) and extensive scrutiny of secondary literature as well as official and (formerly) confidential documentation.

The Socialisation Process, Mechanisms and Agents   Although the neofunctionalists talked rather extensively about socialisation processes, they failed to define the term. Elsewhere, socialisation has been defined as the 'induction of new members [...] into the ways of behaviour that

---

[54] Interview, Brussels, 1996.

are preferred in a society'.[55] Socialisation to the norms of the Council framework is the crucial process through which individuals become members of that society. It is 'the process by which actors internalise norms which then influence how they see themselves and what they perceive as their interests'.[56] Norms are 'collective expectations for the proper behaviour of actors with a given identity'.[57] Very important prevailing norms in the Council framework are 'willingness to compromise and satisfice', collective expectations of 'reciprocity' and 'habits of agreement'. These will be further elaborated and substantiated below. The next sub-section does not so much focus on the norms that are internalised, but on how they are internalised. It is suggested here that socialisation mostly takes place through three mechanisms and agents: Council working groups and committees, Permanent Representations and through holding the Presidency.[58]

Participation in Council Working Groups and
Interaction with Opposite Numbers

Most importantly, norms may be internalised through frequent and prolonged participation in committee or working group meetings. Officials attending the weekly Central Europe Working Group[59] – where most general matters concerning the CEEC, including PHARE, have been discussed – usually sit in the Eastern Europe and Central Asia Working Group too, which also meets weekly. With the formation of the twice weekly Enlargement Working Group there has also been overlap between the latter and the Central Europe Working Group. Moreover, officials come together when there are working group meetings of advisors to the ambassadors, which are held, even if only infrequently, on an *ad hoc* basis, though they take place more frequently in the period prior to European Councils. In addition to that, some of the members of the Central Europe Working Group also attend the PHARE management committee meetings once a month. In total it has been estimated that national officials dealing with PHARE see each other 'at least every other working day on average' in busy periods and sometimes even more

---

[55] Barnes *et al.* (1980: 35).   [56] Risse and Wiener (1999: 778).
[57] Katzenstein (1996: 5).
[58] Much of the subsequent analysis will focus on the role played by new Member States and their delegates and more generally new participants in committees and working groups, as well as new committees in the Council framework. The rationale being that the changes and progress in the internalisation of norms, attitudes and behaviour can most easily be observed in such instances.
[59] The Central Europe Working Group has been renamed after enlargement. It is now called the 'Central and South-East Europe Working Group'. For the day-to-day workings of PHARE the Management Committee has been responsible (see section below in this chapter).

often than their home partners.[60] Officials also tend to see each other informally in between official meetings, in the corridors, for lunch and dinner, or at cocktail parties. Moreover, every six months members of a working group, together with their wives, go on weekend trips to a destination within the country holding the Presidency. This level and intensity of interaction has led to good professional and often personal relationships among officials as well as a strong club 'atmosphere' or 'esprit de corps'. This is by no means applicable to the officials in the Central Europe Working Group alone, but to many other committees and working groups in the Council framework, such as COREPER and the Article 113 Committee.[61]

New members in Council working groups usually behave differently from their colleagues who have been there for some time. It tends to be more difficult to find out where new Member States stand, as their officials cannot be approached as straightforwardly and informally as 'long-serving' members of a working group. As a result, matters cannot always proceed as quickly and smoothly as normal.[62] It takes time for new Member States' officials to adjust to the norms ingrained in the Community's negotiating system, as the style of decision-making is sometimes radically different from that in their capitals.[63] However, 'newcomers are pushed to acclimatise as quickly as possible to the ethos which permeates the Council system'.[64] Early in their membership, Austrian officials, for instance, earned a reputation for delivering rigid instructions and inflexible policy positions in the Central Europe Working Group as well as in the Council framework more generally. However, after only a year of membership, Austria gained a reputation for its ability to compromise.[65]

New members in Council working groups adapt their norms and attitudes in a number of ways. First and probably most importantly, the mere recurrence and continuity of formal and informal interactions has led to the development and internalisation of negotiating habits. As Hayes-Renshaw and Wallace have pointed out, 'where the links between participants are recurrent, [...] the incentives to behave constructively, and according to the codes of conduct, are much greater'. This in turn 'encourages the emergence of stable and predictable relationships

---

[60] Interviews, Brussels, 1996.
[61] For literature capturing this phenomenon in the Council framework generally see Hayes-Renshaw and Wallace (1997); Beyers and Dierickx (1998). On COREPER see e.g., Lewis (1998b) and Barber (1995). On the Article 113 Committee see Niemann (1997a).
[62] Interview, Brussels, 1996.   [63] Cf. Sbragia (1994).
[64] Hayes-Renshaw and Wallace (1997: 235).
[65] See Lewis (1998a); also confirmed by interviews, Brussels, 1996–97.

among the participants, solidifies shared norms and intensifies inter-dependence among the participants'.[66]

Second, the importance of groups in socialisation processes has been emphasised by the social psychology literature. The self-categorisation theory focuses on how individuals are able to act as a group.[67] It sees in-group identification as an adaptive social–cognitive process that makes pro-social relations such as co-operation and unity of attitudes possible. The theory stresses that common fates, social interaction, inter-group competition and common enemies are likely to increase intra-group cohesion, unity of attitudes and mutual acceptance between members.[68] But while the extent of social interaction between the members of the Central Europe Working Group is significant, there are also some elements of 'inter-group competition' and 'common enemies' that are relevant. Although the Central Europe Working Group has fewer 'rivals' than others[69], there have been occasions when feelings of rivalry towards other committees or working groups have made a difference (see below in this chapter).

Permanent Representations

The Permanent Representations of the Member States in Brussels also play an important role in the socialisation process. Governments of newly admitted Member States usually consider it important to expose their officials to the Community's decision-making style and methods as rapidly as possible. According to Sbragia, this rationale explains why Spain, when joining the Community, had the largest Permanent Representation in Brussels. The Spanish government was 'using its COREPER delegation as a mechanism of socialisation'.[70] Equally important is this 'socialising mechanism' for national civil servants moving to Brussels from the Member States that are more experienced in Community affairs. Not only does the work in Permanent Representations foster the acquisition of knowledge over the formal working methods of the Community but it also nurtures the internalisation of norms. As one official from the Central Europe Working Group reported: 'when I changed from Bonn to our embassy in Brussels, I gained a wholly new perspective. All of a sudden I was "on the other

---

[66] Hayes-Renshaw and Wallace (1997: 247).
[67] See e.g. Oakes et al. (1994); Taifel and Forgas (1981).   [68] See: Oakes et al. (1994).
[69] For example, the relations between COREPER and the Political Committee (Kiso, 1997), COREPER and the Article 113/133 Committee (Hayes-Renshaw and Wallace, 1997), or the various sub-Committees of the Article 113 family (Niemann, 1997a). On the question of administrative rivalry in the Council framework generally see also Lewis (2000).
[70] Sbragia (1994: 74).

side" and had to learn from my colleagues in the Permanent Representation how to negotiate back home effectively'.[71] The socialising capacity of Permanent Representations as socialising mechanisms has also been highlighted in the literature. Hayes-Renshaw and Wallace mentioned that officials in Permanent Representations, while engaged in the defence of national positions, tend to develop a sense of collective identity distinct from their interlocutors in the capital, and are sometimes accused of having 'gone native'.[72] Alan Clark, for example, a former British minister called the UK Permanent Representation 'totally Europhile'.[73] It is not surprising therefore that observers attributed the strong *esprit de corps* in the Central Europe Working Group partly to the fact that most of its members were based in Brussels.[74]

The Presidency

The Council Presidency has a socialisation function in forcing the relevant member government to pay more attention, even if only periodically, to EU-wide policy concerns. In addition, civil servants of Member States holding the Presidency also tend to understand better the complexity of issues and the various problems faced by national delegations. As one former chairman of the Central Europe Working Group noted, 'during our Presidency the colleagues in Paris could better understand the daily dilemma we have in terms of searching for compromise. This seems to have made some of them more flexible ever since'.[75] This learning process does not happen entirely by default. Wallace and Edwards have pointed out that chairmen of committees, who are drawn from the Permanent Representations, often welcome their term of office as an opportunity to induce in their home-based colleagues a more co-operative attitude to community negotiations.[76] And a member of the Dutch delegation claimed that their Presidency in the first half of 1997 was used to 're-educate the national administration into Europe, to really go deep; this involved the participation of some 500 to 600 people'.[77] There is some empirical evidence about the impact of the Presidency as a mechanism of socialisation. Wurzel's study on the role of the Presidency has found that holding the Presidency fosters a subtle but important learning process about the European and various national dimensions of policy problems, which induces a more 'European thinking' among national officials and often results in 'European compromises'.[78]

---

[71] Interview, Brussels, 1996.   [72] Hayes-Renshaw and Wallace (1997: 225).
[73] Clark (1993: 138).   [74] Interviews, 1996.   [75] Interview, Brussels, 1996.
[76] Edwards and Wallace (1977: 17).   [77] Cited from Lewis (1998a: 16).
[78] Wurzel (1996: 272, 288).

Decision-styles: Bargaining and Problem-solving A number of authors have distinguished between different styles of decision-making. Richardson, for example, put forward the three-fold classification of 'problem-solving', 'bargaining' and 'confrontation'. Problem-solving emerges through an orientation towards common interests, values or norms which are distinct from the individual interests of participants, and which therefore may facilitate voluntary agreement even when sacrifices in terms of individual interests are necessary.[79] Such a form of decision-making has been emphasised in the neofunctionalist literature on *engrenage*, for example, regarding the notion of 'upgrading common interests'[80]. Bargaining, by contrast, is characterised by the appeal to the individual self-interests of the participants and by resort to threats and promises. Agreement can only be obtained if the anticipated utility is at least as high for each participant as the anticipated utility of non-cooperation.[81] In the literature on EU decision-making many authors, either explicitly or implicitly, still characterise negotiations (especially among Member governments) as bargaining. Most prominently, Moravcsik in his liberal intergovernmentalist (LI) approach describes a process of interstate bargaining that defines the possible responses of the EU political system to pressures from national governments. Other works capturing the EU decision-style in terms of bargaining include (some of) those by Schneider, Schneider and Cederman, as well as Scharpf.[82] I argue that strategic bargaining does not give us a complete picture of the EU decision-making style. For a better understanding of negotiations in the Central Europe Working Group and the Council administrative framework more generally, the notions of 'communicative action' and 'normatively regulated action' have been introduced, further specifying the notion of 'problem-solving' and rendering the concept of social spillover more precise and plausible. Concepts like bargaining, communicative action and normatively regulated action should be seen as ideal types which do not often appear in their pure form.[83]

Communicative Action

The concept of communicative action refers to the interaction of people whose actions are co-ordinated not via egocentric calculations of success but through acts of reaching understanding. In communicative action,

---

[79] Richardson (1982).   [80] Haas (1964a: 66).   [81] Scharpf (1988: 259).

[82] See Moravcsik (1993: 481); Schneider (1994); Schneider and Cederman (1994: 633–62); Scharpf (1988: 260).

[83] Hence, the empirical question to be asked is not whether actors behave in a strategic (i.e. bargaining), communicative or normatively regulated mode, but which mode captures most of the action in a given situation. On this point see Risse (2000: 18). On this question also see Niemann (2004: 387).

participants are not primarily oriented to achieving their own individual success. They pursue their individual objectives under the condition that they can co-ordinate or harmonise their plans of action on the basis of shared definitions of the situation. Agents engaging in communicative action seek to reach understanding about valid behaviour. Habermas distinguishes between three validity claims that can be challenged in discourse: first, that a statement is true, i.e. conforms to the facts; second, that a speech act is right with respect to the existing normative context; and third, that the manifest intention of the speaker is truthful, i.e. that s/he means what s/he says. Preferences are no longer seen as fixed. They can change through argumentative processes in which actors persuade each other on the basis of these validity claims and the better argument predominates. When engaging in communicative action, agents do not seek to maximise their interests, but to challenge and substantiate the validity claims that are inherent in their interest.[84] While agents bargain in strategic interaction, they *discuss, deliberate, reason, argue* and *persuade* in communicative interaction.

According to Habermas, the possibility for communicative action is dependent on a number of factors. First, actors have to share a common life world, i.e. collectively share the same patterns of interpretation of the world. Second, actors should recognise each other as equals and need to have equal access to the discourse. Third, communicative action is dependent on actors' ability to empathise, i.e. to see things through the eyes of the discourse partner. In Council forums such as the Central Europe Working Group, a common life world is shared, for example, through professional proximity, with participants being civil servants having received similar education and training. In addition, a common lifeworld is reinforced as civil servants often also share expertise and, above all, working groups frequently develop a certain 'club atmosphere' or 'esprit de corps'. They all have equal access to the debate during official sessions and generally regard each other as equals. Finally, empathy is greatly facilitated through the high degree of informality which prevails amongst officials in EU decision-making, where restricted sessions, informal meals and collective trips are normal practice giving negotiators considerable opportunity to familiarise themselves with each other's positions and problems.

There is a case to be made for communicative action in the Central Europe Working Group and the Council framework more generally, not as an exclusive explanation, but as one which adds to our understanding

---

[84] Habermas (1981a: 153).

when other accounts, such as bargaining, leave us in the dark.[85] One essential claim of Habermas is that actors seek to reach an understanding about the action situation and their plans of action in order to co-ordinate their actions (by way of agreement). This seems to be a not uncommon characteristic of EC negotiations. The negotiating parties usually try to separate the strategic from the argumentative aspects in order to know where there is scope for real discussion and argumentative discourse. As Peterson has claimed, informal consultations usually allow negotiators to say: 'here is our informal agenda. Do you have one?'[86] Moreover, officials often indicate when they are not behind their instruction by reading them out. As one official remarked 'when I hear other permanent representatives reading out their instructions, I just let it go, we don't even start a discussion'.[87] Even where it is not made so explicit that no argumentative discourse is possible, civil servants tend to understand this, since they tend to know each other well. Many officials dealing with PHARE have noted, for example, that they can ascertain from the tone of their colleagues' voices, or even their body language, to what extent they mean what they say out of conviction or due to instructions.

The purpose of communicative action is less to reach one's own pre-defined goals, than to achieve a mutual understanding on what is true or false and what is right and wrong. Peters has found that conflicts over policy are often about ideas and technical content of policy rather than fixed and firm interests. In these instances participants can learn about their policy options and attempt to create a viable consensus based on effective policy.[88] Lewis, in a paper on COREPER, has pointed out that Permanent Representatives occasionally disregard their instructions because they were given bad arguments to defend.[89] My interviewing with civil servants in the context of PHARE and the Central Europe Working Group, as well as more generally, confirms Lewis's finding on that aspect.[90] This suggests that officials often come to the negotiation table with the disposition to discuss and persuade rather than bargain with each other on the basis of (unchangeable) pre-defined preferences.

Moreover, in line with the notion of communicative behaviour, the better argument indeed often tends to prevail in discussions on the PHARE programme. For example, my evidence suggests that the change towards a greater allocation of PHARE funds towards infrastructure projects eventually won the day because the more reluctant

---

[85] For a more comprehensive and detailed account of the (potential) value of the concept of communicative action for EU negotiations see Niemann (2004).
[86] Peterson (1995: 87).   [87] Quoted from Lewis (1998a: 21).   [88] Peters (1994: 22).
[89] Lewis (1998a: 21).   [90] Interviews, Brussels, 1996, 1997, 1999.

Member States simply had no real arguments to put forward (other than their own potentially insignificant economic gain). The Commission, along with the Danish and German Presidencies, managed to persuade some reluctant Member States on the basis of the (convincing) argument that, after several years of know-how transfer, there was less need of technical assistance.[91] That the quality of argumentation matters in COREPER has been suggested by Barber who wrote that 'the reality is that the ambassador with the best arguments has the advantage, whether he comes from plucky little Luxembourg or united Germany'.[92] And argumentative discourse may also play a substantial role in European Council negotiations where, according to Butler, 'even more than in other Community negotiations those who get their way are those who know their subject'.[93]

The relevance of communicative action regarding the PHARE decision-making process is further underlined by evidence from interviews. A number of civil servants both from Member States and the Commission have characterised the policy styles in terms of communicative rationality without being prodded.[94] In addition, a good indicator for genuine communicative behaviour is argumentative consistency across contexts and forums. By contrast, actors changing their arguments and justification depending on the audience are likely to engage in rhetorical action. In some case it was possible to trace and reconstruct officials' line of arguing in their domestic bureaucratic environment by interviewing their colleagues in national capitals and through the study of (formally) confidential reports. Most of the cases investigated revealed an astonishing argumentative consistency.[95]

My analysis of social spillover among the participants of the Central Europe Working Group, and civil servants in the Council framework more generally, also suggests that processes of communicative behaviour may indeed foster more deeply rooted learning than what I have termed above as 'incentive-based' learning. This can be illustrated, for example, as regards the decision to increase the allocation of PHARE funds towards infrastructure projects during the German Presidency of 1994. In a reasoned discourse officials reached a mutual understanding that after five years of technical assistance and know-how transfer and given the infrastructure challenges in the CEEC, more PHARE funds could be made available on the latter issue. Decision-makers – even from the Member States whose companies disproportionally benefited

[91] Interviews, Brussels, 1996.   [92] Barber (1995: 3).   [93] Butler (1986: 84).
[94] Interviews, Brussels, 1996–97.
[95] Interviews, Brussels, Bonn, London, 1996, 1997, 1999.

from bidding for technical assistance projects – admitted and gradually advocated that this was simply the solution 'which made most sense in terms of the PHARE programme and its beneficiaries'.[96] Unlike one year prior, when the Commission managed to push the first 15 per cent allocation for co-financing infrastructure investment through the Copenhagen European Council, this time negotiators were not pushed, or merely consented to the increase. Instead, they fully concurred; they assented on the basis of common convictions. Instead of merely adapting their positions as at Copenhagen, this time they changed their (more profound) interests. A good indicator for this type of more deeply rooted and complex learning process is that persuaded decision-makers began to apply what they had learned by advocating the very rationale by which they have been convinced across different forums and contexts. Furthermore, given these genuine learning processes, this agreement was uncontested for a number of years until real world developments changed the basis of this mutual understanding.[97]

A few words on the conditions which accompanied instances/periods which were identified as dominated by communicative action. Apart from the common lifeworld, recognition of equals and empathy, communicative action has tended to prevail under the following circumstances: first, when issues were technically complex, expert knowledge is required and discursive inquiry is necessary and validity claims have to be made concerning the right/correct basis for action. Second, when actors lack knowledge, face new problems or experience uncertain situations they are motivated to analyse new information, consider different views and learn. Under such circumstances they are particularly inclined to enter into communicative action as truth-seeking becomes essential. Third, decision-makers need to have the time for lengthy discussions. For a reasoned understanding to develop, time is required, for example, for explicating arguments, for challenging arguments and for reflection. Fourth, for learning processes to take place powerful arguments may not be enough. In addition, persuasive individuals, owing to intellectual capacity or reputation for integrity, reinforce the impact of arguments on preferences. Finally, low levels of politicisation or, more generally, the absence of my hypothesised countervailing pressures seem to be conducive to communicative action. A reasoned consensus reached, for example, in the Central Europe Working Group can be crucially obstructed when negotiators face strong pressure from outside, especially domestic, sources.

[96] Interview, Brussels, 1996.   [97] Interviews, Brussels 1996.

Normatively Regulated Action

Normatively regulated action refers to members of a social group who orient their action towards common values or norms which they have thoroughly internalised. Agents comply with a norm when, in a given situation, the conditions are present to which the norm has application. All members of a group for whom a given norm has validity may expect of one another that in a certain situation they will carry out the actions proscribed. Norms are taken for granted, they are not enacted out of choice, but out of habit.[98] It is argued here that some norms which have been internalised by national civil servants working in the Central Europe Working Group (and in the Council system more generally) are such that they have in fact a common orientation and are not geared towards individual interests of the participants. Such norms include the tendency to reciprocate, the internalisation of a culture of compromise and satisficing, and the acquired habit of agreement.

Reciprocity: A significant degree of mutual trust is required for negotiators to be willing to sacrifice unilaterally, on the understanding that such sacrifice will be reciprocated by others when the occasion arises. It has fostered the development of a habit of reciprocity which has become entrenched in the behaviour of national officials. In the words of Helen Wallace 'expectations of reciprocity have [. . .] become embedded in the negotiating process'.[99] This is different in quality from package deals or side-payment based on individual self-interest calculations alone. This is not to say that such kind of strategic deals do not take place.[100] However, in terms of normatively regulated behaviour, reciprocity may be exercised not out of choice, but out of habit. One way of substantiating the existence of such behaviour is to point to the fact that in many package deals one or more participants lose out,[101] which is hard to explain in terms of egotistic actors alone. The swapping of concessions often takes place implicitly rather than explicitly. As one member of the Central Europe Working Group told the author: 'most of the time we don't talk about "making a deal". If a colleague really can't go any further, but I have some leverage, then I help him out. Without doubt, he would do the same. Sometimes it takes months until he can make up for it'.[102]

Satisficing and compromise: A certain culture of satisficing and compromise has become an inherent part of the negotiating behaviour in the Central Europe Working Group and seems to have become a

---

[98] Habermas (1981a: 127).   [99] H. Wallace (1990: 224).
[100] E.g. Moravcsik (1993: 481).   [101] H. Wallace (1990).
[102] Interview, Brussels, 1996.

widespread norm in the Council framework. Officials have learned 'to accept the need to compromise as an inherent feature of EU negotiation' and 'to embrace that optimal outcomes are impossible'.[103] This is to be distinguished from a self-interested behaviour of safeguarding a final agreement, which also exists. Most delegations in the various working groups usually enter the negotiating room with fall-back positions which partly reflects that a culture of compromise seems to have become entrenched in negotiating practice.[104] As one official put it: 'the positions set up at the beginning are usually not realistic ones, they contain the maximum. It is a bit like putting on a show. Nobody expects to get what they ideally want'.[105] Moreover, group dynamics inducing cohesive behaviour seem to play a certain role.[106] As one member of the Central Europe Working Group said about the outcome of the Essen European Council: 'I was by no means thrilled by the outcome, but went along with it. Those are the rules, if you don't compromise, you cannot be a member of the club'.[107] This general disposition to make concessions has also been noted in the literature.[108] According to Helen Wallace, usually enough participants in Community negotiations are willing in the end to be satisficers rather than optimisers.

Habits of agreement: Finally, and closely related to the culture of compromise and satisficing, habits of agreement developed among the negotiators in the Central Europe Working Group. There is a collective expectation in the various forums that sooner or later an agreement emerges among the participants. Negotiators in various working groups have reported that they feel responsible for progress to be made on the policy issues of their agenda, and that they generally enter into discussions with the disposition to come to a (sound) agreement. So, it is no rare occasion that officials remind their colleagues that 'we are here to agree, not for self-satisfaction'.[109] Moreover, as one official of the Central Europe Working Group put it: 'often a bad agreement is considered better than no agreement'.[110] Habits of agreement seem to be widespread in the Council decision-making system. According to the former UK Permanent Representative, Michael Butler, 'Foreign Ministers know that they have to agree at the end on almost every issue'.[111] In the words of Helen Wallace,[112] 'there is a "can-do" atmosphere, much prompted by the EC experience of turning decision into substance' where 'over a period cooperative modes can be established and habits of transacting business entrenched'.

---

[103] Interviews, Brussels, 1996–97.   [104] Lewis (1998a).   [105] Interview, Brussels, 1996.
[106] Oakes *et al.* (1994).   [107] Interview, Brussels, 1997   [108] Butler (1986).
[109] Participant observation, Brussels, 1996.   [110] Interview, Brussels, 1996
[111] Butler (1986: 75).   [112] H. Wallace (1990: 215, 225).

This section has suggested that decision-making in the case of PHARE (and EU decision-making more generally) goes beyond the concept of bargaining. In order to capture this process adequately the notions of normatively regulated behaviour and communicative action have proved valuable. These findings are echoed by those of Smith[113] who has maintained that EU policy-making concerning Eastern Europe is better characterised by a 'problem-solving' style than by a bargaining style of decision-making.

Socialisation as an Integrative Dynamic   The third (revised) neofunctionalist hypothesis regarding social spillover is that socialisation and learning contribute to overcoming deadlocks and to inducing progress and development during negotiations on the European level.[114] Much of the preceding analysis has already implicitly (and partly explicitly) argued and indicated that socialisation may lead to progress, as integrative outcomes are facilitated by informal channels, mutual trust and familiarity as well as the development of a 'club atmosphere' or 'esprit de corps'. In addition, decision-making characterised by communicative action also suggests that deadlocks can be more easily avoided, as participants enter into the negotiations disposed to comprehending the action situation (and each others' problems), since decision-makers' interests are conditioned by their perception of valid behaviour and since preferences are malleable throughout the negotiation process, during which actors seek a common reasoned understanding. During such processes powerful/convincing arguments and rationales can also register more easily with decision-makers which may also contribute to the avoidance of gridlock. Moreover, negotiations that take place in terms of normatively regulated action, based on collective expectation such as reciprocity, compromise, satisficing and above all on habits of agreement, already imply a logic of consensus formation. That shared norms may advance the integration process in Europe would confirm the findings of Lindberg and Scheingold who argued that the gradual internalisation of the Community's norms may lead actors to 'a realisation of an enlarged common interest, the realisation of which can lead actors to encourage their respective governments to allocate new tasks to the Community system'.[115] Two additional dynamics related to socialisation in the Council framework can be suggested here: inter-committee rivalries and coalition formation.

---

[113] Smith (1999: 171).   [114] E.g. Lindberg (1963).
[115] Lindberg and Scheingold (1970: 119).

Intercommittee rivalries

According to social identity theory, individuals seek to differentiate their own groups positively from other to achieve a positive social identity, which fosters the discrimination of other groups.[116] Such behaviour has been mentioned above. Not surprisingly perhaps, working groups and committees in the Council framework often see themselves in competition with one another. As a result, they usually go as far as possible in resolving problems and reaching agreement because they believe that they are the experts, the only ones who really understand the technical character of issues, or out of prestige or the protection of group interests. Some officials from the Central Europe Working Group suggested, for instance, that their co-operation was enhanced in the period preceding the Cannes European Council decision to raise the overall PHARE budget, as they saw their standing and resources threatened by the proposal to allocate substantial funds to Mediterranean third countries which was pushed in the Mashreq/Maghreb Working Group.[117] Moreover, members of the Central Europe Working Group have sometimes feared that their prestige was at stake if they could not find agreement on an item which subsequently had to be resolved in COREPER. They have also been afraid that technical aspects of a particular issue might be ignored by COREPER, which has often induced civil servants to rally together, reminding each other that 'we are the experts here', which has furthered the feeling of being part of an 'insider-group' and the conviction that 'only we can solve this problem'.[118] Here we have intercommittee rivalries operating as a catalyst for intra-group solidarity and agreement in the working group.

Such intercommittee rivalry seems to be even more prominent in other cases. There are references in the literature which suggest that such competition has fostered progressive outcomes. Hayes-Renshaw and Wallace, for example have noted that, with regard to Article 113–COREPER relations, the Article 113 *Full Members* normally try to 'tie things up' at the level of their committee, so that the ambassadors will not become involved, as they fear that the Permanent Representatives could throw their weight around. Similar observations have been made by Van Schendelen concerning relations between the Agricultural Council and the General Affairs Council, by Kiso as regards the relationship between the Political Committee and COREPER, and by

---

[116] Oakes *et al.* (1994: 42).   [117] Interviews, Brussels, 1996.
[118] Interviews, Brussels, 1996–97.

Niemann concerning the interaction of the various (sub)committees dealing with trade policy.[119]

Coalition formation

Other aspects inducing consensus and progress in EU negotiations are special relationships and coalition formation, which have been recognised as recurrent features of EU decision-making.[120] The basis for the development of special relationships is mutual trust. Confidence in the viability of such a relationship will often be bred by habits of working together. Such habits are important factors in making the shift from an *ad hoc* tactical alignment to a more durable relationship.[121] In the Central Europe Working Group there has been a loose alliance concerning the PHARE programme, bringing the Northern Member States together (as the more progressive or generous) often under the leadership of Germany.[122] As one official put it, 'this sort of occasional but recurrent alliances can sometimes inject a powerful dynamic into the process'.[123] Coalition formation seems to be an even more prominent feature of certain other Council working groups and committees. For example, there is the coalition of seven to eight 'like-minded' (liberal) delegates of the Article 113 Committee who usually get together two or three times a year for an informal exchange of ideas and a discussion of broad strategy. This has given the Article 113 Committee a certain dynamic and often promotes final consensus.[124] As Wallace has pointed out, agreement is facilitated when there are fewer positions or options on agreement.[125]

Possible Countervailing Pressures   In terms of delimiting the concept of social spillover, the pressures which may counter such processes need to be identified. In that respect it is important to look at the relationship between socialised civil servants and their capitals, as socialisation and learning in the Central Europe Working Group and the Council framework more generally may be offset by other demands throughout the formulation and adaptation of national policies. There are three main, partly interrelated and overlapping, sources which could potentially offset socialisation processes in the Council framework. First, opposing views within the lead department in the capital from which the socialised participant of a working group is receiving his/her

---

[119] See: Hayes-Renshaw and Wallace (1997: 90); van Schendelen (1996: 541); Kiso (1997a); Niemann (1997a: 10–11).
[120] Morgan (1986); Beyers and Dierickx (1998).   [121] See Wallace (1985a).
[122] Cf. Jaks (1993).   [123] Interview, Brussels, 1996.   [124] See Niemann (1997a: 12).
[125] Wallace (1985a).

instructions; second, bureaucratic pressures in the form of inter-ministerial rivalries (going against the line of the lead department); finally, political pressures exerted on the socialised official by the domestic political system directly.

As for the first case, David Spence has pointed out that British officials in Permanent Representations often have to persuade their colleagues in Whitehall that the boundaries of negotiability have been reached.[126] This also applies to capital-based officials who are 'members' in Council working groups. Lead departments in capitals may effectively countervail the views proposed by a 'socialised' official in Brussels, but there are a number of ways in which the latter can make an impact. Members of Council committees, such as the Central Europe Working Group, have a sounder knowledge of the various national positions. This is recognised by governments which often request their Permanent Representation to sound out other delegations in order to prepare discussions in capitals. Here, the officials in Brussels have an obvious opportunity to influence their capitals. In addition, officials dealing with PHARE admitted that when reporting back to their capitals they can always highlight certain aspects more than others and thereby steer their capitals in a certain direction.[127] In fact, as one member of the Central Europe Working Groups has pointed out, briefing is a two-way process whereby the officials who attend working groups themselves recommend positions to be adopted and supply briefing material to their capitals.[128] Thus, Lewis has argued that briefings already contain a substantial 'Brussels-element' in them.[129] Moreover, it has been suggested that senior officials, especially the Permanent Representatives, can have a significant direct influence on their ministers, and that instructions can be side-tracked or, to a certain degree, ignored by them.[130]

Second, bureaucratic infighting, either inspired by the pressures that are placed upon ministries by organised interests or by the desire to protect their own departmental interests,[131] poses another threat to common positions facilitated by the socialisation process. It has happened, for instance, that the German Ministry of the Environment opposed an emerging consensus concerning the restructuring of PHARE in the Central Europe Working Group and later in COREPER, although the lead-ministry (economics ministry) was willing to adapt the national position to the mainstream view. However, socialised civil

---

[126] Spence (1993: 49).   [127] Interviews, Brussels, 1997.
[128] Interview, Brussels, 1996.   [129] Lewis (1998a: 19); also cf. Scott (1983: 76).
[130] Butler (1986: 77); Lewis (1998a).   [131] Cf. e.g. Bulmer and Paterson (1987).

servants can skilfully side-track instructions that are based on the demands of other departments. For example, one official admitted, he would sometimes speak last in a meeting and thereby indicate that he would not terribly mind being outvoted, as happened in the above case. And, on another issue, the same official spoke out enthusiastically in favour and hence actively influenced the debate, even though he was asked to come out cautiously in favour.[132] In addition, officials from more and more ministries have become increasingly open to arguments such as 'danger of stalemates' or 'facing isolation'. This is largely due to the Europeanisation trend, whereby more and more ministries participate in Brussels negotiations.[133] A growing number of officials from different ministries have taken part in Council working groups and have learned about the negotiating realities in multilateral negotiations and are thus more prone to respond positively to the above arguments.[134]

Finally, political pressures exerted by domestic political systems may obstruct the impact of the socialisation process on outcomes. National civil servants may be subject to considerable demands from industry, interest groups, opposition parties or other domestic political pressures.[135] This may especially be the case when they are based in their capitals and therefore close to the national political machinery, but it also occurs to Brussels-based officials.[136] However, officials seem to have found ways of coping with such pressure. As one official dealing with PHARE explained: 'in such cases I can usually explain quite plausibly to our industry that decision-making in Brussels is complex and one's own voice of limited influence. When citing the European context, they often let me off the hook quite easily'.[137] Hence not only national governments but also national civil servants play two-level games.[138] Similarly, socialisation effects can unfold when there are several competing domestic demands. They can be played out against each other by taking a line in the working group that leads to agreement, which can later be justified by pointing to the strong demands of other sectors.[139] The above analysis has shown that several kinds of countervailing pressures exist. Although they may lessen the impact of socialisation, it is unlikely that they can entirely offset the process, as

---

[132] Interviews, Brussels, 1996–97.
[133] For such understanding see Rometsch and Wessels (1996). On the various meanings of the term Europeanisation see Olsen (2002: esp. 921ff).
[134] Interviews, 1997–98.   [135] Cf. e.g. Moravcsik (1993, 1998).
[136] See Spence (1993: 48ff).   [137] Interview, Brussels, 1996.
[138] On two-level games see especially Putnam (1988).
[139] Interviews, Brussels, 1996–97.

there are ways in which these countervailing pressures can, to some degree, be overcome.

Cultivated Spillover

The Commission's Mandate for the Co-ordination of Western aid In the section on exogenous spillover earlier in the chapter we have seen the importance of externalisation pressures, whereby G7 member states authorised the European Commission to take on the task of co-ordinating aid to Poland and Hungary. Such pressures were strengthened by Delors' 'politicking' and 'skilful manoeuvring' in order for the Commission to obtain the mandate for the co-ordination of a common aid policy.[140] As Ross holds, the attempt to translate new East–West dealings into enhancements of the Community's foreign policy capabilities was a clear Delorist goal.[141] Despite much public surprise in Brussels and the rest of Europe, the co-ordination idea was by no means a new one.[142] 'Jacques Delors had been asking the Twelve for months to coordinate relations with the Communist Bloc'.[143] In a speech before the EP in January 1989, Delors put particular emphasis on this point. The desire to have joint discussions with the United States on East–West questions was first mentioned by Delors in February in an interview with the *Wall Street Journal*. In April Delors called for the co-ordination of export credits to the East which irritated several Member States.[144] In June Delors went to Washington, where he brought up the matter again during talks with President Bush. 'Insiders claim that it was Delors' own powers of persuasion about Eastern Europe over lunch with Bush which led the Americans to consider giving the Community the important new foreign policy role'.[145] Hence, it seems safe to assume that pressures stemming from the Commission's cultivation efforts have added to the exogenous factors described earlier in this chapter.

The Commission at the Copenhagen European Council The Copenhagen summit, apart from the Twelve's commitment to future accession, also paved the way for a gradual but fundamental change in the orientation of the PHARE programme. Since its initiation in autumn 1989, operation PHARE had concentrated on the disbursement of

---

[140] Ross (1995: 48).   [141] Ross (1995: 138).
[142] For a different view see Pelkmans and Murphy (1991: 130).
[143] Ehlermann (1989: 23).   [144] *Financial Times*, 25.04.89.   [145] Ross (1995: 63).

technical aid in support of the political and economic reform process in the East. However, with the agreements reached at Copenhagen the PHARE programme also began to develop into a medium-term financial instrument with improved possibilities to promote infra-structure development in co-finance with the international financial institutions.[146]

The move towards infrastructure investment was one of the most controversial decisions taken in the course of the programme. At the Copenhagen European Council the Commission successfully initiated and defended the introduction of co-financing infrastructure from PHARE funds.[147] This step was regarded as necessary by the Com-mission as, after up to four years of know-how transfer, there was less need for technical assistance in the CEEC, which explicitly requested a diversion of PHARE money away from technical assistance towards infrastructure.[148] Despite resistance from a number of Member States, the Commission was determined to push its initiative through. In this case the Commission acted like a true policy entrepreneur.[149] It was able to draw on its superior expertise, it negotiated skilfully and was persistent. 'Political engineering and leadership by the Commission' have been described as 'key factors in the reformulation of policy at Copenhagen'.[150] Important in that respect was the considerable support for this initiative within the Commission. Commissioner Brittan had responded very favourably to the suggestion from the PHARE directo-rate. In addition, Delors was also sympathetic. He believed in the importance of trans-European networks as a means of fighting unem-ployment and fostering competitiveness in Europe, as manifested in the White Book on competitiveness.[151] The strong support by both Brittan and Delors meant that the Commission acted very cohesively as an institution. This aspect of Commission cohesion has been singled out in the literature as an important potential asset of the Commission.[152] The Commission used two different strategies in order to upgrade the common interest and achieve its objectives.

First, and most importantly, it made efficient and skilful use of the Community's machinery. During the negotiations on the working group

---

[146] At Copenhagen, the Twelve agreed to make 15 per cent of the PHARE annual budget available for this purpose. As we saw earlier, infrastructure later became an important part of the Union's pre-accession strategy.

[147] This was later extended at the Essen European Council (see section on functional spillover).

[148] See Commission (1993a).

[149] On the notion of 'policy entrepreneur', see, for example, Majone (1993, 1996).

[150] Sedelmeier and Wallace (1996: 375).   [151] Interview, Brussels, 1996.

[152] See Nugent (1995: 611).

level and COREPER, the Commission 'softened up' the British, Dutch and Irish opposition, while waiting for a 'window of opportunity'.[153] The Commission knew long in advance that the CEEC would feature highly on the agenda and that the summit would in all probability produce a clear statement on accession. This provided a good opportunity to bring the issue of PHARE's use for investment purposes to the forefront due to its link with accession. Brittan and Delors managed at a late stage to persuade the Danish Presidency to put the issue on the agenda for the last day at Copenhagen.[154] One senior Commission official recalled that the papers with the agenda arrived in the delegations early in the morning, only a few hours before the meeting, which left little time for a well-prepared response. 'Once it was on the table, it was clear that it would go through'.[155] The same official also asserted that the issue of infrastructure would never have passed in this form in the normal Council framework, as this would have allowed too much controversial discussion, which would have diluted the original Commission proposal.

Second, in its argumentation the Commission seems to have used the rationale of functional and technical pressures as a method of persuasion. An important argument for the use of PHARE money was its reference to the decision of the Edinburgh Council that EIB loans could be allowed to cover up to 75 per cent of the total costs of infrastructure projects. If, in practice a level of 70 per cent could be achieved, this would still leave 30 per cent to be financed by the countries themselves. It was further pointed out that the governments concerned and the international financial institutions considered that local contributions could reach perhaps 15 per cent of the costs through the provision of land and other local costs, thus leaving a further 15 per cent of own financing to be found.[156] Hence, it was argued that PHARE money was necessary to fill this gap. This argument is said to have gained increasing acceptance on the working group level and COREPER and thus softened national positions and upgraded the common interest.[157]

Countervailing Forces

On the issue of making PHARE funds available for co-financing infrastructure projects moderate to fairly considerable countervailing pressures were at work. A number of Member States were against this measure, most notably the United Kingdom, Ireland and the Netherlands.[158] They did not want to see the share of technical assistance

---

[153] On this notion, see e.g. Majone (1996).   [154] Interview, Brussels, June 1996.
[155] Commission interview, Brussels, June 1996.   [156] Commission (1993a).
[157] Interviews, Brussels, 1996.   [158] Cf. Smith (1999).

reduced, partly because they still regarded technical assistance as the top priority, and partly because their domestic consulting industries were very successful in securing technical assistance projects under the tendering procedure and as their companies benefited from it out of proportion. The United Kingdom and the Netherlands also faced moderate direct pressure from the consulting industry which further reinforced their stance.[159] As one official put it, 'Britain and the Netherlands and perhaps Ireland would have remained firm in their opposition had it not been for the very forceful and persuasive action by the Commission'.[160]

The Commission and its Cultivation of Political Spillover   Apart from making use of its negotiating skill and its capacity to generate ideas that reshape the perspectives of other parties, the Commission has also made its voice heard through the cultivation of political spillover. This can mean two things: first, the Commission cultivates relations with governmental and non-governmental elites for the purpose of using them as short-term allies, for example, in order to have backing for certain proposals; second, and more explicitly referred to by Haas and Lindberg, there may be co-optation, the process whereby the Commission seeks to pull national elites into its sphere of influence by cultivating long-term relations.

The Cultivation of Long-term Alliances with National Elites
As for co-optation, a tentative conclusion may be drawn: co-optation seems less a conscious strategy than the addition of many *ad hoc* consultations, or simply normal Commission practice. In general, Commission officials denied the application of deliberate long-term strategy in their cultivation of relations with non-governmental elites. In fact, the example of 'closure', i.e. the termination of the consultation process at the point when Commission officials no longer regarded it as effective,[161] in the case of FEACO, suggests that the Commission may prefer to pursue *ad hoc* rather than seek long-term alliances with organised interest. Lindberg, however, saw evidence for a co-optation strategy in the Commission's efforts to remain in good standing with the press, which contributed to the pro-integrative climate of the late 1950s and early 1960s.[162] Throughout the PHARE programme co-optation was most clearly evident in 1992–93 when the programme was severely criticised by the European Parliament and the media for being too cumbersome. As a number of Member States pushed for a

---

[159] Interviews, Brussels, 1996.   [160] Interview, Brussels, 1996.
[161] Mazey and Richardson (1994: 178).   [162] Lindberg (1963: 71).

dissolution of PHARE and its replacement by bilateral aid programmes, DG I established a PHARE information unit in 1992 which was set up to protect the integrity of the programme. This public relations exercise contributed to a generally more favourable attitude towards the Commission's management of PHARE in the following years.[163]

As for governmental elites, there is potential for co-optation, in view of the very frequent interaction between national civil servants and Commission officials. The Commission is represented at all levels, from the working groups to the European Councils, and also increasingly within the context of CFSP. For its drafting work the Commission has installed around 600 groups of independent experts, of which at least 70 per cent are civil servants from Member States acting in a 'non-official' capacity.[164] More specifically applicable to PHARE, over 10 percent of A-level staff in former DG 1A of the Commission consisted of seconded civil servants detached for a three year period by Member States' governments.[165] As one Commission official put it, 'once they return to their national ministries, seconded national officials tend to be much more positive and understanding about the Commission's involvement and policy line regarding PHARE'[166].

The Cultivation of Short-term Alliances with National Elites[167]
When pursued on an *ad hoc* basis, Commission efforts are more easily traceable and also acknowledged in the literature.[168] Monnet himself had been concerned with the establishment of a small non-hierarchical organisation, capable of cultivating contacts with national officials in order to drill their expertise in the European interest. In its proposals concerning the PHARE programme, the Commission has often used formal or informal channels to sound out Member States' interests. This allowed the Commission to design proposals in such a manner that major quarrels could be avoided, and support for its initiatives more easily secured.[169] In addition, throughout the PHARE programme the formation of *ad hoc* coalitions – that between Delors and Bush

---

[163] Interview, Brussels, 1996.
[164] These numbers apply to the late 1980s (Wessels 1990).
[165] Interview, 1996. Also cf. Hooghe (1996).
[166] Interview, Brussels, 1996. However, the co-optation hypothesis has been contested by a number of authors who suggest that there are strict limits on the extent to which national officials could be drawn into the Commission's sphere of influence because of co-optation on the part of Member States *vis-à-vis* Commission officials (Coombes 1970; Pinder 1991a: 32).
[167] Again, this sub-section overlaps with that on *engrenage*, especially in terms of coalition formation.
[168] See e.g. Kohler-Koch (1996); Wallace (1986).
[169] Interviews, Brussels, June 1996; c.f. Lindberg (1963: 71).

constituting the most prominent one – has repeatedly served Commission policies.[170]

Similar to the Commission's efforts regarding national governmental elites is its use of organised interests for short-term support of its policies. Neill Nugent has pointed to the Commission's knowledge and expertise as one of its prime sources for influencing decision-making in the Community.[171] *Ad hoc* consultations of non-governmental elites are an important device of the Commission in that context. This has also become evident in the case of the PHARE programme. For example, the Commission frequently consults umbrella organisations, such as EUROCONTROL (the European organisation for air traffic control) for technical information and advice, including the occasion when the Commission proposed radar equipment for the international airport in Albania. My findings suggest that the more organisations sre allowed to become involved in the preparation of projects, the greater the stake they feel they have in them, and the more they tend to defend the proposals *vis-à-vis* others, such as Member States.[172] This is similar to Haas' concept of engagement, except that, in that context, he was referring originally to governmental elites.[173] Commission officials dealing with PHARE also frequently consult institutions, such as the World Bank, the EBRD or the EIB. 'When we say that the EBRD is of the same opinion or has already agreed to co-finance something, it goes down particularly well'.[174] This is largely due to the fact that representatives of Member States sit on the board of those banks, and once they have agreed on a project there, it would be difficult to object to it later in the PHARE management committee, which deals with policy implementation.

The Cultivation of Alliances with Epistemic Communities
Epistemic communities, which have been defined as networks of professionals with recognised expertise and competence in a particular domain and an authoritative claim to policy-relevant knowledge,[175] have played an important role in several areas of PHARE. Apart from the field of nuclear safety, they also seem to have existed and have had some influence in areas such as the environment and energy in general.[176] The

---

[170] However, such a process is not one-sided. Spence has pointed out that Member States also influence the Commission for their own ends, in the case of Britain with the UK Permanent Representation as the 'lobbying arm of Whitehall departments' (Spence 1993: 66).

[171] Nugent (1995).   [172] Interview, Brussels, June 1996.   [173] Haas (1958: 522).

[174] Interview, Brussels, 1996.

[175] For a definition and exploration of the concept see Haas (1992: esp. 1–4).

[176] Interviews, Brussels, June 1996.

field of nuclear safety provides the most clear-cut evidence for the existence of an epistemic community, which seems to have had considerable influence on the establishment of nuclear safety as prioritised sectors within PHARE and TACIS. The nuclear safety 'programmes', which are sectoral programmes within PHARE and TACIS, gained financial priority alongside other sectors such as the environment and infrastructure. In 1995–96, the nuclear safety programme was the largest financial component within TACIS and one of the largest within PHARE.[177]

Epistemic community formation began in 1991 after nuclear scientists at the Kozluduy nuclear power plant in Bulgaria pushed the 'alarm button' by pointing out the dangerous state of the plant. As a result, officials at Kozluduy asked the World Association for Nuclear Operators for help. This led to an expert mission by the International Atomic Energy Agency (IAEA) of Vienna. The mission clearly established that there were indeed enormous problems at Kozluduy, as had been hinted at by the experts in Bulgaria.[178] This initial risk analysis gave rise to demands from nuclear safety experts for relevant information and information exchanges. The emerging community of experts gradually managed to consolidate bureaucratic power and institutionalise its influence within the European system of governance.[179]

The epistemic community is made up of experts from European national regulatory authorities, such as the Bundesministerium für Umwelt in Germany, technical safety organisations like the 'Atomic Energy Authority-Technology' in the United Kingdom, plant operators, such as EDF in France, engineering companies, like Siemens in Germany, and Commission experts. Moreover, there is the Nuclear Safety Expert Group, which draws together experts from universities, research institutes and public and private safety organisations. This network of knowledge-based experts is 'not as coherent and clearly defined as the seven wise men of Greece'.[180] Nonetheless, a good deal of information is exchanged across borders and professional disciplines. For example, the Twinning Programme Engineering Group (TPEG), funded by the Commission, brings together experts from nine different nuclear operators and nine different countries.

Haas has pointed out four defining characteristics of epistemic community members:[181] (1) a shared set of normative and principled beliefs,

---

[177] See Commission (1996b).   [178] Commission (1996b: 2).
[179] This development is much in keeping with Haas's account of epistemic community formation, which follows a sequence of uncertainty, interpretation and institutionalisation (1992: 3).
[180] Commission interview, Brussels, June 1996.   [181] Haas (1992: 2–4).

which provides a value-based rationale for the action of community members; (2) shared causal beliefs, which are derived from their analysis of practices leading to a central set of problems which then serve as a basis for problem-solving; (3) shared notions of validity, i.e. internally defined criteria for weighing and validating knowledge in the domain and (4) a common policy enterprise. My interviews suggest that the above described community of knowledge-based experts shares a common set of values that are centred around the importance of adherence to strict nuclear safety measures and the prevention of a 'nuclear holocaust'. Common causal beliefs lie in the acceptance that the safety standards in Eastern European and ex-Soviet nuclear power plants were insufficient, and that something had to be done in order to prevent nuclear accidents. From this follows the policy enterprise. There was agreement that in order to preserve Europe from a nuclear disaster the oldest and most unsafe plants gradually needed to be closed down. Experts also agreed that the most modern plants should receive funding in order to bring them to Western safety standards. Members of the community also seemed to share common validity tests, as they had undergone similar education, and its Western European members had experienced similar safety practices and standards in their countries.[182]

There are many grounds for suggesting that the very evolution that led to the nuclear safety programmes within PHARE and TACIS was initiated by an epistemic community. After the results of the Kozluduy mission were revealed, the Commission reacted by passing funds through the management committee to be allocated for further studies as well as the implementation of technical assistance for the improvement of safety standards at Kozluduy and elsewhere.[183] Within the Commission nuclear experts had considerable influence in convincing the PHARE directorate of the necessity for action. The nuclear experts within the Commission partly managed to do so because of the backing of the wider epistemic community.[184] The movement towards further prioritisation of nuclear safety within PHARE and TACIS was also promoted by the community of experts. In July 1992 at the Munich G7 summit, the heads of government discussed the results of a research document that was drafted by national experts in the field of nuclear safety of the seven most industrialised countries. On the basis of this document the heads of government invited the Commission to increase the amounts earmarked for the PHARE and TACIS nuclear safety initiatives.[185]

---

[182] Interviews, Brussels, 1996.   [183] Interview, Brussels, 1996.
[184] Interview, Brussels, 1996.   [185] *Agence Europe*, 4.7.1992.

As a result 29 MECU were set aside for nuclear safety within PHARE in 1992.[186] Moreover, it is the management committee that gives a green or red light to a certain budgetary line. According to one Commission official, the management committee never authorised a budget line without the approval of the Nuclear Safety Expert Group. It was further pointed out that the Commission made its financial proposals on the basis of the implementation and requirements of previous years, drawing directly on the expert knowledge and support provided by the G7 document, the TPEG and the Nuclear Safety Expert Group.[187]

It has been held that Peter Haas and the other contributors to the 1992 special issue of *International Organisation* left some questions unanswered. Most importantly, they failed to specify under what circumstances epistemic communities would make a policy impact.[188] Risse-Kappen identified some of those conditions. While attaching minor importance to the type of issue area, he attributes much significance to the degree of institutionalisation. The more regulated the inter-state relationship by co-operative international institutions, the more epistemic communities are likely to flourish and the less should national governments be able to constrain them.[189] David Cameron asserts that the existence of the European Union encourages and facilitates the activity of epistemic communities, and transnational actors more generally, to a far greater extent than might exist with an arbitrary collection of states. The dense network of Community institutions is likely to provide both rationale and opportunity to come into contact, and also increases the availability of channels they can use to target decision-makers on the national as well as supranational level.[190] Thus, the high level of institutionalisation within the Community facilitates access of epistemic communities to decision-makers.[191] Taking this line of thought further, as Lindberg and others pointed out long ago, the impact of the Community institutions, and therefore the regulation of state behaviour, is largely dependent on how these institutions assert themselves.[192] Consequently, it can be argued that strong, active and assertive central institutions foster the growth and development of epistemic communities and ease their access to the decision-making

---

[186] Commission (1996b: 3).   [187] Interview, Brussels, 1996.
[188] Risse-Kappen (1995a: esp.16).
[189] Note that Risse-Kappen talks about transnational relations more generally in this context. However, in another chapter of the same volume he establishes that the type of transnational actor makes little difference for the above conclusion (Risse-Kappen 1995b: 310). Further work on the conditions under which epistemic communities define the preferences of (EU) decision has been done by Zito (2001: 585ff).
[190] Cameron (1995: 74).   [191] Also cf. Risse-Kappen (1996: 31).
[192] Lindberg (1963: 8).

level. More directly, the flourishing of epistemic communities is promoted by the fact that central institutions seek to cultivate relations with them for their own purposes.

The Commission (as also other central institutions) can make use of epistemic communities for its own ends and ultimately benefit from their existence. This is where cultivated spillover comes in. Lindberg and Scheingold pointed out that the Commission is in a privileged position of centrality and authority, capable of directing the dynamics of relations with different national groups.[193] As Mazey and Richardson[194] have noted, Commission officials are necessarily 'brokers of interest', trying to mobilise transnational coalitions in favour of policy change. In this case, the Commission drew on the expertise of the epistemic community and sought its backing in order to get its proposals through the management committee. Moreover, the Commission managed to further reinforce and steady its bargaining position by stabilising relations with the epistemic community through promoting its institutionalisation. A number of organisations such as TPEG came about through Commission initiative or are funded partly through PHARE.[195] Other analyses have revealed even greater use and support of epistemic communities for the Commission. As Mazey and Richardson, for example, have observed in the field of environmental law and other sectors where the Commission had no specific Treaty mandate to initiate policies, the Commission gradually attained a *de facto* policy role which it partly acquired through assistance and support from interest groups and epistemic communities.[196]

The Commission and its Dominance of the PHARE Management Committee   The Commission's executive role has increased substantially, as the Community has developed beyond the scope originally envisaged in the Treaty of Rome.[197] The PHARE programme is a good example of such a development. The various types of committee structure imposed upon Commission decision-making, known as 'comitology', are a set of arrangements providing for the implementation of Community law which have developed parallel to but outside the original Treaty provisions. In the case of the PHARE programme a 'management committee' is responsible for the implementation of aid. Although under this type of committee Member States can defer Commission proposals to the Council, this still leaves the Commission a

---

[193] Lindberg and Scheingold (1970: 284).   [194] Mazey and Richardson (1997a).
[195] Interview, Brussels, June 1996.   [196] See: Mazey and Richardson (1997a).
[197] Ludlow (1991: 106–7).

great degree of autonomy, as Member States can only trigger referral of a proposed measure to the Council by adopting an unfavourable opinion by qualified majority.[198, 199]

The PHARE management committee comes into play at two stages.[200] It approves the allocation of the overall PHARE budget to particular sectors and may thus influence the shape of the programme. In addition, individual projects are written up in detail by the Commission in the form of financing proposals which are submitted to the management committee for opinion and approval.[201] There are several reasons why the Commission virtually dominates the PHARE management committee. First, its far greater knowledge and relevant expertise, in comparison to national representatives, are a major reason for the Commission's dominance of the committee. The Commission, through its responsibility for the routine management of the programme and throughout the preparation of proposals, is able to accumulate a much larger volume of information and expertise in its interaction with external experts hired by the Commission, experts from the recipient countries and other international institutions. By contrast, national representatives are rarely experts in the field and often know little more than what is presented to them on paper, and they usually have limited relevant experience to draw on.[202] Few Commission proposals are really controversial. When Member States have technical reservations concerning certain projects, the Commission is often in a position to refute their amendments and to convince Member States since it tends to have a better overview of all technicalities involved.[203]

Second, it has been pointed out that the Commission's key advantage in management committees is that the negative opinion required to trigger a referral to the Council is often difficult to achieve because Member States usually have too many differences to gather a qualified

---

[198] Docksey and Williams (1994: 127).
[199] On the level of Commission constraint concerning the different types of comitology committees, see Steunenberg et al. (1996, 1997) as well as Docksey and Williams (1994). By contrast to the rationalist view of comitology as a control mechanism (Franchino 2000; Pollack 2003), Joerges and Neyer (1997) draw on Habermas's account of deliberative democracy and constructivism to argue that comitology committees provide a forum for expert deliberation and problem-solving.
[200] The following account describes the procedures up to 1996–97. Some changes have been introduced since with a view to the increased accession focus. On this point see especially Geurts (2000) and Bothorel (2000).
[201] Commission (1992a).   [202] Interview, Brussels, 1996.
[203] Interviews, Brussels, 1996.

majority[204] against a Commission proposal.[205] Management committees provide the Commission with an additional advantage. Even if
critics can muster a qualified majority in the committee itself, this is not
the end of the story. When after a negative opinion, a proposal is
transferred to the Council, it is possible that the same qualified majority
cannot be found again due to the political rather than technical
approach in the Council.[206] When the Commission is confronted by a
strong alliance against itself, it usually modifies or withdraws the proposal. However, when the Commission thinks that the political constellation in the Council is favourable it would let the proposal go to the
Council level.[207]

The Commission is in the chair and manages the process of the
meetings. Most important, in this context, is its power over the agenda.
The Commission has often adopted a strategy of organising the agenda
in the order of least controversial to most controversial. 'Anything that is
really rubbish gets to the bottom. [. . .] At the end of the meeting when
they all want to go home, they rush through something worth 70 MECU
that is bad, whereas they were discussing something worth 20 MECU
for two hours that was actually quite good'.[208] A good example of the
Commission's strategy is the PHARE Management Committee meeting
of March 1996, where the Commission chairman withdrew one badly
written and insignificant proposal to satisfy the Member States. Subsequently, Member States were more willing to give in on a politically
controversial proposal concerning the Kozluduy nuclear power plant
which the Commission was eager to pass.[209]

One reason why the Commission usually succeeds in passing its
proposals in the PHARE Management Committee without causing
much controversy lies in the fact that Member States have already
agreed to the main guidelines of what is being proposed by the Commission. They have given their consent to the legal basis on which the
programme rests. In addition, they have conceded, for example, to the
pre-accession strategy at European Councils level, and once it gets to
the level of the discussion of individual projects, Member States have

---

[204] As pointed out my methodology section, I have only chosen cases which are ruled by
unanimity. This is true also for this case study and especially for all decisions taken in
the Council framework. QMV here only applies to policy implementation and thus
does not affect the larger/political design of the PHARE programme.
[205] Docksey and Williams (1994: 127–8).
[206] Ludlow (1991: 107); Docksey and Williams (1994: 178–88).
[207] This has happened, for example, in the case of a proposal for an income support
programme to Albania in 1992, which successfully passed the Council (interview,
Brussels, 1996).
[208] Commission interview, Brussels, 1996.   [209] Interview, Brussels, 1996.

already agreed to areas of prioritisation in the indicative programmes. Moreover, the Commission often seems to pursue a strategy of subtly or openly reminding the Member States that they have already consented to the broad framework in order to win their consent for individual projects more easily. As one Commission official put it, 'once we press buttons like pre-accession, it is very hard for Member States to reject a proposal because they know what their governments agreed on in Copenhagen and Essen'.[210] Hence, overall it can be concluded that even in the tighter procedures of the management committee, the Commission has a strong presumption in its favour and 'Commission officials have only themselves to blame if they cannot carry Member States with them'.[211]

Involvement of the European Parliament in Shaping PHARE   While Haas particularly stressed the role of the Commission, the revised neo-functionalist framework encompasses the supranational institutions more generally. Following this wider view, the European Parliament has been an important actor in the context of the aid agreements for the CEEC and the NIS. Parliament has made its voice heard, especially through its budgetary and informal powers both *vis-à-vis* the Commission and the Council. Informally, the EP has also managed to assert itself through its traditionally close relationship with the Commission. This, to some extent, compensated for the weak legislative standing of Parliament in EU–CEEC relations.[212]

Parliament's Budgetary Powers and PHARE

During the course of PHARE's existence the European Parliament has frequently made use of its budgetary powers[213], the area where its powers are most advanced. Parliament has the last word on the money allocated to the PHARE programme out of the overall Community programme, as PHARE is part of non-compulsory expenditure. Throughout the early history of the programme the European Parliament expressed its full support for PHARE and called for both the expansion and extension of aid.[214] In line with the strong overall support of its aims, Parliament acted as a spur for an increase of the PHARE budget in the early period. In autumn 1989, at the conception of

---

[210] Moreover, what used to be called 'economic restructuring' was later sold by the Commission under 'pre-accession', while the content of such proposals did not (substantially) change (interview, Brussels, 1996).
[211] Ludlow (1991: 107).
[212] According to Article 235 EC (now Article 308 EC), which forms the legal basis, the EP only requires to be consulted.
[213] See e.g. Hartwig (1997).   [214] European Parliament (1991: 138).

the programme, Parliament ensured that the 200 MECU proposed by the Commission – to ensure the implementation of the measures envisaged in the PHARE regulation – was augmented to 300 MECU.[215] Similarly, while the Commission proposed 2.35 billion ECU for the three-year period from 1991 to 1993,[216] the Community ended up giving more than 2.8 billion ECU, which was largely due to Parliament's use of its budgetary powers.[217]

The European Parliament has also used its budgetary powers another way. In 1992–93 Parliament increasingly criticised the management and structure of PHARE and TACIS. Concern over implementation, for example, has been voiced in numerous written and oral questions to the Commission. After no immediate action was taken by the Commission, the European Parliament put 385 MECU of TACIS funds into the reserve.[218] During the budgetary procedure, the EP faced resistance from the Council, which tried to re-establish the TACIS funds before Parliament finally froze the funds through the decision in its second reading. The money frozen in TACIS appropriations was only released after the Commission had shown improvements in the criteria set up by the EP, which required that further improvements had to be made before the 1995 budget was finalised.[219]

European Parliament also used its budgetary power to initiate policies, two of which have become integral parts of the PHARE programme, namely the 'Democracy Programme' and 'Cross-border Cooperation'. The former originated in a Parliamentary debate of July 1990, where McMillan-Scott, the former spokesman of the European Democratic Group in the then Political Committee, pushed for the promotion of civil society and democratisation in the CEEC. This led to a report drawn up by the Political Affairs Committee on a proposal to establish a 'European Democracy Fund', with McMillan-Scott as the *rapporteur*. Eventually 5 MECU were earmarked by Parliament in the PHARE budget to be specifically used for this purpose.[220] This was later raised to 10 MECU.

---

[215] Pinder (1991b).   [216] *Börsen-Zeitung*, 23.02.1990.
[217] Interview, Brussels, 1996.   [218] European Parliament (1994a: 161).
[219] On the latter point see European Parliament (1994b: 84). However, overall interaction between the EP and the Commission has not been confrontational concerning budgetary matters related to PHARE. Parliament as the Community's budgetary authority and the Commission as the eventual executor of the agreed budget are intimately involved with one another at the practical and political levels throughout the procedure (Westlake 1994a: 231). For example, especially in the early period of the PHARE programme, Parliament used informal contacts in order to find out where the financial limits were on the Commission's capacity to implement PHARE funds in a meaningful way without wasting too much money through badly designed proposals (interview, Brussels, 1996).
[220] European Parliament (1995a).

In contrast to the democracy programme, cross-border co-operation was not Parliament's brain child. Originally, it was an idea developed and promoted by the German government. However, Germany failed to persuade other Member States of the usefulness of the initiative, as a result of which cross-border co-operation threatened to disappear from the PHARE agenda. Yet, in 1993 German parliamentarians started to promote cross-border co-operation in the EP, which finally led to the establishment of a specific budget line for this initiative in the Community budget.[221]

Parliament's Informal Powers

Apart from Parliament's influence on the shape of the PHARE programme which is derived from the powers it has been given in the Treaties, the EP has also managed to make an impact in other ways. For example, the EP can activate the public as an ally by cultivating contacts with the media or the organisation of parliamentary hearings. Those are means the EP can use to put pressure on the Commission or member governments. In 1994 and 1995 there were two Parliamentary hearings concerning the effectiveness of assistance to the CEEC and the NIS. One hearing was specifically on assistance for the conversion of military industries for civil purposes. 'This was done in order to alert the public that something needed to be done in this area.'[222] Following the Parliamentary hearing, this issue started to receive substantial media attention and was also brought onto the agenda at the negotiations on the latest TACIS regulation. Subsequently, the conversion of defence-related industries became one of the priorities within TACIS,[223] which some observers have attributed to the attention created by the Parliamentary hearing.[224]

Parliament in Coalition with the Commission

Another way in which the European Parliament can assert itself, which is not to be found in the Treaties, is through 'coalitions' with the Commission. Both institutions are to some degree dependent on each other. While the Commission needs the EP in its search for the popular legitimisation of its policies, Parliament sees the Commission as a partner *vis-à-vis* the Council.[225] Moreover, as they are both kindred supranational institutions and as they both share the same federal vocation, Parliament and Commission have been described as 'natural allies'.[226]

---

[221] Interview, Brussels, 1996.   [222] Interview, Brussels, 1996.
[223] Council (1996a: 6).   [224] Interviews, Brussels, 1996.
[225] Westlake (1994a: 225).   [226] Ludlow (1991: 115); Westlake (1994b: 42).

An example of an informal alliance between the Commission and Parliament can be found in the 1996 negotiations on the TACIS regulation under the consultation procedure. Both institutions tried to reinforce each other's interest in these negotiations *vis-à-vis* the Council. 'Only together Parliament and Commission were able to safeguard some of their interests'.[227] Although it knew that it was already difficult enough to reach agreement in the Council, the Commission, in its compromise proposal, took up a number of Parliament's amendments, including some Parliamentary amendments on the tendering procedure.[228]

On the other hand, the EP tried to help the Commission in its two opinions. According to one official, the Commission had informally contacted Parliament to ask for support, as some Member States' positions threatened to curtail the Commission's powers over the management of the TACIS programme.[229] In its first reading Parliament amended the Commission's proposal in a way that not only corresponded with its own interests, but also with those of the Commission. The EP opted for an 'advisory committee', thereby attempting to enhance the Commission's powers in the day-to-day running of the programme.[230] This was again stated by the EP in its second opinion. Although the Council rejected most of Parliament's amendments in this case, a coalition between the two central institutions could prove beneficial not only for the EP, but also for the Commission, and constitute an integrative force which has so far received little academic attention.

The Role of the Presidency as an Institutionalised Mediator   Ernst Haas pointed out that the use of an institutionalised mediator usually leads to upgrading the common interest of the parties involved in multilateral negotiations. In the context of the ECSC and the EEC, he saw this role fulfilled by the High Authority and the European Commission. However, to move beyond the lowest common denominator in such negotiations, the mediating services do not necessarily have to come from the supranational institutions, but could simply be provided by 'a single person or board of experts with an autonomous range of powers'.[231] At the time of his writing Haas did not foresee that this role could be taken up by the Council Presidency, as the Treaty of Rome provided the Presidency with modest powers.

---

[227] Interview, Brussels, 1996.   [228] Commission (1996a: 11).
[229] Interview, Brussels, 1996.   [230] *Official Journal*, C323, 04.12.95.
[231] Haas (1961: 368).

The contrasting roles played by the Spanish and Italian Presidencies during the 1996 negotiations on the TACIS regulation highlight the importance of genuine mediation on the part of the Presidency, especially where unanimity is required. As opposed to the PHARE regulation, the TACIS regulation is limited in time and had to be renewed for the second time in 1995–96. Discussions started under the Spanish Presidency. However, the Spaniards were unable to find a solution that could accommodate the various national interests. This is largely due to the fact that the Spanish Presidency attempted to push through its own interests rather than mediate between the clashing views on the Commission proposal.[232] Spain suggested, for instance, that firms which already had a lot of experience or had already won a certain number of contracts should be excluded. New and inexperienced firms, like Spanish ones, should have greater chances to win contracts. The negotiations under the Spanish Presidency ended in a deadlock.[233]

The subsequent Italian Presidency, however, managed to work out a compromise between the opposing national positions. First, it modified the Spanish proposal and took a much more neutral stance. Throughout the Spanish Presidency, the Italians were aligned with the interests of the Southern states and were perhaps even the hard-liners together with the Spanish.[234] But, as Edwards has noted, in the search for compromises, the Presidency often has to sacrifice its own national position.[235] When it took up its Presidency, Italy moved away from that position and took a much more moderate stance. This was clearly a signal which showed that other parties also had to become more flexible.

In addition, the Italians also put pressure on Member States to reach a consensus quickly because the old regulation had already run out in December 1995. Although the old regulation had been prolonged, no money could be made available without the new regulation which meant that no projects could be contracted and the implementation of assistance was effectively hampered. The Italian Presidency repeatedly reminded the Member States that any further delay would be to the detriment of the NIS whose interests were supposed to be at stake rather than vested Member States' interests.

Finally, the Italian Presidency found a formula which all member governments and the Commission could accept. While greater emphasis on the environment, nuclear safety and cross-border co-operation satisfied the northern states, the southern Member States were generally content about the better tendering opportunities given to the less

---

[232] Interview, Brussels, 1996.   [233] *Agence Europe*, 05.12.1995.
[234] Interview, Brussels, 1996.   [235] Edwards (1996).

experienced applicants. In general, all Member States, including the Commission, welcomed the greater focus on transparency on the level of the tendering procedure.[236] It can be argued that the compromise worked out by the Italian Presidency managed to upgrade common interests, as all negotiating parties compromised their original positions, but still felt that they gained something. A similar outcome was anticipated by Haas in terms of the Commission's mediating efforts.[237]

Conclusion

The above analysis has indicated the general usefulness of neo-functionalist insights for explaining the emergence and development of the PHARE programme. Exogenous and cultivated spillover pressures based on virtually non-existent countervailing forces convincingly explained the origins of PHARE. Functional and, less importantly, cultivated spillover pressures account for the development of PHARE into an important instrument within the Community's pre-accession strategy. Cultivated spillover also largely explains the expansion of PHARE funds for co-financing infrastructures, which was possible even in face of more substantial countervailing forces. The concept of culti-vated spillover has also provided an important conceptual linkage for the accommodation of epistemic communities which have been very influ-ential in establishing nuclear safety as an important part within the PHARE programme. Moreover, it can be tentatively concluded that social spillover provided a significant lubricant for the development of PHARE, without being able to establish any clear-cut causality. It is also worth mentioning that in most cases the *combination* of revised neo-functionalist dynamics accounted for the occurrence of a certain out-come. For example, the emergence of PHARE has been explained by three factors (strong exogenous spillover, aided by cultivated spillover pressures, along with virtually absent countervailing forces), all of which were necessary, but only together were they sufficient in (convincingly) explaining the outcome.

My analysis challenges the empirical and theoretical findings of Haggard and Moravcsik who asserted that the Commission had played a marginal role in initiating and shaping EC aid for the CEEC. Moreover, the PHARE programme has proven to be far broader and much more viable than they anticipated.[238] It developed into the single largest

---

[236] *Agence Europe*, 26.01.1996.   [237] Cf. Haas (1961: 368–9).
[238] Haggard and Moravcsik (1993: 280). They argued that PHARE had proven 'a narrow and transitional task'. My account is further substantiated by that of Sedelmeier and Wallace (1996) which was written at the same time as the first version of this chapter

source of know-how transfer to the CEEC, showed considerable flexibility in adapting to the changing phases of economic and political transition in the East and obtained a central position in the Union's reinforced pre-accession strategy. In that sense it could be argued that the Community managed to minimise what Christopher Hill – in his conceptualisation of Europe's international role – coined the capability–expectations gap. Although the demands and expectations in the Community to co-ordinate and provide effective aid were substantial, the Community took on this role, acted swiftly and proactively, provided significant funds, repeatedly adjusted the programme in face of changing circumstances and tied it to its wider objective by incorporating PHARE into its strategy of accession. Hence, in this case, capabilities, which for Hill mean 'cohesiveness, resources and operational capacity',[239] were largely able to meet the expectations of outside *demandeurs* and the Community's more enthusiastic supporters. One tentative specification of Hill's concept is that the gap between expectations and capabilities may be most easily bridged in EU/EC external relations where the Community has a significant (although rarely an exclusive) competence, as opposed to areas in which the Community is only a marginal actor such as in CFSP.[240]

(Niemann 1996) and stresses the importance of an active Commission in shaping PHARE. These findings are also broadly echoed by those of Smith (1999) who suggests that a combination of constructivism and neofunctionalism is useful for explaining EU policy towards Eastern Europe.

[239] Hill (1993: 321).

[240] However, Holland (1995) has suggested that this gap can also be bridged in CFSP, as highlighted in his case study of the Joint Action on South Africa.

3   Negotiations on the Reform of the Common Commercial Policy

The Common Commercial Policy and Article 113/133[1]

The Common Commercial Policy (CCP) is one of the oldest and most integrated policy areas of the European integration project. It was named in Article 3 of the Treaty of Rome as one of the main policies of the European Economic Community. As Member States were linked in a customs union, it was essential for them to draw up common policies regarding their commercial relations with the rest of the world.[2] The Treaty of Rome was revolutionary in the sense that it granted the new supranational entity an external personality with the authority to set out, negotiate and enforce all aspects of trade relations with the rest of the world.[3] This was to be achieved through a common trade policy based on the principles of a common external tariff, common trade agreements with the rest of the world and the uniform application of trade instruments across the Member States. The core elements of the CCP and the mechanisms through which it is to be conducted were set out in Articles 110 to 115 of the Rome Treaty. Although the Treaties of Maastricht[4], Amsterdam and Nice as well as the

---

[1] Article 113, which contains the central provisions of the Common Commercial Policy, after the renumbering of the Treaty of Amsterdam became Article 133. I will therefore refer to Article 113 during my analysis of the negotiations of the 1996–97 IGC and to Article 133 when I talk about the outcome of those negotiations (i.e. the Amsterdam Treaty provisions). I also refer to Article 133 in the subsequent sub-case analyses, i.e. my investigation into the IGC 2000 and the Convention/IGC 2003–04.

[2] Cf. Devuyst (1992: 68); Eeckhout (1991: 5ff).

[3] Although the European Coal and Steel Community (ECSC) had a number of external implications, there was no explicit treatment of policy-making for external economic relations at Community level in the Treaty of Paris.

[4] In the Maastricht treaty, Articles 111, 114 and 116 were repealed and Articles 113 and 115 were amended. For a detailed description and analysis of the changes made during the Maastricht Treaty revision see Devuyst (1992) and Maresceau (1993). Article 113, as amended by the TEU, is worth quoting in full length, since it is the focus of subsequent debate and analysis.

  1. The common commercial policy shall be based on uniform principles, particularly in regard to changes in tariff rates, the conclusion of tariff and trade agreements, the

Constitutional Treaty made some amendments, the main principles of the CCP have largely remained the same.

Article 113, the centrepiece of the external trade policy, provides that the Council will give a mandate to the Commission to open negotiations with third countries, in which the Commission acts as the sole negotiator. This mandate may include directives the Commission must respect in fulfilling its task. The Commission is 'assisted' during negotiations by the Article 113 Committee which is not largely 'consultative', as the Treaty provisions suggest, but also watches over the Commission's shoulder during negotiations.[5] Once negotiated, the Commission will initiate an agreement with third countries on behalf of the Community if it regards the outcome of negotiations satisfactory, but the right to conclude the agreement rests with the Council acting in principle by qualified majority but in practice usually on a consensual basis.[6] The role of the European Parliament is very modest in this field.[7] It is merely informed by the Commission and the Council of the conduct of external trade negotiations and may be voluntarily asked for its opinion before the formal ratification of an international agreement.[8]

The Controversy Over the Scope of Article 113

Many authors have pointed out that the Community's Common Commercial Policy was rather poorly drafted, especially with regard to definition and scope.[9] They deplore the fact that the Treaty of Rome only included a non-exhaustive list of examples of subjects belonging to

achievement of uniformity in measure of liberalisation, export policy and measures to protect trade such as those to be taken in case of dumping or subsidies.

2. The Commission shall submit proposals to the Council for implementing the common commercial policy.

3. Where agreements with one or more States or international organisations need to be negotiated, the Commission shall make recommendations to the Council, which shall authorise the Commission to open the necessary negotiations. The Commission shall conduct these negotiations in consultation with a special committee appointed by the Council to assist the Commission in this task and within the framework of such directive as the Council may issue it. The relevant provisions of Article 228 shall apply.

4. In exercising the powers conferred upon it by this Article, the Council shall act by a qualified majority.

[5] Meunier and Nicolaïdis (1999).   [6] Martin Westlake (1995).

[7] The role of the EP would be substantially augmented, if the Constitutional Treaty was ratified and entered into force.

[8] This is to be distinguished from agreements concluded under Article 228 which require the European Parliament's assent and where Parliament has the right to be consulted.

[9] E.g. Bourgeois (1987); Ehlermann (1984).

the CCP but contained no clear definition of the boundaries of this policy. As a consequence of this lack of a precise definition, the external trade policy has been subject to recurrent disputes between the Commission, the Council, Member States and the Parliament. The changing nature of international trade considerably exacerbated the dispute over the definition of the scope of the CCP. The Commission's motivation to expand its powers under Article 113 largely stemmed from the changing multilateral trade agenda. At the Uruguay Round (UR) which had been launched in 1986, negotiations covered issues such as services, intellectual property rights and investment. The Commission and some Member States disagreed on who was competent on these 'new' trade issues.

In its case law, the European Court of Justice has been rather progressive, especially until the mid-1980s. It ruled, for example, that the Community's treaty-making power is not restricted to express powers granted in the Treaty, but also extends to implied powers in all areas covered by the Treaty, and emphasised the open nature of the CCP.[10] However, the Court failed to settle the institutional controversies between the Commission and the Council in the 1980s,[11] so that the Commission attempted to put an end to the permanent debate surrounding the scope of Article 113 during the Maastricht IGC. In its proposal, the Commission ambitiously aimed at an exclusive common policy in the field of external economic relations which, in addition to trade in goods, also sought to include trade measures related to services, intellectual property, investment, establishment and competition. The majority of Member States rejected the Commission proposal, and also refused to include services under the scope of the CCP, as envisaged by the Luxembourg Presidency's draft treaty.[12]

Frictions over competence in external trade policy continued among the Commission and a number of Member States, especially concerning the question of who was entitled to sign the Final Act concluding the Uruguay Round and the WTO agreement. In April 1994 the Commission submitted a request to the Court of Justice, with a view to obtaining a definitive ruling on the matter. In its Opinion 1/94 the Court of Justice ruled that both the Community and its Member States are jointly competent[13] to conclude international agreements of the type (and

---

[10] See e.g. the Court's ruling in the *ERTA* case (22/70) and its Opinion 1/78. Cf. Gilsdorf (1996).

[11] Devuyst (1992: 72f).

[12] On the Commission CCP proposal see Commission (1991b).

[13] The Court has on several occasions said that the Member States and the Community can 'share' competence in a particular area. The principal consequence of shared

scope) of the General Agreement on Trade in Services (GATS) and Trade-Related Intellectual Property Rights (TRIPS).[14] It did not rule on investment. The Court also left a number of questions unsolved, for example by highlighting (again) the open nature of the Common Commercial Policy. Moreover, the Court demanded a duty of co-operation and unity of representation in matters where the Community and Member States are jointly competent, without, however, specifying how such unity of representation was to be achieved. In the aftermath of the Court's ruling in 1994, negotiations between the Commission and Member States on a code of conduct also came to nothing.[15] Against this background, the Commission decided to submit a proposal for an extension of Article 113 within the framework of the Amsterdam IGC.

There are several reasons for choosing negotiations on the reform of Article 113/133 as a case study. First, empirically it makes for an interesting case as little has been written about it from a political science perspective.[16] Second, it is valuable from a methodological point of view because the Amsterdam IGC (and to a lesser degree the Nice IGC) constitutes a deviant case. In comparison to my other cases, the outcome of Amsterdam on Article 113 is close to the *status-quo ante*. As pointed out above, more can be learned about the dynamics of integration when we examine cases with varying outcomes. Finally, from a theoretical angle, the Amsterdam CCP case is intriguing. Why have Member States refused to extend or perhaps even rolled back[17] competence in one of the Community's oldest and most integrated areas? Moreover, given the changes of the world economy and certain linkages with the internal market, it appeared – at least from some distance – that considerable exogenous as well as functional spillover pressures could instigate a reform of the CCP. The latest Treaty revision exercise is equally interesting: the Convention and 2003–04 IGC have managed to achieve something like a break-through concerning the extension of competence

competence is that the Member States still have power to enter into agreements and to take action in the areas in question, subject to duties deriving from the Treaties. See MacLeod and Hyett (1996: 63).

[14] However, the Court found that the Community has exclusive competence in the areas of cross-frontier services and measures prohibiting the release for free circulation of counterfeit goods – goods imitating a genuine article that is usually sold under a trade mark. On this point see Bourgeois (1995: 770–71).

[15] In the meantime, multilateral negotiations on 'unsolved business' (of the Uruguay Round) in the area of services was conducted under unanimity, with the Commission as the exclusive negotiator.

[16] Among the few exceptions there are Meunier and Nicolaïdis (1999, 2000); Meunier and Nicolaïdis (2002).

[17] The roll-back view has, to a certain extent, been advocated by Meunier and Nicolaïdis (1999).

to the Community in contested areas, such as services, intellectual property and investment, which the Maastricht, Amsterdam and (to a lesser degree) Nice IGCs failed to achieve. Hence, there is the important question concerning the factors accounting for this difference in outcome.

The Intergovernmental Conference 1996–97

The Provisions of Amsterdam

After the Commission had put forward an ambitious proposal in July 1996 asking for an external economic policy competence going beyond services, intellectual property rights and investment (Commission 1996f)[18], the eventual outcome at Amsterdam was very modest. The result of the IGC negotiations was a new paragraph (5) in Article 133, according to which 'the Council, acting unanimously on a proposal from the Commission and after consulting the European Parliament, may extend the application of paragraphs 1 to 4 to international negotiations and agreements on services and intellectual property insofar as they are not covered by these paragraphs'.

The extension may encompass any type and area of services and intellectual property, and hence is not confined to GATS and TRIPS. Moreover, apart from the WTO/TRIPS Agreement, other international conventions and agreements which recognise and protect intellectual property rights as such – for instance those concluded in the context of World Intellectual Property Organization (WIPO) – should be covered.[19] Investment is not included within the scope of the new provision. The most significant difference compared to pre-Amsterdam provisions was that the new paragraph enabled the Council to extend the application of Article 133 to services and intellectual property rights by unanimity without having to go through another IGC.[20] Through this provision the Community can (thus) obtain 'fast-track' competence.[21] There has been disagreement amongst legal observers as to whether competence could be extended permanently and generally, in relation to a named international body, or (only) on a case-by-case basis.[22] Overall, observers commonly agreed that the progress made during the IGC

---

[18] The ambition of the proposal is best viewed as bargaining strategy. What the Commission really aimed for was an extension of Article 113 to services, intellectual property and investment, which also became the toned down official Commission position from October 1996 (interview, 1999).

[19] European Policy Centre (1997a: 97).   [20] Cf. e.g. Sutherland (1997: 30).

[21] Petite (1997: 21); Elsig (2002: 123).

[22] Cf. Krenzler and da Fonseca-Wollheim (1998: 239); European Policy Centre (1997b: 97–98).

1996–97 negotiations was minimal. This can be substantiated by judging the outcome against a number of different benchmarks.

Measured against the benchmark of the *status-quo ante* practice, some observers asserted that Amsterdam meant progress. It has been held that, despite the unanimity required in the Council, the new provision was likely to facilitate swifter action, and improve unity and efficiency in international representation of the Community and Member States.[23] With the benefit of hindsight, these more optimistic interpretations can be challenged as paragraph 5 was never used.

However, by the Commission's own standards the outcome of Amsterdam could hardly be described as a success that goes much beyond the *status quo ante*. The Irish Presidency report outlined several possible options which were subsequently discussed at the Conference.[24] In declining order of ambition, they were: (1) the possibility of bringing all measures involving the liberalisation and protection of services, intellectual property rights and investment under Article 113; (2) transfer of competence of only certain matters which would be clearly defined and limited in scope; (3) the eventual outcome of Amsterdam (with the added advantage of the Council deciding by QMV instead of unanimity); and (4) no Treaty change (while improvements could possibly be pursued through a Code of Conduct). The Commission argued in favour of option (1) until March 1997 when it realised that this option was not attainable and started to accept an outcome along the lines of option (2). When the list of exceptions concerning areas and issues to come under Article 113 grew and its own role in the area of goods became challenged, the Commission and a number of Member States began to prefer option (3). The eventual outcome was somewhere between options (3) and (4), thus indeed fairly close to the *status quo ante*, when viewed across the range of possible results.

Those observers who judged the outcome of Amsterdam against the benchmark of a changing world economy and multilateral trade agenda as well as extra-Community expectations have been particularly critical of the progressiveness of the new Article 113 (5). The failure to reformulate Article 113 to include services and intellectual property in the normal conduct of international trade policy was considered by many as a setback. Moreover, it was doubted that the new paragraph 5 would give the EU a stronger and more united voice in international negotiations.[25] Moreover, in the legal academic community it was

---

[23] European Policy Centre (1997a: 98); cf. Coglianese and Nicolaïdis (1998): 14–15).
[24] Irish Presidency (1996c).
[25] See e.g. Patijn (1997: 39); Brok (1997a: 45); Meunier and Nicolaïdis (1999); Tyszkiewicz (1997: 51); Richardson (1997: 53)

pointed out that at the 1996–97 IGC the Community was denied competence that the rest of the world already took for granted.[26] Overall, we have seen that, on most accounts, the outcome of Amsterdam was very modest.

After having analysed the outcome of Amsterdam, the following sections will examine the strength and relevance of the five hypothesised dynamics behind the potential, but ultimately unsuccessful, extension of Article 113/133, i.e. exogenous, functional, political, social and cultivated spillover, followed by an analysis of countervailing forces that manifested during the Intergovernmental Conference 1996–97.

Exogenous Spillover

Exogenous[27] factors were the most important ones pushing for an extension of Article 113.[28] The factors at play here were globalisation[29] and, closely related, 'changes in the world economy', as well as subsequent developments in the multilateral trade regime and the international trade agenda. Globalisation has fostered changes in the world economy, such as the increasing importance of trade in services, in intellectual property rights and foreign direct investment, issues which have begun to feature much more prominently on the multilateral trade agenda since the Uruguay Round. For services and intellectual property rights, the Community largely shares competence jointly with Member States, as ruled by the Court of Justice in 1/94. The Commission has traditionally argued that the scope of Article 113 needs to be interpreted in a dynamic way. As trade policy changed and trade in goods lost in importance, the Community powers under the Common Commercial Policy became gradually eroded. Subsequently, we will look more closely at the growing importance of services, intellectual property rights

---

[26] Hilf (1995: 251).

[27] Aspects which have been described here as exogenous are to some extent endogenous, i.e. related to the European integration process. For example, the multilateral trade agenda and the structures of the new trade regime have been partly influenced by the European Union. However, these factors are treated here as exogenous because they are largely out of the hands of the Union, and also because it is possible/probable that individual Member States had pursued similar policies as the European Union.

[28] This view is shared by the other academic analyses. See for example: Meunier and Nicolaïdis (1999).

[29] In terms of trade, globalisation can be defined as 'the increasing tendency for anything but the simplest product to consist of components made in a range of countries, reflecting most appropriate technology and favourable cost. One of its effects is the relocation and integration of production processes among countries. Globalisation implies therefore a degree of reciprocal action and interdependence ... ' (Goode 1997: 102). For different definitions and understandings of the term, see, for example, Smith and Baylis (1997); Hirst and Thompson (1996).

and investment, resulting from globalisation and the changing world economy, before further explicating the (potential) implications of these exogenous changes.

Trade in Services   Services differ from goods in a number of ways. Boone and Kurtz distinguish services from goods by the following set of characteristics: 'Services are intangible, services are inseparable from the service provider, services are perishable, standardisation of services is difficult, buyers are often involved in the development and distribution of services ... '.[30] In the early to mid-1990s – the period most relevant for decision-makers, perceptions concerning the Amsterdam negotiations – services accounted for 20 per cent of all world trade, and for 26 per cent of EU external trade.[31] The growing importance of services in the world economy was apparent by the conclusion of a General Agreement on Trade in Services (GATS) during the Uruguay Round. While the UR achieved historic results in terms of market access liberalisation in important services areas, services liberalisation was by no means completed. The GATS created a framework of continuing negotiations on the liberalisation of the supply of services which meant that the question of external competence for the conclusion of international services agreements also continued to be a very important issue after the Uruguay Round.

Liberalisation of UR commitments in some major sectors including audio-visual services, financial services, maritime transport and telecommunications was very limited or non-existent.[32] These issues became subject to specialised sectoral negotiations as 'outstanding business' of the Uruguay Round. It was hard to imagine (also at the time of the IGC 1996–97) that future multilateral trade rounds would not make this important sector part of the agenda.[33] The growing importance of trade in services both in volume and in terms of the multilateral trade agenda has significant implications. Given the absence of an exclusive external competence, such developments may have a considerable impact on the 'internal' formulation of the Community's commercial policy with regard to services, a point further elaborated below.

Trade and Intellectual Property Rights   Intellectual property is information with a commercial value. Intellectual property rights (IPRs)

---

[30] Boone and Kurtz (1992: 370).   [31] (Krenzler, 1996: 6).
[32] Dyer *et al.* (1997: 217).
[33] Interviews, Brussels, 1996, 1997. Eventually, services indeed became a major issue, not only in the 'GATS 2000' negotiations but also at the Doha Round. See subsequent sub-cases for further details.

have been defined as a mix of ideas, inventions and creative expression on which there is a public willingness to bestow the status of property. IPRs mainly comprise industrial property and copyrights. Industrial property principally concerns the protection of inventions through patents and trade marks. Copyrights are usually described as pertaining to 'literary and artistic works'.[34] As trade in intellectual property rights substantially increased in previous decades, incentives to breaches of IPRs also rose. It was estimated in the mid-1990s that the European Union lost at least 10 per cent of the value of its exports to copyright piracy.[35] As a result of these trends, IPRs were included in the UR negotiations. The TRIPS agreement attempts to regulate and standardise international property rights in order to prevent the above-mentioned abuses and so create a fairer trade market. With the agreement on TRIPS and the establishment of the WTO, trade remedies (sanctions) can be made available to enforce the protection of intellectual property rights. Thus, IPRs became a frequent item in WTO dispute settlement. A shared competence could have problematic implications for the defence of Community and Member States' interests, as will be elaborated below in this section.

Trade and Investment   Foreign direct investment (FDI) has become a significant area of growth in the global economy and one of particular importance to the European Union. Figures from the early to mid-1990s indicated that 36 per cent of world-wide FDI inflow originated from the European Union and that the European Union received about 19 per cent of world inflow.[36] As a result of the global increase in FDI, Trade-Related Investment Measures (TRIMS) were included for the first time in the UR. The Community has a vital interest in trade and investment, as restrictive national measures (e.g. rules on the share of goods to be produced at home) have a direct negative impact on trade. The agreement on TRIMS obligates members to scrap their trade-related investment standards, but it leaves important practices untouched. For example, it does not grant foreign investors 'national treatment', namely the right to be treated as well as local firms.[37]

Post-Uruguay Round efforts have been widely regarded as necessary, for instance, concentrating on the development of comprehensive investment rules, the long-sought 'GATT for Investment'.[38] Trade and investment, from the viewpoint of most experts at the time of the Amsterdam IGC, were likely to reappear on the WTO negotiating

---

[34] Hoekman and Kostecki (1995).   [35] Adamantopoulos (1997).
[36] United Nations (1995).   [37] Kreinin and Schmidt-Levine (1997).
[38] On post-UR requirements and expectations, see, for example, Bhagwati (1996: 28).

agenda in the future. It was agreed at Marrakech in 1994 to review the issue within five years. A gradual liberalisation of trade-related investment measures could thus be expected over time.[39] In 1/94 the Court did not rule on the issue of investment. The Treaties contain wide-ranging provisions on investment (Article 56). According to the Commission, those provisions can justify an exclusive external Community competence on investment. However, this has been disputed by the legal service of the Council and several Member States.[40] Given the growing importance of investment, and the fear of a weakened Community (and Member State) position in any future negotiations, as will be further explicated below, the Commission sought an exclusive competence in this area.

Perception of the Importance of Exogenous Factors by Decision-Makers Structural pressures, such as exogenous ones, are impotent, unless actors pick up on them. My analysis suggests that globalisation, developments in the world economy and subsequent changes of the international trade agenda have been the most important (pro-reform) arguments for decision-makers when considering the issue of extending Article 113. For example, they were the only explanatory arguments used by the Irish Presidency in its Draft Treaty and in prior texts, by Commission President Santer in speeches and commentaries during and after the IGC, and the few statements by the European Parliament or MEPs that dealt with the issue. Moreover, they were considered the main arguments in all Commission papers and speaking briefs, by opinion leaders in business circles, by NGOs, Brussels Think Tanks and in the few articles in the media that devoted attention to the Common Commercial Policy. As far as member governments are concerned, there are few official documents available which go into detail about the origins of the problem. However, those documents which do analyse the issue more explicitly confirm this trend.[41]

---

[39] Interviews, Brussels, 1996, 1997. This view has been shared by Adamantopoulos (1997: 81).

[40] Interviews, Brussels, 1999.

[41] Following the order in the main text, on the Irish Presidency see: Council (1996c); Irish Presidency (1996c); on Commission President Santer see e.g.: Santer (1996: 4); on the EP and concerning MEP statements see: Randzio-Plath (1995); and Brok (1996); as regards Commission papers see e.g.: Commission (1995d); Commission (1996c: 30); concerning business opinion leaders see: Sutherland (1997: 30); on Think Tanks see: European Policy Centre (1997a); for press articles see, for example: Barber, *Financial Times*, 5.9.96; finally as regards member governments see, for example: Belgian Government (1995).

Probable Implications for EU Decision-making (as viewed by the Commission and 'Progressive' Member States)   What is the impact of the increasing importance of services, intellectual property rights and investment, and the growth of multilateral negotiations in those areas for EU trade policy decision-making, in terms of the 1996–97 IGC? The fact that more and more important trade negotiations take place outside the area of goods means that more and more negotiations have to be conducted under so-called mixed competence. Most bilateral and multilateral negotiations now contain one or more elements of services or sectors where the Community and Member States share competence. Negotiations thus follow the 'Victor Hugo principle', according to which one drop of water is sufficient to cloud a glass of *Pernod*. Similarly, one drop of, say, services is sufficient to expand the EU decision-making rules for trade in services, namely mixed competence, to the whole substance of negotiations.[42] According to this view future big liberalisation rounds would have to be negotiated and concluded under mixed competence.[43] This would have two important implications (which also apply to negotiations under mixed competence more generally): decisions are taken by unanimity and the Commission may not be the sole negotiator. The Commission and some 'progressive' Member States, such as the Benelux, in particular, have suggested that these two aspects entail significant problems, which in their view constitute pressures for reform.

As for the former, unanimity can have a number of detrimental effects on decision-making. First, unanimity tends to drive negotiations towards the lowest common denominator due to Member States' veto power. Second, the unanimity requirement often provides the Community's negotiating partners with the possibility of influencing each Member State, by offering certain concessions in order to prevent or hinder the formation of a common EU position. Third, and closely related, the unanimity requirement gives those Member States that have little interest in an agreement the power to make agreement conditional on onerous or unrelated demands being met.[44] This has indeed happened on occasion in the past, for example, with Portugal during the Uruguay Round.[45] The Portuguese only agreed on the results because substantial subsidies and grants for trade adjustment assistance were made available for the textile sector.[46] Fourth, there is the time factor. Before it can wrap up an international negotiation, the Commission

---

[42] Krenzler and da Fonseca-Wollheim (1998: 229).   [43] Brittan (1996).
[44] Petite (1997).
[45] At the final stages of the Uruguay Round the Community and the Member States had agreed on the unanimity principle. See Paemen (1996).
[46] Cf. Woolcock and Hodges (1996).

must usually secure three decisions from the Council of Ministers, each involving unanimity. These include an agreement on the terms of the mandate, adoption of the mandate and finally the conclusion of the agreement. The process of decision-making is generally slower under conditions of unanimity and has been estimated to take two and a half years on average.[47]

The second major implication of mixed competence is that, legally speaking, the Commission is not the sole negotiator for the Community and Member States. In theory, the latter can intervene throughout negotiations, either individually or as represented by the Presidency. In practice the Commission and Member States have sought to avoid this. The problem of the representation of the Community and Member States in external trade negotiations was around since the beginning of the Uruguay Round. It was not solved by the Court in 1/94. Although the ECJ demanded that there was a duty of co-operation to ensure the Community's unity of action and efficient external representation it did not state how this was to be achieved. After the conclusion of the UR negotiations, a code of conduct was reached on the post-Uruguay Round negotiations on services, according to which the Commission should continue to negotiate (under unanimity) on behalf of the Community and the Member States.[48] Negotiations on a general code of conduct for participation in the WTO had, however, failed on several occasions. However, the Spanish Presidency proposal of December 1995 (according to which the Commission acts as the sole negotiator)[49] has been taken as a basis for negotiations. Some Member States have claimed that the Commission's role as the sole negotiator is undisputed, thus rendering an extension of Article 113 unnecessary.[50] The Commission, in contrast, has emphasised that the situation had become worse since the UR. Member States threatened to act independently in the WTO, if their positions are not fully covered by the Community. A decision by the French National Assembly indicates that this was not only considered, but actually aimed at.[51] In the negotiations on maritime transport, Denmark and Greece expressed themselves independently, in addition to the Commission and the Presidency. The implications can vary. As one Commission official pointed out: 'it is enough when Member States just highlight a certain aspect more than

---

[47] Barber (1997).   [48] Council (1994b).
[49] According to the final text which did not pass COREPER in December 1995, Member States can be present at meetings but only speak when a Member State considers that the Commission has presented the situation in a confusing manner or where the Commission renounces to express itself (Spanish Presidency, 1995).
[50] Interview, Brussels, 1999.   [51] Krenzler and da Fonseca-Wollheim (1998: 231).

the Commission, without saying anything substantially different. Still, the character of the Community position will be influenced, and a delicate balance envisaged by the Commission in its position may be upset'.[52] Outside the WTO framework, negotiations on intellectual property rights, for instance in WIPO, and on investment issues, as in the OECD, are conducted by Member States themselves. In such cases, Member States often negotiate against each other, which makes it easy for Japan and the United States to play one Member State off against another. As an official put it: 'In the WTO such a dissonant choir of 15 voices would be a catastrophe'.[53] According to one Commission interviewee, 'it is quite clear that as far as the WTO is concerned, legal confirmation of what is today only a *de facto* situation, subject to be questioned at any time, would significantly improve the standing of the Commission as a sole negotiator'.[54]

During the 1996–97 IGC negotiations, a solution on the basis of a code of conduct was rejected by the Commission and several Member States because such an instrument can only be non-binding and revocable, a so-called gentleman's agreement. Such agreements may not be particularly durable when important political interests of Member States are concerned.[55] Moreover, the conclusion of a Treaty can only be conducted by the entity which has the legal right to deal with the issue in question. Hence, the decisive phase of the conclusion would fall outside the scope of a code of conduct. Therefore, it has been argued, unity and coherence of representation of the Community and Member States cannot be found through a code of conduct on any lasting or reliable basis.[56]

The Commission has pointed out that, in its view, mixed competence has another (detrimental) implication. It suggested that the Community would probably experience great difficulties in dispute settlement cases in the areas of GATS and TRIPS, since it cannot cross-retaliate by taking sanctions in the goods sector, as the Community has competence in that area.[57] Often, however, third countries (especially Lesser Developed Countries) can be hurt most in the area of goods. Hence, it has been argued that it does not make sense for Member States to enter into dispute settlement cases in the new trade areas on their own. Their purposes would be better served if competence for the disputed areas was transferred to the Community. Thus, the change in the multilateral

---

[52] Interview, Brussels, 1997.
[53] Quoted from an internal Commission paper: Commission (1996g).
[54] Interview, Brussels, 1998.
[55] Also cf. Krenzler and da Fonseca-Wollheim (1998: 5f).
[56] Interviews, Brussels, 1997, 1999.   [57] Kuyper (1995: 114).

trade regime – which brought services and intellectual property under the WTO dispute settlement procedure and opened up the possibility of cross-retaliation – added further pressure towards an extension of the CCP, at least as perceived and framed by the Commission.[58]

Different Perception Concerning the Impact of the Pre-Amsterdam Rules As mentioned earlier, exogenous pressures, like functional ones, are only as influential in a particular decision as they are perceived by key players who then act upon their perception and conviction. A number of Member States did not view the probable consequences pointed out above as severely limiting the coherence, effectiveness and proactiveness of EU trade policy. While the Commission questioned the ability of the Community and Member States to negotiate effectively in the WTO due to the unanimity requirement and the unresolved question of representation, the overarching argument of the reluctant Member States was that the Community has managed to negotiate successfully in the WTO in areas where powers are shared, thus denying the rationale for a change of the *status quo* because of transformations in the world economy.[59] This view was expressed, for example, in a detailed Report of the Italian Presidency to the European Council on the progress of the conference. Here, the Presidency suggested that the Community and Member States are able to act as one in the field of CCP, also regarding services and IPRs.[60]

The Commission and the 'progressive' Member States expressed concern about the feasibility of negotiating future major trade liberalisation rounds under current rules, as 'a small national tail could be wagging the large European dog'[61], as all matters, including goods would be concluded under mixed competence (following the 'Victor Hugo principle'). However, it was argued by some Member States that under the current division of competencies no problems arose for a successful conclusion of the Uruguay Round, especially concerning the new GATT-topics (GATS and TRIPS)[62], but also concerning the post-Uruguay Round negotiations.[63] In this context, it

[58] Also cf. Irish Presidency (1996c).
[59] Of course, some Member States that are regularly out of set with the majority, like France on audiovisual services, were reluctant to give up their veto on the new trade issues (cf. section on countervailing forces).
[60] Italian Presidency (1996: 104).   [61] Brittan (1996).
[62] However, it should be noted that it was agreed to negotiate, as if Article 113 applied.
[63] There seems to be some disagreement also in the academic literature as to whether the Community can act coherently and effectively under mixed competence. Compare, for example, Young's (2001) positive assessment with Elsig's (2002) rather sceptical one.

was pointed out by some Member States that the sole representation by the Commission in negotiations was and is for all areas uncontested.[64]

The Commission pointed out during the IGC negotiations that the unanimity requirement could blackmail or excessively restrict the negotiator and that 'no negotiator can do worthwhile deals with his hands tied behind his back'.[65] While most Member States accepted this argument, some, however, noted that if the Commission stuck to its negotiating mandate it did not have to fear lack of unanimity for the conclusion of an agreement. Following this logic, the problems for the Commission during trade negotiations would be outweighed by an uncomplicated conclusion of the agreement.[66] Moreover, some reluctant Member States argued that despite the generous competencies of the Commission on issues governed under the scope of the CCP, it did not (always) represent the interests of the Community convincingly and that often it gave in too easily to the United States, thus requiring Member States to 'keep the Commission on a short leash'.[67]

The above analysis suggests that the implications of globalisation and changes in the world economy, although recognised as important driving forces, did not really create any problems which justified an extension of the CCP to include services, IPRs and investment from the point of view of several Member States. This suggests that those exogenous pressures, even though they are the most important ones perceived to be at work, were not very/entirely convincing here. However, as will be revealed later, the non-persuasiveness of these exogenous pressures in terms of their impact on the decision of reforming Article 113 was partly due to certain countervailing pressures, such as sovereignty-consciousness and distrust in the Commission on the part of several Member States. This was further compounded by a clumsy approach on the part of the Dutch Presidency during the IGC and reinforced by the implications of the 1/94 ruling of the ECJ and, perhaps to a lesser extent, by the anticipation of further functional spillover. In comparison to these considerations, exogenously created problems seem to have lost much of their gravity.

---

[64] Bundesministerium für Wirtschaft (1996). As pointed out in the previous section this has been doubted by the Commission and others.
[65] Brittan (1996).   [66] Interview, Brussels, 1999.
[67] Interview, Brussels, 1997. It was felt, for example, that the Commission lacked forcefulness, on the question of the Community joining the Japanese–American semiconductor agreement. Although the Commission had exclusive competencies and the 15 behind it, it could not match the United States in the negotiations in Lyon (interview, Brussels, 1998).

Functional Spillover

Functional Spillover versus Exogenous Pressures   Pressures stemming from functional interdependencies are not always easily distinguishable from exogenous factors. Some might argue that what have been described above as the result of globalisation and changes in the world economy are due rather to the functional interdependence of sectors. It is true that sectors such as goods and services cannot always easily be separated.[68] However, here functional interdependence is not the driving force in creating a problem – i.e. the absence of effective EU internal decision-making rules and effective external representation due to an increase of shared competence between the Community and Member States – which then needs to be solved according to the logic of functional spillover. In the case of services, for example, the mere interdependence of sectors (goods and services) was not enough to create a real problem. Things worked well until globalisation and changes in the world economy and international negotiations became more pronounced.

Functional Spillover, the Internal Market[69] and 'implied' External Powers   There has been a long-standing controversy over whether the treaty-making power of the Community (its external competence) should reflect its internal jurisdiction. According to the doctrine of parallelism, as it is often called, it would be illogical for the Community to have internal law-making power with regard to certain policies and yet be unable to conclude international agreements in that field.[70] It is therefore frequently argued that external power is 'implied' in the Community's internal power.[71] More specifically, two arguments can be made in that respect. First, common rules laid down internally could be (adversely) affected by international obligations, if Member States acted individually to undertake obligations with third countries. This is essentially the *ERTA* doctrine laid down by the European Court of Justice in *Commission v. Council* [1971]. Second, external power could flow by implication from measures adopted by the institutions as well as from express provisions in the Treaty creating an internal power in so far

---

[68] As pointed out by Goode (1997: 202).

[69] One issue that has been omitted from this analysis is the potential danger of trade deflection in the area of services as a rationale for extending the scope of the CCP during the IGC negotiations. My interviewing suggests that this issue was not on decision-makers' minds. Apart from decision-makers' perceptions, in Niemann (2000) I suggest that the danger of trade deflection was indeed very slim concerning trade in services (also cf. Timmermans 1987).

[70] Hartley (1994: 168).   [71] MacLeod *et al.* (1996: ch. 2).

as the participation of the Community in the international agreement is necessary for the attainment of one of the (internal) objectives of the Community. This is, in a nutshell, the principle stated by the Court of Justice in its opinion 1/76.[72] Both doctrines imply a certain functional logic originating from the internal Community sphere and pushing for an expansion of powers to the Community into the external realm.

The question now is how strong those two functional arguments were with regard to the areas of services and intellectual property. The Commission used the above arguments, amongst others, when submitting a request to the Court with a view to securing a definitive ruling on the dispute concerning competencies for the signing of the Uruguay Round Final Act and WTO Agreement. In terms of services[73] neither argument is very convincing. As far as the argument following from Opinion 1/76 is concerned, one needs to ascertain whether an exclusive external Community competence in the area of services is necessary for achieving the Community objective of realising the freedom to provide services by the nationals of the Member States within the common market. This (functional) necessity is rather doubtful. In its Opinion 1/94 the Court was faced with this question and held that there was no 'inextricable link' between the two.[74]

The Commission argued in 1994 that the proper functioning of the internal market would be prejudiced if the Community did not have exclusive competence to conclude the GATS. The argument was based on the *ERTA* doctrine, according to which, each time the Community lays down common rules, the Member States no longer have the right to undertake obligations with third countries which affect those rules. This, following a certain functional logic, would have to be the case because common internal rules could be affected if Member States remained free to negotiate with third countries. However, in 1/94 the Court was unconvinced of such functional imperative, as the Community had not adopted internal legislation for all service sectors.[75] The Court

---

[72] Opinion 1/76 (*European laying-up fund for inland waterway vessels*), [1977] ECR 741.

[73] The chapters on establishment and services in the Treaty confer on the nationals of the Member States the right of establishment and the freedom to provide services (see Articles 43–55 EEC Treaty). They contain no provisions dealing with the right of nationals of third countries to establish themselves for the first time in the territory of a Member State or with their right to provide services. Hence, those chapters do not confer on the Community an exclusive competence to conclude agreements with third countries to liberalise access to the services market. On this point see Arnull (1996: 354).

[74] Opinion 1/94: para. 86.

[75] The single market in services started slowly but gathered pace. By the mid-1990s progress was significant in liberalising transport and financial services, but more modest in other service sectors. Significant barriers remained in air transport services, TV

interpreted the functional necessity rather narrowly in this case, as it had applied the *ERTA* doctrine in the past where Community legislation was not complete.[76] However, the functional rationale was certainly less clearcut and evident than had been the case with full (or fuller) harmonisation. The Court therefore ruled in 1/94 that competence to conclude GATS was shared between the Community and the Member States.

As far as intellectual property is concerned, the same reasoning applied. The functional necessity of the Opinion 1/76 principle was disputable, as the realisation of the internal Community regime (harmonisation of intellectual property rights) did not really have to be accompanied by agreements with third countries in order to be effective. The ruling of the Court of Justice in 1/94 echoed this.[77] In addition, the *ERTA* logic did not apply. Internal harmonisation in the field of intellectual property was only partial at best[78] which meant that agreements of individual Member States could hardly affect the internal regime. This was also pointed out by the Court in 1/94.[79]

It can thus be concluded that functional arguments derived from the internal market and the 'implied' powers doctrine do not really make sense with regard to services and intellectual property. Even the Commission legal service argued that, when referring the dispute concerning the WTO Agreement to the Court of Justice, the Commission's arguments based on implied powers were 'a bit far-fetched, stretching the theory [of implied powers] to the maximum'.[80] This helps to explain why the Commission no longer attempted to persuade Member States to extend Article 113 on the basis of the alleged necessity of safeguarding the functioning of the internal market during the 1996–97 IGC. Moreover, the Commission did not use this argument because it did not expect the Member States to buy a line of reasoning which the Court had comprehensively rejected.[81]

---

broadcasting services and advertising (Monti, 1996). The internal harmonisation of services progressed rather slowly due to considerable differences in national regulatory policies. Over the years practices and market structures had developed which effectively precluded suppliers from other EU Member States from gaining access to domestic markets (cf. Mayes 1997).

[76] See Opinion 2/91 (ILO) [1993] ECR I-1061. On this point also see O'Keeffe (1999).

[77] That the Court acted accordingly due to a weak functional link that has essentially been held by Bourgeois (1995: 775).

[78] For example, harmonisation in the areas of trade marks as well as the protection of undisclosed information, industrial designs and patents has been partial or non-existent (Arnull 1996: 356).

[79] Opinion 1/94: para. 103.   [80] Interview, Brussels, 1999.

[81] Interview, Brussels, 1997.

Functional Spillover and the Institutional Pressure of Further Enlargement   A modest functional logic was at work through pressures stemming from the decision on future enlargement, taken at various European Councils since Edinburgh in 1992. Although an exogenous event, enlargement after those internal commitments largely became an endogenous source of pressure for reform of EU decision-making procedures. It was more the internal EU agenda and the way this was marketed within and outside the Union than the actual direct and indirect demands from applicant countries which put the Union under pressure to reform its institutions and decision rules. Following Lindberg's definition of functional spillover, once enlargement became an internal goal (one integrational step), problems were created (anticipated) in terms of decision-making and co-ordination among the Member States under unanimity (exerting pressure for an extension of QMV in trade matters which would have been another integrational step). Unanimity was already regarded as problematic with 15 delegations by some players. This logic of anticipated problems was argued in various Commission papers on the modernisation of Article 113.[82] Horst-Günter Krenzler, Director General of DG I until December 1996, also held that QMV for services, intellectual property rights and investment was needed to maintain the functioning of EU trade after enlargement.[83]

However, the Commission remained the only player using enlargement as a (subsidiary) argument in favour of amending Article 113. Eventually, this functional argument never gained much strength. There are two reasons for this. First, as one official from a 'pro-change' delegation put it: 'Enlargement was not terribly important during the 113 negotiations. The problem was already there. It did not take another 10 countries to realise it'.[84] Second, as Michiel Patijn pointed out: 'in the end it was the lack of urgency that made the Conference decide on only partial reform. No enlargement is foreseen before 2003–2005'[85]. This indeed seems to have been the prevailing mood among decision-makers at the Amsterdam IGC. As already pointed out, functional pressures are only as strong as they are perceived by actors. In this case, the functional argument was largely powerless, because the functional connection was viewed as less pressing with enlargement still at least half a decade away. However, this rationale grew more pressing in subsequent IGCs.

---

[82] See Commission (1996h).   [83] Krenzler (1996: 6).   [84] Interview, Brussels, 1998.
[85] Patijn (1997: 38). Also cf. Devuyst (1998: 626); Moravcsik and Nicolaïdis (1999: 78).

Anticipation of Functional Spillover: an Obstacle to the Extension of Article 113   One important argument used by the more reluctant Member States was that there may be a transfer of internal competencies from the Member States to the Community in some fields coming under exclusive Community competence externally. Hence, they were afraid that external liberalisation could foster a process of internal liberalisation, and that the Commission could use the backdoor of Article 113 to regulate in areas which fell under Member States' competence.[86] The Commission responded to such fears by arguing that it did not propose any changes in the internal decision-making provisions in terms of competencies. Thus, for the translation into Community law of a Treaty that was concluded under QMV, unanimity would still be required, if this was foreseen in the internal decision-making rules. However, some Member States remained suspicious. As one official maintained: 'it was conceivable that the Commission could have gained the power to sell Member States restrictions [laid down in the GATS schedule of concessions] in the Millennium Round in exchange for market access for some third countries. With an extension of Article 113 to services, such a decision could theoretically be taken by QMV'.[87] My interviews with (Commission) officials and review of (formerly confidential) documents at the Commission IGC Documentation Centre suggest that the Commission was genuine about its concern of enhancing its external competencies only, and that the 'risks' of prejudging internal competencies were viewed as insubstantial. Internal communications within the Commission suggest that there was an awareness of potential moderate internal repercussions. As one Commission official explained: 'external economic policy and the internal market cannot be separated without overlap. Every external economic policy decision has a certain effect on the internal market. But some delegations exaggerate these overlaps'.[88]

It is doubtful whether fears of possible related pressures for internal harmonisation alone were decisive in inducing several Member States to

---

[86] Elsig (2002: 40).   [87] Interview, Brussels, 1999.
[88] Interview, Brussels, 1999. It was further admitted by the Commission that the external can influence the internal. For example, should the Community take on an obligation of non-discrimination *vis-à-vis* third countries in the WTO, it would have to follow this obligation also for the internal market. It was pointed out that rules like 'most favourite nation' have been there in the goods sector, and the implications on the internal market were not felt as a dramatic loss of sovereignty. The relationship between external rules and Community level rules would not be different in the new areas, as has been the case so far in the goods sector. Repercussions to the internal market would not be considerable, but would be limited to the implementation of general trade principles, such as most favourite nation (interview, Brussels, 1999).

come out against an extension of Article 113. Such fears on the part of Member States have to be viewed alongside other factors, such as their lack of trust in the Commission in the area of the Common Commercial Policy, the related aspect of 'bureaucratic protectionism', the ruling of the Court in 1/94, as well as the diffuse notions of Member States' sovereignty-consciousness and an unfavourable integrationist climate.[89] The above argument seems to be in line with the neofunctionalist concept of functional spillover. When Member States fear that the external realm could have implications for internal policies, they implicitly (if not explicitly) accept the functional spillover logic, i.e. that pressures from one area (external policy) could create problems in the internal realm which in turn create pressures for internal harmonisation.[90]

Social Spillover

Another aspect which contributes to the explanation of the minimalist outcome at Amsterdam is the lack of social spillover. My analysis has identified five reasons which help explain why socialisation and learning processes did not unfold in the same way as in other areas (cf. Chapter 2). The first factor is the nature of the subject area combined with the background of negotiators. The negotiations on the extension of Article 113 were rather technical in nature. However, there was little opportunity for specialists to come in for individual topics during the actual debates.[91] While negotiators were at ease with institutional and CFSP questions, they usually found the issue of Article 113 'complex' and 'requiring some pertinent legal and trade–political background'.[92] Some negotiators observed that there was not much real debate going on. The IGC representatives usually presented the positions which they were instructed to present and then reported back home about the reactions of others.[93] This was partly due to the fact that most IGC

---

[89] See my analysis below on countervailing forces. In addition, it has been disputed that Member States' fears were always genuine. The *Bundesministerium für Wirtschaft* in particular has been singled out for having deliberately overemphasised the impact on the internal realm, in an attempt to hide conveniently behind the potential dangers involved (interview, Brussels, 1999).

[90] For further thoughts on this point, see the functional spillover section in the conclusion.

[91] With the exception of allowing Commission to bring in DG I Director-General Horst Günter Krenzler in September 1996 to explain why the Commission thought it necessary to modernise Article 113.

[92] Interviews, Brussels, 1997, 1998.

[93] Concerning the Reflection Group the mere presentation and repetition of national positions has been noted by Devuyst (1998: 619).

representatives had little expertise in commercial policy themselves.[94] In terms of 'communicative action' there was little scope for argumentative processes in which actors could persuade each other simply because truth-or validity-seeking is very difficult when actors lack the requisite expertise to evaluate each others' validity claims. Given the near impossibility of any real argumentative debate amongst negotiators, any progress was dependent on bargaining or compromising Member States' strategic positions.

Second and closely related to the previous point, too little time was devoted to the CCP issue which was not, in any case, regarded as a high priority issue at the IGC, certainly in comparison with institutional questions, or 'material' dossiers such as JHA or CFSP. As one official has noted: 'when we discussed external policy for an hour, we spent 55 minutes on CFSP and five minutes on Article 113'.[95] There was neither enough time to get to know in depth each other's problems on the issue, nor to engage in an extensive argumentative debate about the pros and cons of reforming the CCP. Thus, the lack of time devoted to the issue certainly obstructed reasoned/argumentative debate in terms of communicative action. It also provided (too) little scope for the occurrence of more deeply rooted learning processes.

The third explanation for weak socialisation processes is related to the negotiating group. The IGC Representatives Group[96] took up its work in January 1996. It was rather heterogeneous in composition and worked together only for one year and a half, which does not compare with the life span of other Council committees and working groups such as the Central Europe Working Group, COREPER or the Article 113

---

[94] With the exception of the Swedish (Gunner Lund), Finnish (Antti Satuli) and Belgian (de Schoutheete) representatives. This judgement is based on the almost unanimous account of several observers (interviews, Brussels, 1997, 1999).

[95] Interview, Brussels, 1999.

[96] The Representatives Group was comprised of six ambassadors (from Austria, Belgium, Finland, Luxembourg, Spain and the United Kingdom), four other senior diplomats who were socially part of that group (Denmark, Italy, Greece, Ireland) and five junior, or quasi-politicians (Germany, France, Sweden, Portugal, Netherlands). The group was completed by Commissioner Oreja (assisted by Deputy General Director Trojan) and occasionally two members of the European Parliament, Elmar Brok and Elisabeth Guigou. The formal IGC negotiations took place on three levels. Much work was done in the IGC Representatives Group. At the political level, Foreign Ministers met once a month, and heads of government at European Councils, especially the Amsterdam summit where the final package was negotiated. In contrast to the negotiations leading to the Single European Act and the Maastricht Treaty, the contribution of Foreign Ministers was rated as less significant which led some observers to the conclusion that the Amsterdam Treaty was effectively negotiated at two levels, by IGC Representatives and Heads of Government, with the latter settling the leftovers of the Representatives in a marathon session at Amsterdam.

Committee. Although nine out of the fifteen Member States' representatives to the IGC had already participated in the Reflection Group, there was some disruption in terms of socialisation, as 'new members had to be "incorporated" into the group'.[97] Nevertheless, there is some evidence for the development of a certain *esprit de corps* in the IGC Representative's group.[98] However, on balance it seems that the development of common norms or habits was not comparable to those in the Central Europe Working Group or COREPER.[99]

Fourth, as Patijn has noted with regard to the IGC discussions on Article 113, 'underlying the debate about thin dividing lines between Community and national competencies was a basic distrust by some Member States of the role of the Commission in representing the Community in international negotiations and keeping the Member States abreast of what is going on'.[100] This has been confirmed by Ludlow and others[101]. The reason for this basic distrust of the Commission can be found in a number of events in the past when the Commission negotiated without the necessary transparency *vis-à-vis* Member States, as happened most importantly in the negotiations leading to the 'Blair House Agreement'[102], but also when the Commission presented Member States with *faits accomplis*, as in the Information Technology Agreement (ITA)[103], or when Member States were 'deceived' by the Commission, as in the case of 'Bananas' at the end of the Uruguay Round.[104] Much of the distrust *vis-à-vis* the Commission was focused on Sir Leon Brittan, with some governments holding him personally accountable for 'being left in the dark about strategic decisions'.[105] Moreover, many disliked his personality and manner: 'even

---

[97] Interview, Brussels, 1997.   [98] Interview, Brussels, 1997.
[99] Interviews, Brussels, 1997.   [100] Patijn (1997: 39).
[101] Ludlow (1997: 52). This has also been corroborated by interviews (1997, 1999).
[102] In November 1992 the Commission made a pre-agreement on agriculture with the United States. The Commission was accused by France of having been too accommodating at Blair House, especially on the issue of oil seeds. A year later the deal was re-opened due to French pressure.
[103] The breakthrough on the ITA negotiations happened at the Singapore Ministerial Conference in December 1996. During the negotiations at Singapore the Commission also entered into a side-agreement of spirits in order to persuade the United States on the ITA. Some Member States claim that they had not known about the side-agreement when they agreed on the ITA (interview, Brussels, 1997).
[104] At the end of the Uruguay Round the Commission negotiated a framework agreement with several Central American states. Member states were very divided on the issue and there would not have been a qualified majority in favour of this (Germany and Belgium amongst others were against it). Eventually, the Commission put Bananas into the general tariff schedules of the UR without clarifying this with Member States. Hence, in order to vote against the Bananas issue, Germany and others would have had to veto the entire package.
[105] *Financial Times*, 09.03.99.

admirers say his high-handed style [...] alienated potential allies who could have been won over with a little tact or charm.[106] However, distrust of the Commission is more widely spread in trade policy and not just directed against Sir Leon.[107] There were a number of accusations of some Commission officials in DG I having treated officials from Member States delegations 'in an aloof and arrogant manner'.[108] These findings fit with the broader analysis on social spillover which has so far mainly focused on relations between Member States. They underline the importance of trust during multilateral negotiations and also show that strong countervailing pressures may off-set socialisation processes in the negotiating forum. IGC representatives, although generally acknowledging the development of a certain club atmosphere in the negotiating group, noted that reports from colleagues in the capitals concerning the Commission had influenced their own attitude *vis-à-vis* the Commission on this issue. However, here the notion of trust goes beyond the strict forums in which the negotiations were conducted, as the national positions on the Article 113 question were heavily influenced by trade policy officials from the capitals who left the IGC representatives little room for manoeuvre and kept a close eye on this dossier. Hence, habits of agreement and other co-operative norms directed towards more progressive European outcomes had little chance to occur in this case, especially due to countervailing pressures from capitals based on Commission distrust.

Finally, related to Member States' distrust of the Commission, there is the wider issue of 'bureaucratic politics'.[109] It has been pointed out by many actors involved in the IGC Article 113 question that one serious problem throughout the negotiations was the adverse influences of ministries in Member States, including some lead departments on trade issues, coming out against an extension of the CCP. There are two main reasons for this: first, distrust of the Commission, as described above; and second, the phenomenon pointed out by Taylor, Pinder and others in the EC context, namely that civil servants tend to try to hold on to their powers.[110] In addition, it seems to have been the case that some national officials thought that they could deal with services and intellectual property 'just as well as the Commission', in terms of expertise.

---

[106] *Financial Times*, 09.03.99.
[107] This is also evidenced by the fact that the Blair House Accord, which is usually referred to as the most important cause of French suspicions of the Commission, was negotiated by Commissioners Andriessen and MacSharry, prior to Sir Leon taking over the external relations portfolio from Andriessen.
[108] Interview, Brussels, 1999. [109] Cf. Allison (1971).
[110] Taylor (1983); Pinder (1991a). Several Commission officials have noted this concerning their opposite numbers from national ministries (interviews 1997).

The Article 113 *Titulaires*[111] of Germany, the Netherlands and Portugal are said to have held *status quo* views for the above reasons and to have influenced their national positions accordingly. Adverse bureaucratic politics acted as strong countervailing pressures to *engrenage*. This made a genuine debate on the benefits of reform difficult due to tight instructions given to some IGC Representatives. Adverse bureaucratic pressures are also partly responsible for the fact that Germany did not have a co-ordinated position until three weeks before the Amsterdam Summit[112] and for the introduction of the shopping list approach by the Dutch Presidency[113] which enormously complicated the negotiations and invited further bureaucratic politics (see below). Under such circumstances, feelings of responsibility towards achieving progress in the negotiations that appeared to become somewhat ingrained in the IGC Representatives' Group (see chapter on JHA) had no chance to unfold and drive the negotiations towards a more integrationist outcome.

Political Spillover

Although spillover may occur with the participation of non-governmental elites, Haas emphasised the importance of their active involvement for the integration process in Europe. He held that integration in a particular sector leads the interest groups concerned to move part of their activity, focus and expectations gradually to the European level. As they become aware of the benefits of integration, interest groups will promote further integration. The revised neofunctionalist account does not accept the predictive logic that all interest groups would undergo a learning process whereby they shift their expectations to the European level. Haas was much less clear on this issue than many scholars suggest.[114] A careful analysis of Haas suggests that he did not imply that all organised interest would swiftly shift its identity or expectations to the European level, but only those interest groups that operate within integrated sectors.[115] This is echoed by the findings of Risse-Kappen.[116]

---

[111] The *Titulaires* (or Full Members) of the Article 113/133 Committee are usually the highest senior civil servants responsible for trade policy in their respective national administrations.

[112] The *status quo*-minded German Article 113 *Titulaire* managed to influence other ministries to come out against reform and subsequently hid behind their positions (interview, Brussels, 1999).

[113] One observer even used the word 'sabotage' to describe the input of the Dutch 113 Titulaire.

[114] E.g. Tranholm-Mikkelsen (1991); and cf. Cram (1996).

[115] Haas pointed out that industrial groups operating in areas which have not yet been integrated tend to oppose any kind of European public authority with powers to direct them (Haas 1958: 294).

[116] Risse-Kappen (1996: 66).

He argues, the more a particular policy sector has been integrated and the more decisions in this area are governed by majority rule, the more likely it is that the policy-making process is characterised by transnational and transgovernmental coalitions among private, subnational, national and supranational actors rather than intergovernmental bargaining.

How does this square with the empirical evidence of the 1996–97 IGC and the negotiations on the amendment of Article 113? Although most of organised interest which took up the issue came out in favour of extending the scope of Article 113,[117] on the whole there was little effective pressure exerted by interest groups. However, despite the fact that the CCP is one of the most integrated of EU policies, services, IPRs and investment have not been fully integrated, be it internally or externally. As one official pointed out, 'it should not be forgotten that services, etc. are relatively new commercial issues. Many companies have not fully realised the enormous potential benefits from external trade liberalisation in those areas and the necessity for Europe to speak with one voice'.[118] That there was a lack of awareness on the part of organised interests has also been suggested by Krenzler who argued that, in speeches to economic associations and in talks with entrepreneurs in Germany, one could detect that they were surprised that the Community did not actually have an exclusive competence in the areas under discussion.[119] Also interesting in this respect is that the moderate pressure in favour of reform that was exerted by organised interests during the IGC came from European and some national umbrella organisations in the area of industry and commerce, while little pressure has been recorded by umbrella organisations that represent the interests of services operators and companies.

There is another related explanation for the lack of attention and involvement on the part of interest groups in the new trade issues. As Ipsen has pointed out, the lack of transparency and complexity of the GATT system goes some way to explain why producers, consumers, exporters and importers did not know the GATT rules, even those which favoured them, and also explains why there was no pressure group formation.[120] This is all the more true in terms of the new multilateral trade regime, set up after the Uruguay Round with the adoption of the GATS and the TRIPS, which are both subject to complex rules, as well as the establishment of the World Trade Organization, which has

---

[117] See e.g. ERT (1997); UNICE (1997).
[118] Interview, Brussels, 1997.   [119] Krenzler (1996: 5–6).
[120] Ipsen (1994: 722).

brought services and intellectual property under the complicated rules and procedures governing the settlement of disputes.

Finally, as already pointed out in the previous chapter with regard to the PHARE programme, groups such as the European Roundtable of Industrialists (ERT) do not invest as much energy in issues which are rather sectoral and fragmented. As one observer pointed out, 'although trade in services and the commercial aspects of intellectual property rights are by no means peanuts, this does not compare in importance and scale, to the 1992 project'.[121]

It is also worth pointing out that European umbrella organisations came out more in favour of progress than when most of their constituent members had expressed themselves individually.[122] Moreover, some interest groups on the national level, such as the *Bund Deutscher Industrie* and the *Deutscher Industrie- und Handelstag*, were divided in terms of their support for a modernisation of Article 113. While the European departments were clearly in favour, as they saw the benefits of speaking with a single voice, the departments for general external trade questions were more cautious.[123] As pointed out particularly in the context of social spillover, greater 'proximity' and involvement with the Brussels arena seem to induce pro-European learning processes.

All in all, this outcome seems to be consistent with (revised) neo-functionalist theory, in which the level of integration of a sector serves as a tool for anticipating the intensity of interest group focus and expectations at the European level. In an area which is still in the progress of being integrated, interest group attention was weak to moderate. One may argue that interest group involvement and attention was proportionate to the awareness of the benefits of integration. In addition, we have identified two further aspects which specify what we can expect in terms of interest group involvement and attitude: (1) transparency and complexity of (multilateral) regime and (2) importance (and potential benefits) of the issue that is negotiated. Those factors seem to be useful and necessary for (further) delimiting and specifying the logic of political spillover.

Cultivated spillover

The role of the Commission   Neofunctionalism saw the outcome of the integration process partly dependent on the Commission's will and ability to assert itself and push for further integration and to upgrade common interests.[124] The main argument of this section is

---

[121] Interview, Brussels, 1999.   [122] Interview, Brussels, 1999.
[123] Interviews, Brussels, 1997, 1999.   [124] E.g. Haas (1964a: 78).

that the Commission did not manage to assert itself on the Article 113 question during the IGC, despite an extensive lobbying campaign in an attempt to rally support on this issue. This was due to factors related to both its standing before, and performance during the IGC, as well as a lack of internal cohesion, along with a number of (subsidiary) conditioning factors which were unrelated to the Commission's doings.

First, neofunctionalism's emphasis on 'process' allows us to look at developments before the beginning of the IGC, in order to explain the Commission's role during the conference. Most important, in this context, was the lack of trust in the Commission pointed out earlier. Once a number of Member States had become generally suspicious of the Commission, the latter's possibility of influencing the important debate on the scope of the CCP had greatly diminished. Given the position the Commission found itself in, one Commission official admitted that 'the question of modernising Article 113 should never have been tabled in the first place; or at least it should not have been tabled by the Commission itself, but under the name of another delegation'.[125]

This brings us to the Commission's 'performance' at the Conference itself. Before the IGC started, the Commission took up a very modest tone.[126] In a speech before Parliament in March 1995, Commission President Santer said: 'At Maastricht we talked about "competencies" .... In 1996, I have the feeling we will talk a lot more about "how best to do things". I wish the Commission does not present itself as a *demandeur* of new competencies'.[127] Officials in DG I found this of 'little help' or even a 'handicap' which forced the Commission to present the case 'in a less straight-forward manner'.[128] Given its initial approach, some Member States were irritated when the Commission made it explicit a year later that it was effectively 'asking for new competencies in disguise'. The fact that it merely wanted to 'update' or 'modernise' the Common Commercial Policy was seen as sheer rhetoric by them. In fact, some officials even seemed to see this approach as a confirmation that the Commission could not be trusted.[129]

The previous point leads us to the wider issue of Commission cohesion. The general cohesion of the Commission has usually been pointed out as one of the strengths of the Commission compared with other

---

[125] Interview, Brussels, 1999.
[126] See Niemann and Edwards (1997).   [127] Santer (1995).
[128] Interviews, Brussels, 1999.
[129] Interview, Brussels, 1999; Interview, 1997. Also cf. Meunier and Nicolaïdis (1999: 494).

players.[130] Santer's remarks in 1995, which were not helpful to the ambitions of DG I, constitute only one aspect of a general lack of cohesion within the Commission on the issue during the IGC. In addition, there were some problems between DG I and Sir Leon and his cabinet. DG I was the driving force behind the Commission's quest for Article 113 reform. Although he was the Commissioner in charge of the Common Commercial Policy, Sir Leon did not support the initiative of DG I's Director-General at the time, Horst-Günter Krenzler, and his staff. At the beginning of the Conference, Leon Brittan was the only Commissioner in the College against putting the Article 113 question onto the IGC agenda, before subsequently coming round to the idea, albeit not very enthusiastically at first.[131] Perhaps even more importantly, the Commission's Legal Service was rather against the initiative throughout the Conference. This was largely because its Director-General was discouraged after he had put his own person on the line when submitting the WTO case to the ECJ and because he was irritated by the way that DG I had been 'selling out Member States', particularly France, from where he is also said to have been under pressure 'not to cover up for DG I again'.[132] The IGC Task Force, although not opposed to DG I's initiative, was somewhat sceptical of it. As DG I had no representative sitting at the IGC table where both the Task Force and the Legal Service were present, it was clearly in a disadvantaged position to make sure the issue attained sufficient attention. When things were going in the wrong direction during the Conference in March 1997, DG I suspected the Task Force to have allowed discussions to go towards the shopping list approach[133] which was rightly regarded as dangerous by DG I and allegedly did not represent the co-ordinated Commission position.[134]

Finally, it can be argued that the Commission held on to its demands for too long. It did not manage to avoid the shopping-list approach, which it might have done, if it had put forward a scaled down proposal that would have at least brought some tangible improvements for the Commission. There was some scope for such a formula. First, one rather visionary Commission official suggested – after 'alarming reports' about Council Secretariat drafts on Article 113 had reached the Commission – that the Commission had to respond quickly by presenting its

[130] Nugent (1995).
[131] Some observers in the Commission speculated that Sir Leon was against tabling the 113 issue at the IGC because he anticipated the difficulties the Commission would have in reforming the CCP at that stage (interview, Brussels, 1999).
[132] Interview, Brussels, 1999.   [133] Cf. my discussion below.
[134] Interview, Brussels, 1999.

own alternative. He analysed quite correctly that a very important concern of Member States was that an extension of Article 113 could lead to QMV decisions in areas strictly concerning their own legislation and on which the European Community had not acted internally. He pointed out that it was a key concern for the Commission to safeguard unity of representation in the new areas. Hence, in an internal paper he presented two possible options[135]: first, a unanimity requirement when agreements result in legislative changes in the Member States; second, and slightly less favourable to the Commission, a unanimity requirement for agreements on areas where Member States retain internal competencies. These two suggestions would have implied that the negotiating mandate could be given to the Commission by QMV, with the proviso that, should the final agreement to be negotiated require legislative changes, then unanimity would be required for the conclusion. By tabling such a 'compromise' counter-proposal, the main Commission aims could have been preserved, while satisfying the concerns of the reluctant and distrustful Member States. However, this attempt came too late, as the shopping list was put on the table, while the Commission was in the process of making up its mind internally. Second, as pointed out by officials outside the Commission, the other significant concern of some Member States was the question of 'transparency'. Had the Commission suggested or put forward a declaration dealing with this issue, as promised at the beginning of the negotiations, it may have influenced the reluctant Member States positively. 'Without such assurances, it made it really easy for some governments to say no to what was on the table'.[136] The Commission may have underestimated some Member States' concern in that area, and thereby wasted a chance to attain a more favourable outcome.[137]

In conclusion of this section, the Commission – after having overplayed its hand in the years prior to the IGC – faced an uphill struggle during the IGC, which was made even more difficult by the clumsy strategy it pursued throughout the conference, as well as its lack of institutional cohesion. In view of this constellation it is not surprising that the Commission did not manage to assert itself. Moreover, a number of accompanying factors, which were partly outside the influence of the Commission, made

[135] Commission (1997b).   [136] Interview, Brussels, 1998.
[137] Interview, Brussels, 1999. While the Commission regarded this issue rather as a 'secondary front', with the real battle fought over unanimity, some Member States did consider the issue of transparency to be a very important one. Officials pointed out that a veto would not have allowed them to 'pull the handbrake' in cases such as Bananas (cf. p. 324), as it had never come to a vote (as an individual issue). Hence, they felt that there was a necessity for enhanced transparency, keeping Member States abreast at every stage of the negotiations.

things even more difficult for the Commission to make itself heard: there was little to no support from any of the big Member States, a factor which has been judged important for effective Commission leadership.[138] Along the same lines, there was little support from the European Parliament.[139] More support from that end as well as from the rather silent Brussels interest group community could have made it easier for the Commission to assert itself on the 113 question. Finally, the Commission negotiator, Marcelino Oreja, had only minimal interest in[140], and little understanding of, the issue so that he allegedly merely read out his speaking brief during the negotiations. This led observers to judge his performance on the Article 113 dossier as 'rather poor'.[141]

The preceding analysis is consistent with the revised neofunctionalist framework which does not suggest that the Commission always manages to assert itself and act as a policy entrepreneur. When the Commission fails to do so, it logically follows that integrational steps become less likely. One purpose of my case analysis is to identify conditions which delimit the various spillover concepts, a task that has been partly advanced for the concept of cultivated spillover above.

The Role of the Court of Justice
Theorising Opinion 1/94:   Opinion 1/94 can be captured by revised neofunctionalism.[142] In its modified form, neofunctionalism is freed

---

[138] George (1991: 144–5).

[139] See section below. Coalition formation with powerful Member States and with the EP have been described as substitute forms of legitimacy (Héritier 1998: 13.).

[140] One official recalled overhearing a conversation between Oreja and Michel Petite (director at the IGC task force at the time) almost half way through the negotiations in which Oreja asked his advisor 'what this Article 113 business is all about' and 'whether we really need it' (interview, Brussels, 1999).

[141] Interview, Brussels, 1999.

[142] Also cf. my analysis on p. 45. Given the minimalist nature of 1/94 (see my analysis earlier in this chapter), (neo-) realism, intergovernmentalism or rational-choice institutionalism seem obvious choices for conceptualising the role of the Court. Moravcsik (1995) and Garrett (1995) see the ECJ as an agent controlled by Member States who delegate to the Court the implementation of imperatives. Opinion 1/94 appears to confirm this: Member States were broadly against an expansion of Community powers; in face of such pressure, the argument would go, the Court decided upon shared competence rather than exclusive Community competence for most services and IPRs. However, there is insufficient evidence for this realist proposition here to substantiate this correlation. Going beyond intergovernmentalist theory, one has to distinguish between judges seeking to please the bastions of political power and judges paying attention to some prevailing value-consensus in society (cf. Koopmans 1986). The latter is necessary in order to avoid the erosion of judicial authority and legitimacy (Rasmussen 1988: 28ff). During the WTO case there was substantial media presence which articulated the post-Maastricht sentiment of a limited expansion of the Community's powers. Giving way to such predominant transnational societal consensus is slightly, but importantly, different from the realist conception of the ECJ 'obeying' member governments' preferences. See

from its predictive straight-jacket by regarding the various dynamics as explanatory tools which, when present, can make informed guesses about outcomes. Without claiming that integrational dynamics are present all the time, an important part of this analysis is to ascertain the factors under which spillover can be expected to take place. Along the same lines, revised neofunctionalism would argue that under the 'wrong' conditions, which lead to the non-existence of spillover pressures, outcomes are expected to be minimal. Such is the underlying argument of this sub-section, which will subsequently be substantiated by looking at the different aspects of neofunctionalist theory of the Court.

First, as pointed out in Chapter I, the Court-driven legal integration is partly due to the ECJ's upgrading of common interests by justifying its decisions in light of the common interests as enshrined in the general objectives of the Treaty. It can be argued that the ruling in 1/94 would have been more progressive, had the Court opted for this method of teleological interpretation, which is usually associated with the 'ever-closer-union' leitmotif. Why did the Court choose not to do so? There are two interrelated reasons for this. One is politicisation, the other is perceived self-interest coupled with countervailing forces. As for the former, Weiler has argued that the period of depoliticised case law of the ECJ is over. There is now a higher degree of political, academic and popular scrutiny than in the past. Political awareness of the Court of Justice has risen due to a number of landmark decisions since the 1960s, as well as the return and increase of QMV since the mid-1980s. While the unanimity requirement diffused any sense of threat and loss of power on the part of member governments, with QMV they no longer feel in absolute control of the legislative expansion due to the loss of the guaranteed veto and thus tend to take a hard look at the general issue of legislative expansion. Public opinion has also become more sensitive in a number of Member States.[143] Moreover, the academic world has become more critical of the Court and less cautious in its estimation of the Court's activism.[144] All these factors contributed to a politicisation of the Court's rulings. The WTO case submitted by the Commission in 1994 was highly politicised, with the media portraying the case as a struggle between the Commission and the Member States.[145] Under such circumstances law can no longer possibly

also Stone Sweet and Caporaso (1998: esp. p. 129) for an analysis which highlights the limitations of a principal-agent analysis of the Court and implicitly supports many of the neofunctionalist postulates.
[143] Weiler (1991, 1994).   [144] Rasmussen (1988: 36ff).   [145] Bourgeois (1995: 763).

function as an effective mask for politics, which has been pointed out as an important precondition for Court-induced spillover.[146]

As for the argument of self-interest, a number of authors have pointed out that the ECJ has such an institutional self-interest.[147] The argument is that 'any court has to calculate its activism nicely because miscalculation is likely to provide clashes with other organs of government' which could lead to court-curbing counter-measures.[148] My findings suggest that some (few) member governments may have indeed entertained certain considerations to that effect which can be explained through a mixture of the countervailing forces of sovereignty-consciousness and domestic constraints and diversities. My interviews tentatively suggest that this may have been anticipated by the Court. Hence, it can be argued that a more cautious interpretation in 1/94 and a number of other recent cases is in the long-term self-interest of the Court.[149] As the 1996–97 IGC was only two years away, there was also an opportunity for Member States to cut the wings of the Court of Justice in the not so distant future, although given the need for a unanimous decision at the IGC, these dangers were limited.

Second, the Court has been singled out as an important agent for recognising and acting upon functional pressures.[150] In 1/94 the Court ruled very much on the basis of strictly functional grounds. It rejected the Commission's argument of 'implied powers' because internal powers were not '*inextricably linked* to the exercise of implied external powers'.[151] Hence, weak functional pressures, constraining a 'progressive' ruling, further explain the minimal outcome of Opinion 1/94.

Finally, there are some subsidiary but not unimportant considerations which may help to explain the Court's departure from previous case law on the scope of the CCP. There were a number of new judges involved in the ruling, who 'by nature had a more open ear to national concerns, before they become a victim of the socialisation process with their colleagues'[152]. Rasmussen has argued that the ECJ's teleology is, to some extent, due to the development of certain European orientations on the part of the ECJ judges.[153] There are other explanatory factors which are largely unrelated to neofunctionalist theory of the Court. For

---

[146] Burley and Mattli (1993: 44).   [147] Burley and Mattli (1993).
[148] Rasmussen (1988 : 34).
[149] Interviews, 1997, 1999. That supranational institutions may anticipate the reactions of principals, as framed by principal-agency analysis, has been noted by Pollack (2001: 230). While for Pollack this is a measure for a lack of institutions' autonomy, in terms of my framework this (substantiated through the underlying explanation of countervailing factors) is part of the delimitation of the concept of cultivated spillover.
[150] Burley and Mattli (1993: 43, 65).   [151] Hilf (1995: 254).
[152] Interview, Brussels, 1999.   [153] Rasmussen (1988: 28).

example, the Belgian judge rapporteur was known as not being very well disposed towards the Commission and for generally interpreting the law narrowly. He wrote most of the draft judgement which served as a basis for the Court's deliberations.[154] In addition, the Court had to operate under considerable time pressure.[155] Finally, it has been pointed out that the legal arguments advanced by some of the Member States, especially those in the UK memorandum, were of very high quality and well presented.[156]

Implications of Opinion 1/94 for the IGC negotiations on Article 113:   The role played by the European Court of Justice in Opinion 1/94 was detrimental to the course of extending Article 113. Although the Court's ruling is, of course, in the first instance an interpretation of an existing Treaty, it also tends to be a comment on how the law should develop. In its ruling the Court showed that it had not endorsed important arguments in support of bringing services and IPRs within the scope of the Common Commercial Policy. It could be argued that due to the 1/94 ruling the Commission's wish for an extension of Article 113 lacked critical legal endorsement by the very institution that had supported a dynamic–integrationist interpretation of Article 113 and EC law in general.[157] If even a generally activist ECJ did not want to 'extend' the Community's competencies to include all modes of services and IPRs, why would the Member States take this decision (even if the Commission put forward additional arguments during the IGC)? This, at least, was the reasoning of some national officials.[158] The Court's ruling in 1/94 provided the more reluctant Member States with a strong argument, 'a good shield behind which they could hide'. France, for example, repeatedly said that it wished to stress the importance it attached to the 1/94 ruling.[159]

As pointed out at the beginning of this chapter, the Court's ruling in 1/94 explains, to some extent, why the issue appeared on the agenda again so soon in the first place. The Court emphasised the dynamic (open) nature of the CCP[160] and agreed with the Commission on the need to preserve the Community's unity of action and effective presentation in trade negotiations. The Court required close co-operation between

---

[154] Interview, Brussels, 1999. Dehousse has pointed to the central role that may be played by judge rapporteurs in the Court's decisions. See Dehousse (1998: 13).
[155] Bourgeois (1995).   [156] Interview, Brussels, 1999.
[157] On previous integrationist ECJ case law in the area of the Community's trade policy, see Pescatore (1979), Emiliou (1996b) and Chalmers (1996).
[158] Interview, Brussels, 1997.   [159] Interview, Brussels, 1998.
[160] Opinion 1/94: para. 41.

Member States and the Commission, without, however, offering any guidance as to how the necessary co-operation may be ensured.[161]

The Role of the Council Presidency   At an IGC, the role of the Presidency is supremely important. In its role of institutionalised mediator and promotional broker it is *the* institution responsible for progress of the negotiations. All in all, on the issue of amending Article 113, the various Presidencies did not help much in the Commission's quest for an extension of the CCP. Discussions on the topic started under the Italian Presidency. Italy wasted little political energy on the issue and was also not particularly progressive in terms of its substantive approach.[162] This was reflected in its progress report on the Intergovernmental Conference, in which it described the existing situation as satisfactory and suggested that the European Union was able to act as one in the fields of services and intellectual property.[163] In a Presidency note of May 1996, it merely suggested a provision on the assurance of unity, but not an extension of competencies. On the whole, the CCP did not get much space in the otherwise detailed and comprehensive text.[164] Later, during the Irish and Dutch Presidencies, Italy turned out to be one of the advocates of widening the scope of Article 113. This suggests that the Italian Presidency did not hold back the issue due to national interest considerations, but because it simply did not get round to considering the issue in great depth and due to a lack of ambition.[165]

Although the Irish did not devote significantly greater attention to the issue than the Italians, they were generally supportive of extending Article 113 which was reflected in several Presidency notes.[166] In the Draft Treaty prepared by the Irish Presidency in December 1996, a new Article 113a was included which provided for 'a limited extension of external Community competence in ... the fields of services, intellectual property and direct foreign investment'.[167] The three areas were to come under the scope of Article 113 and the Council was to decide by QMV, on a proposal by the Commission acting as the sole negotiator. This was to apply to negotiations in multilateral international organisations, and hence was not to be restricted to negotiations in the WTO. At the same time, it was made clear that there would be no transfer of internal competence from Member States to the Community. Also a declaration was foreseen to ensure that negotiations would be conducted with maximum transparency *vis-à-vis* Member States. Apart

---

[161] Emiliou (1996a: 297).   [162] Interview, Brussels, 1999.
[163] Council (1996b).   [164] Italian Presidency (1996).
[165] Interview, Brussels, 1996.   [166] E.g. Irish Presidency (1996c).
[167] Council (1996c).

from the declaration on transparency, the Irish Draft Treaty was more or less in line with the goals of the Commission.[168]

The Dutch Presidency was less supportive than the Irish. In its April 1997 text, it proposed QMV and external representation by the Commission acting as the sole negotiator.[169] This part of the Presidency proposal was welcomed. On the question of the scope of application, however, the Dutch *Titulaire* in the Article 113 Committee, who was responsible for drawing up the provisions on external economic policy, restricted it to negotiations in the WTO (i.e. no longer in all international organisations, as in the wider Irish proposal), without informing the Commission of his intentions. Once the text came out, Trojan, then the Dutch Deputy-Secretary General of the Commission, called Patijn, the chairman of the Representatives' Group, who thought that this had been co-ordinated with the Commission and made sure that a *corrigendum* came out widening the scope to negotiations in multilateral international forums. But as pointed out by one interviewee: 'The problem with *corrigenda* is that every Member State and every ministry is looking particularly carefully what it is about. In this case the wider approach was quickly put under pressure and eventually was not tenable'.[170]

Second and more importantly, given the persistent resistance of a number of Member States, including France, the United Kingdom, Portugal and Spain, and to some extent also Germany, the Dutch had drawn up a protocol of exceptions.[171] This was severely criticised within Commission circles. Above all, it was feared that this would open the door to arbitrary exceptions. Even worse, the Dutch Presidency suggested a number of exceptions and then wrote ' ... ' which was 'an invitation for other delegations to press for more exceptions or to allow their ministries to ask for special treatment'.[172] In the following weeks most delegations 'bombarded the Presidency with requests for exceptions', turning the protocol of exceptions into a 'shopping list'.[173] It has been argued that the Dutch approach greatly facilitated the manifestation of bureaucratic politics as it 'became more and more difficult for governments to contain their ministries'. 'Although there had been underlying "protectionist" tendencies by ministries in most Member States throughout the Conference, these were now presented with a concrete outlet'.[174] Hence, on the basis of the above evidence, it appears that the

---

[168] Interview, Brussels, 1999.   [169] Dutch Presidency (1997f).
[170] Interview, Brussels, 1999.
[171] It has been suggested that this approach was originally the idea of the Council Secretariat (interview, Brussels, 1999).
[172] Interview, Brussels, 1998.   [173] Interview, Brussels, 1999.
[174] Interviews, Brussels, 1999.

Dutch Presidency made a considerable misjudgement by introducing the shopping-list approach, as other options seem to have been available.

The shopping-list approach eventually led to the abandoning of discussions on a permanent extension of Article 113. The proposed text on Article 113 was 'too laborious and draught with exceptions. A number of participants thought that the value added to the proposed long amendment, which was coupled with an additional protocol and a number of declarations, in the attempt to rationalise and simplify the CCP, was doubtful'.[175] In the words of one official, 'water was added to wine until it was undrinkable. So, eventually it had to be poured down the drain'.[176]

The Role of the European Parliament   The European Parliament was not a very vigorous supporter of the Commission's quest for an extension of its competencies under Article 113.[177] Parliament's 'Draft Constitution of the European Union' did not mention the Article 113 *problematique* at all. Parliamentary resolutions on the IGC were almost silent on the topic.[178] In its most important contribution, the Dury/Maji–Weggen Resolution on the convening of an Intergovernmental Conference, the EP did not mention the extension of Article 113 as an explicit aim. As one official pointed out, 'the European Parliament is generally critical of Article 113 as it does not foresee any involvement of Parliament'. The fact that the EP was not outrightly supportive may have taken some legitimacy away from the Commission proposal.[179]

On the other hand, Parliament was very explicit about its own institutional ambitions. In the Dury/Maji–Weggen Resolution, the EP sought to simplify procedures relating to external economic policy by 'introducing co-decision, especially for Article 113' and by 'extending assent to all international agreements and measures to be taken in the area of economic sanctions'.[180] Although the EP later reduced its demands during the negotiations, no longer demanding co-decision, it still did not unequivocally support the extension of Article 113, but pursued a *quid pro quo* strategy, making its support for the Commission conditional on having its own demands supported by the Commission.[181] The Commission for its part was not very enthusiastic about the

---

[175] European Policy Centre (1997b: 97).   [176] Interview, Brussels, 1999.

[177] However, one has to distinguish between the Committee on External Economic Relations, which was generally supportive, and other Committees such as the Cultural and the Economic and Monetary Committee which were rather against it (interview, Brussels, 1997, 1999).

[178] With the exception of one line in the Martin–Bourlanges Resolution (EP 1995b: 7).

[179] Interview, Brussels, 1999 and 1997.   [180] European Parliament (1996a: 15).

[181] Strangely, after the IGC Parliament expressed its regrets about the failure to extend Article 113 and claimed to have supported the issue (EP 1997a; 1997b: 375–8).

prospect of the assent procedure. Although most Commission officials seem to have had few problems with it, even pointing out that the procedure might come in handy sometimes, allowing reference to be made to the EP during negotiations, similar to the United States' frequent reference to Congress, on the whole assent would limit the Commission's margin of manoeuvre, as it would have an additional player on its back.[182] Parliaments failure to strongly support the Commission constitutes another, although admittedly rather small, explanatory piece fitting into the 'IGC 113 puzzle'.

Countervailing Forces

So far we have looked at the potential dynamics of integration. On the other side of the equation we have countervailing pressures in the revised neofunctionalist framework. Firstly, there is the diffuse pressure of the general anti-integrationist climate[183] which arose in the early to mid-1990s and is reflected in less pro-European popular opinions and more sceptical media coverage of the European Union in some countries. Whether the more Eurosceptic policies of some Member States are a result of that development (or vice versa), or largely unrelated, is uncertain. However, part of this anti-integrationist climate has been a closer scrutiny of the competencies of the Commission, which for many had become an aloof, high-handed and politically unaccountable institution.[184] In view of this predominant climate, it was always going to be difficult for the Commission to upgrade its competencies on external trade.

Second, and more concretely, domestic constraints provide some useful insights for explaining the restrictive outcome of Amsterdam. The new trade issues do not stop at the borders, such as issues of tariffs and quotas, but extend behind borders into the state and thus concern national laws and domestic regulation.[185] Hence, these issues also tend to be more politicised. To shed competences to the Community under these circumstances is more difficult. For example, during the IGC negotiation France asked for a derogation on cultural services in order to safeguard its cultural diversity policy behind which there is strong public support and strong lobbies.[186] Domestic constraints in some goods

---

[182] Interview, Brussels, 1997, 1999.
[183] It is striking for example that the support of EU/EC membership after 1994 has on average been about 15% lower than from the mid 1980s until the early 1990s. Compare Eurobarometer No. 25–35 with Eurobarometers No. 41–61.
[184] E.g. Papademetriou (1996: 63).
[185] See Smith and Woolcock (1999: 440–1); Young (2000: 101).
[186] Interviews, 1997, 1999.

issues also affected the debate on the extension of competence concerning the new trade issues. One way of avoiding QMV on agriculture or textiles – which are substantially politicised issues in France and Portugal respectively – in horizontal trade negotiations was, following the 'Victor Hugo Principle'[187], to keep unanimity for the new trade issues.

Finally, there is the more diffuse issue of sovereignty-consciousness which arguably constituted the strongest countervailing pressure in this case. The intrusion of the new trade issues into domestic spheres close to the heart of national sovereignty had increased the sensitivity in terms of delegating powers to the Community on these issues. Meunier and Nicolaïdis have shown that several countries, including France and the United Kingdom, came out against an extension of Community competence, contrary to their national interest, and joined the 'sovereignty camp', largely on ideological grounds.[188] Both France and the United Kingdom are very competitive in terms of trade in commercial services internationally and have a positive trade balance in this sector. Their interest would have been best served by a Community with exclusive trade competence, since its collective negotiating position cannot be held up by the Member State least ready to confront international competition. Also in the case of Denmark, the traditional ideological bias against an expansion of Community competence outweighed its traditional liberal stance.[189] The phenomenon of bureaucratic politics is also relevant here as officials in national ministries became agents of sovereignty-consciousness, either for ideological reasons or in the attempt to maintain personal or departmental competencies. This ideological basis for opposing a progressive reform of Article 113, and delegations' sovereignty concerns more generally, have been strongly spurred by the distrust *vis-à-vis* the Commission. Moreover, sovereignty-consciousness was further legitimated and reinforced by the ECJ opinion in 1/94 and the introduction of the Dutch Presidency's shopping-list approach which provided an outlet for bureaucratic pressures. The shopping-list approach itself had been fostered (in the first place) by adverse bureaucratic pressures from the Dutch *Titulaire*.

As pointed out in my analysis of opinion 1/94, countervailing forces did not only impact during the IGC negotiations, but also impeded more progressive outcomes and conditions in the run-up to the Intergovernmental Conference which later adversely affected spillover pressures during the Treaty revision negotiations. All in all,

---

[187] One unanimity aspect in horizontal trade negotiations leads to unanimity on the whole package. See also the analysis above in this chapter on exogenous spillover.
[188] Meunier and Nicolaïdis (1999: 485–7).   [189] Meunier and Nicolaïdis (1999).

countervailing forces manifested as (very) substantial during the Amsterdam IGC.

Conclusion

The failure to reform Article 113 at the Amsterdam IGC has been explained as the result of overall fairly weak dynamics combined with strong countervailing pressures. Exogenous pressures, which constituted the strongest dynamics, were not convincing enough to a minority of reluctant Member States. Moreover, these structural pressures were not supported by sufficiently assertive agency. Functional arguments were less pressing. The anticipation of further functional spillovers (prejudging the internal sphere) may have even been an obstacle to reform. In addition, organised interests never really caught on to the idea, and socialisation processes were offset by several factors. Moreover, the central institutions (and the Council Presidency), traditional agents of integration, barely fostered the issue, and at times even hindered an extension of the CCP. The dynamics were opposed by strong countervailing factors. There was above all the issue of sovereignty-consciousness, complemented by domestic constraints due to increasing politicisation of the new trade issues and a diffuse anti-integrationist climate.

The findings of this chapter correspond with revised neofunctionalist theory. In the absence of effective functional, political, social and cultivated spillover – the functioning of which was further restricted by certain countervailing pressures – the outcome at Amsterdam was a very modest one. This underlines the importance of neofunctionalist dynamics. When absent, and even further impaired by strong countervailing forces, there is little chance of progressive outcomes.

The Intergovernmental Conference 2000

At the Nice IGC external trade policy formed part of the broader issue of the extension of qualified majority voting, which was added to the IGC agenda at first hesitantly and later more decisively. The Common Commercial Policy first appeared on the list of items discussed under QMV in February 2000 and was formally included on the IGC agenda at the Feira European Council of 19–20 June 2000. During the negotiations Article 133 turned out to be one of six controversial QMV issues and stayed a contentious item until about halfway through the summit of Nice.

The Nice Provisions

The Nice provisions[190] have brought some integrative progress in terms of the breadth (scope) and depth (level) of the Common Commercial Policy. Most importantly, the Community has gained 'explicit' competence for the negotiation and conclusion of agreements relating to trade in services and commercial aspects of intellectual property.[191] Qualified majority voting applies to these areas. However, several important exceptions have also been introduced where unanimity is still applicable: (1) areas in which unanimity is required for the adoption of internal rules or where the Community has yet to exercise its competence; (2) where an agreement would go beyond the Community's internal powers, notably by leading to harmonisation in areas for which the Treaty rules out such harmonisation. Agreements which relate to trade in cultural and audiovisual services, educational services, human health services have been explicitly excluded; (3) the negotiation and conclusion of international agreements in the field of transport.

In addition, the Nice provisions contain some further important drawbacks: (1) foreign direct investment was not included within the scope of Article 133; (2) unanimity is still required for the negotiation and conclusion of horizontal agreements (like the Doha Round), if one of the above derogation areas forms part of the negotiations. Furthermore, ratification by the Member States is needed in such cases; (3) the European Parliament remains excluded from decision-making in the Common Commercial Policy and has not even obtained a formal right of consultation. At least, under the new Article 300 (paragraph six) EC, the EP is now entitled to obtain an opinion from the Court on the compatibility of an envisaged international agreement with the EC Treaty; (4) Member States are still allowed to maintain and conclude agreements with third countries or international organisations in the fields of trade in services and commercial aspects of intellectual property (in so far as agreements comply with Community law and other relevant international agreements).

---

[190] See Article 133 TEC as amended by the Treaty of Nice. For detailed legal commentaries on the external trade provisions of the Nice Treaty see for example: Krenzler and Pitschas (2001); Pescatore (2001); Herrmann (2002).

[191] New competences are conferred on the Community, (only) insofar as these topics were not previously covered by Article 133 EC or an implied power. Hence, cross-frontier services and the protection against counterfeit goods at the Community's external border – which were found by the Court in 1/94 to fall under the scope of the CCP – are not affected by the new provisions (and therefore also not by the QMV derogations below).

Given these derogations and drawbacks, commentators both in the legal community and in the policy-making community have generally viewed the progress made as rather modest. While Andrew Duff talks about 'important and possibly overriding exceptions', Elmar Brok regards the progress made through the extension of the CCP 'decisively qualified through the multitude of safety clauses'.[192] The Commission itself acknowledged that 'the progress made in improving the operation of the EU's trade policy is modest'.[193] Legal commentators have concluded, for example, that 'the Treaty of Nice only represents a small step forward in strengthening the Community's capacity to act on the international scene. Nice was not a breakthrough at all.' Among the various exceptions and drawbacks, the necessity to negotiate and conclude future horizontal agreements under the unanimity requirement has been particularly criticised.[194] In addition, many authors have lamented the complexity of the Treaty text which does not meet the growing demands for greater simplicity and transparency and generally disapproved of the quality of drafting which has also been described as 'legal bricolage'.[195]

Exogenous Spillover

Exogenous pressures, i.e. the development of the world economy and the corresponding shape of the international trade agenda, which constituted the chief (structural) driving forces for CCP reform at the Amsterdam IGC, remained substantial (and had perhaps even very slightly grown from the last Treaty revision) and continued to be the most important dynamics behind the extension of Article 133 during the Nice Intergovernmental Conference. Services, intellectual property rights and investment remained important features of the international and especially the EU trade agenda. With the 'GATS 2000' negotiations that started in January 2000 and important unfinished business from the Uruguay Round, including maritime and air transport as well as the impact of electronic commerce on the sector, services stayed particularly prominent in the WTO framework. The European Union also pushed for the inclusion of intellectual property rights and investment, and a host of other issues, to become part of a more comprehensive multilateral trade round. The inclusion of investment on this agenda, or the

---

[192] Duff (2001: 14); Brok (2001: 88 author's translation).
[193] Commission (2000b: 2), quoted in Young (2001: 21).
[194] Krenzler and Pitschas (2001: 312 for quote; 2001: 311 on horizontal agreements).
[195] Pescatore (2001: 265) for quote. Also see Hermann (2002: esp. 16) and Leal-Arcas (2004: 13).

WTO agenda more generally, was particularly pressing, given the failure to reach an agreement on investment in the framework of the OECD in 1998 (MAI negotiations). Intellectual property also remained an important topic in the WTO, not least because many of the Dispute Settlement cases were (and still are) related to this issue.

As described at the beginning of this chapter, in most of these areas, the Community shared competence with Member States. Under such mixed competence, unanimity applies to the conduct and conclusion of negotiations. In the case of horizontal agreements such as a comprehensive Millennium Round, which the European Union was advocating at the time and which later manifested in the Doha Round, discussion of any mixed competence item would expand this legal basis to the whole agreement. The Commission in particular has repeatedly suggested that mixed competence and unanimity are, among other factors, to be associated with lowest common denominator agreements, potential abuse of the veto option and increased potential for third parties to play 'divide-and-rule' games. A number of Member States did/do not view mixed competence as a problem. However, changes in the international trade agenda and the implications associated with shared competence in services, intellectual property and investment, was the rationale most frequently stated by actors in their plea to extend the scope of Article 133 or QMV in external trade policy.[196] The importance of exogenous pressures has also been recognised, to some extent, in the academic discourse.[197]

Functional Spillover

Overall functional pressure had increased since the Amsterdam IGC. Most importantly in that respect, the pressure of enlargement[198] had grown. While there was still a lack of urgency in terms of forthcoming enlargement in the minds of negotiators during the 1996–97 IGC, enlargement had become much more concrete with the launch and confirmation of the enlargement process at the Luxemburg European Council of 1997 and the Helsinki European Council of 1999 respectively, and with the aim to welcome new Member States from the end of 2002 onward. The pressure on the CCP in terms of services, intellectual

---

[196] See, for example, the argumentation by Commission President Prodi (2000a: 3). This has also been confirmed through interviews with officials in Brussels, July 2004.

[197] E.g. Meunier and Nicolaidis (2000: 341–3); to a lesser extent this rationale is acknowledged in van Dijck and Faber (2000: esp. 321–2, 330–1).

[198] Although facilitated and triggered by exogenous events, enlargement after several internal commitments (e.g. Copenhagen European Council of 1993 largely became an internal goal and thus an endogenous source of pressure for reform of EU decision-making procedures. Cf. IGC 1996–97 CCP case, section on functional spillover.

property and investment, as on other policies partially or wholly governed by unanimity, is obvious: with 25 Member States and the corresponding diversification of interests and increased heterogeneity of political cultures, decision-making is (significantly) more prone to paralysis. Position papers by Member State delegations and EU institutions suggest that there was indeed an increased sense of urgency as regards looming enlargement.[199] Interviews mostly substantiate this growing concern but also reveal that enlargement was only one out of several competing concerns of Member States and that strong countervailing pressures may well be overriding in particular policy areas, a point that will be revisited below.

Functional pressures stemming from the internal market had also grown since the 1996–97 IGC. The doctrine of implied powers, also referred to as parallelism – according to which common rules laid down internally could be (adversely) affected, if Member States act individually to undertake international obligations – to some extent increased the rationale for an exclusive Community competence for external trade policy. Internal legislation in services and intellectual property had continued to grow. The internal market in telecommunications, for example, was almost complete at the time of the IGC negotiation. However, in most other areas internal legislation was either still incomplete, or lacking effective transposition and implementation.[200] Hence, from an implied powers perspective, an exclusive external trade competence across *all* services and intellectual property and investment did *not* follow. However, implied powers or parallelism in a broader sense did, to some extent, inform policy-makers and legal drafters during the IGC. The Commission services of DG Trade have referred to the doctrine of parallelism as 'the guiding principle of the new Article 133', the purpose of which is 'to align the decision-making mechanism for trade negotiations on internal decision-making rules'.[201] Therefore, QMV was codified for services and intellectual property except where internal Community rules require unanimity or where no harmonisation has taken place at Community level.[202]

The anticipation of functional pressure, which acted as a moderate obstacle to CCP reform during the Amsterdam IGC (due to fears that the Commission could use the backdoor of Article 133 to 'regulate' areas of Member State internal competence), still played a role albeit a

---

[199] Commission (1999: 6); French Presidency (2000b: 1)
[200] See e.g. Commission (2000a).   [201] Commission (2000b).
[202] However, this logic was not applied wholly consistently. Trade agreements in the field of transport remained subject to unanimity, although this sector is governed by QMV internally and there is considerable internal harmonisation.

diminished one. Member States' fear was (slightly) reduced due to the progression of the internal market, which provided less scope for the prejudgement of internal competences. Nevertheless, the anticipation of this type of potential functional spillover gained further substance when coupled with other countervailing pressures, as will be indicated below.

Social Spillover

At the Intergovernmental Conference 2000 socialisation processes could not unfold in the area of external trade policy. Several factors, most of which were also at work during the Amsterdam IGC, are responsible for this lack of social spillover pressures: (1) The nature of the subject area, along with the background of negotiators, was detrimental for making progress through argumentative debate. Neither the IGC Representatives, nor Foreign Ministers, nor Heads of State and Government, who dealt with the CCP issue at Nice, had the requisite knowledge and expertise to fully engage in a sensible discussion on this fairly complex subject. (2) Even though qualified majority voting was perhaps the most discussed topic in the Representatives Group, and despite the fact that the CCP was one of six rather prominent issues on the QMV agenda, there was simply not enough time available in order to engage in an extensive reasoned debate on the perceived opportunities and risks of extending QMV in external trade policy. This trend was even more pronounced in the ministerial sessions, where *all* IGC issues *together* were usually discussed for only one hour.[203] Moreover, the agenda at the Nice summit was very full with many unresolved issues[204], so that Article 133 could not be properly discussed. (3) The fact that the Representatives Group, which constituted the main negotiating arena of the Nice IGC, only met about thirty times and had a life span of less than a year did not allow for the development of very intense socialisation processes, certainly not comparable with committees or working groups in the Council framework.

(4) Tight, inflexible and sometimes competing or contradictory instructions resulting from the demands of various national ministries (usually other than trade or foreign ministries) hampered genuine exchange on the pros and cons of QMV in trade policy. As one official put it, 'any emerging consensus achieved on the merits of the problem of unanimity in services was to be destroyed by yet another "input" of

---

[203] Gray and Stubb (2001: 20)
[204] Gray and Stubb (2001: 13). On the superficial nature of the 'debate' on another issue (reweighting of Council votes) at Nice see *The Economist* (16/12/00: 26).

some national ministry'.[205] Hence, bureaucratic politics, aggravated by some prevailing distrust of the Commission in several national ministries, impaired processes of social spillover. (5) The negotiations on some institutional topics, although largely left to the Nice summit, 'rubbed off on the discussions in the Representatives Group and damaged the atmosphere among delegations'. Other observers stated that they had never witnessed 'such basic distrust' among Ministers and Heads of State and Government as during the last part of the Nice IGC.[206] Against this background socialisation processes and reasoned debates had little chance to unfold.

Political Spillover

Political spillover in terms of non-governmental elites remained modest, perhaps even slightly below the level of the Amsterdam IGC. Although there was support for the extension of external trade policy among some segments of organised business interests[207], some important players remained rather uninvolved. The European Roundtable of Industrialists, though generally in favour of extending Community competences in the Common Commercial Policy, invested little political energy in the issue.[208] This lack of involvement has been explained by the fact that the CCP was fairly hidden within the broader QMV agenda. Moreover, there is still a certain lack of knowledge and awareness surrounding the CCP competence issue on the part of organised interest. One official has pointed out that 'industry is not bothered so much, if the Commission negotiates under shared competence or exclusive competence, as long as the deals are struck. So far things have worked fairly well under shared competence. Perhaps some major failure is needed to wake up industry'.[209]

Cultivated Spillover

The Role of the Commission   Overall the Commission's assertion and impact on the CCP debate was rather mixed, although it was (somewhat) more effective on this issue than at Amsterdam. From the very start, the Commission was on the defensive. In the run-up to the

---

[205] Interview, Brussels, July 2004.
[206] Duff (2001: 19 for quote); also see Gray and Stubb (2001: 11).
[207] See e.g. UNICE (2000) and AMCHAM (2000).
[208] This judgement is shared by the Corporate Europe Observer that generally tends to, if anything, overemphasise the influence of business lobbies. See *Corporate Europe Observer* (2000).
[209] Commission interview, Brussels, 2004.

IGC 2000, the Commission found itself in an unfavourable position. After the resignation of the entire Santer Commission in March 1999 and the difficult early days of the new Prodi Commission, it was obliged to give priority to administrative reform and to putting its own house in order. Moreover, in the Nice IGC, the Commission was, to some extent, object rather than subject in the negotiations. An augmentation of the Commission's role and competences was, perhaps apart from Article 133, not part of the IGC agenda. Instead, reform of the Commission became part of haggling processes in order to fix the overall IGC package. The Commission, itself an item on the agenda, was increasingly sidelined by Member States, that on occasion decided more about, than with, the Commission, which left the latter in a difficult position to play an active and autonomous role.[210]

On trade policy, the Commission's ability to influence the debate was hampered by the prevailing lack of trust in the Commission, stemming from the Uruguay Round. Although overall this lack of trust had diminished with the departure of Sir Leon Brittan as Trade Commissioner, some delegations remained suspicious of the Commission in terms of a strict abidance of its mandate and a fair representation of Member States' views at international trade negotiations. New Trade Commissioner Lamy's (alleged) exceedance of his mandate at the Seattle Ministerial Conference by accepting the setting up of a biotechnology working group was, therefore, grist to some Member States' mills. Concerning the IGC negotiations themselves, the Commission has been accused of having retreated from its ambitious first proposal a few weeks before the Nice summit and thereby, as the guard of the Treaties, alleviated Member States of their bad conscience, which subsequently felt free to further water down CCP reform proposals.[211] However, my findings suggest that no tactical/strategic mistake was made by the Commission. It simply responded to the negotiating realities, and instead 'created an opening for the more reluctant Member States to accept at least a partial changeover to QMV in services and intellectual property'.[212]

On the positive side, the Commission's IGC opinion of January 2000 provided a good starting point for discussion.[213] In this paper it also tried to avoid the possiblity that QMV issues were negotiated on a case-by-case basis. It suggested that QMV should become the rule and

---

[210] Cf. Grabbe (2001: 1); Monar (2001a: esp. 115–16).

[211] This claim has been made by Maurer (2001: 138).

[212] Interview at the Council Secretariat, July 2004. This view was confirmed by other interviewees.

[213] Interview at Council Secretariat and at the German Permanent Representation, Brussels, 2004. Cf. Commission (2000c).

presented (objective) criteria for determining which issues should be excepted from this rule. 'Only this type of approach stood some chance of avoiding painstaking line-by-line haggling. However, eventually Member State sensitivities in trade, JHA, tax and other policies manifested as too significant. As a result, these issues had to be discussed on a case-by-case basis.'[214] In addition, the Commission managed to establish more cohesion on trade policy as compared to the Amsterdam IGC. Lamy and his cabinet, DG Trade, the Legal Service and the IGC Task Force all pulled in the same direction and managed to speak with one voice.

Finally, at the Nice summit the Finnish delegation and the Commission made sure that QMV in external trade policy was not completely scrapped. According to some observers, without their interventions at the summit, the outcome 'would have probably been still worse, or even remained at the Amsterdam provision'. Through intense behind-the-scenes negotiations the Commission and the Finish delegations managed to bring the French, who were the most reluctant party in terms of reforming Article 133, on board.[215] Eventually, it was Commissioner Lamy, Finnish Permanent Representative Antti Satuli and Jean-Claude Piris, Director-General of the Council Legal Service, who worked out the final text at Nice.[216]

The Role of the Presidency As pointed out earlier, the role of the Presidency is particularly important in the IGC context. While the Portuguese Presidency fulfilled its role as an honest broker and furtherer of common interests, the French Presidency failed in that respect. The Portuguese Presidency in the first half of 2000 took a relatively ambitious approach on the issue of qualified majority voting and saw to it that the CCP appeared on the QMV agenda. The Portuguese Presidency also tried to avoid case-by-case examination of policies potentially switching to QMV, although in a less bold fashion than the Commission, by establishing criteria according to which changes to QMV could occur.[217] However, eventually it could not prevent the gradual slide into case-by-case analysis especially of the more sensitive issue areas, such as the CCP.

---

[214] Interview, Brussels, 2004.
[215] Beach (2005: 169).
[216] Interview Brussels, July 2004; on this point also see Gray and Stubb (2001: 21). It has been pointed out by Beach (2005: 128–9) that the Commission, the Presidency and the Council Secretariat have informational advantages at IGC summits, because their representatives sitting at the table have very closely followed (or been involved in) the negotiations, more so than foreign ministers and heads of government, who solely represent national governments in the meeting room.
[217] See Portuguese Presidency (2000a).

The French Presidency can be criticised on several accounts. On a general level, it failed to demonstrate its impartiality. It advocated, quite explicitly, a shift in the balance of power towards the larger Member States.[218] This further spurred the looming mutual resentment and lack of trust in the final stages of the IGC among big and small Member States and 'spilled-over' to other issue areas. It also discredited the Presidency's potential position and role as an honest broker. Second, as regards Article 133, unlike the Presidency's expected role, the French did not take an ambitious (or at least neutral) approach on the issue and failed to modify its own national interest in the search for a far-reaching solution in the 'European interest' (or at least for the sake of a mutually acceptable compromise). Instead, in the last stages of the IGC, the French Presidency insisted on the preservation of unanimity in several sectors, above all cultural services.[219] This was, of course, rather inviting for other delegations to oppose the extension of QMV in other aspects and areas of the Common Commercial Policy. Third, the French Presidency can be criticised for a lack of leadership on external trade policy. It failed to gradually narrow down the debate towards one option that could be decided upon.[220] During the Nice summit there were still at least three different options on the table, which substantially inhibited agreement. Some of the reasons for the French line taken during its Presidency will be taken up below in the section on countervailing pressures.

The Role of the European Parliament   The European Parliament was more supportive of the extension of Article 133 than in the previous IGC. The EP's stance basically mirrored that of the Commission on the Common Commercial Policy and augmenting its role in trade policy became one of its more important objectives. However, its impact on the debate was limited. Although the role of Parliament had further augmented from the last IGC – this time the two EP Representatives, Brok and Tsatsos, were not only allowed to exchange views with IGC Representatives before official meetings, but were allowed to attend the Representatives Group as observers – the EP failed to make much use of this increased room for manoeuvre. Parliament failed to submit a substantial opinion before the start of the IGC. During this defining, i.e. agenda-setting period, where its impact on the debate was arguably the greatest, the EP was simply unable to take up detailed positions. When its opinion came on 13 April[221], almost three months after the

---

[218] Gray and Stubb (2001: 11).
[219] Cf. Lequesne (2001); Gray and Stubb (2001); Beach (2005: 148).
[220] Also see Maurer (2001: 138).   [221] European Parliament (2000).

Commission's opinion, many other players had already submitted their papers, as a result of which Parliament's resolution did not have the desired impact. Moreover, it has been argued that the EP failed to sufficiently focus on important objective (like the CCP)[222]. However, it has been pointed out that the presence at the Representatives' negotiating table provided more ample opportunity to 'remind Member States that trade is the only policy area [in the Community framework] where Parliament was not even required to be consulted'. This, according to some observer, may have contributed to further raising awareness on the issue for future Treaty revisions.[223]

Countervailing Forces

Sovereignty-consciousness was an important countervailing pressure at the IGC 2000, however, arguably slightly weaker than during the Amsterdam IGC. France, the United Kingdom and Denmark were little inclined to delegate competence to the Commission for ideological reasons. Sovereignty-consciousness was to a lesser extent than during the last IGC reinforced by some remaining lack of trust in the Commission. This also raised further (but – compared with the IGC 1996–97 – weaker) doubts concerning delegating powers to the Commission in France but also in countries like Portugal and Greece. Sovereignty-consciousness sparked by some Commission distrust can, to a large extent, explain provisions on unanimity for areas where this decision-mode is required internally (to prevent potential Commission attempts to introduce liberalisation through the back door) and the unanimity requirement for horizontal agreements with which some governments felt more 'at ease'. The insistence of France on the 'cultural exception' is partly illuminated by the specificity of French national identity, the perceived threat to this identity and the importance of culture therein. In terms of French perceptions of national identity, no loss of sovereignty in such sensitive areas as culture could be accepted.[224]

On specific trade policy issues, bureaucratic politics played an important role. For example, it has been reported that officials at the French Ministry of Economy, Finance and Industry blocked the issue of investment from coming under the scope of Article 133. Moreover, officials from Dutch, United Kingdom, Danish, Greek, German and Austrian national transport ministries are said to have been very reluc-

---

[222] Cf. Gray and Stubb (2001: 9–10).   [223] Interview, Brussels, 2004.
[224] On the importance of the issue in terms of French national identity cf., for example, *Le Monde*, (31/10/00); *Le Monde* (07/12/00); *Le Monde* (10/04/01).

tant to introduce QMV for trade in transport services, mainly in order to avoid having to cede competence to their respective economic ministries. In some cases, such as the Netherlands and the United Kingdom, the perceived competitive advantages of these countries in air transport services under the current regime played an even bigger role, prompting a defence of their constituents' interests.

This brings us to the role of domestic constraints. These have played an important role here as 'trade negotiations were increasingly coming to concern matters traditionally seen as part of domestic policy'.[225] For example, the unfortunate, cautious as well as defensive role by the French Presidency on the CCP, particularly on cultural services can, to some extent, be (further) explicated by domestic constraints. Within the context of cohabitation[226] and looming elections in 2002, neither Chirac, nor Jospin could allow himself to be viewed as giving in on such an important issue as cultural diversity.[227] Hence, their 'competition' significantly contributed to such minimalist French Presidency position and approach, especially on trade in cultural services. Domestic constraints further mattered on the latter issue, as many of the about 4.5 million jobs[228] in the French cultural sectors would be endangered through WTO level liberalisation.[229] The issue of culture also became such a strong countervailing pressure because of diversity, or more precisely due to French distinctness. Distinct French national identity and particular structures of its economy did not allow France to give up its veto in this domain. In addition, the importance of the agricultural sector in France, backed by strong lobbies, adds to the sovereignty-consciousness explanation on the unanimity requirement for horizontal agreements. The latter provision ensures a French veto when agriculture is discussed at multilateral trade rounds.[230] Finally, the integrationist climate remained at a similarly low level as during the previous Treaty revision.

---

[225] A senior French official quoted in Rollo and Holmes (2001).
[226] On the problems resulting from cohabitation during the French Presidency, see, for example: Lequesne (2001); and Moscovici, Pierre in: Le Monde (18/11/00).
[227] Interview, Brussels, 2004.   [228] See Le Monde (22 /04/02: 16).
[229] The exception on educational services and social and human health services, was introduced by the French Presidency, in order to have a 'cover' for its exception on cultural and audiovisual services, by stating all areas for which there is a prohibition of internal harmonisation and thereby provided a post hoc overall rationale for these exceptions. The rationale is not wholly consistent: audiovisual services do not follow this logic. There is harmonisation in this area, for example, through the Television without Frontiers Directive (89/552/EEC).
[230] Interview, Brussels, 2002.

Conclusion

All in all, the IGC 2000 negotiations on the Common Commercial Policy were characterised by stronger overall dynamics. Exogenous pressures were as strong as at Amsterdam, if not stronger, due to the further development of the trade agenda. Functional pressures stemming from the internal market, and particularly from enlargement, had also become fairly substantial. Some aspects of cultivated spillover (Commission and EP) had also been reinforced, albeit to a limited extent. On the other hand, social and political spillover pressures remained at about the same low/modest level as during the IGC 1996–97. Combined, these dynamics can explain the limited furtherance of Community competence and extension of qualified majority voting. These pressures were countered by a number of spillback forces that were of similar strength as during the Amsterdam IGC. While suspicion in the Commission had decreased, the politicisation of some issues in the domestic context had grown. Countervailing pressures significantly further our understanding of the many qualifications and exceptions of Community competence and qualified majority on external trade policy at the Nice IGC.

The Convention and the Intergovernmental Conference 2003–04[231]

The Laeken European Council decided to depart from the more standard methods of preparing EU Treaty reforms and chose to convene a Convention on the Future of Europe.[232] The idea of a Convention was first suggested by the European Parliament and later supported, above all, by the EP, the Belgian Presidency and the Commission. The Common Commercial Policy was identified by members of the Convention early on as one of the issues that required further discussion. Within the Convention Working Group on External Action, the CCP was of secondary importance in comparison with the Common Foreign and Security Policy. The Draft Treaty that came out of the Convention

---

[231] My analysis of the last Treaty revision negotiations concerning Title IV and the CCP stretches from pre-negotiations (including the Convention) to the signing of the Constitutional Treaty. The ratification process – which continues at the time of writing – does not form part of this study. However, it would be interesting to assess, if the current difficulties along this process (after the referendums in France and the Netherlands) may be explained through this framework, particularly by drawing on countervailing forces. Even if the Constitutional Treaty does not come into force, it will serve to describe a certain state in the evolution of the European integration process (Wessels 2005: 11).

[232] Presidency Conclusions (2001).

had already provided for the changes outlined below. The Common Commercial Policy only played a subordinate role at the IGC 2003–04 where the provisions of the Draft Constitutional Treaty agreed upon at the Convention were watered down only insubstantially.[233]

The New Article III-315 (ex Article 133 TEC)

The Treaty provisions on the Common Commercial Policy have substantially progressed in terms of breadth and depth. The following are the most important advances: (1) foreign direct investment is now included under the scope of the CCP in addition to services and intellectual property; (2) services and intellectual property (and also investment) now fall within the exclusive[234] competence of the Community; (3) the European Parliament has obtained co-decision on legislative acts, i.e. for measures implementing the Common Commercial Policy. In addition, consent by the EP is required for most types of international agreements; (4) mainly following from the second point, *horizontal agreements* involving services, intellectual property and investment may now be decided more easily by QMV[235]; (5) exceptions for unanimity have been further narrowed. Unanimity in the external realm is still required on services, intellectual property and investment, where unanimity is required for the adoption of internal rules. However, the derogation regarding cultural and audiovisual services has been made subject to 'where these risk prejudicing the Union's cultural and linguistic diversity' and social, education and health services now also come under unanimity only 'where these risk seriously disturbing the national organisation of such services and prejudicing the responsibility of Member States to deliver them'.[236] These explicit derogations have become narrower and the burden of proof to invoke these exceptions lies

[233] A rather narrow derogation on social, education and health services was (re)introduced during the IGC. Also investment belongs to those policies (alongside with services and intellectual property) for which unanimity applies externally where this is required for the adoption of internal rules. Cf.: Article 133 (6) TEC, Article III-217 (4) (Draft Constitutional Treaty) and Article III-315 (4) (Treaty establishing a Constitution for Europe).

[234] The Treaty of Nice had made the competence on services and intellectual property 'explicit'. However, legal scholars seem to agree that competences in these areas were still shared between the Community and Member States. Cf., for example, Krenzler and Pitschas (2001: 302); Herrmann (2002: 13, 19).

[235] When those areas that are specifically excepted are included in horizontal agreements, unanimity still applies. Antoniadis (2004) has suggested that horizontal agreements are likely to be concluded by unanimity in the future because the derogation on cultural diversity may be invoked relatively easily. A more 'optimistic' view has been taken by some of my interviewees (interviews, Brussels, 2004).

[236] See Article III-315 (4) of the Constitutional Treaty.

with those Member States that want to apply them[237]; (6) following from the second point, national parliaments are no longer needed for the ratification of future WTO agreements (involving the new issues).

The new Article III-315 provides a substantial degree of further integration. Interviewees and scholars have generally agreed on the progressiveness of this latest CCP Treaty revision.[238] The implications for EU trade negotiations are that unanimity would become rarer, thus decreasing the danger of lowest common denominator agreements, reducing the scope for possible abuse of the veto option resulting in disproportionate demands by veto-countries, and also limiting the potential for third parties to play 'divide-and-rule' games. Moreover, the sole representation by the Commission in services, intellectual property and investment is now also codified in the Treaty, providing further certainty for the Commission. The (significantly) augmented powers of the EP were overdue, given the democratic deficit in this area. Parliaments' new role, should the Treaty enter into force, does not (necessarily) weaken the efficiency of the CCP. In contrast, some observers have suggested that the EP could be conveniently used as a bargaining chip. The Commission could strengthen its bargaining position in international negotiations by referring to the requirement of EP consent, as practised by US negotiators with regard to Congress.[239]

Exogenous Spillover

Exogenous pressures continued to be as strong as during the previous Treaty revision. The mismatch between international trade policy realities and the internal provisions under Article 133 was growing. The inclusion of services and intellectual property as well as issues such as 'trade and environment' on the comprehensive agenda of WTO negotiations under the Doha Round, which got underway in early 2002, further exacerbated this disparity.[240] However, with the entering into

---

[237] This opinion is generally shared by officials in the Commission and Council Secretariat: Interviews, Brussels, July 2004.

[238] Interviews, Brussels, July 2004. Cf. Antoniadis (2004); Cremona (2003).

[239] This view was held by most interviewees. On the other hand, the involvement of the EP could further contribute to a politicisation of the Community's external trade policy and threaten to hamper the internal policy-making process (cf. Smith and Woolcock 1999: 451).

[240] Issues such as investment and 'trade and competition' also, for a long time, seemed to form part of this agenda and were strongly advocated by the European Union (e.g. Commission 2003a). Only by July 2004, it became clear that these issues would not be negotiated within the Doha Round. Hence, during the Convention and the IGC 2003/04 the mismatch rationale also applied to these two issues. In any regard, these issues are/were likely to reappear in the WTO (or another) context.

force of the Treaty of Nice in February 2003, part of this gap has been closed due to the Community's increased competences on services and intellectual property. On the other hand, horizontal agreements, like the Doha Round, were still to be negotiated and concluded under unanimity if one of the many derogation areas was to be included which was looming (large) at the time of the Convention and the IGC 2003–04. That exogenous pressure played an important role at the last Treaty revision is further substantiated by the frequent and prominent usage of this rationale in the argumentations in favour of a (further) extension of Article 133, especially by the Commission.[241]

Functional Spillover

Overall, functional pressures further increased after the IGC 2000. For example, the pressure of enlargement became even stronger and also more urgent as the Seville European Council of June 2002 expected the Accession Treaty to be signed in spring 2003 and anticipated the participation of new Member States in the 2004 EP elections.[242] Therefore, decision-making in the Council with 25 Member States was now an imminent reality, which put substantial pressure on those trade policy issues subject to unanimity. Enlargement became one of the most frequent rationales used to substantiate the need for further CCP reform.[243]

Moderate additional functional pressures were created by the Laeken European Council Declaration on the Future of Europe. Herein, the Heads of State and Government restated and reinforced a number of aims. In order to achieve these goals, further action, i.e. a deepening of certain policies, such as the CCP, was necessary (or at least the most logical solution), hence creating pressures for further communitarisation. The first objective stated in the Laeken Declaration was the strengthening of the Union's role in the world. In order to achieve this collective goal, improvements in the decision rules of several policies, such as the CFSP, the CCP and development co-operation was 'at least a logical corollary, if not a necessity'.[244] The second set of aims of Laeken was greater simplification in the decision-making and workings of EU institutions and policies. Given the complexity of the Nice provisions on Article 133, the CCP was an obvious candidate for improvements along these lines. Streamlining and rationalisation of external trade policy provisions can, of course, go both ways: re-nationalisation or

---

[241] See, e.g. Lamy (2002a: 2, 2003).   [242] Presidency Conclusions (2002: 6).
[243] Cf. e.g. Lamy (2002b).   [244] Interview, Brussels, July 2004.

supranationalisation. However, given the various other pressures, including the aim of a more effective Union in the world, the bias was clearly in favour of the Community method. Finally, Heads of State and Government called for greater democracy and transparency. In terms of the CCP this aim could, again, have repercussions in two different directions: either greater involvement of national parliaments or a more substantial role for the European Parliament. And again the bias was in the latter direction, given the overall tendency and pressure towards more Commission competence and more QMV which is well complimented by stronger EP involvement under the tried and tested Community method. The functional tensions created by these three sets of aims should not be exaggerated, as they had been formulated at various European Councils before without having much impact. The difference this time was two-fold. These objectives were arguably emphasised more strongly than in previous European Council Presidency conclusions[245] and the members of the Convention took them more seriously than officials preparing previous IGCs.[246]

Pressure from the internal market, which played a moderate level during the IGC 2000, was diminished. At Nice, the doctrine of implied powers or parallelism had provided a rationale for establishing QMV for trade in services except for those areas where internal Community rules require unanimity or where no harmonisation has taken place at Community level (or where derogation areas formed part of horizontal agreements). One remaining anomaly was transport services[247]. As a result, it was argued to drop the explicit derogation on transport during the Convention.[248] This reasoning, together with other pressures for further communitarisation, was initially followed in early Convention drafts[249], which excluded the Nice exception on transport, but this could not be maintained later on. Finally, the anticipation of further functional spillover played no (detrimental) role this time, since the Nice provisions – prohibiting the conclusion of an external agreement if it includes provisions which would go beyond the Community's internal

---

[245] Cf. Presidency Conclusions of the following European Councils: Cannes (point IV), Madrid (pp. 1, 3), Helsinki (point I), Feira (point I) and Laeken.

[246] Interviews, Brussels, July 2004.

[247] Transport is governed by QMV and there is considerable internal harmonisation. Another, less clear-cut, anomaly is the audiovisual sector. Although there is a prohibition for harmonisation in this sector and though it is governed by unanimity, some harmonisation has taken place through the Television without Frontiers Directive (89/552/EEC). Moreover, in the Constitution, culture has been transferred to QMV internally, suggesting a departure from the doctrine of parallelism (cf. Antoniadis, 2004).

[248] Interview, Brussels, July 2004.   [249] Cf. Praesidium (2003: 52–5).

powers – provided a safeguard for the concerns that some Member States had had during the Nice and Amsterdam IGCs.

Social Spillover

One of the most substantial changes from the previous two Treaty revisions was the much greater favourable impact of socialisation, deliberation and learning processes in the Convention. This provided a futile ground for exogenous and functional spillover rationales. It also constituted an environment in which countervailing forces could exert themselves less easily. In comparison to other forums that have priorly prepared Treaty revisions, the Convention provided the following conditions, favourable to socialisation and communicative action processes: (1) The Convention started off with an initial listening (and reflection) phase during which expectations and visions could be freely stated. It generated a deeper understanding for other ideas and perceptions, softened pre-conceived opinions and generally created considerable openness of mind.[250] With people seriously listening and reflecting, good arguments could also register more easily. (2) The Convention negotiating infrastructure – with more than 50 sessions that both the Plenary and the Praesidium held over a period of 18 months – also induced the development of an 'esprit de corps' that captured both the Plenary and the Praesidium.[251] Most people 'had or developed substantial responsibility for the success of the project'. Some initially more sceptical members of the Convention, such as Erwin Teufel representing the German *Länder*, are even said to have changed their outlook during the process towards more European/pro-integrative attitudes.[252] And one of the most important common norms that developed during the process was 'to really solve the problems at hand and to arrive at the best possible solution'. In addition, the consensus principle, which was suggested by Giscard d'Estaing and accepted as the mode of reaching decisions, prevented people from just taking their diverging positions, without trying to find common answers and solutions in a mutual process.

(3) Another important aspect was that the members of the Convention, including representatives from Member States, by and large, could

---

[250] Cf. Checkel (2001a: 562) who has suggested that the absence of strongly ingrained beliefs/opinions is conducive to arguing/persuasion.

[251] For the ascertainment of an *esprit de corps* in the Plenary see Göler (2003: 17). Concerning the Praesidium: interview with Klaus Hänsch (EP member of the Convention and the Praesidium), July 2004. On the two subsequent quotes: interviews, Brussels, 2004.

[252] Interviews, Brussels, 2004. See also *Die Tageszeitung* (14.6.2003: 9).

act freely without having to stay within a certain (externally set) brief, as during an IGC.[253] (4) Perhaps most importantly, based on the pervious points, the atmosphere, spirit and negotiating structure in the Convention did not allow (or at least made it very difficult for) a member of the Convention to reject something without justification, explanation and entering into a discourse where his or her factual and normative validity claims would become subject to scrutiny. During an IGC, by contrast, negotiators can often simply say 'no' to something without having to give reasons. Hence, bargaining behaviour was substantially discouraged. (5) During the Convention one important source of countervailing pressures was (largely) shut out: bureaucratic politics and resistances were in a much less favourable position to counter the deliberation process in the Convention because the representatives of Heads of State and Government did not, unlike at an IGC or in the Reflection Group preparing the Amsterdam IGC, have to go through the process of inter-ministerial co-ordination for the formation of national positions. The various departments could only assert their views – which were, however, not binding to government representatives – out of their own initiative.[254]

Following from the previous points, the strength of the argument considerably mattered, while the hierarchy, status, affiliation, i.e. power of the negotiator were less relevant. As the might of the better argument increased in importance, the many convincing exogenous and functional spillover rationales, which did not succeed in unfolding during previous IGCs, now managed to make an impact. As one official put it, 'we had had good arguments for the extension of Article 133 all along – be it concerning the changing trade agenda, enlargement or the single market. However, for the first time, we had the feeling that people were really considering these points and their implications'.[255] As a result, more deeply rooted learning processes seem to have occurred during which actors not merely adapted their short-term strategies and positions to reach the same goals, but some agents' very interests and preferences themselves seem to have changed in the process.[256]

---

[253] This point has also been confirmed by Maurer (2003a: 134). But also cf. Magnette and Nicolaïdis (2004: 393).

[254] On this point, see: Maurer (2003a: 136).   [255] Interview, Brussels, July 2004.

[256] 'Hard' evidence concerning this type of learning is sparse. One strand of evidence points to the altered attitudes of some French nationals in the Convention regarding the value of having an exclusive Community competence on external trade. Some individuals, for example, began to increasingly argue the rationales which they had earlier contested, which is one indicator for more reflexive learning processes (interviews, June 2004).

Moreover, in an open process, in which the participants are eager to find the best solution to common problems, in which learning processes occur and people are persuaded by the better argument, negotiators tend to concur fully in the common results achieved. On the Draft Constitutional Treaty there was 'overall, with only few reservations, great satisfaction with what had been achieved'. This judgement applied especially to policy (as opposed to the institutional) issues, such as the CCP.[257] This broad consensus, behind which (almost) all could stand, of course, substantially increased the weight and impact of the Convention text and made it difficult for negotiators at the IGC to (considerably) depart from this consensus.[258] Indeed, the concurrence in, and the satisfaction with, the Convention consensus, including the one on external trade policy, had made an impact on the IGC in three interrelated ways: first, Member States had been very much part of this consensus. The Intergovernmental Conference 2003–04 was negotiated on the level of Ministers and Heads of State and Government only. And these two levels had, either directly or indirectly, participated in the Convention process. Heads of State and Government had sent their representatives – who, in many cases, were the Ministers who later negotiated the IGC. Second, there was a general feeling that the Convention had done a good job and the dominant policy discourse suggested that the Convention text should be kept as much as possible.[259] Third, and closely related, due to the substantial bonding strength of the CCP provisions and the Draft Constitutional Treaty more generally, the Convention text on most (non-institutional) issues, including external trade policy, became the basis for further negotiations at the IGC. In a way, it turned into the default setting[260], which is difficult to change at an Intergovernmental Conference. As a result, the IGC 2003–04 hardly reopened debate on the Common Commercial

---

[257] Interviews: Brussels 2004, and by telephone 2004.

[258] Interestingly in this respect, on the issue of institutions quite a number of important decisions were taken in the Praesidium, while many papers of the Convention Secretariat were not distributed and while there was less debate in the Plenary. At the end, representatives of some of the smaller Member States who had also not been represented in the Praesidium did not really concur in the decision, also because they did not entirely feel part of the decision. As a result, these smaller Member States were also the first to demand a reopening of the institutional package during the IGC.

[259] Statements to this effect can be found in various press articles (e.g. *Frankfurter Allgemeine Zeitung* (16/06/04: 1; 18/06/03: 2); *The Guardian* (14/06/03)) by members of the Convention such as Joschka Fischer, Peter Hain, Johannes Voggenhubber, Alain Lamassoure, Valery Giscard d'Estaing, etc. See also the opinions of the *European Parliament* (2003b: 7) and the *Commission* (2003b) concerning the IGC. Also overall *organised interests* (e.g. Eurochambres 2003) defended the outcome of Convention. For positions taken by *civil society* see, for example: Act4Europe (2003).

[260] Beach (2005: 199).

Policy and made only one noteworthy change by (re)introducing a derogation on social, educational and health services, which is however more narrow than the one in the Treaty of Nice.

What has been presented above as socialisation, deliberation, arguing and learning needs to be further substantiated. After all, what appears to be the power of the better argument may not have been genuine reasoning, but strategic arguing or rhetorical action, i.e. the use of arguments to add cheap legitimacy to one's case. Due to space limitations my evidence has to be somewhat cursory here. On a general basis, interviewees – who were either themselves members of the Convention, advisors to Convention members or civil servants working in the Convention Secretariat – characterised the decision-style in the Convention in terms of true deliberation, arguing and reasoning. They either did so without being prodded, or in few cases, when proposing four different characterisations ('truthful arguing/reasoning', 'bargaining', 'confrontation/compulsion' and 'strategic arguing'), they consistently opted for the first one. In addition, when analysing the Plenary discussions and when reconstructing the debates in the External Action Working Group and in the Praesidium, it is striking that speakers were anxious to explicate their proposals, to consider the pros and cons and to reflect their proposals against the criteria set up in the run-up to the Convention at Laeken. Also more generally, other preliminary studies of the decision-making style at the Convention have also found that deliberation and communicative action capture much of the Convention decision mode.[261]

Second, one indicator for 'true' communicative action is that 'bad' arguments and mere strategic positions, even by supposedly 'powerful' actors, which make no sense in terms of generally acknowledged criteria in a reasoned discussion, were not accepted during the Convention. For example, the French cultural exception, which was supported by the French nationals in the Convention and also some other members, was already catered for in a general passage about unanimity rule for external policy where unanimity was required internally. An explicit derogation was therefore not necessary and also not desirable in terms of simplification. As a result, during the Convention, this derogation was not accepted because it made no sense to the vast majority of members and was therefore kept out of the text. Only at the very end, after the Thessaloniki European Council, which was supposed to be only for some legal tidying-up, the Praesidium took the cultural

---

[261] Cf.: Göler and Marhold (2003: esp. 323 ff.); Göler (2003: esp. 27); Maurer (2003a: esp. 132 ff.).

exception on board, largely for strategic reasons, i.e. to win the support of the French on the overall package. Not without reason has this stage been called 'IGC-pre-negotiations'. It was no longer characterised by the deliberative spirit of the Convention.

Third, and related to the previous point, members of the Convention, including government representatives, abstained from pointing to their rank, status or qualification or other sources of power when making their arguments, and thereby avoided adding extra (non-discursive) authority to their statements.[262] Fourth, consistency across different forums and contexts is a good indicator for truly argumentative behaviour, while actors changing their arguments and justifications depending on the interaction partner are likely to engage in rhetorical action.[263] It was possible to trace some actors' lines of argumentation across more than one forum, i.e. also outside the Convention. Overall, there has been an astonishing consistency in argumentation between the statements in the different Convention forums and also outside the Convention.[264]

Political Spillover

Political spillover somewhat grew during the Convention, but did not exceed a moderate level of pressure, although the integration and involvement of organised interests and civil society has never been greater during any Treaty revision exercise. This was achieved through several means: a forum, which allowed non-governmental organisations and interests to provide written contributions to the Convention; the establishment of eight contact groups to allow for an exchange of views with specific sectors of society; finally, public hearings, which gave civil society and organised interests a chance to address the Convention Plenary directly. Moreover, the European Social Partners[265] had one

---

[262] On the value of this indicator of communicative action see Risse (2000: 18). Concerning my evidence, Göler and Marhold (2003: 325–6) have come to a similar conclusion in their study of two Convention Working Groups

[263] Cf. e.g. Risse (2000) and Checkel (2001a).

[264] One example, where this could be traced perhaps most thoroughly is the case of Pascal Lamy, who was not a member of the Convention, but was heard in the Working Group on External Action as an expert and participated in the discussion. Cf., for example, Lamy's (2002a) account in the Working Group and speeches in other forums (e.g. Lamy 2002c; 2003).

[265] They were represented by the Union of Industrial and Employers' Confederations of Europe (UNICE), the European Trade Union Confederation (ETUC) and the European Centre of Enterprises with Public Participation and of Enterprises of General Economic Interest (CEEP).

observer each in the Convention. Some members of the Convention also seem to have been rather positive concerning the chances of organised interests and civil society to influence the discussions in the Convention.[266] Eventually, UNICE, the ERT and some few national associations, such as the *Bundesverband der Deutschen Industrie* (BDI) and the *Bundesverband der Deutschen Arbeitgeberverbände* (BDA), submitted written contributions to the Convention in which they expressed their support for a further extension of Article 133.[267] Overall, there seems to have been a slight increase in their activity from previous Treaty revisions. However, the level of organised industry's activism was not enormous and their role was not viewed as decisive on external trade policy by anyone involved in the Convention or subsequent IGC. Their contributions had the most impact during the first few months of the Convention when members were still in the process of making up their minds. However, papers and statements of organised interests 'were merely few out of many different inputs'.[268] Some Commission officials have interpreted this overall trend as the results of certain learning processes on the part of industry concerning the benefits of greater integration of non-goods trade issues into the CCP, with yet further scope for increasing their awareness.[269]

Counter to the positions taken by business interest groups, the post-Nice process saw, for the first time, a noticeable input from anti-globalisation movements and NGOs, opposing the extension of Community competence in external trade policy. They spoke out against further Community competences because of the lack of democratic legitimacy in this area and the danger of creating a 'bosses Europe'. However, they generally supported an increased role of the European Parliament.[270] The intensity and impact of their campaign should not be exaggerated. However, overall, 'to some extent it cancelled out or neutralised the efforts and lobbying by business groups' (concerning the question of community competence).[271] By generally supporting the Draft Constitutional Treaty, both business groups and (parts of) civil society contributed to reinforcing the bonding strength of the Convention text and thus also to a far reaching overall outcome, including external trade policy results.[272]

---

[266] Cf. Maurer (2003a: 133).
[267] See e.g. ERT (2002: 2, 4); UNICE (2002: 6); BDA and BDI (2001: 8).
[268] Interview, Brussels, July 2004.
[269] Interview at the European Commission, DG Trade, Brussels, July 2004.
[270] For quote, see Libertarians Against Nice (2002); also see O'Brien (2001).
[271] Interview, Brussels, July 2004.
[272] Cf. e.g. Eurochambres (2003); Act4Europe (2003).

Cultivated Spillover

The Role of the Commission   As far as the Commission is concerned, its influence on external trade policy matters has been greater
than during the Amsterdam and Nice Treaty revisions. Most observers
agree that the Commission's starting position at the Convention was a
very good one. Its representatives were, unlike at an IGC, equal participants. They enjoyed very substantial infrastructural backing and were
both also 'first-tier' members of the Praesidium.[273] Moreover, Barnier
had already gained IGC experience in 2000 as the Commissioner
responsible and Vitorino had represented the Commission in the EU
Charter negotiations. In addition, the more deliberative process of the
Convention constituted a promising platform for Commission assertion
(see below). However, assessments concerning the overall leadership
role of the Commission at the last Treaty revision diverge: while it has
been argued that the Commission played itself out of the picture by
failing to adopt timely, coherent and co-ordinated positions[274], it has
also been held that it played a 'leading role during the Convention'.[275]
As for the Common Commercial Policy, the Commission did manage
to assume a leadership role. The partial incoherence, alluded to above,
between the official Commission opinion and the so-called 'Penelope'
paper (initiated by Commission President Prodi) contained no contradictions in the field of external trade policy. Concerning the CCP issue,
the negotiating infrastructure was favourable for the Commission. The
Commission had established good contacts with Jean-Luc Dehaene,
who chaired the Working Group on External Action and also the
external relations issues in the Praesidium, and who was himself an
advocate of greater Community competence on trade policy. This
helped in terms of making sure that the issue was put on the Working
Group's agenda and in terms of drafting the Working Group's
recommendations.
Perhaps most importantly, as pointed out above, the deliberative
decision style in the Convention meant that the well-founded arguments
of the Commission – for example, on the changing trade agenda, concerning enlargement, on simplification and legitimacy – were, in contrast to most IGC negotiations, listened to and reflected upon, and that
they finally largely prevailed. As one Commission official put it, 'as
opposed to the last IGCs, people at the Convention were eager to really
discuss the pros and cons of more Community competence. [In this

---

[273] On the latter point see Beach (2005: 200).
[274] Concerning this judgement see Beach (2005).
[275] Goulard (2003: 381, author's translation).

kind of environment,] we could finally influence the debate because the best arguments made the biggest impact. And the Commission and other supporters of extending Article 133 simply had the best arguments'.[276] Hence, socialisation and communicative action processes had greatly facilitated the Commission to successfully act out (or cultivate) exogenous and functional spillover pressures. In this respect, it also helped that the Commission had greater expertise in, and better overview of, the subject matter. Commissioner Vitorino, who represented the Commission on the issue, was in close contact with Trade Commissioner Lamy during the Convention and the IGC. Vitorino has been repeatedly praised for his remarkable grasp of trade policy matters. He played a very active part in preventing a watering down of the progressive Working Group CCP provisions in the Praesidium (see below). In addition, Lamy was heard as an expert in an important session of the Working Group on External Action.[277]

Other factors further contributed to the Commission's augmented role in the last Treaty revision. The Commission had invested a lot of attention and political capital in the IGC and especially in the Convention. The Commission Task Force was stocked up to twelve officials. Contacts were made and cultivated with important, often like-minded, actors, such as MEPs, particularly during the Convention, and the German and Dutch delegations during the IGC. At the Convention, it certainly helped that the Commission had been for some time the only party (apart from the Parliament itself and civil society) that had supported an enhanced role of the EP in trade policy. This made it 'even easier for many MEPs to support the Commission on more Community competences regarding trade'.[278] Without forming an open alliance, the preferences of the Commission and the EP complimented each other such that mutual support on trade policy was a natural corollary.

The Commission's approach and strategy in the subsequent Intergovernmental Conference was not to reopen the consensus reached during the Convention.[279] Due to the bonding strength of the Draft Constitutional Treaty, the Convention text was taken as the basis for further considerations on all non-institutional issues. On the whole, the consensus reached on the Common Commercial Policy was a solid one to which the various delegations, by and large, remained dedicated. Yet, with stronger domestic, especially bureaucratic, constraints than during the Convention, some delegations attempted to obtain further exceptions to QMV. During the IGC, the Commission particularly

---

[276] Interview, Brussels, 2004.   [277] Interview, Brussels, July 2004.
[278] Interview at the European Parliament, 2004.   [279] Commission (2003b).

collaborated with the governments of Germany and the Netherlands who became allies in preventing the CCP from being watered down. Avoiding a dilution of the Convention text on external trade relations was relatively easy at the IGC. Due to the bonding strength of the Convention provision (and the dynamics behind the extension of Article 133), the IGC negotiating infrastructure which facilitates defending the *status quo* and hampers enforcing change, for once, worked in the Commission's favour. Any changes to the provisions on the table had to be supported by very substantial political impetus.

The Role of the European Parliament   In contrast to past Treaty revision exercises, in the Convention the European Parliament managed to assert itself to a much greater extent. EP representatives in the Convention were, unlike during IGC negotiations, fully legitimate and equal participants, they were used to working in a parliamentary-like environment and they were familiar with the EU machinery. Overall, Parliament provided a very significant source of leadership for a more pro-integrative and simplified outcome,[280] also concerning the reform of the Common Commercial Policy. Apart from the afore-mentioned favourable starting position, the EP was influential at the Convention for a number of reasons. First, apart from the small Commission delegation, the sixteen representatives from the EP formed the most coherent and the best organised fraction of the Convention.[281] This is largely due to the fact that EP Convention members already possessed institutionalised and functioning working structures to prepare for meetings in the framework of the Convention.[282] As a result, large coalitions could be built with proposals signed or amendments backed by more than ten MEPs.[283] Second, representatives of the EP were, apart from the Commission representatives (on some issues), the most active fraction in the Convention in terms of making proposals, participating in the debate and liaising with other Convention members.[284] For example, they played a prominent role in the meetings of the political families which 'functioned as a catalyst for the advancement of good ideas and the rejection of bad ones'.[285]

More specifically on external trade policy, the mainstream of the EP delegation strongly supported a far-reaching extension of Community competences accompanied by a substantial augmentation of

---

[280] E.g. Beach (2005: 207–9).
[281] However, two of its members, Bonde and Muscardini, did not effectively form part of this group, due to their rather 'eurosceptic' views.
[282] On this point see Maurer (2003a: 137).   [283] Beach (2005: 208).
[284] See Duff (2003: 3).   [285] Duff (2003: 5, author's translation).

Parliament's involvement. On the latter issue the EP was successful for several reasons: first, in an open and reasoned debate, Parliaments' arguments were bound to make an impact. External trade was one of very few EC/EU policy areas in which the European Parliament had hardly any role. Given the Laeken declaration's emphasis on legitimacy, the EP's claim became even more convincing. Moreover, in view of the fact that public health and consumer issues were increasingly discussed at WTO level, a role for the European Parliament was all the more important. In addition, despite its virtual exclusion from the making of the Common Commercial Policy, Parliament had shown an active interest in trade policy over many years and generally taken a constructive approach. The EP was not usually far off from the EU mainstream and often showed understanding for Member States' concerns in its reports and resolutions.[286]

EP representatives strongly supported an extension of Community competences and QMV on external trade, while the Commission firmly backed co-decision for all CCP legislative acts. In the Working Group on External Action, MEPs actively pushed for a far-reaching reform of Article 133.[287] When Convention President Giscard d'Estaing sought to redraft the progressive CCP provisions of the Working Group report, it was the chairman of the Working Group Dehaene, decisively backed by EP representatives in the Praesidium Brok and de Vigo as well as Commissioner Vitorino who made sure that the external trade provisions were not watered down.[288]

In the dying days of the Convention, the EP turned into the strongest supporter of the Convention text and thus contributed to its bonding strength with regard to the subsequent IGC negotiations.[289] At the IGC following the Convention, the European Parliament was endowed with yet more rights in terms of participation. While the two EP participants at the Nice IGC were still 'observers', this time they were 'representatives' and had speaking rights on all issues. The two representatives Klaus Hänsch and Inigo Mendez de Vigo (later replaced by Elmar Brok) participated at every ministerial session, and Pat Cox, the President of the European Parliament, at each session at the level of Heads of State and Government. 'One can say that the European Parliament is now on the same level as the Commission [in terms of IGC participation rights]'.[290] The overall approach of the EP to the IGC was 'to respect the consensus reached by the

---

[286] See Bender (2002: esp.197–202); also cf. Smith and Woolcock (1999: 447).
[287] Interview, Brussels, July 2004.   [288] Interview, Brussels, 2004
[289] E.g. Beach (2005).   [290] Interview with Klaus Hänsch, Brussels, 2004.

Convention'.[291] The European Parliament thus became the Convention 'cheerleader' at the IGC.[292] As for the Common Commercial Policy, Parliament contributed to the Commission-led endeavour to prevent a thinning out of the CCP provisions, which was also supported by several Member States, including most outspokenly Germany and the Netherlands.

The Role of the Presidency   The role played by the various Presidencies had a moderate impact on the CCP outcome. The Belgian Presidency in the second half of 2001 was, along with the EP, the Commission and some Member States, a strong supporter of convening a Convention for the preparation of the IGC. The Belgian Presidency has particularly been credited for reaching agreement, despite considerable reservations, on a very broad mandate for the Convention.[293] External trade policy as well as many other policy areas would have probably fallen prey to a more restricted mandate.

Most assessments of the Italian Presidency during the second half of 2003 have been rather mixed or even downbeat.[294] 'Italy wasted precious time at the beginning of the Intergovernmental Conference denying the existence of deep divisions between the Member States'.[295] In addition, it has been suggested that the Italian Presidency should have held more extensive bilateral talks with delegations in the run-up of the Brussels summit.[296] At the summit itself, the Presidency has been criticised for having engaged almost exclusively in bilateral confessionals, that as a result there was too little time for discussion in the Plenary, that no real compromise was offered by the Italians and that what was offered came at a very late stage.[297] The Italian Prime Minister, Silvio Berlusconi, negatively affected the negotiations due to his over-confident style and lack of credibility.[298] These criticisms notwithstanding, the somewhat poor performance of the Italian Presidency only marginally reinforced the failure of the Brussels summit. More fundamental factors are behind the breakdown of negotiations, as we will see when considering countervailing factors below.

---

[291] European Parliament (2003b: 7).   [292] Beach (2005: 209).
[293] Göler (2002: 104) in particular has given credit to the Belgian Presidency for the broad mandate.
[294] E.g. Dinan (2004: 41); cf. Quaglia (2004: 47–8).   [295] Dinan (2004: 41).
[296] Reinhard Rack, at a conference of the Renner Institut on the IGC 2003–04, Vienna, 30 January 2004, conference summary, p. 2 (http://www.renner-institut.at/download/texte/eu-pb30.1.04.pdf last accessed on 15 July 2004).
[297] On these latter points see *Die Tageszeitung* (2003).
[298] Dinan (2004: 41); cf. Quaglia (2004: 47–48).

Finally, the Irish Presidency has been praised in terms of objectivity, organisation and leadership.[299] In contrast to the Italians, the Irish Presidency went on a 'tour of capitals' early on in order to gain a more complete picture of Member States' most substantial concerns. The Commission, with which the Irish held close contact, was invited to join the second phase of the tour. On this occasion, the Commission and the Presidency gained better insights into the real underlying concerns of the Swedish and Finnish governments regarding social, educational and health services in the area of the CCP. This facilitated the compromise derogation that is now in the Constitutional Treaty, which satisfies both the respective governments and the Commission (because of its narrow phrasing). Due to very good organisation, timing and leadership, the Irish also managed to successively close discussion on all but some few outstanding issues before the Brussels summit in June 2004, which made the final agenda manageable.[300] The Irish Presidency managed to successfully conclude the negotiations, albeit under considerably more favourable conditions than the Italian Presidency, as we will see below.

Countervailing Forces

During the Convention phase countervailing pressures were much weaker than during an Intergovernmental Conference. There are several reasons for this: first, due to the absence of inter-departmental co-ordination, representatives of national governments were not curbed by the influence of various functional ministries. Bureaucrats, who have been identified as important agents of sovereignty-consciousness and also constitute a principal source of domestic constraints, were thus largely shut out from the process. This change in the negotiating infrastructure has been recognised as 'a very important factor facilitating progressive agreements'.[301] Second, more generally, although the members arrived at the Convention with certain domestic or institutional socialisations and frames guiding their behaviour, all in all, they were able to negotiate freely without significant restrictions.[302] As a result, domestic factors – while constituting important sources of information and feedback mechanisms – were far less constraining for

---

[299] See e.g. Rees (2005: 56); cf. Dinan (2005: 39).   [300] Cf. Irish Presidency (2004).
[301] Interview, Brussels, 2004.
[302] The general freedom and independence of action has been confirmed by several interviewees, including Klaus Hänsch (Brussels, July 2004), and the following study: Maurer (2003a: 134–7). However, some few members of the Convention, such as UK parliamentarian Gisela Stuart, are said to have been under the influence of their governments.

members of the Convention than for negotiators in an IGC. Regarding external trade policy, the strongest countervailing pressures during the Convention were domestic constraints faced by (and through) French members on the issue of cultural diversity. This pressure mounted when the draft texts of April, May and June 2003 did not provide for a French cultural exception.[303] Largely as a result of this pressure, the Praesidium decided after the Thessaloniki European Council to include the cultural exception in the text, as otherwise it would have been very difficult for the French government to support the Draft Constitutional Treaty.

The greatly reduced countervailing pressures also had an impact, beyond the Convention, on the entire Treaty revision exercise. Due to the considerable bonding strength of the Convention described above, the results of the Convention had a much greater significance than normal IGC pre-negotiations or preparation exercises. When the IGC formally began in October 2003, countervailing pressures, for example through national ministries, gathered greater strength. As far as the Common Commercial Policy is concerned, these had little chance to register as the Convention text on Article 133 was, by and large, the result of a strong and genuine consensus, of which either Foreign Ministers (themselves) or representatives of Heads of State and Government had been part. Hence, the Convention text became the default. Given this situation, for countervailing forces to make an impact on the provisions, they had to be stronger than during normal/previous IGC negotiations. But on the whole, the countervailing forces which impacted on the CCP were weaker than during former IGCs. Distrust of the Commission had further waned, partly due to the replacement of Sir Leon Brittan by Pascal Lamy as Trade Commissioner, and partly because more than ten years had passed since the most controversial events during the Uruguay Round which had given rise to the significant distrust in the Commission. In addition, pressure from functional departments endangering the CCP compromise was less intense than during previous Treaty revisions. This is partly attributable to the fact that the IGC was largely conducted on the political level and partly because of the relative short duration of the IGC as a result of which it was more difficult for departments to have their voices heard in the formation of national positions.

The strongest countervailing pressure during the IGC on the CCP issue came from the Swedish and Finnish delegations. They sought (and obtained a narrow) exception to qualified majority voting in the field of

---

[303] On the public and media pressure in this period, see, for example, *Le Monde* (16/05/03; 13/06/03; 27/06/03).

trade in social, education and health services. The two delegations argued that their domestic high-quality provisions concerning these services could be prejudiced by an international agreement in these areas. The Swedish and Finnish reservations to QMV in these domains can be explained by a mix of sovereignty-consciousness and domestic constraints and diversities. The issue of trade in 'public' services was raised by various national Parliamentarians (from various parties) in the Finnish Parliament during the Convention and IGC and thus effectively tied the hands of the government, which of course needs to go through Parliament to ratify the Treaty. The Swedish situation was similar. The issue of social, education and health services became part of the Swedish IGC paper and was approved by the Swedish Parliament. In addition, the (ideological and sovereignty-conscious) maxim that public services should remain in state control was widely accepted in the Swedish government (less so by the Conservative opposition). In addition, the new Finnish government led by the Centre Party was perhaps less Europhile than the Lipponen government, certainly with regard to the issue of external trade competences, and thus took a more sovereignty-conscious approach.[304]

The IGC as a whole threatened to fail during the autumn and winter of 2003–04 due to unsuccessful bargaining on the larger institutional questions and particularly on the issue of Council voting. As failure to resolve this conflict would have also brought down the revision of external trade policy, the substantial countervailing pressures jeopardising the entire Constitutional Treaty shall be briefly looked at. Due to scope limitations, I will concentrate on what was by far the greatest conflict, i.e. the issue of Council voting and the positions of Spain and Poland which blocked agreement by strongly objecting to the double majority proposed in the Convention text on this issue. Both countries sought to stick to the Nice provisions which gave them, in the view of many observers, a disproportionate amount of votes in the Council. Polish resistance, which was the more fervent one, can largely be attributed to a mixture of strong sovereignty-consciousness and significant domestic constraints. As for the latter aspect, the government of Leszek Millar was under very strong domestic pressure.[305] Millar was leading a minority government and was dependent on EU-critical opposition for the implementation of crucial legislation. Pressure from the parliamentary opposition to defend the Nice formula was reinforced by strong public and media pressures. This led

---

[304] Interview (by telephone), 2004.
[305] On domestic pressures facing the Millar government see Kranz (2003: 7ff).

to the dictum 'Nice or Death' which the government indirectly accepted due to the pressure that was mounted on it. Second, after four partitions in the country's history and forty-five years under Soviet influence, there was a widespread scepticism and suspicion as regards giving up part of Poland's recently recuperated sovereignty. And the Convention formula was interpreted as a further loss of Polish national sovereignty, even as a 'threat to the independence of the Polish nation'.[306]

Sovereignty-consciousness and, to a lesser extent, domestic constraints provide important insights for explaining the position taken and the role played by Spain during the IGC. For the Spanish government, the Convention formula meant shedding more sovereignty, as it aggravated Spain's ability to block decisions under qualified majority voting. The Aznar government's sentiments were increased by Spain's augmented foreign policy profile[307], which was supposed to be accompanied by an according representation in the Council. Moreover, the Spanish position on the issue of Council voting was reinforced by Aznar's personal ideological (national interest) disposition. Domestic constraints were present in the form of the Spanish economy's reliance on EU funds from the Union's structural and agricultural policies. In order to safeguard, to some extent, Spanish influence on these (for Spain) vital policies , the Nice formula was sought to be kept. That these countervailing pressures largely pertained to the Aznar government's perception can be seen by the relative ease with which the Zapatero government could change the Spanish position. Contrary to the Polish case, sovereignty-consciousness was not a structural pressure but one which was more confined to Aznar, most of his government and part of the political elite. Countervailing pressures decreased significantly after the Spanish election, as the Zapatero government held different ideological views and felt less constrained by domestic factors. Being isolated and also facing more critical media coverage[308], the Polish government became more induced to alter its position on the issue of the Council voting system, which made agreement on the Constitutional Treaty possible in June 2004.

---

[306]   *Warsaw Voice* (05/05/03).

[307]   On the increased Spanish foreign policy weight see, for example: *Frankfurter Allgemeine Zeitung* (21/09/03: 12).

[308]   On the changing media coverage in Poland, see, for example: *Frankfurter Allgemeine Zeitung* (12/12/03: 3).

Conclusion

The outcome of the last Treaty revision can be aptly explained by taking account of the dynamics pushing for an extension of the Common Commercial Policy and the factors resisting such dynamics. After the partial reform of Article 133 during the Intergovernmental Conference 2000, spillover pressures had gathered further strength. Functional spillover pressures, particularly through enlargement, and exogenous spillover, creating pressure from a changing world economy and an evolving world trade agenda, provided important structural pressures. These two structural pressures were reinforced by political and, more importantly, cultivated spillover. In contrast to the past two CCP Treaty revisions, cultivated spillover pressures played an enhanced role. These were important in terms of activating and initiating functional and exogenous spillover arguments, supporting and pushing the Convention idea in the first place and by asserting, more generally, their institutional (integrative) interests.

An important link between these structural and agency pressures was social spillover. Convincing arguments built on the exogenous and functional spillover rationales could register with actors due to important processes of socialisation, deliberation and arguing. Social spillover can also largely explain the bonding strength of the Convention text, which came about due to learning processes and participants' (including Member States' representatives') concurrence with the results. Given the strong overall support of the Draft Constitutional Treaty, the basic default condition at the subsequent IGC to some extent changed from one in which a far-reaching solution would not happen in the event of no agreement (as in the case of a 'normal' IGC preparation exercise) to one where the progressive outcome would persist unless a strong fraction of Member States seek to reopen the issue. This partly/largely explains the relative ease with which many aspects of the Convention text survived the IGC, including the negotiations on external trade policy and on visa, asylum and immigration policy.[309]

The story would be incomplete without considering countervailing pressures. On the whole, spillback forces were (substantially) weaker than at the Amsterdam and Nice Intergovernmental Conferences. This facilitated the stronger ignition and dissemination of integrational

---

[309] The changing default condition has been pointed out in my methodology section of Chapter 1 (section concerning the specification of variables) as an important intervening variable. This altered variable has thus been flagged and also been incorporated in my estimation of key causal variables for this sub-case as well as the Convention/IGC 2003–04 sub-case within the next chapter.

dynamics. Wherever countervailing forces were strong – as in the case of France on the issue of cultural diversity, or as regards Sweden and Finland on social, education and health services – they also made an impact. It has also been important to consider the broader countervailing pressures that threatened overall agreement at the last IGC. Wider countervailing forces also continue to accompany the ratification process of the Constitutional Treaty, which after the referendums in France and in the Netherlands has been seriously set back.

4 Negotiations on the Communitarisation of Visa, Asylum and Immigration Policy

Visa, Asylum and Immigration Policy

Visa, asylum and immigration which form part of the wider policy field of justice and home affairs (JHA) are relatively new areas of European policy-making. The original text of the Treaty of Rome did not contain any provisions on the co-ordination or harmonisation of visa, asylum and immigration matters. The necessity to deal with these issues in a European context was first mentioned in the Tindemans Report of 1975. However, it received more significant attention during discussions concerning the elimination of internal border controls, following the European Council in Fontainebleau in June 1984. As a result, the Single European Act of 1986, which mandated the creation of an area without internal frontiers, was accompanied by a political declaration stipulating co-operation in matters of entry and stay of third-country nationals.[1] To continue discussions on compensatory measures necessary for the abolition of frontier controls, the Ad Hoc Group on Immigration was set up in 1986 which, as its greatest success, conducted negotiations leading to the signing of the Dublin Convention of 1990. With the Maastricht Treaty, asylum and immigration as well as most of visa policy came into the Union framework, which attributed this policy to the sphere of intergovernmental co-operation within the third pillar of the Treaty on European Union (TEU). Only two aspects of visa policy in Article 100c came into the EC Treaty.[2] However, under Article K.9 (the *passerelle* provision) there was the possibility of bringing JHA issues into the Community sphere if the members of the Council unanimously agreed to do so, but this provision was never used. With the entering into force of the Amsterdam Treaty in May 1999, policy on visa, asylum and

---

[1] Nanz (1994).

[2] Article 100c has empowered the Community, acting unanimously and after consultation of the European Parliament, to determine the third countries whose nationals require a visa in order to enter the Community. Since 1 January 1996 the Council acts by qualified majority on these issues.

187

immigration became part of the Community framework. The Treaty of Nice which is in force since February 2003 brought about rather complex (potential) alterations of decision rules. These, however, resulted in only very modest steps towards further deepening them. By contrast, in the Constitutional Treaty Member States agreed on substantial supranationalisation of decision rules by introducing the Community method into almost all areas of visa, asylum and immigration policy.

There are several reasons for choosing the IGC negotiations concerning visa, asylum and immigration policy as a case study. Empirically as well as theoretically it is an interesting case, not least because justice and home affairs have been described 'as a possibly decisive battlefield in the struggle between the predominance of the nation-state and supranational integration in Europe'.[3] While close to the heart of national sovereignty and thus thought of as one of the least suitable fields for the workings of the spillover logic,[4] it has arguably become the most dynamic area of European integration. In addition, after having tested neofunctionalism in the area of external relations, we are now looking at the internal[5] dimension of EU policy-making. As pointed out by Caporaso, it is more impressive if a theory holds across diverse settings.[6] From a methodological point of view, the IGC negotiations on visa, asylum and immigration policy constitute a valuable case: it increases the spectrum of values on the dependent variable by providing for two sub-cases with progressive results and one sub-case with a rather minimal decision outcome. As pointed out in Chapter 1, more can be learned about the strength of our independent variables when we examine cases with varying outcomes. The subsequent sections will analyse the results of the three sub-cases and particularly the factors accounting for variation.

The Intergovernmental Conference 1996–97

The Provisions of Amsterdam

The changes brought about through the Amsterdam Treaty[7] begin with a redefinition of one of the Union's principle objectives in Article B. While the old Article B sought to 'develop close cooperation on justice and home affairs', the Amsterdam provision is much fuller and more

---

[3] Monar (1998a: 137).   [4] Cf. Hoffmann (1964, 1995).
[5] Of course, the visa, asylum and immigration policy also has external implications (cf. e.g. Monar 2004b).
[6] Caporaso (1995: 457–60).
[7] This section can only summarise the provisions of Amsterdam. For a full account see Council (1997a, b, c).

specific. It describes the Union as 'an area of freedom, security and justice, in which the free movement of persons is assured in conjunction with appropriate measures with respect to external border controls, immigration, asylum and the prevention and combating of crimes'. With the Amsterdam Treaty the old third pillar has been divided into two parts: the first part, which constitutes the focus of this analysis, became Title IV of the TEC on 'visa, asylum and other policies related to the free movement of persons' which shifted into the community sphere. The second part, the substantially reduced third pillar (Title VI TEU), is composed of police and judicial co-operation in criminal matters and remains largely intergovernmental. The new Title IV TEC did not immediately create 'an area of freedom, security and justice', but rather established mechanisms and a timetable for the progressive establishment of such an area.

Article 61 of Title IV constitutes a general obligation on the Council to adopt – within a period of five years after the entry into force of the Amsterdam Treaty – the necessary flanking measures aimed at ensuring the free movement of persons. Article 62 established a five-year timetable for the Council to adopt measures to abolish any controls on persons, regardless of whether they are citizens of the Union or third-country nationals, and to agree on measures to harmonise the control regime applying at the external frontiers of the Union, including visa rules. Article 63 established a five-year timetable for new measures on asylum, refugees and displaced persons, and immigration policy. The actual content of the measures to be taken was not specified, but the main thrust in each case was to establish minimum standards, rather than – as intended earlier throughout the Conference – common rules, for the treatment of immigrants, asylum seekers and refugees.[8] Article 64 states: 'This title shall not affect the exercise of the responsibilities incumbent upon Member States with regard to the maintenance of law and order and the safeguarding of internal security'. 'The legal significance of this Article as a possible counterbalance to the preceding article is not explicit, but it was clearly not intended to contradict the commitment to abolish internal border controls'.[9] Article 65 stipulates measures in the field of judicial co-operation in civil matters having cross-border implications. Article 66 provides the Council with a legal basis to ensure co-operation between the administrations of the Member States and the Commission.

Article 67 is concerned with voting rules and the powers of Commission and Parliament on the above provisions: during a five-year

---

[8] Cf. Duff (1997).   [9] Dodd *et al.* (1997: 14).

transitional period decisions are taken by unanimity in the Council on an initiative of either the Commission or a Member State and after consultation of the European Parliament. Five years after the entering into force of the Treaty, the Commission is to obtain an exclusive right of initiative. At the end of the transitional period the Council decides unanimously whether all or part of the areas of the new title will be decided by qualified majority and co-decision. After five years the Council may also review the provisions relating to the Court of Justice.

The provisions on short-term visa issues form an exception: the list of third countries whose nationals must be in possession of visas and a uniform format for visas is decided by QMV after a proposal from the Commission and after consultation of the EP. After the five-year period provisions on procedures for issuing visas by Member States and rules for a uniform visa would automatically be taken by QMV and co-decision, on a proposal of the Commission.

Article 68 deals with the role of the Court of Justice. It limits the application of Article 234 (ex Article 177) concerning references by national courts to the Court for preliminary rulings on questions of Community law. Only the highest national courts are entitled to refer cases to the Court of Justice for preliminary ruling. The ECJ has no jurisdiction over internal border control measures relating to the maintenance of law and order and the safeguarding of internal security. The Commission and Member States are entitled to seek rulings from the Court on questions of interpretation of Title IV. However, they cannot use this power to re-open judgements already made by the courts of the Member States.

Article 69 makes the whole of Title IV subject to the two Protocols concerning the United Kingdom and Ireland and the Protocol on the position of Denmark. The title does not in principle apply to the United Kingdom and Ireland. However, both countries may choose on a case-by-case basis to participate in certain initiatives. The Council decides by unanimity whether or not to accept the involvement of the United Kingdom or Ireland.[10] Moreover, the Council may adopt a measure without the United Kingdom and Ireland if it has been proven impossible to adopt it with them within a reasonable period. Ireland, as opposed to the United Kingdom, has the option of revoking the Protocol in order to participate fully. The two countries have negotiated the right to maintain border controls.[11] Denmark has a general opt-out

---

[10] See Amsterdam Treaty, Protocol on the Position of the United Kingdom and Ireland.
[11] See Amsterdam Treaty, Protocol on the Application of Certain Aspects of Article 7a of the Treaty Establishing the European Community to the United Kingdom and to Ireland.

from the new Community framework, except for some aspects of visas.[12] However, as Denmark has since become a signatory to Schengen, it can decide to implement measures that build upon the Schengen *acquis*.[13] Denmark is entitled to withdraw from all or part of the provisions of the Protocol at any time.[14]

Different Interpretations of the Value and Progressiveness of the New Provisions Interpretations of the progress made through the new provisions of Amsterdam vary depending on the benchmark that is used. First, compared with the *ex-ante* practice, almost all observers have asserted that Amsterdam marked a significant advancement. It has been remarked, for example, that Amsterdam 'certainly is a net gain',[15] or 'decisive progress'[16] or even 'a substantial qualitative leap'.[17] All Community institutions have gained powers, for some analysts they are even 'big winners'.[18] The *rapporteurs* of the European Parliament on the Amsterdam Treaty noted that 'before the Maastricht Treaty there were no issues more characteristic of the governmental sphere of activity than justice and home affairs, which were regarded as attributes of national sovereignty. While the EU Treaty enshrined intergovernmental co-operation between the Member States, the Amsterdam Treaty signifies a shift towards integrationism through communitarisation'.[19]

Second, judged against the expectations held prior to the IGC, Title IV should be viewed as a real achievement, given Member States' reluctance to use the '*passerelle*' provision, the (at best) mediocre overall integrative climate and the fact that no provision in Title VI of the Maastricht Treaty expressly provided for revision in 1996.[20] O'Keeffe and van Outrive, for example, thought that a communitarisation of third pillar issues would be unlikely.[21] And Michiel Patijn concluded after the IGC that the Intergovernmental Conference had succeeded in transferring asylum, visa and immigration policies to the first Pillar 'against all odds'.[22]

---

[12] See Amsterdam Treaty, Protocol on the Position of Denmark.   [13] Petite (1998a).
[14] It should also be mentioned that the Schengen system has been incorporated into the Community legal order by means of a protocol annexed to the Treaty. It provides for the unification of two parallel legal systems (Petite 1997: 9). This was done by 'gluing' Schengen 'in an ungainly manner onto both the first and third pillar' (Duff 1997: 53). With the integration of part of the Schengen *acquis* into the first pillar, there has been a very significant overlap between Articles 61–69 TEC and those Schengen provisions that went into the Community pillar.
[15] Brinkhorst (1997: 49).   [16] Brok (1997b: 377).   [17] Schnappauff (1998: 17).
[18] Rupprecht (1997: 269).   [19] European Parliament (1997b: 24).
[20] Bieber (1995: 384).   [21] See O'Keeffe (1995b: 895); Van Outrive (1995).
[22] Patijn (1997: 38).

Third, compared with the institutional demands and requirements necessary to meet the Union's objectives, the Amsterdam Treaty seems to have brought mixed or moderately positive results. Most commentators agree that the failure to switch to QMV on a broader scale has been the greatest deficiency of the IGC provisions concerning asylum, immigration and external borders. Monar has pointed out that majority voting would only become possible after five years 'if – and this is a big if – this move finds unanimous backing in the Council'.[23] Hence, it has been concluded, the unanimity requirement 'creates the risk that the progress noted above will be virtual rather than real [...and] the revisited Pillar III remains a half-way house'.[24] However, there have been more optimistic voices emphasising that the shift to QMV, if it comes, would not require another IGC. Moreover, for some QMV looks like a 'postponed certainty'.[25] Müller-Graf even concludes that 'the changes reflect the demands for reform within the scholarly community'.[26] The truth is probably that it was at the time 'premature to predict whether effective results in the field of justice and home affairs [could] be achieved' from the new decision rules.[27]

Fourth, measured against the various other options considered during the work of the Reflection Group and the Intergovernmental Conference, the outcome achieved at Amsterdam must be considered as progressive. Many different scenarios were brought up and discussed during the IGC.[28] With increasing level of ambition and progressiveness they were the following: (A) the *status quo*. This implied waiting for more experience with the existing third pillar before proceeding with further institutional changes. This view was not seriously held by any delegation, except perhaps the United Kingdom at some stages. (B) Strengthening the co-operation arrangements provided for in the old Title VI of the TEU without fundamentally changing their nature or scope. This was the line taken by the United Kingdom and Denmark. The proposals for reform in that respect were very modest. The most 'far-reaching' suggestion was to reduce the number of decision-making levels.[29] (C) A 'new Third Pillar'. This implied no (explicit) transfer of competencies to the Community pillar, but the use of certain Community elements, ranging from closer involvement of the EP and a greater role for the Court to a super-qualified majority in the Council on

---

[23] Monar (1998a: 138). Also cf. Moravcsik and Nicolaïdis (1998).
[24] Brinkhorst (1997: 49).   [25] Kiso (1999: 262).
[26] Müller-Graf (1997: 271; author's translation).
[27] European Policy Centre (1997a: 114).
[28] E.g. Italian Presidency (1996); European Parliament (1995c).
[29] United Kingdom Government (1996a).

some issues. Variations on this were manifold. This type of option seems to have been supported, at least at times, by Ireland, Sweden, Spain and France.[30] (D) 'Pillar I bis'. This was a proposal by the French government which fell well short of real communitarisation by limiting the role of the Community institutions. It also sought to introduce a body consisting of national parliaments into the Union as a second parliamentary chamber. This option was at times also supported by Denmark.[31] (E) Communitarisation of certain areas, while restricting the use of some Community methods. This scenario was often linked to the 'timetable solution',[32] which sought to introduce, or at least envisage amendments for a later stage. The new provisions on Title IV TEC would fall into that category. Germany, although previously prepared to go further, was the single most persistent advocate of this solution at the Amsterdam summit, supported by Austria. (F) The final option was a full-fledged communitarisation of visa, asylum and immigration policies. This option was supported by the Benelux countries, the Commission and the European Parliament. Measuring the outcome along the lines of other possible options highlights that the Amsterdam provisions of Title IV were indeed far-reaching.

Finally, compared with other provisions of the Treaty of Amsterdam – like the very modest improvements on institutional matters and CFSP – visa, asylum and immigration fared very well, despite strong countervailing pressures and pessimistic expectations. The new Title IV was considered by many 'the main improvement'[33] or 'the most important area of reform in the Amsterdam Treaty'[34]. In general, therefore, despite the only mixed or moderately positive results obtained by Amsterdam in view of the challenges facing the Community, the 1996–7 IGC has brought about significant progress through Title IV, compared with prior expectations and other provisions of the Treaty, and perhaps more importantly when measured against the provisions of the Maastricht Treaty and other options considered at the Amsterdam IGC. Hence, in overall terms, the outcome is judged here as a far-reaching one.

Functional Spillover

This section essentially argues that functional pressures, stemming from the objective of free movement of persons, constitute the most important dynamic for the communitarisation of external border control, asylum and immigration policy at the 1996–97 IGC. In a nutshell, the

---

[30] Interviews, Brussels, 1998–99.   [31] Kiso (1999: 124).   [32] Bieber (1995: 386).
[33] Hoyer (1997: 71).   [34] Müller-Graf (1997: 271).

argument goes as follows: in order to realise the free movement of persons, certain flanking measures have to be taken in the areas of external border control, asylum and immigration policy to compensate for the elimination of intra-EU borders.

The Free Movement of Persons   Already in the Treaty of Rome the free movement of persons was inscribed as one of the principles on which the Community is based. Article 3c contains the famous 'four freedoms', and talks about 'an internal market characterised by the abolition [...] of obstacles to the free movement of goods, persons, services and capital'. The idea of abolishing border controls at the Community's internal frontiers has been on the agenda since the Tindemans report of 1975. It proposed the abolition of border controls as one of the measures to make the Community more of a reality for its citizens.[35] The adoption of the Schengen Agreement on the gradual abolition of controls at the common frontiers by five Member States in 1985, and the SEA of 1986, aiming for the realisation of an internal market by the end of 1992, prompted renewed debate on the subject, and reinforced the objective of a free movement of persons. Article 8a (now Article 18 TEC), introduced by the SEA, provides for an 'internal market [which] shall comprise an area without internal frontiers in which the free movement of ... persons ... is ensured ... '. The progression from Article 3c marked a *'double saut qualitatif'*.[36] First, there was now a definition of what those barriers to the free movement of persons were. Prior to that, it had been unclear as to whether or not being stopped at a border in order to prove one's identity constituted a barrier to free movement. Second, a deadline was set, by which time this objective was to have been realised. The principle of free movement of persons was further reiterated by the Maastricht Treaty where it was stated as the primary objective for co-operation in the field of justice and home affairs (Article K.1). Moreover, outside the Community framework, the principle was strengthened through the signing and entering into force of the Schengen convention in 1990 and 1995 respectively by an increasing number of Member States.[37]

There are several reasons for attaching such significance to the free movement of persons. First, it is arguably this freedom which has the most direct bearing on the lives of individual citizens amongst the four freedoms.[38] Closely related to this point, Hoogenboom has argued that

---

[35] Donner (1993).
[36] On this and the following point see de Lobkowicz (1994: 101–2).
[37] See den Boer (1997b).   [38] See Fortescue (1995: 28).

'if the internal market were regarded merely as a form of economic co-operation in the narrow sense of the word, it would be difficult to justify a common attempt to achieve integration'. However, 'the rules that govern the internal market are expressly concerned with more far-reaching interests than purely economic ones'.[39]

Second, as argued by the Commission in its *White Paper on the Internal Market*, from an economic perspective, the proper working of the internal market would be jeopardised, unless this principle were to be put into practice. 'The reason for getting rid of [...] controls between Member States is [...] the hard practical fact that the maintenance of any internal frontier controls will perpetuate the costs and disadvantages of a divided market'.[40] The abolition of border controls are important to business, as controls impose an unnecessary burden on industry due to delays, formalities, transport and handling charges, thus adding to costs and damaging European competitiveness.[41]

Third, the free movement of persons needs to be translated into reality in order to avoid further discrimination of non-EC nationals. One of the dominant legal norms in both the Community and the Member States would otherwise be infringed, i.e. the prohibition of discrimination. It is worth mentioning in this context that there has been a long-standing debate as to whether the free movement of persons also applies to third-country nationals. The Commission pointed out that the phrase ' ... free movement of [...] persons' in Article 8a EEC Treaty referred to all persons whether or not they are economically active and irre-spective of their nationality.[42] This view was shared by the European Parliament[43] and a large majority of Member States and most legal writers.[44] Some Member States, in particular the United Kingdom and Denmark regularly rejected this interpretation of Article 8a and held that the free movement was confined to EC nationals and that limited documentation checks on persons entering any of these countries from another Member State were compatible with Article 8a.[45]

It is also worth pointing out that the functional link between the free movement of persons on the one hand, and common/co-ordinated immigration and asylum policies on the other could go both ways. Not only does the prospective free movement of persons require certain

---

[39] Hoogenboom (1993: 503).   [40] Commission (1985: 6).   [41] Butt Philip (1994: 171).
[42] Commission (1992b).   [43] European Parliament (1993a: 13).
[44] E.g. Timmermans (1993).
[45] With the Amsterdam Treaty this debate seems to have been settled in favour of the Commission interpretation (Dodd *et al.* 1997), as the new Article 62 talks about the abolishment of 'any controls on persons, be they citizens of the Union or nationals of third countries, when crossing the borders'.

flanking measures, as has been commonly held, it has also been argued that the absence of such flanking measures postponed the free movement of persons indefinitely.[46] The two arguments can be viewed as two sides of the same coin.[47]

Spillover Pressures Arising from the Abolition of Border Controls
Eradicating the internal borders of the Community is more a political than a technical problem. In theory, it is possible to abolish internal border controls without any compensation in the form of co-operation in the areas of external border controls, asylum and immigration. Member States could pursue a policy of continuously decreasing the intensity and effectiveness of their frontier controls, at the price of a diminished capacity to protect essential public interests or at the price of increased controls inside their own territory which are, however, more costly and less efficacious.[48]

The most obvious functional link is between the abolition of internal borders and increased co-operation in terms of external border controls. States are unlikely to waive the power of internal controls, unless they can be provided with an equivalent protection with regard to persons arriving at the external frontiers. In the words of Statewatch, there is an 'intrinsic' relationship between the abolition of intra-Union border controls of persons and the crossing of external borders[49], not least because it is difficult to conceive of systematic internal border checks which allow nationals of Member States to pass blindly and which would still include controls of third-country nationals.[50] Hailbronner has made the link to visa policy. He notes that, if one is prepared to accept that the Internal Market requires the abolition of internal border controls, this necessitates a shifting of border controls to the external borders and also a common visa policy, regulating short-term admission to EC territory.[51] This is echoed by statements of Member States' politicians, such as Michel Barnier, the French 1996–97 IGC Representative, who claimed that illegal immigration had increasingly come about through false tourists and false students. Once they were legally inside the European Union, they were relatively free to move between the Member States. Hence, the European Union had to respond by

---

[46] Müller-Graf (1997: 272).
[47] Guiraudon (2000: 254f.) somewhat contests the free movement/internal market logic because it stems from the *future* planning of the single market. Elsewhere, I have argued (in greater depth) that functional rationales also tend to work *in anticipation of upcoming* necessities or pressures (cf. Niemann 2000: 14–15).
[48] Donner (1993: 8).   [49] Statewatch (1999).   [50] As D'Oliveira (1994: 266).
[51] Hailbronner (1994: 982–3).

putting into place uniform visas, requiring comparable rigour in terms of entry conditions.[52]

The functional link to immigration and asylum policy is also a strong one. In order to create a common external frontier for the internal market, common policies on immigrants, asylum seekers and refugees are necessary. Otherwise, the restrictive efforts of one Member State, for example, would be undermined by diverging (liberal) policies of other Member States, as 'the free movement of persons also means free movement of illegal immigrants' or rejected asylum seekers.[53] The need for uniform criteria of jurisdiction became apparent in view of the fact that within Western Europe an estimated 30 per cent of all applicants were seeking asylum in more than one European country, and that a significant proportion of rejected asylum seekers stayed in the country as illegal immigrants.[54] With the elimination of controls at internal Community borders, the detrimental effects of insufficiently co-ordinated measures to execute asylum policies would be multiplied for the Community. Unlawful migration to another country and the disappearance of dismissed applicants for asylum would be made easier, along with the danger of people taking advantage of different regulations and undercutting national immigration rules.[55] Thus, following this logic, national solutions were no longer sufficient, as 'they would ask too much of the individual state'.[56]

The Dublin Convention in September 1997, to some extent, tackled the problem of asylum shopping (i.e. asylum applications in several countries).[57] However, by determining the first entry state as the one having to deal with the application of an asylum seeker, this provision created a (serious) problem of arbitrariness, given Member States' differing standards of reception and varying interpretation of the refugee status. As a result, minimum standards on the reception of asylum seekers were necessary. This is reflected in the Amsterdam provisions laid down in Article 63 concerning minimum standards on the reception of asylum seekers in Member States, minimum standards with respect to the qualification of nationals of third countries as refugees and minimum standards on procedures in Member States for granting or withdrawing refugee status. In order to arrive at this and other flanking

---

[52] Michel Barnier (1995 : 8); Hix and Niessen (1996: 11).
[53] de Lobkowicz (1994: 104).   [54] Hailbronner (1992: 923).
[55] See Hailbronner (1992: 921).   [56] Schelter (1996: 21–2).
[57] Yet, neither the Dublin Convention, nor the Regulation 343/2003 replacing it ('Dublin II'), may be wholly successful in terms of reducing multiple applications or secondary movements within the European Union. Cf., for example: Immigration Law Practitioners' Association (2001).

measures a greater degree of Community methods and legal instruments was required, so as to make co-operation more efficacious, to enable co-operation to move beyond the lowest common denominator and to avoid lengthy national ratification processes. In short, a communitarisation of this policy area was necessary.

Functional Pressure from within: the Deficiencies of the Third Pillar Preventing Effective Co-operation   For conceptual purposes one distinction should be highlighted again here. One can distinguish between pressures – resulting from the dissatisfaction of collective goal attainment – inducing (further) integrational steps in other policy areas, and pressures generating increased co-operation in the same field. To distinguish these two phenomena, the former has been referred to as (functional) 'spillover pressure', and the latter one as (functional) 'pressure from within'. So far we have talked about functional spillover in the former sense, i.e. the resolution of dissatisfaction (non-realisation of free movement of persons) by resorting to collaboration in another area (JHA). However, there is also a case to be made for functional 'pressure from within'. At the time when the debate on the revision of the Maastricht Treaty started, Member States had co-operated on matters of asylum and immigration policy in a largely intergovernmental fashion, for about a decade. Since the creation of the third pillar, especially, an integrated scheme for collaboration in matters of justice and home affairs had been in place. Despite the existing goal of the provision of flanking measures concerning the free movement of people, effective and successful co-operation gradually became an end in itself.[58] From that perspective, the considerable (structural and institutional) weaknesses of the third pillar, which will be elaborated below, became a major stumbling block towards effective co-operation, thus creating functional problems from within.

There has been an overwhelming consensus in the literature concerning the 'failure' of the third pillar in the run-up to the Amsterdam IGC. According to this general view, the JHA pillar contained 'major weaknesses' and 'glaring defects'.[59] It 'has not worked efficiently'[60] and 'surprisingly little has been achieved', both in terms of the provision of flanking measures and in terms of the more diffuse objective of effective JHA co-operation in itself.[61] The most important flaws of the third pillar

---

[58] Interview, Brussels, 1999. Cf. also Monar (2001b). This is also reflected in the wording of the TEU. Title I, Article B which defines the Union's objectives, states, in a rather general way, as the fourth objective 'to develop close co-operation on justice and home affairs'.

[59] O'Keeffe (1995b: 919).   [60] Justus Lipsius (1995: 249).   [61] O'Keeffe (1995b).

can be summarised as follows: first, there have been overlapping competencies between the first pillar and the third pillar. For instance, the rules governing the crossing of external borders (Article K.1(2) TEU) are closely linked to the abolition of internal borders in the internal market and the EC competencies in the area of visa policy. A communitarisation of issues where there is such a link to existing EC competencies promised to increase the efficiency of measures and the coherence of action taken by the Union.[62]

Second, the legal instruments of the third pillar – joint positions and the promotion of joint co-operation, joint action and conventions – which had largely been taken over from the CFSP, were widely regarded as flawed. For example, there was some uncertainty concerning the legal effect, particularly concerning joint actions.[63] Problems were also caused by conventions, the only undisputed legally binding instrument, as they not only have to be agreed by consensus but also have to be ratified by Member States according to national procedures, which may imply a referendum.[64] These difficulties had the effect of a 'downward spiral'. Member States tended to tone down their ambitions and to use instruments which were of a lesser binding nature, such as joint positions, as well as instruments which had no official stature in the JHA pillar, such as recommendations, protocols, conclusions and declarations.[65] As a result, no convention had entered into force before the conclusion of the Amsterdam IGC, while much of the other work done in the area consists of non-binding resolutions. With the transfer of matters to the first pillar, use could be made of the time-tested and well-tried Community instruments, so the argument went. Regulations are directly applicable, and while in many cases directives are needed, which are implemented by the Member States themselves, there are deadlines for implementation.[66] Faster progress could thus be expected on implementing the flanking measures set out in Title IV.

Third, the unanimity requirement was always assumed to have been a severe obstacle to the adoption of measures under the third pillar. The qualified majority voting option, through the '*passerelle*' provision (Article K.9), which allowed the Council, acting unanimously, to bring issues within the scope of the Community, was very difficult to invoke,

---

[62] Monar (1997).   [63] O'Keeffe (1995b).   [64] den Boer (1997a: 505).
[65] den Boer (1997a).
[66] Interview, Brussels, 1999. Moreover, another advantage of the Community approach, which is worth mentioning in this context, is the potential use of Article 169 TEC, through which the Commission may bring a case against a Member State before the Court, in case of faulty or insufficient implementation of a directive or an obligation under the Treaty (interview, Brussels, 1999).

and in fact never had been, because it was subject to a 'double-lock' procedure, requiring unanimity at Council level (in order to invoke it) and unanimous ratification by Member States. The restrictions affecting the use of the *passerelle* were serious, as this was the Article which had always been pointed to as proof of the dynamic nature of the third pillar, and had been particularly relied upon by those who saw it as a 'cure' for the defects of the third pillar.[67] Under the provisions of Amsterdam, the introduction of QMV became subject to a unanimous decision by the Council after five years, which makes it far from certain that the unanimity problem will be remedied. However, for those areas transferred to the first pillar, the absence of QMV is less grave than before, since several other benefits of communitarisation, such as Community instruments and judicial review, can be reaped automatically, without any *passerelle* required. Yet, in terms of QMV, functional pressures have only partially been acted upon.

Fourth, the third pillar essentially lacks a generalised system of judicial review.[68] As the third pillar affects individual rights, a strong claim could thus be made to seek judicial review in the areas covered by it. Failure to do so would leave the Union open to the charge that in areas governed by the third pillar it does not provide for an adequate system of legal remedies, that it is not a system governed by the rule of law and that individual rights are not adequately protected.[69] The pressure at work here seems to be a functional one, not from another sector but from within the same sector. The third pillar provides a (significant) integrational step for visa, asylum and immigration policy, but one which is dysfunctional due to the lack of judicial review it created; it constitutes a 'half-way house', a situation in which the first integrational step of bringing JHA under the pillar structure of the Union needed to be followed by another one, namely greater jurisdiction of the Court of Justice over (certain) third pillar matters.[70]

Fifth, under Article K.4, the Commission was supposed to be fully associated with the work of Title VI. However, it was in fact 'quite unclear to what extent the Commission is actually associated with the work in the third pillar, and with the work of the K.4 Committee .... It has been suggested that the Commission has the status of *observateur privilégié*. If this is so, it would scarcely seem to meet the requirement of Article K4(2) ... '.[71] Due to the generally greater effectiveness associated with the involvement of the Commission in EC decision-making – for example in terms of its better overview of legislation, growing

---

[67] O'Keeffe (1995b: 900).   [68] Drüke (1995).   [69] O'Keeffe (1995c).
[70] Cf. Hailbronner (1992: 937).   [71] O'Keeffe (1995b: 903).

expertise and its strategic position being centrally located within a web of policy networks[72] – there was some pressure towards greater involvement of the Commission 'not as a privileged observer, but as an actor in the process'.[73] Moreover, under the provisions of Title VI of the TEU, the Commission had a non-exclusive right of initiative in the areas referred to in Article K.1 (1) to (6), hence including external borders, asylum and immigration. Although this provided already greater impetus than giving no right of initiative to the Commission, there is reason to believe that the classic Community method provides for greater effectiveness and consistency. For example, as Horst-Günter Krenzler and Fraser Cameron argued with respect to the CFSP at a conference in Brussels in 1997[74], a shared right of initiative tends to have the effect that nobody feels responsible to provide some impetus.[75] Finally, as Krenzler and Schneider have pointed out with regard to CFSP, a non-exclusive right of initiative for the Commission means that responsibility for greater consistency in the Union's policy is shared between the Commission and the Council which 'is not an ideal basis for conducting a more consistent policy'.[76] Hence, it seems that there was also some (functional) pressure towards a non-exclusive right of initiative for the Commission in order to provide the decision-making system with greater impetus and consistency, both as an aim in itself and with the objective of developing the necessary flanking measures established by the Treaty of Amsterdam.

Perceptions of Political Elites As already pointed out in the previous chapters, functional pressures are only as strong as they are perceived and acted upon by agents. The functional arguments described above were widely embraced not only by the scholarly community but also by the political elites, including those directly or indirectly involved in the IGC decision-making process. There is some evidence of such perceptions in the secondary literature. Guyomarch noted that 'the government of almost every EU Member State has become increasingly afraid of its inability, acting alone, to deal with the effects of the removal of internal border controls on persons ... '.[77] Moreover, den Boer

---

[72] E.g. Nugent (1995); and Marks, *et al.* (1996).   [73] O'Keeffe (1995b: 905).
[74] Conference organised by the *Institut für Europäische Politik*, Brussels, May 1997.
[75] However Marks *et al.* (1996: 357–8) have argued that, in areas where the Commission has an exclusive right of initiative, this has in practice become increasingly shared with the Presidency, the Member States and the European Parliament. This would somewhat weaken the above argument. Moreover, they hold that a *de facto* 'shared' right of initiative may even benefit the Commission, as it gives the Commission allies for integrationist initiatives.
[76] Krenzler and Schneider (1997: 136).   [77] Guyomarch (1997: 141).

pointed out that politicians, senior police officers and civil servants argued that the removal of border controls would have negative repercussions for the internal security situation of the Member States, and hence that international crime and illegal immigration would rise without compensatory measures. 'Although few of these arguments were based on reliable statistics on the effectiveness of border controls for law enforcement purposes, they tended to have great rhetorical appeal'.[78] Finally, Anderson *et al.* have found that in the professional and policy-making community 'structural fatalism', which is their way of referring to the functional spillover logic, 'is subscribed to widely, if often tacitly'.[79]

Apart from the assessments concerning decision-makers' perception found in the secondary literature, there is plenty of primary evidence suggesting that functional pressures were recognised and also seen as paramount (in comparison with exogenous pressures) in the considerations of the political elites. Some conclusions can be drawn from the careful study of such primary sources. First, a large majority of member governments acknowledged and/or propagated the functional linkage and considered it as the prime reason for reforming the JHA pillar.[80] Only a minority of sources regarded functional and exogenous pressures as equally important[81], and few sources gave greater weight to exogenous factors[82]. Second, nearly all sources representing, or – in the case of Presidency texts – at least reflecting, the views of the Member States as a whole put considerable emphasis on the functional logic.[83] Moreover, the reports of the Reflection Group suggest that even before the opening of the Conference there was widespread support for a reform of the methods and instruments of the third pillar. This was largely based on functional pressures from within, namely, the dissatisfaction with the attainment of the Union's objectives, and more generally the inability to co-operate efficaciously. The progress report of the chairman of the Reflection Group states that 'a large majority feels that the provisions of the Title [VI] are inappropriate. They see the

---

[78] den Boer (1994: 184).   [79] Anderson *et al.* (1995: 88).

[80] See e.g. Benelux (1996a, b), Dehaene (1996), Finnish Government (1996), French Government (1997), Barnier (1995), Chirac (1996), Juppé (1996), de Charette (1996, 1997), German Government (1996), Kohl and Chirac, (1995, 1996), Kinkel (1995), Kinkel and Dini (1997), Greek Government (1996), Italian Government (1996), Spanish Government (1995), UK Government (1996b).

[81] See e.g. Mehaignerie (1994).

[82] Luxembourg Government (1995); United Kingdom Government (1996a).

[83] See, for example, Irish Presidency (1996a, b), Dutch Presidency (1997a, b), Council (1996b) and to a somewhat lesser extent Reflection Group (1995a, b).

results as clearly defective ... '.[84] Finally, it is worth mentioning that functional arguments were also recognised as well as considered to be the most important pressures by the Community institutions[85] and organised interest.[86]

But, it has been suggested by a few observers that the free movement of persons logic was not as compelling as some decision-makers and scholars believed. It has been pointed out that the intra-EU borders (or borders in general) have always been permeable and that the abolition of border control makes less difference than is widely held. One good example of the permeability of borders in the pre-Schengen area is the case of the abduction and murder of the German representative of the employers association, Hans-Martin Schleyer, by the *Rote Armee Fraktion* (RAF). The RAF managed to cross the border to France, despite the huge efforts made to lock the borders.[87]

One official admitted that when his country held the Presidency and a distinction had to be made between matters going to the first pillar and others staying in the third, 'we made a somewhat arbitrary separation and said that those related to the free movement of persons should be communitarised, as we had to find a logic for justifying this separation. The truth is that crime and drug-trafficking are also related to the free movement of persons'.[88] Others admitted that the argument in favour of the free movement of persons 'contains an element of rhetoric'.[89] However, regardless of how flawed or rhetorical the argument is, what ultimately matters is that decision-makers (and those who informed them) bought the argument, and the above analysis leaves little doubt that they did.

Exogenous Spillover

Another structural pressure, influencing the area of justice and home affairs at Amsterdam, was exogenous spillover. Although less powerful here than functional spillover, exogenous factors interacted with and reinforced functional ones in driving Member States and Community institutions towards the communitarisation of the third pillar. Hence,

---

[84] Reflection Group (1995b).
[85] See, for instance, Commission (1995d, c, 1997a), Santer (1995, 1996), Oreja (1997), European Parliament (1995c, d; 1996a, 1997b).
[86] See e.g. UNICE (1995); ETUC (1995a, b); Euro Citizen Action Service (1996); ERT (1997).
[87] Interview, Brussels, 1999. The *logic* (as opposed to the *perception*) of the free movement argument has been contested in the literature. Cf. Huysmans (2000: 759); Bigo (1996).
[88] Interview, Brussels, 1999.   [89] Interview, Brussels, 1999.

functional and exogenous forces are viewed here as parallel and complementary rather than divergent or substitutional dynamics.

What constitutes exogenous pressures? Exogenous pressures are
understood here as large numbers of asylum seekers, immigrants and
refugees entering the Community and staying there, legally or illegally.
This, combined with rising levels of unemployment in Western Europe,
resulted in the perceived need to limit the number of third country
nationals seeking asylum in and immigrating, legally or illegally, to the
Community.[90] For instance, in 1992 the then British Foreign Secretary,
Douglas Hurd, pinpointed migration 'as one of the most serious, perhaps the most serious problem' for Europe.[91] The need for a common
EU response to those problems was a mixture of the perception of a
common threat and the (related) inability of individual nation-states to
cope with these problems single-handedly. National immigration and
asylum policies have become ineffective, especially because 'no single
country in Western Europe is capable of regulating migration flows
without influencing those in other countries'.[92] Achermann has pointed
out that European states confronted with the growth of asylum applications and illegal immigration have adopted ever stricter asylum and
immigration regulations, which however, have not been successful
because 'restrictions in one country have only led to more asylum seekers in other countries until those countries adopted the same or even
stricter rules'. As a result, it was recognised that 'solo runs' did not help
and that co-operation was needed.[93] Hence, underlying this issue was,
at least to some extent, the nature of the asylum and immigration problems that went beyond the governance potential of individual nation-
states. Regional integration was viewed as a more effective buffer against
exogenously originated problems of international migration.

Exogenous Dynamics Reinforced by Functional Tensions   Although
sound in themselves, these exogenous dynamics are, to some extent, based
on, and exacerbated by functional pressures. The free movement of
persons is partly responsible for the fact that EU Member States can no
longer handle the immigration problem single-handedly in their effort to
preserve the well-being of their peoples. 'In a Europe in which borders
become increasingly permeable, illegal immigrants can practically
move without control from one Member State to another. In order to
fight illegal immigration, therefore, [...] national solutions are not

[90] Cf. Baldwin-Edwards and Schain (1994: 7).   [91] Quoted in Collinson (1993: 115).
[92] Baldwin-Edwards and Schain (1994: 11).
[93] Achermann (1995: 129). On competitive national policy-making also see Uçarer (2001:
291–4) as well as Lavenex and Uçarer (2002: 20).

sufficient. They would ask too much of the individual state'.[94] And Laurens Brinkhorst, the draftsman of an EP working document on the process in the field of justice and home affairs, has explained: 'At the 1996 IGC it will be a matter of great urgency to deal with these matters at the European level since national measures are becoming increasingly ineffective as a result of the abolition of the internal borders of the EU'.[95] Hence exogenous and endogenous-functional rationales for a common Community approach were (and continue to be) inextricably linked.[96]

Perceived Importance as an Integrational Dynamic   Although the exogenous pressures described above are complementary to and linked to functional ones, this does not prevent us from examining their integrational strength. In terms of sheer numbers, migratory pressures seemed to diminish. Throughout the Community (apart from the Netherlands and the United Kingdom), the number of asylum applications – perhaps the best statistical indicator available[97] – was in the process of falling since 1991.[98] Hence, 'despite the prediction in the press in 1989–90, the "invasion" of Western Europe ha[d] not taken place ... '.[99] However, more important than actual figures were the perceptions of political elites and the public who continued to view it as a significant problem. As pointed out by Butt Philip well before the start of the Amsterdam IGC, immigration policy was set to become more and more of an EU affair, partly as the consequence of 'the shared perceptions of [...] threatening external pressures [which] work themselves through'.[100] Despite decreasing numbers of asylum seekers, the perceptions concerning the seriousness of the 'problem' on the part of political elites by no means changed in the mid-1990s. Rather, some passionately talked about the growing migratory pressures in the future.[101]

Although the exogenous pressures pointed out above have been regarded as secondary (in terms of their influence on the development of

---

[94] Schelter (1996: 21–2; author's translation).
[95] European Parliament (1995c: 30).
[96] It is also worth pointing out that the very reason why immigrants seek to come to the Community in high numbers is partly an endogenous one, i.e. related to the European integration project itself. Economic integration has significantly contributed to peace and prosperity in Western Europe and thus added to its attractiveness in terms of immigration.
[97] There are no reliable data concerning illegal immigration (see Collinson 1993).
[98] Papademetriou (1996: 71).   [99] Baldwin-Edwards and Schain (1994: 7).
[100] Butt Philip (1994: 188). This account was shared by the Ad Hoc Group on Immigration. See Ad Hoc Group on Immigration (1991: 3).
[101] See e.g., Cederschiöld (1996); Nassauer (1996).

the justice and home affairs area) in the literature[102], and hence more as an 'indirect rationale for intensified co-operation',[103] they acted as an additional and complementary dynamic for increased integration in this area, especially regarding *restrictive* policies.[104] This is also true for the 1996–97 IGC negotiations. Most contributions of Member States' governments[105] mentioned the problem of migratory pressures as one of the reasons for upgrading co-operation in this area. The means available to respond to the external challenges were viewed as insufficient. In this context, it is often difficult to distinguish whether the challenges referred to are the realisation of free movement of persons or external ones. In the contributions of member governments these two are often not clearly distinguished.[106] Interviews with national officials in Brussels also suggest that the challenges were partly seen as exogenous in nature and that these complemented the two functional rationales and thus acted as an additional spur for intensified co-operation.[107]

Social Spillover

Social spillover may have had an impact on JHA issues at the IGC in two respects. First, justice and home affairs is a relatively new field of European policy-making, for example, compared with the CCP. The question in that regard is how fast and to what extent those decision-making structures, as well as actors and forums, allowed socialisation, learning and communicative action processes, and thus co-operative behaviours, to take place *in the policy-making domain*. In essence, the minimal occurrence of such processes and behaviours increased the pressure for further institutional reform towards communitarisation at the Intergovernmental Conference. Second, there is the question of socialisation processes occurring *at the IGC itself*, and thus possibly contributing to consensus formation and more integrative outcomes. On the whole, a modest development in that respect seems to have occurred.

---

[102] A large majority of authors have viewed exogenous pressure as secondary, or complementary, to the functional one. See, for example, de Lobkowicz (1994); Butt Philip (1994); Morgan (1994); O'Keeffe (1995a); Joly (1996). Few authors have put more emphasis on exogenous pressures. See: Collinson (1993) and Kiso (1999: 12ff).

[103] den Boer (1994: 182).

[104] As regards the development towards restrictive European-level policies see e.g. Geddes (2000a).

[105] See e.g., Luxembourg Government (1995); United Kingdom Government (1996a).

[106] E.g. Spanish Government (1995).   [107] Interviews, Brussels, 1997, 1999.

Socialisation Processes in the Policy Area of Justice and Home Affairs   A few years after the entering into force of the Maastricht Treaty most commentators seemed to suggest that socialisation processes had not been very far-reaching. For example, it was proposed that 'some of the national bureaucracies have taken rigid and dogmatic positions, hampering any progress, despite the obvious fact that a close co-operation is badly needed ... '.[108] Moreover, apparently ministers and officials in the third pillar had not (yet) realised 'the need to make concessions and to seek compromise'.[109] This sort of behaviour, although happening occasionally in other policy areas, was far from the habits of agreement and reciprocity described in the PHARE chapter.

There are a number of explanations for the seemingly modest level of internalised co-operative behaviour. First, as Fortescue has pointed out, 'the third pillar [was at the time], after all, still very young and the ministers and officials concerned ha[d] been working within the new framework for a very short time compared with other colleagues more used to First or even Second Pillar activity'.[110] Moreover, the K.4 Committee 'was rather heterogeneous in composition when it took up its work'.[111] This confirms the analysis of social spillover in the other previous chapters, namely that socialisation processes do take time, and that a newly created forum with new members does not display the same level of collaborative norms.

Second, due to the variety of issues to be dealt with, third pillar co-operation has, in most Member States, involved representatives from at least four different ministries: justice, interior, finance and foreign affairs. 'This variation of origin at the inauguration of the K.4 Committee made co-operation initially unwieldy and stagnant' according to the German K.4 official at the time, Klaus-Dieter Schnapauff.[112] Moreover, clear political responsibility sometimes tended to vanish in problems of co-ordination and competencies between these ministries.[113] Hence, one could not have expected the same cohesion as between officials and ministers involved in the second pillar. 'Foreign

---

[108] Justus Lipsius (1995: 249).   [109] Fortescue (1995: 26).

[110] Fortescue (1995: 25). However, there had been intergovernmental co-operation on justice and home affairs since 1975, the most significant of which was within the Trevi Group.

[111] Interview, Brussels, 1999. The new members of the K.4 Committee came from various forums such as the Co-ordinators Group, the Trevi Group, the Ad Hoc Committee on Immigration and the Schengen Committee. Moreover, some rather well-functioning structures and established clubs, such as the Trevi Group which was known for its 'wining and dining culture' were abolished. In contrast, the third pillar arrangements were viewed by senior police officials as more bureaucratic, less efficient and less intimate (interview, Brussels, 1999). See also on this point: den Boer (1996).

[112] Quoted in Kiso (1999: 183).   [113] Monar (1995: 246).

ministers are already a "club" with fewer problems concerning the internal division of competencies'.[114] This is also in line with the findings earlier on in this book where the detrimental impact of bureaucratic rivalries has been described.[115] Further fragmentation occurred as some delegations, such as those of Germany and Finland, designated their member of the K.4 Committee separately for each item on the agenda.[116] This made the formation of personal contacts and an *esprit de corps* more difficult.

Finally, as suggested by Fortescue, 'interior ministers, as their name suggests, were probably always going to be among the least enthusiastic about agreeing to have their habits changed by external pressures coming from the Union'.[117] In this context, Westlake has pointed out that 'it is an ill-kept secret that many interior Ministries felt that they were dragged into the third pillar and subsequently felt no driving compulsion to make it work'.[118] Hence, a certain degree of resentment on behalf of JHA ministers and officials lingered on for some time, which adds to our explanation of the malfunctioning of socialisation processes.

The insufficient development of socialisation and learning processes has been referred to as one of two main features 'most unconducive to progress'.[119] In essence, the minimal occurrence of such processes until the mid-1990s increased the pressure for further institutional reform towards communitarisation at the IGC. Few policy-makers suggested that the cumbersome, rigid and often uncooperative policy process in the area of JHA was a natural reflection of still insufficiently developed socialisation and learning processes, and that the new system needed more time to develop.[120] Instead, the intergovernmental institutional set-up was usually solely blamed for this. By largely ignoring the socialisation dimension, most actors naturally focused on the question of decision rules and competencies, which increased the pressure in terms of communitarisation. Hence, somewhat paradoxically, the minimal occurrence of socialisation and learning processes spurred the reform of the old third pillar.[121]

Social Spillover and the Intergovernmental Conference 1996–97   In the IGC Representatives Group, which is the focus of this analysis, there was some scope for social spillover. Meetings were held frequently,

---

[114] Wessels (1994: 332).   [115] Cf. pp. 48–9, 93–4 of this study.
[116] Papademetriou (1996: 76); Kiso (1999).   [117] Fortescue (1995: 26).
[118] Westlake (1995: 240).   [119] Fortescue (1995: 27).
[120] See Justus Lipsius (1995: 249). Only the UK Government (1996a) seemed to have come to this conclusion.
[121] Interviews, Brussels, 1997, 1999.

usually once a week from Monday morning until Tuesday evening. On Monday evenings, the representatives had dinner together in a less formal atmosphere without interpreters, which, according to one official, 'allowed us to get to know each other better, not only professionally, but also personally'.[122] In addition, each Presidency organised trips to attractive destinations in their country, where 'serious work was combined with sightseeing and relaxed get-togethers'. According to one official, substantial progress was made during their trips to Toledo, Cork and Nordwijk, especially on difficult and sensitive topics.[123] Apart from regular dinners and organised trips, there was also a lot of bilateral informal contact between the representatives. Several members of the group noted that there was 'something like a club-atmosphere', in which 'basic relationships of trust' evolved. As one official put it: 'there was a feeling that we were very much responsible for the [outcome of the] conference. This collective responsibility was a source of motivation for making progress'.[124]

On the whole, however, socialisation processes seemed less evident in the Representatives Groups than in other, permanent working groups or committees. Members of the Representative Group, who at the same time were also members of COREPER, pointed out that the group was rather heterogeneous at the outset, and although a significant club atmosphere developed, relations never got as close as between the ambassadors in COREPER, which was also attributed to the limited (eighteen months) lifespan of the group.[125]

Having said that, the scope for social spillover was still more significant than regarding the CCP case at the IGC 1996–97. Although we are talking about the same forum, the conditions for socialisation, learning and communicative action were more favourable. First and most importantly, unlike in the negotiations on the extension of Article 113, the moderate socialisation processes occurring in the Representatives' Group and the progression of the negotiations in the JHA field more generally, were little offset by competing bureaucratic pressures from the interior and justice ministries, which barely interfered with the JHA negotiations conducted by foreign ministries.[126] This was partly due to the lack of familiarity of JHA officials and ministers with the EU

---

[122] Interview, Brussels, 1999.   [123] Interview, Brussels, 1997.
[124] Interviews, Brussels, 1999.   [125] Interviews, Brussels, 1997, 1999.
[126] Interview, Brussels, 1999. It has been reported that JHA ministries later resented the extent of the progress achieved at Amsterdam in the areas of visa, asylum and immigration. In Denmark, the United Kingdom and Ireland JHA ministries are said to have been more involved. Hence, it may be no coincidence that these countries have opt-outs in this field (interviews, Brussels, 1997).

and IGC machinery. As one official noted, 'they were too introspective' and 'took surprisingly little interest in what was happening at the IGC, while working on less important day-to-day issues'.[127] Other observers noted that JHA senior officials did not know how to best assert themselves in the JHA debate, unable (or lacking the familiarity) to network effectively on the European level, to build potent alliances with other capitals and exert direct pressure on the negotiators.[128] Perhaps most importantly in that respect, the (Irish and) Dutch Presidencies played their hand rather cleverly by putting forward an Action Plan Against Organised Crime, a sexy topic with much public appeal, which attracted JHA officials' and ministers' attention and at the same time diverted their political energy away from the IGC.

Second, unlike the CCP debate in the Representatives' Group, where the basic distrust against the Commission hampered socialisation, learning and argumentative discourse on trade topics, the issue of trust did not pose a particular problem on JHA issues. Third, while very little time was reserved for discussing external trade policy, justice and home affairs was one of the major items on the IGC agenda. Thus, contrary to the CCP case, there was more time available for communicative action processes to unfold.

In line with the general neofunctionalist argument that social spillover facilitates consensus and may lead to an upgrading of common interests, a number of other mechanisms seem to have been at work in the Representatives Group which eased such a process. For example, participants could test ideas and say things that they would not normally wish to say in more formal settings. Moreover, officials noted that socialisation processes and reasoned discussions helped in the sense that one could get access to one's peers' motives, which is often the first step to solving a problem. As Manfred Scheich, the Austrian IGC Representative, remarked, 'through private talks with Niels [Ersboll] I could finally understand why the Danes made so much fuss about the communitarisation of asylum and immigration policy'.[129] The understanding and knowledge of the severity of the domestic problems facilitated a swift acceptance of the special provisions for Denmark. In addition, a substantial degree of reciprocity as a collective understanding about appropriate behaviour seemed to have developed in the Representative Group. For example, as one official mentioned, 'after we were granted our (Title IV) opt-out, it was clear to our delegation that we should be accomodating on other issues. Here, as often, there was no explicit talk about making a deal or returning concessions'.[130]

---

[127] Interview, Brussels, 1999.   [128] Interview, Brussels, 1998.
[129] Interview with Manfred Scheich, Brussels, 1997.   [130] Interview, Brussels, 1997.

Enmeshment and socialisation processes also fostered coalition behaviour and special relationships which in turn often acted as catalysts for consensus. In the Representatives Group, the Frenchman, Michel Barnier and the German, Werner Hoyer, are said to have had particularly close relations and to have met regularly for informal discussions. Moreover, socialisation eased the formation of a flexible Benelux alliance which was often joined by Finland, Austria and Italy, and most of the time shared the views of the Commission. Coalition formation provoked further alignment and facilitated consensus-building 'because it is easier to find a solution between two or three blocks than fifteen different and fragmented positions'. Moreover, alliances also provided an impetus for the progression of negotiations. 'Although we were negotiating in a pluralistic setting, group-formation has its effects because mass still makes an impact'.[131]

Political Spillover

On the wider question of communitarisation of visa, asylum and immigration policy, interest groups asserted only fairly modest pressure on member governments and central institutions in favour of a more supranational set-up. Most NGOs were sceptical of a Community competence in those areas for a long time, as member governments did for many years play a two-level game, 'putting forward more restrictive policies, while putting the blame for such policies on Brussels'.[132] Only since the mid-1990s did many NGOs begin to understand that the Commission pursued a more balanced and liberal course than most Member States which appealed to the wider NGO human rights community. Moreover, NGOs began to see that communitarisation would also entail other benefits such as enhanced democracy and judicial review. Hence, subsequently, NGOs came out more strongly in favour of communitarisation,[133] however, too late for a concerted campaign. As one activist put it, 'we contributed to the general climate but Member States came to the right conclusions themselves'.[134]

The above echoes the writings of Haas, who held that integration in a particular sector would lead the interest groups concerned to move part of their activity, focus and expectations gradually to the European level. As they became aware of the benefits of integration, they would promote

---

[131] Interviews with Manfred Scheich, Brussels, 1997.   [132] Interview, Brussels, 1999.
[133] See e.g., Standing Committee of Experts on International Immigration, Refugee and Criminal Law (1995, 1997), Justice (1996a, b), European Council on Refugees and Exiles (1995).
[134] Interview, Brussels, 1999.

further integration. Haas did not imply that all organised interests would swiftly shift their identity or expectations to the European level, but only those interest groups that operate within integrated sectors.[135] The field of justice and home affairs as of the mid-1990s can hardly be called an integrated sector. However, the tendency described above supports the general direction of the neofunctionalist concept of political spillover, as the increasing prominence of JHA on the European level induced them to take a greater interest in the relevant issues which led them 'to realise the potential advantages and to see through governments' efforts to portray Brussels as the bad guy'.[136]

While the workings of political spillover can only be *anticipated* with regard to the wider issue of communitarisation of visa and migration policy, on a number of smaller issues interest group development and pressure did make a difference.[137] First, there is the issue of anti-discrimination which is related to immigration policy. Due to past (and present) immigration the European Union is populated by people from many different ethnic backgrounds. Before and during the IGC, NGOs have lobbied in favour of an anti-discrimination clause in the Treaty, since a legal basis for concrete action was thought to be lacking. They argued that this issue should be dealt with on the European level as individual Member States lacked courage to take appropriate action and because some of the problems, such as cross-border publications, have interstate dimensions.[138] A coalition of over 250 NGOs, churches and trade unions across the EU as well as European-wide umbrella organisations, active in the areas of human rights, migration and anti-racism, the so-called Starting Line, pushed strongly for Community wide anti-discrimination legislation, and formulated its own treaty amendment[139] with active support from the European Parliament[140] and to a lesser extent also from the European Commission.[141] It succeeded in persuading the Kahn Commission, the Consultative Commission on Racism and Xenophobia, to adopt its proposal.[142] Kahn – its chairman is a personal friend of French President Chirac – and the other fourteen members of the Kahn Commission also had very good contacts.[143] A

---

[135] Haas (1958: 294).
[136] Interview, Brussels, 1999.
[137] On the development of interest groups in this area also see e.g. Geddes (1998, 2000b); Guiraudon (2000: 294).
[138] Justice (1996b: 19).   [139] Starting Line Group (1994).
[140] European Parliament (1995b).   [141] Commission (1994c, 1996c).
[142] Consultative Commission on Racism and Xenophobia (1995).
[143] The Starting Line had also cultivated relations, for example, with Jack Straw, then Labour shadow minister for justice and home affairs, Ignaz Bubis, leader of the Jewish Community in Germany, who was very close to Kohl, Carlos Westendorp, chairman

further indication for the effectiveness of the Starting Line campaign for an anti-discrimination clause is the fact that the European Parliament made reference to and endorsed its proposal in a number of its resolutions.[144] It has generally been recognised, also outside the NGO community, that the efforts of the Starting Line were crucial in bringing about Article 13 on anti-discrimination.[145]

Another example of NGO-induced change in the wider area of JHA in the Amsterdam Treaty are matters affecting third-country nationals. NGOs have argued for third-country nationals to be granted European citizenship and for measures under the first pillar to ensure equal treatment of Union citizens and third-country nationals. The new Treaty does not include a provision granting European citizenship to non-EU nationals, but Title IV does mean progress for the rights of third-country nationals. For example, Article 61 provides for the adoption of measures safeguarding the rights of third-country nationals. And Article 62 calls for measures to be taken removing all controls on persons crossing internal borders. NGOs argued that the 10 million legally resident third-country nationals are in a second-class category compared with Member State nationals, as regards Community rights, and that differential treatment of third-country nationals feeds racism and xenophobia. Moreover, it was regarded as unjust to exclude third-country nationals, some of whom have lived all their lives in an EU Member State, from the economic benefits of free movement rights in the Union. Advancing this issue on the European level would mean that the Commission, the EP and the ECJ would each have a role.[146] Although a less clear-cut case than the previous one, there is evidence which suggests that interest groups – alongside the Commission and Parliament – have been influential on this issue, supported by the broader case law of the Court of

---

of the Reflection Group and Elisabeth Giugou, one of two MEPs who represented the EP in the Reflection Group (interview, Brussels, 1999).

[144] E.g. European Parliament (1996b).

[145] Interviews, Brussels, 1999. Article 13 reads as follows: 'Without prejudice to the other provisions of the Treaty and within the limits of the powers conferred by it up the Community, the Council, acting unanimously on a proposal from the Commission and after consulting the European Parliament, may take appropriate action to combat discrimination based on sex, racial or ethnic origin, religion or belief, disability, age or sexual orientation'.

[146] See Churches Commission for Migrants in Europe (1995); European Union Migrants' Forum (1995). Moreover, NGOs as well as the Commission also recognised the functional rationale that making a distinction between EU citizens and third-country nationals does not make sense in terms of a right of free movement because 'when crossing intra-Community frontiers people do not have their nationality written on their forehead', thus making a differentiation for the enforcement of controls on non-Union citizens very difficult (interview, Brussels, 1999).

Justice.[147] NGOs pursued the strategy of ambitiously demanding Union citizenship to third-country nationals. Knowing that Union citizenship was not feasible they rightly hoped and anticipated that Member States would take at least a first step. NGOs managed to form a loose transnational alliance[148], including interest groups from most Member States, which lobbied their respective governments.[149]

The transnational coalition pushing for an anti-discrimination clause (and to a lesser extent also the coalition advocating increased rights of third-country nationals[150]) can be conceptualised as an advocacy coalition. It fulfils the requirements laid down by Sabatier and Jenkins-Smith.[151] It consisted of actors from a variety of private and also of governmental organisations (such as the EP, Commission and national officials) who shared a set of policy beliefs and sought to realise them by influencing multiple governmental institutions over time. Moreover, advocacy coalitions, like these, are glued together by common beliefs rather than by common interests, as in 'material' interest groups. As hypothesised in Chapter 1, with increasing importance given to the European level of governance over time, advocacy coalitions develop the perception that their beliefs and interests need to be articulated and better served on the European level. As one NGO representative explained: 'as we can have a wider impact through EU legislation, it was clear that we had to take the Brussels avenue and boost the competencies of the Community. The Community institutions are therefore often our natural allies'.[152]

Cultivated Spillover

The European Commission
Starting Position, Approach and Strategy
It has been argued that the Commission itself was to some extent responsible for the growing pressures to bring about increased cooperation on JHA after the SEA, given the prominent role it played in

---

[147] See the section on the Court of Justice below in this chapter.

[148] This alliance included the Meijers Committee, the Kahn Commission, the Churches Commission for Migrants in Europe, the European Union Migrants' Forum, the Churches' Commission for Racial Justice, the European Co-ordination for Rights of Immigrants to Family Life, Justice and many others.

[149] Interviews, Brussels, 1999. The most important channels for the exertion of pressure were with Michiel Patijn, the Dutch chairman of the Representatives' Group, Elmar Brok and Elisabeth Giugou, the members of Parliament's Civil Liberties Committee. Good contacts were also cultivated with the forthcoming Labour government, the Irish Presidency, the German ministry of interior and the Commissioner for Foreigner's Affairs of the Senate of Berlin (interviews, Brussels, 1998).

[150] To a lesser extent because there was less involvement from governmental organisations.

[151] Sabatier and Jenkins-Smith (1993: 225).   [152] Interview, Brussels, 1999.

shaping the 1992 project.[153] There is some evidence which suggests that it was a conscious strategy of the Commission to promote the elimination of internal borders in order to reap spillover in the form of EC policies on immigration and other areas related to the free movement of persons. According to Papademetriou, 'in Delors' thinking, the move to abolish frontiers between EC countries would in turn convince Member States of the need to cooperate on admission and border control measures, thus creating a context for subsequent efforts to bring immigration policy into the institutional framework of the EC'.[154] Although the Single European Act did not mention the aim or necessity of common immigration and asylum policies, Article 8a of the SEA set policy goals that realistically could not be fully realised without Community-wide policies on asylum, immigration and external border control.

Given Member States' reluctance to cede power to the Community too quickly in such a sensitive area, the Commission essentially faced two options: first, the 'doctrinaire' approach which – favouring a *communautaire* framework – advocated that the Commission should attempt to bring as many JHA issues under Community competence as possible. This approach implied a policy of non-cooperation with the Member States in the various intergovernmental forums. Second, the 'gradualist' approach which can be characterised as pragmatic and involved the acceptance of the intergovernmental nature of JHA co-operation. It implied that the Commission would co-operate with Member States in order to maximise its powers.[155] In the early years of justice and home affairs co-operation, the Commission tended to pursue the doctrinaire approach.[156] At the same time, Member States were intensifying their interaction by way of intergovernmental co-operation in this field. Thus, the Commission was confronted with a choice – 'take the "doctrinaire" approach and stand its ground on the issue of competence and risk being excluded from the whole process or accept the intergovernmental nature of Member States' co-operation and embrace a "gradualist" approach which would at least provide it with a seat at the table'.[157] From the late 1980s the Commission began to pursue the gradualist

---

[153] Sandholtz and Zysman (1989).
[154] Papademetriou (1996: 22).   [155] Myers (1995).
[156] See Monar (1994). Examples of this can be found in the Commission's White Paper on completing the internal market (Commission 1985), in which the Commission committed itself to proposing seven directives in the field of controls on individuals, including such sensitive matters as the co-ordination of national rules concerning the right of asylum. It was the intention of the Commission that these matters should be dealt with in the Community arena (Myers 1995).
[157] Myers (1995: 282).

strategy.[158] It opted for practical rather than legal doctrine or – in the words of Commissioner Bangemann – 'making progress rather than fighting time consuming battles for competence'.[159] Although this provoked furious reactions from the European Parliament, most observers agree that the adoption of the gradualist approach was the right decision by the Commission, as pushing too hard might easily have proven counterproductive.[160] Especially after the Maastricht Treaty, that granted the Commission means of influence in JHA for which it had struggled more than twenty years in EPC, the Commission had to act cautiously and use the new instruments very prudently. Any political activism could have caused a loss of trust on the part of the Member States and proven detrimental in the long-run.[161] The gradualist approach taken by the Commission was reflected in the initiatives it launched after the Treaty on European Union entered into force. For example, the Commission's report to the first Justice and Home Affairs Council on the possibility of applying the *passerelle* procedure under Article K.9 TEU to asylum policy was rather careful in substance.[162] The Commission concluded in its report that the time for an application of Article K.9 had not yet come. According to Monar, the Commission wanted, for tactical reasons, to avoid a polarisation of Member States on the question of communitarisation at least before the start of the IGC.[163]

As pointed out by Myers, apart from being prudent, the Commission needed, at the same time, to demonstrate that it could bring some added value into JHA policy-making. According to Myers, the Commission was successful in that respect. It generally presented well-researched, creative and balanced proposals.[164] The approach and performance of the Commission had important implications for the Intergovernmental Conference. Myers argued that on the question of future communitarisation of JHA, 'the performance of the Commission in this area will undoubtedly be taken into account. [...] Faced with well-researched, reasoned and perhaps innovative proposals from the Commission, the Member States may feel themselves able to entrust the Commission with more and more power in these politically sensitive areas ... '.[165]

---

[158] According to Myers (1995: 283) this strategy was formally adopted in 1995.
[159] Quoted in Monar (1994: xx).   [160] See e.g. Wessels (1994: 233).
[161] Monar (1994). The Commission's limited activism was also due to the fact that Member States tended not to act on its initiatives (interview, 1999).
[162] See Commission (1993d).
[163] Monar (1997). A similarly cautious approach can be found in its Communication on a comprehensive action programme (cf. Commission, 1994c).
[164] In its February 1994 communication, for example, it struck a fine balance between 'liberal' and 'restrictive' measures which was acceptable as a basis for discussion by all delegations and 'set the terms of the debate in convincing but pragmatic manner' (Myers 1995: 296).
[165] Myers (1995: 298).

Not only had the Commission managed to manoeuvre itself into an advantageous position in the area of justice and home affairs before the IGC, it also did not take any chances in its approach to the Conference itself. The Commission's overall pre-IGC approach was a more modest one than it had been under Delors, due to Member States' scepticism and the fact that the Commission's success depended on its ability to focus on a manageable number of goals and objectives.[166] One official described the Commission's approach as follows: 'it is not that we were not ambitious. We decided to be reasonably cautious at the beginning, set priorities and be selective, and not put forward, as at Maastricht, a grand package'.[167] The Commission concentrated on 'reform' (rather than revolution) in a few areas. The Commission's approach to the Amsterdam IGC can be characterised as 'between utopia and honest broker', pursuing 'the highest possible realistic line'.[168] After institutional questions and CFSP, the third pillar was at the top of the Commission's priorities. The Commission invested even more resources and political capital on JHA matters throughout the Conference, as success became more feasible than in other areas.[169] Although the Commission may have been cautious and selective on substance, it was rather assertive concerning methods and style of defending its ideas, by constantly reminding Member States of the expansive logic of functional pressures, making use of its knowledge and expertise, and by cultivating contacts and alliances with politicians and interest groups. Overall, Commission leadership has been regarded as an important factor explaining the communitarisation of visa, asylum and immigration policy.[170]

Cohesion

The general cohesion of the Commission has usually been pointed out as one of the strengths of the Commission compared with other players.[171] The previous chapter regarding the CCP at the Amsterdam IGC has shown that a lack of cohesion can be considerably detrimental for the Commission's leadership role. In this case, however, the Commission was much more united and cohesive. All relevant divisions of the Commission were in favour of, and actively supported, the communitarisation of visa, asylum and immigration policy. The JHA Task

---

[166] Dinan (1997).   [167] Interview, Brussels, 1997.   [168] Petite (1998b: 21).
[169] Interviews, Brussels, 1998, 1999.
[170] Interviews, Brussels, 1999; Beach (2005: 134–5; 143).
[171] It has been pointed out, for example, that Commissioners have more time and opportunity to develop consensual positions on important issues than national ministers and heads of government, and that the Commission President has considerably greater potential for forging cohesion than is the case with the six-monthly rotating Presidency. See: Nugent (1995).

Force, despite rumours of its head having been hesitant at the beginning, came out strongly in favour of this course.[172] Similarly, Commissioner Gradin, after a period of acclimatisation, soon came round to the idea in the summer of 1995. DG XV, after initial scepticism[173], also came to favour this approach with constructive support from Commissioner Monti. Early difficulties between the two Commissioners over other issues were also overcome in 1995–96. Finally, the IGC Task Force envisaged a communitarisation of visa, asylum and immigration policy from the very beginning.[174] The IGC Task Force skilfully co-ordinated the work and input of the JHA Task Force, DG XV, the cabinets of Gradin and Monti as well as the Legal Service. All substantial reports and contributions were the product of a co-ordinated effort led by the IGC Task Force, mainly drafted by the latter in co-operation with the JHA Task Force. The advantages of such cohesion are viewed as the ability to act swiftly and hence proactively, to lobby effectively, to be less vulnerable *vis-à-vis* Member States' 'divide and rule' strategies, and the capability to act assertively at the negotiating table.[175]

Setting and Shaping the Agenda

Many authors have noted that in the Community framework, where the Commission has an exclusive right of initiative, an important source of power is its agenda-setting ability.[176] As Wallace put it, 'any practitioner of negotiations well recognises the crucial power of the drafter of the texts'.[177] Although at Intergovernmental Conferences the Commission is only one of many actors making proposals, it can still substantially influence the debate. Most generally, Community institutions do matter in shaping the perceptions of national actors and in changing the context of the rational pursuit of interests.[178]

It is argued here that the Commission was capable of influencing Member States' agendas and interest formations. It has done so in a number of ways: first, as alluded to above, the Commission's own performance in day-to-day policy-making may have influenced Member States' perceptions concerning the vital question of third pillar communitarisation. Second, Peterson has pointed out that the relatively early stages of the decision-making process are of critical importance to

---

[172] Interview, Brussels, 1999.
[173] Allegedly in the beginning DG XV was afraid to lose staff to another DG as a result of communitarisation (interview, Brussels, 1999).
[174] Interview, Brussels, 1999.   [175] Interviews, Brussels, 1999.
[176] See e.g. Marks (1993); and Matlary (1997).
[177] H. Wallace (1990: 215).   [178] Cf. e.g. Bulmer (1994); Sandholtz (1993a).

the eventual policy outcomes.[179] The main sources for the IGC negotiations were the formal submission from EU governments and institutions. Few actors already submitted contributions to the Reflection
Group, the exceptions being the European Parliament and the European Commission.[180] The Commission report to the Reflection Group
as well as its later formal contribution to the Intergovernmental Conference were often regarded, even by national officials, as 'the best' and
'by far the most comprehensive contribution'.[181] Moreover, the two
reports of the Reflection Group seem to have been influenced by the
contributions of the European Parliament and especially the Commission. They not only made reference to these papers but used a similar
reasoning to explain the rationale for communitarisation.[182] The
Commission's contributions concerning the communitarisation of visa,
asylum and immigration policy during the IGC negotiations were
regarded as innovative and well-balanced and thus influenced the debate
on important points, such as drawing the line for the scope of
communitarisation.[183]

There is a third way in which the Commission helped to shape the
agenda, namely by planting a proposal with another delegation. As
some delegations are more suspicious of ideas and proposals originating
from the Commission, it is more likely for the Commission to achieve
policy advances when a proposal is issued under the name of another
Member State.[184] Former Commissioner, Lord Cockfield, claims that
the Commission operated in such a way with respect to the 1992
initiative.[185] During the IGC negotiations on JHA, the Commission
allegedly used this agenda-setting strategy on several occasions,
for example by tabling a proposal under the name of the Irish
Presidency.[186]

The Commission can also influence the agenda and more generally the
progression of negotiation by a good timing of its proposals. At the IGC
negotiations on justice and home affairs, the Commission got the timing
of their proposals right. The Commission first softened Member States
up to the idea of (at least a partial) communitarisation of the third pillar

---

[179] Although Peterson (1995) referred to 'policy-making' rather than treaty reform, it is
hypothesised here that the early stages are equally vital for the macro-level of decision-
making.
[180] It has been pointed out by several officials that their national positions only took real
shape throughout the term of the Irish Presidency in the second half of 1996
(interviews, Brussels, 1997).
[181] Interviews, Brussels, 1997–98.
[182] Cf. Reflection Group (1995a) and Commission (1995d).
[183] Moravcsik and Nicolaïdis (1999: 72).   [184] Cf. Nugent (1995).
[185] Cockfield (1994).   [186] Interview, Brussels, 1999.

in its first two reports.[187] Once the idea had found a reasonable acceptance amongst Member States, the Commission put forward its concrete
proposals; first on procedure and then on the technicalities of communitarising the third pillar, at a time when Member States failed to make
much progress.[188] Finally, the Commission can shape the agenda by
cultivating contacts with governmental elites, as will be discussed below.

Cultivation of Functional Spillover and Exogenous Pressures
One important way of softening Member States up to the idea of
communitarisation was by emphasising functional pressure, and to a
lesser extent exogenous pressures. The Commission began to cultivate
the functional spillover rationale from the very start. As pointed out
above, the Commission's insistence in its White Paper on the internal
market regarding the necessity of some legislative proposals, if checks at
internal borders were to be abolished, may have contributed to getting
the ball rolling in the first place. In subsequent years the Commission
missed few opportunities to emphasise the internal market logic.[189] In
its contributions to the Reflection Group and to the IGC, the Commission made both kinds of functional arguments: it pointed to the free
movement of persons objective as well as to the more diffuse goal of
developing close co-operation in the area of justice and home affairs.
Both aims, it argued, would be unattainable without at least partial
communitarisation.[190]

A variation of (and going beyond) the cultivation of functional spillover was to remind Member States that they wanted to complete the
internal market and that they had already recognised the necessity
therefore of developing certain policies. These tactics have been
employed by the Commission on many occasions, as in its explanatory
memorandum to the draft external border convention and visa regulation accompanying the proposals.[191] In order to further strengthen its
case of communitarisation the Commission additionally cultivated the
exogenous arguments of 'migratory pressures'. This rationale has often
been connected to and wrapped up with the free movement of persons
argument.[192] As pointed out earlier, functional and exogenous pressures
always need players who act upon them and point out the functional
logic to those taking the decisions. The Commission, it is argued here,
became an important agent of the spillover logic and thereby provided
an impetus for its unfoldment.

[187] Commission (1995d, 1996c).   [188] Interview, Brussels, 1999.
[189] See e.g., Commission (1988: 2, 1991a, 1993c, e, 1994c).
[190] See e.g., Commission (1995d, 1996c, 1996d, e).
[191] Commission (1993e: 1).   [192] Commission (1994d, 1996c).

Expertise, Better Overview and More Detached Position

In the Community framework 'the Commission ... is the main single source of technical expertise and the main repository of information about the content and impact of most EU policies. With expertise and information being key power resources, the Commission is thus advantageously placed to make itself indispensable to policy initiatives and developments'.[193] The extent of the Commission's knowledge and expertise varies considerably depending on the issue area. Where EU policy competence is long established, such as in commercial and agricultural policy, there is naturally a greater expertise than in emerging, and frequently under-resourced, areas of Community competence. Justice and home affairs doubtlessly fall into the latter category. However, over the years the Commission partly made up for the deficiencies it had in this field. After the Maastricht Treaty came into effect, the Commission changed its internal organisation, and created the Directorate F within the Secretariat General, which then changed into the JHA Task Force, still under the Secretariat General.[194] The Commission's staff gradually expanded in this area. Its expertise was gradually built-up, particularly through the use of ready-made national experts.[195]

Although one could argue that at the time of the IGC negotiations the Commission had fewer comparative informational advantages in JHA than in other policy areas, the expertise it had acquired was still viewed as substantial and advantageous during the IGC. Beach has argued that its technical expertise and its legitimacy of being the 'guardian of the treaties' put the Commission in the right position to propose and see through a transferral of JHA policies to the first pillar, 'a solution that would not have been successful had it come from any other actor'.[196]

The Commission also sought to exploit more clear-cut comparative advantages it had *vis-à-vis* Member States. One such potential advantage was the overview that the Commission had over the developments in the various Member States and their legal systems. Myers has noted the significance of this. 'The Commission, removed from the straitjacket of one single national perspective, may better be able to see which concerns are common to many or all of the Member States'. But he sees even more important implications for the Commission in the long-run. 'If the Commission is able to compare and contrast the data it collects [...] it can offer individual Member States wider perspectives of which they might not otherwise be aware'.[197]

---

[193] Nugent (1995: 608).
[194] Later DG Justice and Home Affairs was established in 1999, along with further staff expansion.
[195] Interview, Brussels, 1999.   [196] Beach (2005: 135).   [197] Myers (1995: 287, 289).

The Commission's detached position and overview of national legislations was also important for progress concerning the negotiations on the communitarisation of visa, asylum and immigration policy at the IGC. As one official put it, 'national officials were always saying that something had to be done, but they could not table any sensible proposals for remedies'.[198] The problem for representatives from Member States was that their national administrations were very conservative and traditional in their thinking in terms of sovereignty. In addition, 'they were too familiar with their own legislations, unable to go beyond merely taking photographs of each other's legislations and to bring some real dynamic into the debate, whereas the Commission did not always fall back into a national approach, as it did not carry such baggage and was free of such intrinsic national thinking'.[199] Several observers suggested that the Commission's more distanced perspective and holistic approach enabled it to advance the substantive debate and to work out a compromise which was acceptable to all delegations.[200]

Cultivation of Alliances with Policy-making Elites

The Commission further seeks to assert itself and find support for its ideas and proposals through the cultivation of contacts with governmental and non-governmental elites. For the Representatives Group the Commission decided to appoint Oreja, Commissioner for Institutional Affairs, rather than Secretary General David Williamson, who had represented the Commission during the 1991 IGC. The choice of Oreja proved to be a reasonably good one, as his standing added further weight to the contributions of the Commission in the Representatives Group.[201] Oreja's presence was especially beneficial for the Commission throughout the Reflection Group, as he could make use of his contacts in the Spanish government and because his friendship with Carlos Westendorp, chairman of the group, gave him 'access' to Westendorp's private office rather than having to go through the Council Secretariat.[202] Anita Gradin, Commissioner responsible for immigration, home affairs and justice, also made good use of her excellent contacts in the Swedish Social Democratic Party, including direct contacts with the Prime Minister, in view of the slightly reluctant stance taken by Sweden on the communitarisation of visa and migration policy at the beginning

---

[198] Interview, Brussels, 1997.   [199] Interview, Brussels, 1997.
[200] Interviews, Brussels, 1997, 1999.
[201] However, Oreja has been described as 'little charismatic' and 'insufficiently knowledgeable' on certain dossiers, such as the extension of Article 113. On JHA his understanding has been rated as 'quite good' (interview, Brussels, December 1997).
[202] Interview, Brussels 1999; Beach (2005: 134).

of the Conference. Gradin and her Cabinet allegedly managed to turn around the Ministry of Justice which is supposed to have triggered Sweden's acceptance of the idea of communitarisation during the Irish Presidency.[203] In addition, Michel Petite, Director of the Commission's IGC Task Force is said to have 'worked on' the French quite a lot which was considered one reason why the French government eventually gave up the idea of *Pillar I bis*.[204]

As already alluded to above, a good relationship with the Presidency is vital for the Commission. On JHA, co-operation with the various Presidencies during the IGC was good indeed, especially those with the Irish Presidency. The Irish were very open to the Commission's ideas concerning the communitarisation of JHA issues. As one Commission official put it 'most of Dublin II on JHA came straight from our pen'.[205] In addition, the Dutch Presidency allowed the Commission to collaborate closely on JHA issues, and also drew on the Commission during the drafting process.[206]

As for the cultivation of alliances with non-governmental elites, the Commission can act as a 'process manager' or 'interest broker', as it is capable of directing the dynamics of relations with national or transnational interest groups.[207] It has been argued that during this IGC, the Commission did not make much use of such powerful groups such as the ERT to bolster the Commission's position.[208] Nevertheless, there is some evidence for the Commission's attempts and capability to act as a process manager. For example, the Cabinet of Oreja sent out letters to 11,000 NGOs from which he got 7,000 replies. This was done, above all because the Commissioner wanted to be perceived as open by engaging the public and civil society. However, 'a useful by-product' was that 'many, if not most, NGOs ended up supporting much of the Commission's agenda'. This can be of help for Commission proposals because 'obviously when you have the support of a powerful group such as the Kahn Commission on anti-discrimination that is very useful for us. You can always use this in negotiations and make it clear to governments that there is a considerable movement behind it'.[209]

The Council Presidency   The various Presidencies, in their roles as institutionalised mediator and promotional broker, contributed significantly to the changes on visa, asylum and immigration policy during

[203] Interview, Brussels, 1999.   [204] Interview, Brussels, December 1997.
[205] Interview, Brussels, 1997; also cf. Beach (2005: 134).
[206] Beach (2005: 134).
[207] On this point see e.g. Mazey and Richardson (1994); Marks *et al.* (1996).
[208] Dinan (1997: 209).   [209] Interview, Brussels, 1997.

the IGC. Firstly, the Council Presidency has the task to act as the 'honest broker', to act as an intermediary between the various Member States and positions. Presidencies are usually in a good position to gather information about the concerns and difficulties of their opposite numbers. Both the Irish and Dutch Presidencies used many *tête-à-têtes* to sound out their colleagues.[210] Both Presidencies succeeded in their jobs as honest brokers on the communitarisation of visa, asylum and immigration policy, as compromises were found by the Irish and Dutch Presidencies with which all parties could live without feeling pushed to the sidelines.

However, the Presidency job goes beyond that of an honest broker. Particularly at IGCs it is also *the* institution responsible for the progress of negotiations, thus acting as a motor of the integration process, given the more limited role of the Commission compared to normal Community business.[211] At the same time, Presidencies cannot be too ambitious, as Member States would not accept their text as a common basis for further discussion, as happened with the overambitious Dutch 'black-Monday proposal' of 1991 which was still vivid in the minds of the Dutch Presidency negotiators in 1997. Hence, Presidencies need to be 'on the upper end of realism', 'to keep the momentum up at a fairly high, but not too high, level of ambition'.[212] The Irish and Dutch Presidencies managed to do so in a persistent and skilful way. As one participant to the JHA negotiations described: 'often discussions did not get very far. Still the drafts evolved. Although our discussions often had no tangible results, the next time something was on the table containing the useful bits and pieces. Somebody had a clear picture of where we were going. That somebody was the Presidency. It had "masterminded" the negotiations'.[213]

Both the 'Dublin II' and the draft Treaty that went to Amsterdam can be characterised as being 'on the upper end of realism'. The Irish draft treaty foresaw an ambitiously short one-year period to achieve the abolition of internal border controls and necessary compensatory measures. Moreover, measures on immigration and asylum were aimed to be in place within two years after the Treaty had entered into force. These time scales have to be seen in relation to the five-year period which was eventually provided for in the Treaty of Amsterdam. In addition, the draft treaty ambitiously suggested an automatic switch to QMV after a certain initial time period which was not further specified, a

[210] Interview, Brussels, 1999.   [211] Cf. McDonagh (1998).
[212] Interview, Brussels, 1997.   [213] Interview, Brussels, 1998.

non-exclusive right of initiative for the Commission, and enhanced roles for EP and ECJ.

The Dutch Presidency issued four texts before the Amsterdam summit, the fourth one being the Draft Treaty of Amsterdam. The first three were very ambitious, including an automatic switch to QMV after three years,[214] whereas the draft treaty pretty much reflected the final outcome.[215] As mentioned above in the section on social spillover in this chapter, the Dutch Presidency also cleverly managed to divert the attention of senior JHA officials and ministers by pushing the Joint Action on Organised Crime parallel to the IGC, thereby minimising their interference with JHA issues at the Conference negotiated by the more 'progressive' foreign ministries. Moreover, Michiel Patijn, the Dutch representative to the Conference, has generally been regarded to have been an effective chairman of the Representative Group, due to his good grasp of the subject matter, having been chairman of the Schengen Group only six months prior, and his strong determination.[216] Brokerage of the Dutch Presidency is said to have been decisive in winning French acceptance concerning the idea of communitarising visa, asylum and immigration policy, for example by postponing the Commission's monopoly of initiative.[217]

Both the Irish and Dutch Presidencies had enjoyed very good co-operation with the Commission on JHA issues. Tactics varied. Where it was thought that a proposal by the Commission would be outrightly rejected by some Member States, the (Irish) Presidency tabled it under its own name.[218] In situations when the (Dutch) Presidency did not want to put its stance as neutral broker at risk, the Commission pushed ahead, so that they could say to the reluctant states: 'of course, the Commission is going a bit too far. But, look don't they have a point here? Surely, we can work out something in the middle of the ground'.[219]

The European Parliament
The Role Played by Parliament in day-to-day
JHA Policy-making

The European Parliament started to define its position on JHA after the SEA. Parliament reacted to the intergovernmental approach chosen by the Member States and the Commission (as it was perceived by the EP)

---

[214] Dutch Presidency (1997c, 1997d).   [215] Dutch Presidency (1997e).

[216] Interviews, Brussels, 1999. Lindberg Clausen (1997) also noted that on the related issue of the integration of Schengen the Dutch Presidency managed to upgrade common interests and broker a number of formal and informal compromises.

[217] Moravcsik and Nicolaïdis (1999: 79).   [218] Interview, Brussels, 1997.

[219] Interview, Brussels, 1999.

with 'doctrinaire opposition', by pressing for a communitarisation of JHA matters and criticising the Commission for collaborating with Member States, whilst failing to put forward clear policy options.[220] After the TEU came into effect, Parliament became more active by adopting a number of important reports and resolutions on justice and home affairs.[221] However, the EP weakened its position, as its Committee on Civil Liberties and Internal Affairs did not consider the subjects before the Council in sufficient depth. It issued too many reports, members of the Committee often failed to attend meetings and to exercise their right of information by asking detailed questions, so that Council representatives gained the impression that MEPs were not sufficiently interested and therefore rarely provided information that went beyond what was stated in the Council press releases.[222]

After the 1994 elections to the European Parliament, the EP's newly constituted Committee on Civil Liberties and Internal Affairs began to improve its reputation on justice and home affairs matters. The new Committee increased its efficiency and the frequency of its contacts with the Council. Through this more powerful and concentrated approach 'the European Parliament is beginning to create an image for itself in the field of justice and home affairs'.[223] Moreover, there were some clear signs before the IGC that the EP no longer upheld its maximalist position, as it only suggested a partial communitarisation of the third pillar in reports and resolutions.[224]

The role played by Parliament at the IGC

Although the European Parliament only made a moderate contribution on the JHA negotiations, its influence should not be underestimated. Bobby McDonagh, an Irish diplomat closely involved in the negotiations, has given a rather up-beat account of the EP's role, as it helped significantly to maintain ambitions at the highest attainable level.[225] In addition, Parliament has managed to assert itself in a number of respects, especially through its indirect participation at the IGC table, the cultivation of contacts with governmental and non-governmental elites, as well as an informal alliance with the Commission.[226] During

---

[220] In fact, in 1993 the European Parliament took the Commission to the ECJ on grounds of inactivity (e.g. de Lobkowicz 1994).

[221] For example, the Robles Piquer Report of July 1993, in which the EP (1993a) called for all matters listed in Article K.1 TEU to be transferred to the Community realm. See also EP (1993b, 1994c).

[222] Esders (1995).   [223] Esders (1995: 175).

[224] European Parliament (1995b, c, d, 1996a).   [225] McDonagh (1998).

[226] As Christiansen (2002: 43) has pointed out, the European Parliament's influence on IGC negotiations is largely based on informal channels.

the 1996–97 IGC, Parliament was much more actively involved in the negotiations than in previous Intergovernmental Conferences.[227] In contrast to previous IGCs, two MEPs were allowed to take part in an 'exchange of views' at the beginning of each meeting of the Foreign Ministers and the European Council dealing with the IGC. Moreover, Parliament's two representatives met Member States' IGC Representatives for a detailed exchange of views at least once a month. This was seen as a substantial improvement, as 'Parliament could constantly remind national Representatives of its concerns'.[228] The EP's Representatives, Elmar Brok and Elisabeth Guigou, were highly rated, both by national officials as well as their colleagues at the European Parliament. Brok had excellent contacts in the German Chancellery, and via Bitterlich, one of Kohl's advisors, almost direct access to the Chancellor which he is said to have used successfully on the issue of the anti-discrimination clause. Guigou, as a former Minister of European Affairs for the socialist government in France, had good contacts to the socialist and social-democratic camp and was more generally part of the 'foreign ministers club'. Moreover, Brok and Guigou held good relations with the various Presidencies, particularly the Irish.[229]

Parliament can also make its voice heard, although in a more subtle way, by cultivating relations with NGOs, similar to the Commission. In the two public hearings held by the European Parliament in October 1995 and February 1996 more than 500 NGOs came to Brussels to comment on the weaknesses of the TEU. Apart from ensuring a greater degree of transparency and legitimacy, Parliament can use such hearings for its own purposes. As one EP official explained, 'it was convenient because most NGOs were concerned with questions such as environment, employment, equality, animal welfare, and also – to a lesser extent – justice and home affairs, which is also much the concern of the European Parliament. By giving them a voice, we had most of our own issues raised'.[230] The most prominent IGC example in the field of justice and home affairs was the issue of anti-discrimination where Parliament extensively used contributions of NGOs, in particular the Starting Line, to give more weight to its own resolutions and proposals. Parliament further asserted itself through an informal coalition with the Commission. Observers suggested that the fact that the EP's opinion to the IGC closely mirrored that of the Commission on JHA,

---

[227] Cf. European Parliament (1996a: 73).
[228] Interview, Brussels, 1997. Also Moravcsik and Nicolaïdis (1999: 71) have stated that, where they did participate, the EP representatives were effective in the negotiations. Also cf. Beach (2005: 129).
[229] McDonagh (1998).   [230] Interview, Brussels, 1997.

which had come out only a few weeks earlier, was no coincidence. 'It was a message which said: here there is common ground on which we can travel'.[231] Both clearly promoted a communitarisation of visa, asylum and immigration policy, and thus reinforced the impact of each other's stance. Finally, it has been suggested that Parliament somewhat contributed to the Title IV result by indicating that it would make its assent to enlargement conditional on a satisfactory IGC outcome.[232]

The role of the European Court of Justice   The Court of Justice has tended to interpret Community law progressively in the field of immigration policy and the related areas of anti-discrimination and free movement of third-country nationals (which have been considered in the political spillover section). The Court rejected the contention of some Member States that immigration policy fell completely outside the scope of Article 137 EC (ex-Article 118 EC) (co-operation between Member States in the social field). The Court held that migration policies could pertain to the social field within the meaning of Article 118, but only to the extent that they related to the situation of workers from non-member countries in connection with these workers' impact on the Community labour market.[233]

As far as the issue of anti-discrimination was concerned, the Court had always gone beyond the express provisions of the Treaty by holding that there was a general principle of non-discrimination in Community law.[234] The Court of Justice had concerned itself more and more often with action against not only direct but also indirect discrimination in the Union. Since the mid-1970s, the Court had repeatedly referred to the EC Treaty and related Council regulations in decisions that secured non-EU workers many of the same social, employment and fiscal rights as EU nationals, all in the name of removing barriers to free entry, mobility and establishment.[235] The jurisprudence of the ECJ had established that in respect of Turkey/EC Association and Morocco/EC Co-operation Agreements, workers from those third states had directly enforceable rights in respect of employment and social security benefits.[236]

---

[231] Interview, Brussels, 1997.
[232] Interview, Brussels, 1999; cf. Mauver 2002.
[233] See *Germany and others v. Commission* [1987] ECR 3254; cf. Hoogenboom (1993: 507).
[234] See e.g. *Frilli v. Belgium*, Case 1/72 [1972] ECR 457 and *Sotgiu v. Deutsche Bundespost*, Case 152/73 [174] ECR 153.
[235] P. Ireland (1995: 249). Also cf. Geddes (2000a: 52–4).
[236] See the following cases: *Demirel*, Case 12/86 [1987] ECR 3719; *Sivince*, Case C-192/89 [1990] ECR I-3461; *Kus*, Case C-237/91 [1992] ECR I-6781; *Kziber*, Case 18/90.

In other areas the Court managed to narrow the gap between the rights of European Union and third-country nationals which (some) Member States had fought hard to preserve. Since 1990 non-EU nationals who are family members of an EU citizen could rely on that person's rights to achieve and maintain access to the Union and its labour market.[237] The Court also took a stance on third-country nationals who were recruited by a person to provide services in one of the Member States, other than that of the person for whom the services were intended.[238] The authorities of the Member State where the services are being provided may not take any restrictive measures in respect of the employees as long as the service continues. This supports a limited right of free movement, namely to the Member State where the services are to be provided and for as long as the service lasts.

Patrick Ireland concluded that with EU Member States unwilling to grasp the nettle of fundamental, patently necessary immigration reform, the Court of Justice stepped in, supplied a policy and at least forced Member States to react.[239] On the whole, it is difficult to estimate to what extent the Court influenced the debates leading to the Amsterdam Treaty. Observers have noted that it was probably the most influential in the area of anti-discrimination.[240] Its case law was cited by various NGO proposals concerning the anti-discrimination clause.[241]

The Court also directly influenced the IGC debate. In its report to the Reflection Group, the Court made two important points early on.[242] First, in response to debates concerning potential Court-curbing measures, for example in the United Kingdom, the ECJ stressed that it was essential that its functions and prerogatives be safeguarded during the IGC, if the fundamental features of the Community legal order were to be maintained. To that end the Court needed to remain independent and its judgements binding. Second, on the issue of justice and home affairs the ECJ brought into question Article L which limited its jurisdiction in pillars II and III. The Court pointed to the problem of judicial protection of individuals affected by the activities of the Union in JHA. Such protection would need to be guaranteed in such a way as to ensure a consistent interpretation and application of both Community law and of the provisions adopted within the JHA framework. It also maintained that the insurance of uniform interpretation and application of Community law and conventions presupposes the existence of a single judicial body, such as the ECJ itself, which can give definitive

---

[237] *Singh*, case 370/1990.   [238] See *Rush Portugesa* [1990] ECR 1439.
[239] Ireland (1995: 253).   [240] Interviews, Brussels, 1997, 1999.
[241] See e.g. Justice (1996b).   [242] European Court of Justice (1995).

rulings on the law for the whole Community. It has been suggested that the Court's report was generally well received and contributed considerably to the debate on judicial review in the area of JHA.[243]

It can be argued that the ECJ was influential in getting itself chosen to fulfil the need for an international judicial review. As pointed out by Neuwahl, if one accepts that judicial control is desirable, one may ask why this should be done by the ECJ. Apart from having recourse to the Strasbourg institutions in matters coming within their jurisdiction, new courts could be established. However, not only could the creation of new courts lead to overlaps in jurisdiction between new and existing courts, the Court of Justice also has the advantage of being well-established and having a sound reputation.[244] Hence, it could be argued that the history of its jurisprudence and respectability as an institutional actor have enhanced its case for a greater involvement in the area of justice and home affairs, a crucial and particularly sensitive aspect of the wider issue of the communitarisation of visa, asylum and immigration policy, and JHA more generally.

Countervailing Forces

Integrational dynamics have to be seen in relation to the existence and strength of countervailing measures. In the absence of strong countervailing forces even weak integrative forces may drive the integration process forward. Likewise, reasonably strong pressure may not be successful when spillback pressures suffocate them. It is argued here that in the case of the communitarisation of policies on asylum, immigration and external borders, the countervailing forces were fairly substantial, i.e. of medium strength.

One very important aspect is sovereignty-consciousness. Immigration and asylum policy, and more generally, justice and home affairs, touch upon 'fundamental aspects of the traditional prerogatives of States',[245] and therefore belong 'to the core of state sovereignty'.[246] Freedom of action over their own territory and the right to decide freely on the entry and expulsion of aliens are issues 'of national identity'.[247] With the economic recessions in Europe since the early 1970s and rising numbers of refugees in the late 1980s, the political salience and sovereignty-consciousness in the area of asylum and immigration policy further increased, as they became linked to sensitive issues like unemployment

---

[243] Interviews, Brussels, 1999.
[244] Neuwahl (1995).   [245] Monar (1994: 63).   [246] Achermann (1995: 128).
[247] Baldwin-Edwards (1997: 497).

(and also internal security, the maintenance of law and order). It has been held that 'the competent ministers act as policemen of sovereignty'.[248] As pointed out above, during the IGC negotiations, JHA ministers' attention was successfully diverted away from the Conference by the Dutch Presidency through discussions on the politically expedient Action Plan on Organised Crime. This development reduced the impact of sovereignty-consciousness at the 1996–97 IGC.

Similarly inhibiting agents of sovereignty-consciousness (and domestic constraints) are bureaucrats working in national departments. 'When policemen replace diplomats' was the title of a French Senate report in 1998 which sums up the increasing involvement of internal security personnel at the European level dealing with issues such as migration management.[249] During the Amsterdam IGC bureaucrats from various functional ministries attempted to feed their countervailing demands into national positions through the process of interministerial co-ordination. The fact that the French delegation prevailed on limiting the role of the ECJ in justice and home affairs has been attributed to sovereignty-consciousness within the French government in general and within French ministries (e.g. Justice, Interior) more specifically. The Danish opt-out has also largely been explained by sovereignty-consciousness on various levels of national government and administration.

This brings us to the related issue of domestic constraints. The most significant countervailing force emerged in German domestic politics. Chancellor Kohl's refusal at the Amsterdam summit to go along with an automatic switch to QMV after three years is supposed to have been decisive as regards the final provision on voting rules in Title IV of the Treaty of Amsterdam.[250] The Kohl, who at the outset of the Intergovernmental Conference had strongly supported qualified majority voting in the area of visa, asylum and immigration policy, faced opposition within his own party. Especially several CDU *Ministerpräsidenten* of the *Länder*, above all the Bavarian, Edmund Stoiber, opposed QMV for Title IV issues, partly for ideological reasons (i.e. sovereignty-consciousness). They were also against such move because they feared potential detrimental effects of (uncontrolled) migration for their *Länder*, particularly regarding their regional labour markets. Stoiber's intervention, backed by a number of colleagues of other CDU governed *Länder*, is said to have been critical in persuading Kohl to press for a

---

[248] Van Outrive (1995: 395).   [249] On this point see: Guiraudon (2003: 267).

[250] Even though German reluctance was decisive for the final outcome, Kohl was not isolated on this. Austria, France, Denmark and the United Kingdom also had some reservations concerning an automatic switch to QMV after three years (interviews, Brussels, 1999).

toning down of the provisions on JHA matters transferred to the first pillar, particularly an abolition of the envisaged automatic switch to QMV after three years. Kohl needed their support to get the Amsterdam Treaty through the *Bundesrat*. Moreover, on the EMU debate Kohl had to stretch himself to win the support of some CDU *Länder* leaders. Insiders claim that he did not have political support for both EMU and the shedding of more sovereignty over immigration and asylum, which led him to backtrack on the latter issue, given his priority for Economic and Monetary Union.[251]

Diversity – either viewed as an aspect on its own or as a sub-issue of domestic constraints – constituted another countervailing force. Particularly, the existence of different legal traditions in the various Member States has been seen by many as a potential hindrance of policy harmonisation.[252] In addition, specific national interests related to geopolitical distinctness (i.e. constituting islands), as in the case of the United Kingdom and Ireland, obstructed a consistent communitarisation of visa, asylum and immigration policy. This geographical distinctness along with the customs union between the two countries (and British sovereignty-consciousness) can explain the opt-outs for the United Kingdom and Ireland.[253]

Finally, the general integrative climate at the Intergovernmental Conference was not very favourable.[254] National governments and the sub-national actors increasingly stressed the importance of subsidiarity, public appeal for the Community had slightly decreased and the Commission was increasingly seen as high-handed.[255] Although it is a very diffuse countervailing pressure whose influence can barely be traced, it is nevertheless suggested here that it may have had a slight detrimental impact on the integration project, including the communitarisation of visa, asylum and immigration policy.

The findings of this section suggest that countervailing or status quo pressures were fairly considerable. However, given the diversion of ministers' attention away from IGC matters and only partial/specific domestic constraints, they are not judged as 'strong' (but only as 'medium'), which will become clearer when compared with the IGC 2000.

---

[251] Interviews, Brussels and by telephone, July 1997 and April 1999. Also cf. Moravcsik and Nicolaïdis (1999: 68, 75); Devuyst (1998: 615, 620–1, 623); Beach (2005: 120).
[252] See Monar (1997: 335).   [253] See Monar (1998a: 137); Devuyst (1998: 625).
[254] It is striking, for example, that the support of EU/EC membership after 1994 has on average been about 15 per cent lower than from the mid-1980s until the early 1990s. Compare Eurobarometer No. 25–35 with Eurobarometers No. 41–61.
[255] Papademetriou (1996: 63).

Conclusion

The IGC 1996–97 case on visa, asylum and immigration policy can be explained by the revised neofunctionalist framework. In short, 'medium' countervailing pressures were 'overcome' by strong dynamics, which led to considerably progressive results. Of the two structural pressures, functional and exogenous, the former appeared to have been predominant in the considerations of decision-makers at Amsterdam. The functional pressure related to the objective of the free movement of persons was thereby assisted by pressures that arose from the dissatisfaction with the (non-achievement) of the diffuse aim of achieving 'effective co-operation' in this field (functional 'pressure from within'). Exogenous developments have constituted important complementary, though secondary, pressures for a communitarisation of the subject matters discussed here.

As for social spillover, somewhat paradoxically, the minimal development of socialisation processes at the policy-making level and the parallel occurrence of flawed co-operation among Member States, induced only very few players to conclude that the new system needed time to develop. Most concluded that the cumbersome, intergovernmental decision-making procedures were responsible for the lack of progress. While this analysis is unable to establish a clear-cut connection between the two, it nevertheless appears that minimal socialisation in the policy-making domain contributed to the pressures for reform. Social spillover not only mattered as regards policy-making in justice and home affairs but also at the Conference itself. Here there seems to have been some degree of 'club atmosphere' and induction of co-operative attitudes by the IGC representatives which allow the tentative conclusion of a moderate contribution to the progressive outcome.

Political spillover in terms of non-governmental elites has had a limited impact on the communitarisation of visa, asylum and immigration policy. However, on the immigration-related issues of anti-discrimination and the rights of third-country nationals, transnational NGOs, which have also been described as advocacy coalitions, more considerably influenced the provisions of Amsterdam. As far as cultivated spillover is concerned, this analysis suggests that the roles played by the Commission and the various Presidencies, above all, substantially promoted the process of communitarisation. The roles played by the European Parliament and the ECJ further contributed to integration.

Finally, given the perceived and predicted unlikeliness of integration entering the area of 'high politics' as well as the non-applicability of neofunctionalist theory therefore,[256] the findings of the case study are all the more remarkable. Justice and home affairs, the area which for some constitutes 'the ultimate test of "who governs?"', the national or the supranational state',[257] has witnessed a remarkable manifestation of the strength of (revised) neofunctionalist dynamics.

The Intergovernmental Conference 2000

Like external trade policy, justice and home affairs formed part of the broader issue of the extension of qualified majority voting at the IGC 2000. JHA appeared on the QMV agenda right from the beginning of discussions in early February 2000. First pillar JHA issues (Title IV TEC) of asylum, immigration and visa policy, which are the focus of this analysis, were included alongside policies subject to the third pillar (Title VI TEU) of judicial co-operation in criminal matters and police co-operation. During the IGC negotiations leading to the Treaty of Nice, the JHA cluster turned out as one out of six controversial QMV subject areas and also formed part of the Nice summit agenda.

The Nice Provisions

The IGC 2000 has brought about the following Treaty changes to Title IV TEC: first, only Article 65, on judicial co-operation in civil proceedings (with the exception of aspects related to family law), is governed by the procedure referred to in Article 251 (QMV in the Council and co-decision of the EP) since the entering into force of the Treaty of Nice. Second, Article 63, paragraph 1 (measures on asylum) and Article 63, paragraph 2a (on refugees and displaced persons under temporary protection) will change to the procedure of Article 251 subject to prior *unanimous* adoption of Community legislation defining the common rules and basic principles governing these issues.

Hence, a switch to QMV and co-decision was possible before the May 2004 date (set out in the Treaty of Amsterdam), from when the Council was to decide unanimously which areas become subject to the procedure of Article 251. On the other hand, this change depended on the unanimous agreement and specification of comprehensive basic legislation. Therefore, it was asserted in the aftermath of the conclusion of the Treaty that 'it is possible that Nice will lead to a delay of transfer to QMV'.[258] The unanimity requirement for the adoption of legislation

---

[256] E.g. Hoffmann (1995) [1964].   [257] Baker (1993: 442–3).
[258] On this interpretation see: Stuth (2001: 11).

has hampered the legislative process in these areas, as a result of which the important directive concerning minimum standards for qualification of third-country nationals as refugees was only adopted at the last moment, while the directive concerning minimum standards on procedures was delayed even further and could only finally be adopted in 2005.[259]

In addition to these Treaty changes, the contracting parties also decided upon a number of procedural advances in a declaration annexed to the final act. First, they decided to actually do what the Treaty of Amsterdam had foreseen: to switch the procedure of Article 251 from May 2004 in the cases of Article 62, paragraph 3 (measures for freedom to travel of third-country nationals) and Article 63, paragraph 3b (on illegal immigration). Second, the contracting parties agreed to change Article 62, paragraph 2a (standards and procedures concerning checks at external borders) to QMV and co-decision when agreement on the field of application concerning these matters has been reached. Finally, for Article 66 (administrative co-operation in the areas of Title IV) a switch to QMV in the Council and consultation of the EP in May 2004 has been stipulated in another separate protocol. These provisions have arguably facilitated political agreement on the respective measures. However, they are not legally binding. The (final) decision on these changes was to be taken by unanimity.

Moreover, a number of important areas have brought about no advances at all: Article 62, paragraph 1 (abolition of controls on persons at internal borders), Article 63, paragraph 2b (balanced distribution of refugees and displaced persons), Article 63, paragraph 3a (entry, residence and standards of procedure for long-term visa) and Article 63, paragraph 4 (rights and conditions for residence of certain third-country nationals). The provisions on Title IV have generally been viewed as providing rather 'minimal' or 'small' progress.[260] Moreover, the partial and deferred switch to QMV, mostly but not exclusively accompanied by co-decision, subject to different conditions, and only in part legally binding, is a rather complex and intransparent solution.

That the Council later decided to actually switch all areas under Title IV TEC, except measures regarding legal immigration and family law, to the procedure of Article 251 could not be expected when the Treaty

---

[259] Cf. Council (2004a) and Council (2005).
[260] Concerning these verdicts see e.g. Stuth (2001: 11); and Prodi (2000b: 3). Also see Lavenex (2001: 851).

of Nice was signed.[261] Part of the rationale for the December 2004 Council decision can be found in the Convention/IGC 2003–04 negotiations and outcome (see next sub-case).

Functional Spillover

During the IGC 2000, functional rationales were somewhat less potent, compared with the Amsterdam IGC. Pressure from the internal market and particularly the free movement of persons objective was diminished in terms of its rationale for the further communitarisation of visa, asylum and immigration policy. That the free movement of persons had not yet become a (complete) reality by the late 1990s was acknowledged by several sources. However, the perceived deficiencies in terms of realising this principle and the intensity of demanding progress in this area had both diminished compared with the discourse of the early and mid-1990s.[262] Also, this logic was less on the minds of decision-makers, which is reflected by the IGC 2000 documentation, where this logic was hardly cited.[263]

Instead, another internal market pressure increasingly began to unfold its rationale in the late 1990s. Despite substantial progress concerning the completion of the single market, there was still no adequate access to judicial authorities in other Member States for individuals and businesses. As a result the Tampere programme endorsed the principle of mutual recognition as the cornerstone of judicial co-operation in both civil and criminal matters.[264] It also gave the mandate for new procedural legislation in cross-border cases, in particular on those elements which are instrumental to smooth judicial co-operation and enhanced access to law. Decision-making by qualified majority voting would allow faster progress to be made in one of the last loopholes of the internal market. It has been argued that this rationale was also on the minds of (some) policy-makers when transferring Article 66 to the Community method during the IGC 2000.[265]

---

[261] Interviews (2004, 2005). In December 2004, agreement was reached to transfer Articles 62(1), (2a) and (3) as well as Article 63 (2b) and (3b) to QMV and co-decision, but not Article 63 (3a) and Article (63) (4). See Council (2004b).

[262] For sources assessing the realisation of the free movement objective in the late 1990s, see High-Level Panel on the Free Movement of Persons (1997); Commission (1998): for a comparison regarding the early and mid-1990s, see my discussion above on functional spillover regarding the Amsterdam IGC; also see Commission (1995c).

[263] Also interviews, Brussels, 2003, 2004.

[264] Monar (2001b: 755) also sees a functional logic and causal connection between the internal market and the Tampere provisions on judicial co-operation.

[265] Interview, Brussels, 2002.

Overall, the single market/free movement rationale was still frequently referred to as an important reason for more efficient decision-making rules in the Council.[266] However, the single market objective did not dominate the policy discourse to the same extent as during the Amsterdam IGC.

While internal market logics had receded, functional pressures stemming from enlargement[267] had increased. The lack of urgency in terms of forthcoming enlargement during the Amsterdam IGC had, to some extent, given way to different perceptions. The accession of (ten) new Member States had become more concrete with the launch and confirmation of the enlargement process at the Luxemburg European Council of 1997 and the Helsinki European Council of 1999, respectively, and the aim to welcome new members from the end of 2002. With 25 Member States and the corresponding diversification of interests and increased heterogeneity of political and legal cultures, it was feared that those areas which were still governed by unanimity, such as asylum, immigration and part of visa policy, would become substantially susceptible to decision-making deadlocks. Interviews mostly substantiated this growing understanding. However, in JHA – even more than in other policy areas given the already substantial differences in terms of legal traditions, migratory pressures and labour market approaches – diversity among Member States (further growing with enlargement) was also perceived as a concern, causing some reservations *vis-à-vis* QMV, because of the high costs of adjustment in the case of 'minoritisation' in the Council. However, overall the prospect of enlargement added moderate additional functional pressure for (further) communitarisation.[268]

Another potentially strong functional pressure stemmed 'from within', i.e. necessities for increased co-operation in the *same* issue area due to the dissatisfaction with the attainment of collective goals in that sector. The establishment of an area of freedom, security and justice, with Title IV as a significant component part, has become one of the most important projects of the European Union, comprising about 250 planned binding legislative acts (accounting for about 40 per cent of the Union's new legislation)[269] and backed by an effective legitimising political discourse. It is mentioned as one of the Union's core objectives

---

[266] See e.g., Benelux (2000: 5); Portuguese Presidency (2000b: 1). For a comparison with the discourse during the Amsterdam IGC, see my analysis on pp. 202–3.

[267] Although enlargement has an exogenous element, after several internal commitments (e.g. Copenhagen European Council of 1993) it largely became an endogenous source of pressure for reform of EU decision-making procedures.

[268] Interviews, Brussels 2002, 2004.

[269] On these estimations, see: Monar (2000: 18); and Grabbe (2002: 1).

in Article 2 TEU and has been furnished with concrete aims and deadlines through the provisions of the Amsterdam Treaty. These have been backed and concretised by the Vienna Action Plan of December 1998 and further substantiated and, to some extent, exceeded by the conclusions of the Tampere European Council in October 1999.[270] The substantial goals laid down in this area created pressure on the decision rules in the Council. As most of Title IV was still governed by unanimity, it was judged questionable by some whether these objectives could really be obtained without substantial delays.[271] However, the pressures in this respect were still moderate. It was widely argued that the improved provisions of the Amsterdam Treaty, which were perceived as substantial progress by many, had been in use only for a few months, that these needed to be (thoroughly) tried out first, and that it was too early to tell whether they would be inadequate to cope with the problems at hand.[272]

Exogenous Spillover

Pressures exogenous to the European integration process have remained at a fairly substantial level, comparable to that of the Amsterdam IGC. The number of asylum applications had begun to rise again in the European Union after 1996, even if in 1999 it was still only about half the 1992 level.[273] In addition, the decline in legal migration, resulting from more restrictive national approaches, was 'compensated' by increasing illegal immigration.[274] Also, EU unemployment, which was slightly diminishing after 1996, was still at a relatively high level in subsequent years[275] and still viewed as a major problem in EU Member States. Thus, since the 1980s/early 1990s Member States had increasingly opted for rather restrictive national policies. However, tolerating different asylum and immigration regimes in the EU context had invited competitive policy-making among Member States.[276] Restrictive policies in some Member States raised the burden for those with more lenient standards. Hence, member governments and administrations had become gradually aware that these policies could no longer be tackled effectively on the national level, also because of the gradual abolition of internal borders. Hence, European solutions needed to be intensified to prevent disruptive policy competition by determining

---

[270] As for the Vienna Action Plan see: Official Journal (1999: 1–15); for the Tampere programme see: Presidency Conclusions (1999a: 1–6).
[271] On these judgements, see e.g. Prodi (2000b: 3); also cf. Hänsch (2001: 100).
[272] Interviews, Brussels, 2003 and 2004.   [273] Cf. Eurostat (2003).
[274] Greens/EFA (2001: 1).   [275] Cf. Eurostat (2004: 94).
[276] Cf. Achermann (1995: 129); Uçarer (2001: 291–4); Lavenex and Uçarer (2002: 20).

common standards on which all Member States could rely.[277] Further common measures, in addition to the Schengen and Dublin Conventions, needed to be worked out, for example concerning reception standards, the qualification as a refugee and on procedures for granting and withdrawing refugee status in order to continue to even out different recipient standards. And progress in these and other areas can be attained more easily with more supranational decision rules.[278]

Social Spillover

During the Nice IGC, processes of socialisation and communicative action were substantially hampered by several factors. Perhaps most importantly, while at the IGC 1996–97, the Dutch Presidency had successfully managed to divert senior national JHA officials' and ministers' attention to the Action Plan on Organised Crime and away from the IGC, this time national ministries were much more alert and managed to assert their interests to a much greater degree. It has been noted that a substantial fraction of national officials in the area of justice and home affairs have been sceptical of the Amsterdam provisions and that they also sought to limit (further) loss of control.[279] Their views were fed into the formation of national positions through the process of inter-ministerial co-ordination. This led to tight, restrictive and inflexible instructions to IGC Representatives. As a result, a reasoned discussion on the merits of the problem at hand became difficult. In addition, co-operative norms, such as reciprocity, that usually characterise negotiations in the EU context and tend to lead to the realisation of an enlarged common interest were also countervailed by such externally induced constraints.

Second, as already pointed out in the context of the CCP, institutional topics pertaining to the balance of power between small and big Member States had led to substantial distrust among negotiators. Although these issues were largely left to the Nice summit, they also rubbed off on other issues, such as justice and home affairs. Under such circumstances, socialisation and communicative action processes had little chance to unfold. Third, even though substantial time was dedicated to the extension of qualified majority voting in the Representatives Group, there was such a large number of issues that even prominent and controversial ones, like JHA, were dedicated too little time to engage in an extensive reasoned debate on the pros and cons of extending QMV in

---

[277] Märker (2001).
[278] This line of thinking has been confirmed by interviews with decision-makers (interviews, Brussels, 2003, 2004).
[279] See Guiraudon (2003: 279, at 13).

Title IV. Fourth, as already elaborated in the context of external trade policy the shorter lifespan of the Representatives Group was detrimental to the development of intense socialisation processes.

Political Spillover

Pressures stemming from political spillover were very modest during the IGC 2000. NGOs and Think Tanks in the areas of migration, refugees and human rights had supported a communitarisation of asylum, immigration and other JHA issues since the mid-1990s, mainly because they perceived EU institutions (i.e. the Commission and the European Parliament) to pursue more balanced and liberal policies than Member States' governments. In addition, they favoured the enhanced judicial review and greater democratic control which would accompany full-fledged communitarisation. This attitude had not changed. However, NGOs and Think Tanks active in this area were not very active and outspoken on JHA during the IGC, for several reasons: first, JHA as part of the wider issue of the extension of qualified majority voting was fairly hidden on the IGC agenda. Second, despite the 'Dialogue on Europe' initiative by the Commission, in partnership with the EP and Member States, which aimed at an active dialogue with citizens and civil society, the IGC 2000 has generally been perceived as a less open process than the Convention and the Amsterdam IGC (although the contrast with the IGC 1996–97 was perceived as less sharp).[280] Third, generally speaking NGOs in the area of migration and human rights are more concerned with substantive issues (related to the content and objective of policy) than with decision-making rules. The Nice IGC, however, (almost) exclusively dealt with the latter aspect.

Cultivated Spillover

The Role of the Commission   The Commission's assertion and impact on the issue of justice and home affairs was weaker than during the Amsterdam IGC. As pointed out earlier with regard to the CCP case, the Commission was on the defensive from the very start of the Intergovernmental Conference 2000. This was partly due to the resignation of the Santer Commission in 1999 and the subsequent priority of putting its own house in order and also due to the fact that the Commission, itself an item on the agenda, was more object rather than subject to the negotiations, as a result of which the Commission was to

---

[280] Interviews, Brussels, 2004.

some extent sidelined during the IGC. The Commission did cultivate and act out some of the structural dynamics, such as the inadequacy of current decision rules for a timely implementation or swifter progress of the Amsterdam and Tampere objectives (functional pressure from within).[281] However, on the whole it was admitted that more could have been done by the Commission in that respect. In retrospect, it was deplored that energy was wasted on issues that had little chance of succeeding, such as social security, taxation or the public prosecutor, while important issues such as JHA were rather neglected.[282] There was no substantial comprehensive paper by the Commission on the extension of qualified majority voting in the area of justice and home affairs. Such a paper could have further contributed to cultivating the various structural rationales pointed out above. Also slightly detrimental for the Commission was Michel Barnier who was not at all times perceived as the Commission representative at the IGC, 'because people saw him at Amsterdam defending French interests and suddenly he was supposed to represent the Commission, while he was often following or coinciding with the French line'.[283]

The Role of the Presidency   While the Portuguese Presidency accomplished its task as an honest broker and promoter of common interests, the performance of the French Presidency in the important final half of the IGC was detrimental to a progressive outcome on Title IV. Bearing a certain similarity to my analysis concerning the Common Commercial Policy, the French Presidency can be criticised on three accounts; first, its approach concerning the extension of QMV on Title IV was not particularly ambitious, certainly not on the upper end of realism. Even at relatively early stages it introduced fall-back positions.[284] In addition, the French Presidency 'started-off right from the beginning to discuss Title IV sub-article by sub-article, and therefore invited delegations to ask for special treatments on different provisions, which inevitably watered the whole thing down'.[285] Second, the French

---

[281] Cf. e.g., Prodi (2000a: 3). Moreover, the Commission had further contributed to functional 'pressure from within' in this area by (timely) initiating several important proposals for legislation which meant that the pressure was on the Council to find agreement. For an overview of the legislation proposed by the Commission see e.g.: Brinkmann (2004).

[282] Interview, Brussels, 2002.

[283] Interview at the European Commission, Brussels, 2004.

[284] See French Presidency (2000a).

[285] Interview, Brussels, 2004. Some observers argued that bargaining over each sub-article of Title IV was taking things too far and that certain provisions could have been bundled, which might have avoided agreement on the lowest common denominator.

Presidency failed to display an adequate degree of leadership on a number of issues, including the extension of qualified majority voting in the area of JHA. Similar to the external trade issue, the Presidency did not succeed in sufficiently narrowing down the options on the table. It went into the Nice summit still undecided about the basic approach to be chosen and thus still presented two different frameworks – staying within the realm of Article 67 or to work with declarations/protocols – which both provided the possibility for further sub-options.[286] Finally, and more generally, the French Presidency somewhat departed from the principle of impartiality by advocating a shift in the balance of power between big and small Member States.[287] This adversely affected its potential role as an honest broker, especially on institutional topics, but also more generally across all issue areas and also contributed to a deteriorating negotiating climate, especially in the final phase of the IGC.

The Role of the European Parliament   The European Parliament was less influential than in the run-up to and during the Amsterdam IGC. As in the case of the Common Commercial Policy at the IGC 2000, the EP failed to make much of its enhanced role in the IGC proceedings. It missed the change to assert itself during the important agenda-setting phase by submitting its opinion at a time when the issues had already largely been framed.[288] On Title IV, as on all JHA issues, it spoke out in favour of QMV and co-decision. Brok who had been able to assert Parliament's positions, to some extent, during the IGC 1996–97 due to his excellent connections inside the Kohl government, was less effective this time on JHA as on other issues.

Countervailing Forces

Overall, the forces countervailing further communitarisation of Title IV had gathered further strength and should be judged (even) more substantial than during the Amsterdam IGC. With asylum and immigration policy constituting core state prerogatives, sovereignty-consciousness remained an important factor. Mutual trust, for example in the administration and surveillance of external borders and the efficiency of each others judicial systems, which was always one aspect of sovereignty-consciousness, seems to have become an even stronger *problematique*. With the prospect of ten new Member States, additional trust was required in the judicial systems and efficient management of external

---

[286] Cf. French Presidency (2000c: 31–3).   [287] Cf. Gray and Stubb (2001).
[288] For the EP IGC opinion, see European Parliament (2000).

borders on the part of the accession countries. As one official put it, 'with looming enlargement some people became even more sceptical concerning shedding more sovereignty. In discussions, they could rarely pinpoint any direct negative implications. It was rather a diffuse feeling of uneasiness for them'.[289]

National ministers and civil servants, by and large, continued to act as carriers of sovereignty-consciousness. As opposed to the Amsterdam IGC, when JHA ministers' attention had been captured by the Action Plan on Organised Crime and was directed away from the IGC issue of communitarisation,[290] this time ministers were very alert and conscious of the IGC, and thus constituted a (more) potent countervailing force. After the considerable integrational step that was taken at Amsterdam, national bureaucrats sought to limit 'agency loss'[291] during the legislative process and also in many cases continued to be sceptical of further JHA integration at the IGC. Substantial extension of QMV in Title IV was most strongly opposed by France, but also by Germany, Britain and Austria. French and German opposition has partly been attributed to the strong reluctance from (senior) officials in the respective ministries of interior and justice.[292]

Domestic constraints also played an important role in hindering a further communitarisation of Title IV. Asylum and immigration had become topics of very high salience in domestic politics, partly coupled with the predominating high unemployment in most Member States. With elections scheduled or expected in the United Kingdom in 2001 and in Germany and France in 2002, there was a tendency to keep the unanimity rule because opposition parties could have capitalised on this during election campaigns. Particularly in the German government this thinking seems to have prevailed.[293] In Germany, there was additional pressure from several *Länder* governments on the Federal government not to give up the national veto.[294]

Diversity further contributed to countervailing the above dynamics. The existence of different legal traditions, different migratory pressures and different priorities in migration management based on labour market and colonial histories or geographical position – further exacerbating with

---

[289] Interview, Brussels, 2002.   [290] Cf. my discussion on pp. 210, 231.
[291] On this point, see Guiraudon (2003: 279).
[292] Interviews, Brussels and by telephone, 2002 and 2004.
[293] On this point, see for example: Prevezanos (2001: 3). More generally, Givens and Luedtke have argued that high salience leads (especially restrictive) national governments either to block supranational harmonisation of immigration policy or to make sure that legislation is not subject to the scrutiny of supranational institutions. See: Givens and Luedtke (2004: 149–50).
[294] Interview, by telephone, 2002.

enlargement – all spurred the fear to be on the losing end of a qualified majority in the Council, as this could imply very high costs of adjustment for 'minoritised' Member States. Finally, the integrationist climate remained at a similarly low level as during the previous Treaty revision.

Conclusion

The dynamics at work both in the run-up to, and during, the Inter-governmental Conference 2000 were less substantial than during the IGC 1996–97. While exogenous spillover provided a similar rationale as three years prior, functional spillover pressures had changed. The internal market rationale had diminished. In addition, functional 'pressures from within' stemming from the deficiencies of the old third pillar had transformed into new pressures derived from the inadequacy of current rules for the attainment of the Amsterdam and Tampere objectives. The latter forces were still in the initial stages and had not yet gathered significant strength, as the Amsterdam decision rules had not thoroughly been tried. These decreasing functional pressures were, only to some extent, compensated by additional functional pressures stem-ming from enlargement. More grave was the fact that these still fairly substantial structural forces were not adequately acted out by agents in terms of cultivated spillover. The Commission, the French Presidency and also the European Parliament were either unable or unwilling to push for integrative outcomes, to reason out the logics for further communitarisation or to upgrade common Community interests. This was further compounded by the lack of social and political spillover pressures, especially in terms of governmental elites. Their absence removed an important basis for connecting actors with the structural (functional and exogenous) spillover rationales.

These diminished spillover dynamics were met by stronger spillback forces than at the previous IGC, particularly because of greater invol-vement of the generally sovereignty-conscious JHA officials and minis-ters, and strong domestic constraints in an increased number of Member States. This combination of dynamics and countervailing pressures can explain the relatively modest – i.e. low (to medium) – integrative out-come in terms of Title IV in the Treaty of Nice. The distribution of dynamics and spillback forces can also help us to explain the variation in terms of the different outcomes across Title IV. Most progress was made on judicial co-operation in civil matters as one of the last loopholes and deficiencies of the internal market. In this area the principle of mutual recognition was established as a cornerstone and EU laws were to be devised 'only' in the form of procedural legislation concerning cross-border cases, thus arousing fewer concerns about national sovereignty and also mitigating (potential) domestic constraints.

The Convention and the Intergovernmental Conference 2003–04

The Laeken European Council decided to convene a Convention on the Future of Europe, and thus to depart from the more standard methods of preparing EU Treaty reforms. The area of justice and home affairs was identified in the first plenary debate of the Convention as one of the subjects requiring substantial further discussion (and action). JHA became one of the main issue areas at the Convention, which is partly reflected by the fact that a Working Group on Freedom, Security and Justice was established. First pillar issues of visa, asylum and immigration policy (and judicial co-operation in civil matters) were discussed a bit less than third pillar issues of judicial co-operation in criminal matters and police co-operation. The Draft Treaty that came out of the Convention already provided for the changes which are outlined subsequently. First pillar, i.e. Title IV, issues were barely discussed at the IGC following the Convention, as a result of which only cosmetic changes were made to visa, asylum and immigration policy during the Intergovernmental Conference 2003–04.

The New Provisions on Visa, Asylum and Immigration Policy

The Treaty provisions on Title IV issues have substantially progressed in terms of breadth and depth. The following are the most important advances: (1) the Community method – i.e. qualified majority voting in the Council, co-decision of the European Parliament, the exclusive right of initiative of the Commission and jurisdiction of the European Court of Justice – has been introduced for all first pillar issues with only very few exceptions; (2) turning from decision rules to policy objectives, in terms of border control, the new Treaty talks of a 'policy', and with regard to asylum and immigration it uses the term 'common policy', instead of merely 'measures', and thus denotes a higher degree of integration; (3) specific objectives in the three fields have also been extended, including the introduction of a management system for external borders, a uniform status of asylum, a uniform status of subsidiary protection for third-country nationals, co-operation with third-countries for the purpose of managing inflows of people applying for asylum, and the combating of trafficking in persons; (4) the new structure of the Treaty abolishes, at least formally, the division of JHA into two different pillars. The current pillar separation is sub-optimal, not least because of past conflicts concerning the legal basis of cross-pillar measures.

There are few safeguards and exceptions in the new provisions: in the area of immigration policy, a prohibition of harmonisation of Member States' laws has been codified for the promotion of integration of third-country nationals. In addition, Member States' right to determine access to the labour market by third-country nationals shall remain unaffected by the Treaty provisions. Regarding judicial co-operation in civil matters, measures concerning family law will remain subject to unanimity and the European Parliament will only be consulted. It has also been judged detrimental that the Constitutional Treaty followed the system introduced at Amsterdam, whereby individual objectives are listed for each policy area. Not only is it unusual for a constitution to contain such detailed programmatic elements, these catalogues also have the disadvantage that they may be interpreted such that aims that have not been expressly stated may not be subject to Union action.[295] Overall, the new provisions, especially concerning decision rules, have commonly been judged as bringing substantial progress in terms of a further communitarisation of visa, asylum and immigration policy.[296]

Functional Spillover

All in all functional pressures on JHA decision rules had intensified after the Nice IGC. Substantially contributing to this, as in the case of external trade policy, was the ever growing pressure of enlargement with the Accession Treaty (expected to be) signed in the spring of 2003 and with the participation of new Member States in the 2004 EP elections.[297] As a result, decision-making in the Council with 25 Member States was now an imminent reality, putting substantial pressure on issue areas such as Title IV that were (mostly) subject to unanimity. In the Convention, enlargement became a frequently cited rationale to substantiate the need for reforming the decision rules of Title IV.[298] With growing understanding regarding the prospect of decision-making deadlocks in the Council, concern about growing diversity which would increase the costs of adjustment for countries outvoted in the Council had diminished.[299]

---

[295] Monar (2003: 539).
[296] Cf. e.g. Cuntz (2003: 352); Monar (2003: 540ff, 2004a: 130); Zypries (2003: 6).
[297] Presidency Conclusions (2002: 6).
[298] See e.g., Amato (2003: 1); Commission (2002d: 12–13); Hjelm-Wallen (2002).
[299] Interview, Brussels, 2004.

Perhaps equally strong functional pressures were exerted 'from within'. Dissatisfaction with the collective goal of achieving the area of freedom, security and justice – and more particularly the concrete targets set in the Treaty of Amsterdam, the Vienna Action Plan and the Tampere programme – was growing, due to little progress in the legislative process. The European Council of Laeken increased the pressure by reaffirming the commitment to the policy guidelines and objective defined at Tampere and by expressing its concern that 'progress has been slower and less substantial than expected'[300] in the area of asylum and immigration policy. Heads of State and Government at the Seville European Council of June 2002 also saw the need 'to speed up the implementation of all aspects of the programme adopted at Tampere'.[301] Similarly, the 'scoreboard', a bi-annual update established to review the progress concerning the creation of the area of freedom, security and justice indicated the severe problems of complying with the time limits that had been set. In its assessment on the second half of 2002, for example, it concluded: 'eighteen months ahead of the deadline set by the Amsterdam Treaty, only few of the objectives defined for the establishment of a common asylum and immigration policy have been met'.[302] Many observers, both in academic[303] as well as in decision/policy-making[304] circles, have made the unanimity requirement responsible for the lack of progress in this area, which reinforced the pressure for a reform of decision rules. In addition to the lack of progress concerning the Amsterdam objectives, the Tampere programme asked for substantial additional measures.[305] It stipulated important aims, some of which were likely to remain subject to agreement beyond the Amsterdam deadline. Hence, during the Convention improved decision rules in the Council were called for with a view to dealing with possible leftovers from this comprehensive programme after 2004 and further objectives set thereafter.

Similar to the case study on the Common Commercial Policy, the Laeken European Council added additional functional pressure. By putting particular emphasis on greater simplification and efficiency, the Heads of State and Government increased the rationale for JHA reform.

---

[300] Presidency Conclusions (2001: 11).
[301] Presidency Conclusions (2002: 7). Also cf. Fletcher (2003: 558).
[302] Commission (2002e: 4–5).
[303] See e.g. Fletcher (2003: 535); Monar (2003: 545).
[304] See e.g. Belgian Presidency (2001: 5).
[305] These included issues such as the harmonisation of the conditions for refugees concerning entry and stay, the right of residence for third-country nationals who wish to stay in Member States other than their country of residence, standards for long-term visas and residence permits, and provisions with respect to refugee 'burden-sharing'.

Given the complexity of its decision-making rules introduced at Amsterdam and Nice with many inconsistencies and irregularities, Title IV provided much scope for improvement along the lines set out at Laeken. As pointed out earlier, streamlining and rationalisation of halfway/hybrid decision-making provisions can go both ways: re-nationalisation or supranationalisation. However, given the various other dynamics pointing towards further communitarisation, the bias was clearly in favour of the Community method, i.e. QMV in the Council, co-decision of the European Parliament, an exclusive right of initiative for the Commission and full jurisdiction of the European Court of Justice across Title IV. The Laeken European Council had also called for more democracy and transparency. The two solutions at hand, greater involvement of the European Parliament and an enhanced role for national parliaments, were not equal competitors. Given the strong predisposition in favour of the Community method, and especially QMV, through the various dynamics, the logic was clearly to involve the EP more substantially in Title IV. Part of this rational was also that QMV should be accompanied by co-decision. As ministers could be outvoted in the Council, the democratic deficit would be dealt with more effectively through greater EP involvement.

Functional spillover rationales stemming from the single market and the free movement of persons objective had further receded. First, the perceived deficiencies in terms of realising the free movement of persons principle and the intensity of demanding progress in this area had further diminished.[306] Second, the general feeling in the policy-making and also in the academic Community was that issue areas such as asylum and immigration had for some time developed aspects and objectives beyond the abolition of internal borders and the internal market.[307] But, the free movement of persons argument still had some currency in the general JHA debate and also remained on policy makers' minds when drafting certain provisions on the area of freedom, security and justice. The latter is stated as one of the Union's fundamental objectives in Article I-3, characterised as 'without internal frontiers' and mentioned alongside the aim of 'an internal market where competition is free and undistorted'. However, the area of freedom, justice and security is now, unlike the old Title IV, more clearly separated from, and no longer 'annexed' to the fundamental freedoms/internal market provisions and has its own chapter in the Treaty. As far

---

[306] Interview, Brussels, 2004. It should also be noted that the Commission has been conspicuously more silent on the free movement objective since its 1998 communication. Cf. Commission (1998).

[307] Interview, Brussels, July 2004.

as the reasons and rationales for changing the decision rules of Title IV are concerned, the free movement of persons objective played only a subsidiary role at the Convention and the IGC 2003–04.

Exogenous Spillover

Pressures exogenous to the European integration process had very slightly grown since the previous Treaty revision. EU-wide migratory pressures in terms of asylum applications remained fairly constant between 2000 and 2002. Competitive restrictive policy-making of the 1980s and 1990s, in an attempt to solve migratory pressures at the national level, had raised awareness concerning the need for European solutions, as the nature of the problem went beyond the governance potential of individual nation-states. The perceived pressure for *common* asylum measures and decision-making by QMV was still on, as the experience with current Title IV decision rules indicated. For example, progress concerning the directives on procedures and qualification – the core provisions of a common asylum system that could potentially reduce exogenously induced problems by levelling out different national standards – was forthcoming only very slowly under unanimity, and during the Convention no agreement on these measures was yet in sight.[308]

In addition, a new exogenous dimension had arisen. The terrorist attacks of 11 September 2001 had certain implications for asylum and immigration policy, as for the area of justice and home affairs more generally.[309] The link between terrorism and immigration/asylum policy is the assumption that terrorists tend to come from outside and enter the country in question as third-country nationals – as legal immigrants as in the case of some of the perpetrators of 9/11, as illegal immigrants or as asylum seekers. Of course, the Tampere programme of December 1999 already included objectives related to the combat of terrorism. However, 9/11 was certainly a spur to work out EU level provisions, for example, the Common Position on Combating Terrorism[310] or the adoption of the Comprehensive Plan to Combat Illegal Immigration and Trafficking of Human Beings in the European Union.[311] Yet, additional anti-terrorist measures were judged necessary, for example, related to the

---

[308] Brinkmann (2004: 196–7).

[309] On the implications of 9/11 on visa, asylum and immigration policy in the European Union see Guild (2003) and Brouwer (2003).

[310] 2001/930, OJ 2001 L 344/90. It provides that measures are to be taken to prevent terrorists from being granted refugee status.

[311] 6621/02, 26 February (2002). In this plan the JHA Council reached political agreement on the possibility of inserting biometric data on visa documents and the introduction of the 'European Visa Identification System'.

expulsion, extradition and detention of (potential) terrorists. Further progress in this area would be facilitated by the extension of qualified majority voting in justice and home affairs. This rationale for QMV was accepted by a number of interviewees and also articulated less overtly by some policy-makers.[312] But on the whole, 9/11 was perceived only as a modest, and certainly not decisive, extra spur for further communitarisation.[313]

Further pressures, largely exogenous to the European integration process, had evolved as regards immigration and visa policy. In some Member States the political discourse, often in conjunction with growing concern regarding the demographic development in the European Union,[314] increasingly suggested that immigration policy should be liberalised, not least to allow for immigration of the young and well-qualified. Somewhat related to the latter point, there was and still is demand in many EU countries for highly qualified professionals, for example, in the IT sectors, to work in Member States for a number of years. In parallel, there has been talk in the WTO concerning the removal of barriers to the temporary movement of people under the GATS. These developments created pressure for simplified and more straight-forward visa procedures or a GATS visa.[315] However, these developments also do not seem to have had any substantial impact on the communitarisation debate.

Social Spillover

As in the case of the Common Commercial Policy,[316] the Convention paved the way for socialisation and communicative action processes, making a more substantial impact in the area of visa, asylum and immigration policy than during previous Treaty revisions. The conditions for social spillover were equally favourable as in the CCP case during the Convention: (1) the initial listening phase generated a (deep) understanding of members' ideas and softened pre-conceived opinions; (2) more than 50 sessions of both the Plenary and the Praesidium held over a period of eighteen months induced the development of an 'esprit

---

[312] Cf. e.g., Martikonis (2002).   [313] Interviews, Brussels, 2004.
[314] See Iglicka (2002: 327–33). On the political discourse concerning the link between demographic developments and the need for immigration, for Germany see e.g.: *Frankfurter Allgemeine Zeitung* (31/10/01: 4; 30/5/01: 8; 17/01/02: 4); concerning France see e.g.: *Le Monde Economie*, (13/11/01; 16/4/02; 24/9/02); and for the United Kingdom where this concern is less evidently reflected in the political discourse, see *The Guardian* (25/1/01).
[315] Cf. European Services Forum (2001).
[316] Cf. my social spillover analysis in the Convention/IGC 2003–04 CCP case.

de corps' and a strong sense of responsibility for a successful outcome; (3) members of the Convention were in a position to act freely and were largely unbound by governmental briefs or bureaucratic (countervailing) interests; (4) participants, on the whole, had sufficient expertise on justice and home affairs, and there was also ample time available to lead a sensible debate on the pros and cons of further communitarisation of Title IV, especially in the working group; (5) the atmosphere, spirit and negotiating structure in the Convention made it very difficult for members of the Convention to reject something without explanation, or without entering into a reasoned discussion where his or her arguments would become subject to scrutiny.

Under such conditions, bargaining recedes and negotiations are led more with a view to achieve mutual understanding through a reasoned debate. In such an environment good arguments, validated on the basis of accepted criteria, can register more easily with participants, and are therefore more likely to prevail in the discussion. Hence, the structural rationales for further integrational steps in Title IV such as enlargement, the free movement of persons, simplification, legitimacy, the inadequacy of current decision rules for a timely implementation or swifter progress of the Amsterdam and Tampere objectives, etc. now had a much better chance to be taken up by actors, thus unfolding their logic. With members of the Convention changing their views and learning from the rationales and explanations provided in discussions, 'something like a common understanding emerged on Title IV: almost everyone was satisfied, or even convinced by the results'.[317] This concurrence in the outcome substantially increased the weight and impact of the Convention text on visa asylum and immigration policy. In fact, its bonding strength was such that during the subsequent IGC, the text on Title IV issues was not reopened by Ministers and Heads of State and Government.[318]

It is difficult to substantiate the case for communicative action – i.e. to show that a lot of the time genuine arguing and deliberation occurred, as opposed to strategic arguing or rhetorical action (the use of arguments to add cheap legitimacy to one's case) – given scope restrictions.[319] Suffice it to say here that interviewees characterised the negotiations in terms of arguing and reasoning, either without being prodded, or when offered different potential characterisations. In addition, negotiators

---

[317] Interview, Brussels, 2004.
[318] Provisions on judicial co-operation in criminal matters and on police co-operation, which are however not part of this analysis, were altered during the IGC.
[319] But also see indications for socialisation and communicative action processes in the secondary literature: Cf.: Göler and Marhold (2003: esp. 323 ff); Göler (2003: esp. 27); Maurer (2003a: esp. 132 ff.).

generally avoided pointing to hierarchy, status, qualifications or other sources of power when making their statements, and thus refrained from adding non-discursive authority to their arguments.[320] Moreover, speakers' utterances in the plenary seem to be very consistent with their statements in other forums, which reinforces the case of truthful arguing. Finally, and perhaps most convincingly, 'powerful' actors did not manage to prevail in the Convention when their arguments were not persuasive. For example, when the German Foreign Minister and others sought to reintroduce unanimity for the whole area of immigration policy through amendments or in the Plenary discussion, they were not successful as their case was not convincing given the powerful rationales for further communitarisation pointed out above.[321] On the other hand, some German nationals in the Convention argued for an exclusion of Member States' right to determine access to the labour market by third-country nationals from the Treaty provisions. This was eventually taken on board by the Praesidium, partly because it could affect the sensitive area of Member States' labour/employment legislation and was thus considered justified by quite a number of people. However, this provision was also, to some extent, included for strategic considerations, i.e. in order to ensure the full backing of the Convention text by the German government. This does not confirm with the tenets of communicative action, but occurred in the final stages of the Convention – referred to by some as the 'pre-IGC stage' – which was to a much lesser extent characterised by the above conditions.

Political Spillover

Throughout the last Treaty revision, the role of organised interests provided a (slightly) increased, albeit not decisive, impetus for Title IV decision rule reform compared with the IGC 2000. NGOs and, to a lesser extent, Think Tanks concerned mainly with issues of migration, refugees and human rights got more involved in the debates on visa, asylum and immigration policy, due to the fact that JHA figured much more prominently on the agenda than during the Nice IGC, and because the Convention was a more open process and provided more extensive possibilities for involvement than the Nice IGC. On many occasions NGOs in the area of migration, refugees and human rights managed to pool their resources and issued joint position papers

---

[320] This point has been confirmed by several interviewees, including Klaus Hänsch, member of the Convention for the EP: Interview, July 2004.

[321] Cf., for example, Fischer (2003).

and submissions.[322] Apart from pursuing direct contacts, some also attended the public hearings and used the chance to put their views to members of the Convention directly.

All in all, NGOs and Think Tanks active in this area came out clearly in favour of the Community method. Perhaps most consistently, they asked for greater judicial supervision through the European Court of Justice, particularly a system permitting all national courts to refer cases to the ECJ[323] which would enable a timely conclusion of cases and prevent divergences in the implementation of EC law. This would be desirable from the perspective of human rights and a fair and efficient functioning of EU asylum and immigration law. It would enable a more effective challenge to EC legislation in the migration field, as national courts cannot rule invalid Community acts without first obtaining an ECJ opinion. NGOs also uniformly asked for more democratic accountability, which entailed a greater role (co-decision) for the EP. The European Parliament was generally viewed by Rights NGOs as a counter weight to (some) Member States' restrictive policies on asylum and immigration.[324] NGOs and Think Tanks concerned with issues of migration, refugees and human rights also, although slightly less outspokenly, favoured an extension of QMV to ensure more effective decision-making. Also, the unanimity rule is perceived to foster lowest common denominator decisions which tend to favour restrictive measures, while the protection of refugee rights, and integration issues more generally, tend to fall by the wayside.[325]

Overall, decision-makers seem to have taken notice of NGO input on JHA issues. Their views were generally seen as one of several sources of information for members of the Convention. NGO contributions had most leverage during the early, i.e. agenda-setting, stages of the Convention when members were still in the process of making up their minds. In addition to their direct influence during the Convention and IGC 2003–04, NGOs and Think Tanks have since the mid-1990s consistently and regularly contributed to the policy discourse with their calls for more judicial supervision, democratic accountability and decision-making effectiveness. Their influence in that respect is difficult to measure. However, as one member of the Convention put it, 'when you get these views over many years, they do influence your thinking to an

---

[322] See e.g. Standing Committee of Experts on International Immigration *et al.* (2002); Amnesty International *et al.* (2003).
[323] Under the current provision of Article 68 TEC only final courts have the right to refer cases to the ECJ.
[324] Cf. Standing Committee of Experts on International Immigration *et al.* (2002: 12–13).
[325] Interview, Brussels 2004. Also see Uçarer (2001: 303).

extent, especially when you take the views of civil society seriously'.[326] By generally supporting the Draft Constitutional Treaty, NGOs and Think Tanks active in the area of migration and human rights contributed to reinforcing the bonding strength of the Convention text and thus also to a far-reaching overall outcome, including the one on Title IV issues.

Cultivated Spillover

The Role of the Commission   Despite the diverging accounts concerning the Commission's overall performance in the last Treaty revision, it can be held that regarding Title IV issues its assertion and influence had substantially increased compared with the IGC 2000. Three factors mainly contributed to this: first, the Commission actively fostered spillover by making a (more) considerable effort to explain the structural rationales for further integrative steps in the area of visa, asylum and immigration policy, for example, by pointing to the inadequacy of current decision rules for a timely implementation or swifter progress of the Amsterdam and Tampere objectives (functional 'pressure from within'). The Commission did so both by pursuing personal contacts with member governments and other political actors and through interventions and papers at the Convention and other forums.[327] As for the argument concerning functional 'pressure from within', the Commission had also contributed to its very rationale by (timely) initiating the required legislative proposals. The pressure was thus on the Council to find agreement, which further spurred the revelation of problems attached to the unanimity rule.[328]

Second and somewhat related to the first point, in the Working Group on Freedom, Security and Justice, as well as in the Plenary, the Commission was represented by Antonio Vitorino, who was able to influence the debates through his superior expertise, his persuasive argumentation, his reputation as credible and trustworthy, and finally due to the enormous amount of political energy that Vitorino and his cabinet had invested in the Convention and IGC.[329]

Third, the deliberative decision-style which predominated in the Convention meant that arguments and explanations attached to

---

[326] Interview, Brussels 2004.

[327] See e.g. Vitorino, Antonio (2001: 2 ; 2002 : 2).

[328] For an overview of the legislation proposed by the Commission and the progress made in the Council, see e.g.: Brinkmann (2004).

[329] On Vitorino's influence on the JHA debate see e.g., Goulard (2003: 374); Beach (2005: 198). Further Commission expertise was brought to the Convention through invited experts, such as Jean-Louis de Brouwer, Head of Unit, DG, Justice and Home Affairs.

propositions were considered more openly and seriously by participants. It also entailed that good arguments could register more easily
with negotiators. And the Commission could and did make powerful
arguments in favour of a further communitarisation of Title IV by
pointing to the various structural rationales.

The Role of the European Parliament   As in the case of the
Common Commercial Policy, the European Parliament made a considerably bigger impact on the last Treaty revision in the field of visa,
asylum and immigration policy than during the IGC 2000. As pointed
out earlier, members of the EP managed to assert themselves because,
apart from the small Commission delegation, they formed the most
coherent and best organised fraction in the Convention. In addition,
members of the European Parliament were among the most active ones
at the Convention, also in the area of justice and home affairs. They
frequently intervened in Plenary and Working Group debates and
contributed their own papers to the discussion. Klaus Hänsch (PES),
Elmar Brok (EPP), Andrew Duff (Liberals) and Johannes Voggenhuber
(Greens), who all supported the extension of Community competence
and qualified majority voting (as well concerning Title IV issues), also
played a prominent role in their respective political families. On substance MEPs, with few exceptions, were alongside the two Commission
representatives, perhaps the most fervent supporters of the Community
method in all policy areas of JHA, including visa, asylum and immigration. This way, members of the EP pushed several of the above-
mentioned structural rationales for further integration and thus became
active agents of spillover.[330] In the end, MEPs and the European Parliament more generally were among the strongest, if not the strongest,
defenders of the Draft Constitutional Treaty and thus considerably
contributed to its bonding strength.[331]

The Role of the Presidency   The role of the various Presidencies
during the IGC is of lesser relevance to the analysis of visa, asylum and
immigration policy. The mutual agreement on Title IV issues reached
during the Convention was, apart from some cosmetic changes, left
untouched during the Intergovernmental Conference. As described earlier,
the Italian Presidency mildly contributed to the stalemate at the summit

---

[330] See e.g. Brok (2002: esp.1, 4).
[331] Concerning support of the European Parliament for the Draft Constitutional Treaty,
see e.g. European Parliament (2003b: 7); moreover, many/most of the sixty-three
parliamentarians who signed the plea to keep the Draft Constitutional Treaty were
MEPs (cf. *Frankfurter Allgemeine Zeitung* 14/11/03: 1). See also Beach (2005).

meeting of December 2003 which threatened to bring down the entire package and eventually only delayed agreement on the Constitution. Not to forget the Belgian Presidency in the second half of 2001, which was one factor in turning the idea of a Convention into reality and also had an impact on the broad mandate of the Convention.[332]

Countervailing Forces

During the Convention phase, countervailing pressures manifested to a (much) lesser degree than during an IGC. Generally speaking, countervailing forces were still latently present in Member States' political systems including governments and administrations. The big difference was two-fold: (1) the Convention structure and environment shut out most of the looming countervailing pressures; (2) those countervailing forces that made it onto the Convention stage had to withstand the process of deliberation and truth-seeking which largely prevailed. As far as the first point is concerned, although members arrived at the Convention with certain domestic or institutional socialisations and frames guiding their behaviour, all in all they were able to negotiate freely without significant restrictions.[333] As a result, domestic factors, while constituting (important) sources of information and feedback mechanisms, were far less constraining for members of the Convention than for negotiators in an IGC.

More specifically, national civil servants, and also ministers responsible for JHA – who have been identified as important agents of sovereignty-consciousness and who also constitute a principal source of domestic constraints – were largely shut out from the process. Due to the absence of inter-departmental co-ordination, representatives of national governments were not confined by the influence of the various functional ministries. The importance of this change has been particularly emphasised for the German government and administration. In the Nice IGC, the Ministry of Interior was very influential in terms of shaping the formation of the German position along restrictive lines, close to the *status-quo*. During the Convention it was difficult for the Ministry to assert itself due to the divergence from the resort principle and the much greater independence of the German Convention

---

[332] For a more detailed account of the Italian and Belgian Presidencies, see my analysis on these Presidencies in the CCP case study.

[333] The general freedom and independence of action has been confirmed by several interviewees (e.g. interview with Klaus Hänsch (Brussels, July 2004), and also by Maurer (2003a: 134–7). But also cf. Magnette and Nicolaïdis (2004: 393).

members. Only towards the end of the Convention the Ministry is said to have made some impact on the line of the German government.

The German *Länder* also failed to make an equally countervailing impact as during previous IGCs. Erwin Teufel, the *Länder* representative was not a member of the Working Group on Freedom, Security and Justice. As a result he was less capable of influencing the emerging consensus in JHA matters, to which the Working Group substantially contributed. Towards the end of the Convention Teufel and also German government representative Fischer became more vocal in their attempts to modify the emerging consensus.[334] It was, however, more difficult to influence matters at this stage, not least because considerable common agreement had already materialised through discussions in the Working Group and in the Plenary.

As for the second principle explanation, it was more difficult for those countervailing pressures that slipped through the Convention filter to register in an open debate than during a process in which all participants have a *de facto* veto. In a deliberative process, arguments stemming from countervailing pressures become subject to scrutiny along commonly accepted criteria and are also judged against other arguments, i.e. those stemming from the various functional and exogenous spillover rationales. Hence, Fischer and Teufel had, to a greater extent than in an IGC context, to persuade other participants as regards the merits of their arguments. As pointed out earlier, Fischer, Teufel, UK government representative Hain and others who tried to 'water down' the progressive emerging consensus, to a large part did not succeed to assert their proposals, because their arguments were only accepted to a limited extent. Of course, one should not overstate the impact of communicative action in terms of easing countervailing pressures. For example, the decision on the exception in the area of immigration regarding access to the labour market for third-country nationals has been influenced by strategic considerations of the Praesidium. The latter sought to win the overall support of the German government on the Convention text in order to augment its weight in the light of the forthcoming IGC. It is interesting to note, however, that most of the few modifications concerning Title IV issues were made in the final stage of the Convention, which some observers have termed the 'pre-IGC stage', during which some of the above pointed Convention structures which are disadvantageous to countervailing pressures had, to some extent, disappeared.

---

[334] See proposed amendments by Teufel and Fischer to the Draft Treaty (on policies concerning border checks, asylum and immigration) published on the Convention website: http://european-convention.eu.int/amendments.asp?content=848&lang=EN.

Sovereignty-consciousness manifested through a number of Convention members, especially those from Eurosceptic parties or from Member States that were traditionally more cautious in the delegation of sovereignty to supranational institutions. Individuals who spoke out against progressive Title IV decision rules who fit this description include Poul Schlüter, Alternate Representative of the Danish Government, Peter Skaarup of the Danish People's Party or Timothy Kirkhope, MEP (British Conservative). However, they were clearly in the vast minority and their arguments were generally not accepted in processes of reasoning and deliberation. Moreover, some sovereignty-conscious tendencies among Convention members, to a certain extent, eased during the Convention as a result of socialisation and learning processes.[335]

The small number of exceptions to a full communitarisation can be explained by the few islands of strong countervailing pressures that made it onto the Convention stage. Most prominently, exclusion of the right to determine access to the labour market by third-country nationals can be attributed to strong domestic constraints (and some sovereignty concerns) in Germany. Very important in that respect was the pressure from the CDU/CSU opposition which itself has partly been explained by ideological/sovereignty-conscious rationales. The opposition is said to have 'blackmailed' the government not to give in on that question, as otherwise it would block the domestic immigration bill in the Bundesrat. In addition, the German government feared the conservative opposition would exploit the issue by accusing the government of disrespecting national interests and thus spark off a domestic political debate on the issue, on which most Germans were rather sceptical and cautious according to opinion polls.[336]

The reduced countervailing pressures also had an impact, beyond the Convention, on the entire Treaty revision exercise. Due to the considerable bonding strength of the Convention, described above, the results of the Convention had a much greater significance than normal IGC pre-negotiations or preparation exercises. Because of the satisfaction with, and concurrence in, the outcome concerning Title IV issues, there was strong agreement not to reopen the Convention text on visa, asylum and immigration policy. Hence, it was very difficult for any countervailing pressures to manifest to an extent which would have

---

[335] Erwin Teufel, representing the German Länder is said to have undergone such processes (interview, Brussels 2004). Also cf. Die Tageszeitung (14/6/03: 9).

[336] On the pressure by the CDU/CSU opposition see *Frankfurter Rundschau online* (5/7/03; 9/7/03); on German opinion poll figures concerning this and related questions, see *Frankfurter Rundschau online* (3/5/04).

led to a change in the provisions. When the IGC formally began in October 2003, countervailing pressures gathered greater strength. Some pressures, such as bureaucratic constraints, however, could not unfold to the same extent as during former IGCs because the IGC 2003–04 was conducted on the political level and was also shorter, thus providing less scope for the materialisation of spillback forces. But most importantly, because Title IV issues were almost entirely kept off the agenda, countervailing forces were not really brought to bear on these issues.[337]

Conclusion

The theoretical framework outlined in Chapter 1 adds much to our understanding concerning the progressive results of the last Treaty revision on visa, asylum and immigration policy. On the one hand, the dynamics of integration had gathered further strength. Structural (functional and, to a lesser extent, exogenous) spillover rationales had grown. In addition, agents that can typically be expected to act upon these structural pressures, such as the Commission and the European Parliament, were more able to assert themselves. Furthermore, social spillover pressures provided the much needed lubricant between structures and agents during the Convention and constituted an important platform for the unfolding of structural pressures. Convincing arguments built on functional and exogenous spillover rationale could register with actors due to important processes of enmeshment, socialisation, deliberation and arguing. Social spillover also contributed to the bonding strength of the Convention text. Strong support for the Draft Constitutional Treaty changed the basic default condition at the subsequent IGC from one in which a far-reaching solution would not happen in the event of no agreement (as in the case of a 'normal' IGC preparation exercise) to one where the progressive outcome would persist unless a strong fraction of Member States seek to reopen the issue.[338] On the other hand, countervailing pressures were diminished in comparison with the Amsterdam and Nice IGCs. As a result, a stronger ignition and dissemination of integrational dynamics was possible.

The interplay between dynamics and countervailing pressures can also explain the more specific aspects of the final outcome concerning

---

[337] The countervailing pressures that predominated in the last IGC more generally and threatened to bring down the process in the autumn and winter 2003–04 are described in the Convention/IGC 2003–04 CCP case.

[338] This also helps explaining the relative ease with which many aspects of the Convention text survived the IGC, including the negotiations on external trade policy and on visa, asylum and immigration policy.

decision rules. First of all, agreement on the Community method across the whole of Title IV can be explicated as follows: as pointed out above, most pressure was exerted in terms of the voting system in the Council; the deficiency of the unanimity rule in making legislative progress considering the aims of Amsterdam and Tampere (functional 'pressures from within'), coupled with exogenous spillover, internal market, enlargement and efficiency rationales which were taken up by the Commission, the EP and other actors, all pushed for an extension of qualified majority voting. Pressure for co-decision of the European Parliament in the legislative process was exerted through the legitimacy and simplification aims stipulated at Laeken, was acted upon especially by the EP and NGOs, and was also reinforced by the overall QMV logic due to the link which has often been made between co-decision and qualified majority voting. The enhanced jurisdiction of the European Court of Justice can be attributed to the Laeken goal of simplification, the strong support for this reform on the part of NGOs and to the overall rationale for the Community method, which resulted from the pressures for QMV and co-decision. Some actors, like the Commission, also explicitly reasoned in favour of the Community method and the inter-relatedness of these elements.[339] The few aspects which remained close to the *status quo* can be attributed to certain instances of particularly persistent countervailing forces that made it onto the Convention stage, as the case of Germany and specific areas immigration policy have indicated.

---

[339] See e.g. Commission (2002b).

5 Conclusion

The aim of this book has been to restate and develop the original neo-functionalist theory as an approach for explaining outcomes of EU decision-making and to assess the usefulness of the revised neo-functionalist framework in explaining (1) the emergence and development of the PHARE programme, (2) the reform of the Common Commercial Policy and (3) the communitarisation of visa, asylum and immigration policy.

The analysis has indicated the general utility of neofunctionalist insights as a theoretical basis for such an assessment. However, for an adequate understanding of EU decision-making in the above cases, a number of original neofunctionalist assumptions had to be clarified, dropped and reformulated. Taking early neofunctionalism as a starting point, the revised framework departs from it in several ways: a more explicitly 'soft' constructivist ontology has been formulated (and combined with the 'soft' rational-choice ontology of Haas's neofunctionalism) along with a more equal ontological status between structure and agents. Integration is no longer viewed as an automatic and exclusively dynamic process, but rather occurs under certain conditions and is better characterised as a dialectic process, i.e. the product of both dynamics and countervailing forces. In addition, instead of a grand theory, the revised approach is understood as a wide-ranging, but partial, theory. Moreover, the 'end of ideology' and 'unabated economic growth' assumptions, which were particularly time sensitive, have been buried. And while elites are still attributed a primary role for decision outcomes, the wider publics are assumed to impact on the evolution of the European integration process, too.

The explanatory variables of the revised approach have been further developed and specified. Perhaps most obviously, countervailing forces, mainly in the form of domestic constraints and diversities as well as sovereignty-consciousness, have been hypothesised for. Also, exogenous spillover has been included in order to account for the tensions and contradictions originating outside the European integration process itself. In addition, other more established neofunctionalist concepts have been further extended and refined. Functional spillover has been broadened in scope to go beyond merely economic linkages. It departs from a more deterministic ontology and thus reflects a 'soft' functionalism. Functional 'pressure from within' – which captures pressures for increased co-operation within the same, rather than another, sector – has been made more explicit and upgraded as an explanatory tool. So has cultivated spillover, which has also been widened to include the integrative roles played by the Council Presidency, the European Parliament, the European Court of Justice and epistemic communities. The concept of political spillover has also been stretched. Interest groups are taken to be influenced not only by endogenous-functional, but also by exogenous and domestic structures. Advocacy coalitions have also been incorporated within political spillover. The concept of social spillover has been split off from political spillover, in order to (better) explain reflexive learning processes. The concepts of communicative and norm-regulated action have been incorporated to describe and explain socialisation more adequately. Learning and socialisation are no longer seen as constant but subject to conditions.

This chapter reflects upon my analysis in the preceding chapters and offers conclusions on a number of empirical, theoretical and methodological aspects. First, my findings on each of the revised neofunctionalist pressures are summarised and assessed in terms of the presumptions of the revised framework. The various pressures are also linked to the wider theoretical context. In addition, some conditions for delimiting the various pressures that can be extrapolated from my analysis of Chapters 2, 3 and 4 are suggested. These proposed conditions are to be understood as tentative rather than (systematically) probed or tested. The second section of this chapter deepens my analysis in terms of comparison and causality. Third, the revised neofunctionalist framework is integrated more systematically into the wider theoretical cosmos and related more closely to important disciplinary debates. The final section discusses several potential shortcomings and offers some final thoughts.

Analysis of Hypothesised Pressures

Functional Spillover

My tracing and analysis of causal mechanisms and processes in the three empirical chapters has underlined the substantial causal importance of the concept of functional spillover as well as the subsidiary concept of functional 'pressure from within'. Functional pressures were the weakest during the Amsterdam IGC negotiations on the extension of Article 113. Functional arguments derived from the internal market and the 'implied' powers doctrine did not really make sense with regard to services and intellectual property rights. This was not only the opinion of the Court in 1/94, but was also widely accepted within the Commission which henceforth made minimal use of the argument that the CCP had to be extended to safeguard the functioning of the internal market. Functional pressures increased during the last two Treaty revisions, particularly due to the linkage with the goal of enlargement. The latter objective reinforced the logic of QMV and – combined with the Laeken aims of greater legitimacy – also strengthened the rationale for an enhanced role of the European Parliament.

Functional pressures have been the most forceful in the case study on the communitarisation of visa, asylum and immigration policy at the Amsterdam IGC where they contributed very substantially to the far-reaching outcome. Those pressures stemmed primarily from the free movement of persons objective which was considered realisable only if certain flanking measures were taken in the areas of visa, asylum and immigration policy to compensate for the elimination of intra-Community borders. The rationale for changes in the institutional set-up in those areas was that existing (intergovernmental) measures had not been effective in bringing about the required flanking measures. These pressures were further reinforced by functional pressures which arose from the dissatisfaction over the non-achievement of the diffuse aim of developing 'close co-operation' in this field, as stipulated in Article B TEU (functional 'pressure from within'). At the Nice IGC functional pressures, both in terms of the sector-to-sector logic and 'from within', had diminished especially due to the decreasingly perceived internal market logic and because 'pressures from within', related to the Amsterdam and Tampere goals, were not (yet) accepted by decision-makers since the new decision rules had not been thoroughly tested. The last Treaty revision again witnessed stronger functional necessities, partly because pressures stemming from the Amsterdam and Tampere objectives were now considered difficult to attain with existing decision rules and partly due to the steadily increasing pressure of enlargement, along with added weight from the Laeken European Council objectives.

In the case of the PHARE programme, functional spillover also played an important role. The adoption of the pre-accession strategy was largely the result of functional pressures. As the initial commitment for accession at the Copenhagen European Council required an intensified effort to make the CEEC fit for enlargement, the logic was to change the focus and increase the volume of the PHARE programme at the Essen and Cannes European Councils. Later expansions of the pre-accession strategy can also be attributed to the growing commitment of Member States in terms of enlargement, for example, in response to the launching of the accession process in Luxembourg 1997 and with political agreement on the Agenda 2000 (including the financial framework for 2000–06) in Berlin 1999.

Functional 'pressure from within', derived from the original neo-functionalist foundations as a variation of functional spillover, proved to be a useful analytical tool, especially in the area of visa, asylum and immigration policy. While functional pressure from within had not attained a very high explanatory status in the original neofunctionalist formulations, and has been largely ignored by scholars in their analyses of EC decision-making, the revised neofunctionalist framework has firmly integrated this almost forgotten insight. In fact, as in the EU context Member States can often only agree on half-way house solutions and short-term compromises, falling short of the means and methods necessary to attain certain objectives, there is bound to be continuous potential for functional pressure from within.

The theoretical utility of the spillover concept can be enhanced by delimiting it. My analysis in Chapters 2, 3 and 4 has suggested a number of (further) specifications and refinements of the concept of functional spillover as well as conditions under which it is most likely to occur. First, as repeatedly alluded to, functional pressures are only as strong as they are perceived. This is because functional spillover is a structural pressure and structures need agents to translate those pressures. This specification has allowed us to draw member governments closer into (revised) neofunctionalist theory, not least because functional inter-dependencies constitute one source of their preference formation. It also underlines that functional structures make certain actions plausible, but they do not 'determine' behaviour in any mechanical or predictable fashion. If (national) decision-makers are not convinced by a functional logic, pressures are weak. Similarly, even somewhat 'flawed' functional arguments can be powerful. As Chapter 4 has shown, the free move-ment of persons argument seems to have had its limitations, as frontiers have always been permeable anyway. However, it constituted a very strong pressure because decision-makers were convinced by the free movement of persons argument and acted upon it.

The second condition for functional spillover, which is linked to the previous point, is that the original issue area and objectives therein have to be perceived as salient.[1] Both the free movement of persons and the

---

[1] Haas (1961: 372) held more narrowly that it has to be a vital area of welfare.

aim of preparing the CEEC for enlargement have been considered important by decision-makers. Third, as pointed out by Schmitter and by Pierson and Leibfried, functional interdependencies are most likely to occur in the presence of 'high issue density'.[2] They have pointed out that, in contrast to any existing international organisation, the scope of decisions made at the European level runs nearly the whole range of traditional domestic issues. Chiefly responsible for this development has been the massive expansion of Community decision-making in the past fifteen years, largely due to the single market programme.[3] Pierson has demonstrated that with an increase of issue areas on the European level there is an exponential expansion of connections between issue areas. For example, with four issue areas there are six possible connections, while with eight areas the number of potential connections rises to twenty-eight.[4] Hence, this would suggest that there is growing potential for functional linkages and functional spillover processes as the integration process proceeds. This may also explain the resurgence of integration since the 1992 project.[5]

Finally, as the IGC case study on the extension of Article 113 has shown, Member States can sometimes foresee that further integration in one area (external policy) may create problems in other areas which in turn fosters pressures for further (internal) harmonisation. This insight constitutes a useful clarification and refinement of the concept of functional spillover, as it further contributes to bringing member governments, which were often regarded rather passively by neofunctionalism, back in: member governments can anticipate future functional problems and pressures. Although a first integrative step is not regarded as completely undesirable, it is the implications of that step which may persuade member governments to not even take that first step.[6] However, as pointed out by Haas and more recently elaborated by Pierson decision-makers normally have restricted time horizons.[7] Their first concern may be less with the safeguarding of sovereignty than with creating the conditions of continued domestic success. As a result, governments are usually more interested in the short-term consequences of their actions, whereas long-term effects are frequently discounted. Long-term institutional consequences are often the by-product of actions taken for short-term political reasons. This confirms the validity of the original neofunctionalist maxim on 'unintended consequences', i.e. the inability of governments to see the consequences of their actions.

[2] Schmitter (1969:163); Pierson (1998: 40).   [3] See Leibfried and Pierson (1995: 65).
[4] Pierson (1996: 137).   [5] Cf. McNamara (1993: 320–1).
[6] Cf. my analysis on functional spillover in Chapter 3.
[7] Cf. Haas (1970: 627).

It also explains why functional spillover is possible and why visionary and selfless politicians may be an obstacle to the workings of functional spillover.

The causal relevance of the concept of functional spillover, which can be derived from tracing and analysing causal mechanisms and processes in the three empirical chapters, is further substantiated in the second main section of this chapter that intensifies my analysis regarding 'comparison and causality'. Overall, this allows for the conclusion that functional spillover remains the structural backbone of the revised neofunctionalist dynamics.

The value of the concept of functional spillover has also been high-lighted more generally in the literature of the past fifteen years. It has been pointed out by a number of scholars that, although functional spillover is not an automatic process, 'it does have visible effects'.[8] Some recent studies have highlighted the potential integrative force of func-tional pressures, especially in terms of spillovers from the ECSC to the EEC[9] from the 1992 project to EMU[10] and from the single market to the domain of social policy[11] as well as energy policy.[12] In addition, Schmitter has suggested that the potential for further exploitation of functional interdependencies has not been exhausted and may affect areas such as transport, communications and financial services.[13] Moreover, some of the more recent approaches to European integration such as the fusion theory and historical institutionalism have made use of and incorporated the concept of functional spillover.[14]

Social Spillover

The analysis of social spillover which focused on socialisation in the Council framework and more specifically on processes occurring in the Council committees and working groups[15] has indicated that sociali-sation processes do take place amongst national civil servants engaged in the Council framework. New participants are induced to and adopt the norms that predominate in the system, mainly through the socialising mechanisms and pressures exerted by working groups and committees, the Permanent Representations and by holding the Presidency. It has

---

[8] Kohler-Koch (1996: 362).   [9] George (1991: 23ff).
[10] Padoa-Schioppa (1987); Mutimer (1989: 91ff).
[11] Pierson and Leibfried (1995: 441); Jensen (2000: 71–92).
[12] Matlary (1997).   [13] Schmitter (2004: 66).
[14] Cf. Wessels (1997: 288); Pierson (1998: 40f).
[15] For an analysis of wider socialisation and also Europeanisation processes in government departments, see, for example, Bulmer and Burch (1998). Socialisation processes in the Commission are dealt with by Hooghe (1999).

been suggested that norms are internalised through adaptation and habitualisation (i.e. quantity/duration of interaction) and through argumentation and persuasion (i.e. quality of interaction). In addition, Chapter 2 allows for the preliminary conclusion that, contrary to mainstream accounts of EU negotiations, behaviour other than strategic interaction takes place in EU decision-making on the official level, along the lines of normatively regulated and communicative action. Moreover, it has been suggested that socialisation processes, especially by inducing inter-committee rivalries and coalition formation, along with normatively oriented and communicative behaviours may spur agreement and more integrative outcomes.

These findings on the occurrence of socialisation processes are particularly important in two respects. First, with regard to Europeanisation trends, according to which national ministries consider it increasingly important to be present in Brussels to assert themselves[16], the socialisation phenomenon suggests that ministries may not only shift their attention and participation to the Brussels arena, but that this may not necessarily have detrimental effects on EU decision-making and consensus formation, as new players tend to be socialised into the consensual norms of the system. Second, as far as EU enlargement is concerned, socialisation may partly explain why a decision-making system, originally designed by a Community of six, still works, more or less reasonably, with fifteen or twenty-five members. It can be expected that socialisation processes may absorb some of the difficulties that lie ahead in terms of decision-making regarding the most recent accession to the Union as well as future EU enlargements, as new members are likely to become socialised into the club.

The three case studies, and especially the two IGC ones, have pointed to a number of factors specifying and delimiting the concept of social spillover. First, socialisation processes do take time. As the analyses of the different IGC Representative Groups and of the K4 Committee have shown, newly created forums with new members do not display the same level of co-operative norms as working groups and committees that have existed over many years such as COREPER, the Central Europe Working Group or the Article 113/133 Committee. Second, if one member of the 'club', particularly the Commission, is not sufficiently trusted, as in the case of the reform of the CCP especially during the Amsterdam IGC, pro-integrative behaviour on the part of national

---

[16] On this specific understanding of 'Europeanisation' see Rometsch and Wessels (1996). On the various meanings of the term and the usefulness of the concept see: Olsen (2002: 921ff.).

officials is clearly hampered.[17] In addition, when basic distrust among delegations prevails, even on issues not directly related to the one in question, as witnessed during the second half of the Nice IGC regarding institutional dossiers, this tends to rub off on discussions more generally and seems to have disruptive influence on social spillover processes. Third, when strong adverse bureaucratic pressures occur, as in the CCP case, socialisation processes can be obstructed or offset.[18] Fourth, political pressures exerted by the domestic political system may obstruct the impact of the socialisation process on outcomes. National civil servants and administrations may be subject to considerable demands from industry, interest groups, public opinion, opposition parties or other domestic political pressure.[19] The fifth conditioning factor of social spillover is the nature of the subject area combined with the background of negotiators. If negotiations are rather technical in nature and negotiators do not possess enough expertise, as in the case of the extension of Article 113, there is little scope for communicative behaviour whereby actors could persuade each other. Given the near impossibility of any real argumentative debate amongst negotiators, any progress is then dependent on bargaining or compromising Member States' strategic positions. Sixth, and closely related to the previous point, when too little time is devoted to an issue, such as the reform of the CCP at the 1996–97 and 2000 IGCs, there is neither enough time to get to know in depth each other's problems on the issue, nor for engaging in an extensive argumentative debate about the pros and cons. Thus, the lack of time devoted to an issue certainly obstructs the occurrence of socialisation processes. Seventh, too much diversity in origin and fragmentation in delegations further conditions the workings of socialisation processes in committees and working groups. The development of personal contacts and an *esprit de corps* is hampered when officials are of too many different departments and the *porte parole* frequently changes within delegations, as has happened in the K4 Committee. Finally, social spillover may be impeded when officials are *a priori* against changing their norms and habits and feel that they have been dragged into co-operation in the Union framework, as has been the case with JHA officials and ministers during the post-Maastricht/Amsterdam phase.

---

[17] However, Commission distrust is far less detrimental in the various Article 113/133 (Sub-)Committees, largely because the matters agreed upon in the day-to-day decision-making only occasionally involve the issue of competencies and rarely have (significant) integrative implications (interviews, Brussels, 1997). For a more detailed analysis of socialisation processes in the Article 113 Committee, see Niemann (2004: 388ff); and Niemann (1997a: 7ff).

[18] Cf. Taylor (1983) and Pinder (1991a: ch. 2).   [19] Cf. Moravcsik (1993: 487–8).

A comparison across the various chapters shows the above conditioning factors at work and indicates their usefulness for explaining variation in the strength of *engrenage*. Socialisation processes have been found the strongest in the Council committees and working groups (except the K4 Committee) which deal with the day-to-day policymaking. Social spillover is strong in those forums due to their long lifespan. This allows for the adoption of certain norms, homogenous composition of members, substantial (Central Europe Working Group; 113 Committee) or sufficient (COREPER) expertise, enough time to allow for argumentative debate and generally weaker adverse bureaucratic as well as domestic political pressures which, as shown in Chapter 2, can often be positively influenced by socialised national officials. Without having been able to establish any real causality in the PHARE case, it can be suggested that social spillover had a favourable impact on consensus formation and progressive outcomes throughout the development of the programme.

In contrast, as for the JHA case study, the K4 Committee had had a shorter existence, was more heterogeneous in composition and officials were generally unwilling to have their habits changed by pressures coming from the Union. As a result, socialisation processes were limited at the time when the Intergovernmental Conference began, although there were some signs of a gradual emergence of *engrenage*. Somewhat paradoxically, given the implicit neofunctionalist argument that a deficit of social spillover may, if anything, hinder further integration, here the lack in progression of the socialisation process reinforced the impression that the third pillar had failed at the start of the IGC 1996–97.[20] This in turn nourished the functional rationale that Maastricht had provided inadequate supranational methods and instruments to solve the problems at hand. Thus, my empirical analysis suggests that on the level of policy-making more social spillover should facilitate problem-solving and consensus formation. In contrast, on the level of grand bargains, under-developed socialisation processes at the policy-making level in the run-up to an IGC can foster decision-makers' impressions of the need for a greater involvement of the Community institutions and therefore have integrative effects at an Intergovernmental Conference.

The (different) IGC Representatives Groups were again a different matter. Their relatively short lifespan and semi-homogenous composition of the generally more open-minded ministries of foreign affairs provided some basis for the occurrence of social spillover. In the Article 113/133 case (especially at the Amsterdam but also the Nice IGCs),

---

[20] Fortescue (1995).

things turned sour because of the distrust of the Commission, the strong bureaucratic countervailing pressures and the fact that there was no time and little expertise for argumentative debate. Hence, social spillover is believed to have had little to no impact on the moderate reform of the CCP at Amsterdam and Nice. In contrast, during the negotiations on the communitarisation of visa, asylum and immigration policy at the IGC 1996–97, socialisation processes could unfold, to some extent, because of the relative trust in the Commission and much weaker bureaucratic countervailing pressure from JHA ministries, along with more time devoted to the issue and greater expertise on the part of the personal representatives. On the whole, this would suggest that social spillover had a moderate bearing on the partial communitarisation of the third pillar at Amsterdam. During the Nice IGC negotiations on visa, asylum and immigration policy, social spillover processes were hampered to a greater extent than during the previous Treaty revision. This was largely due to the stronger countervailing pressures resulting from the greater involvement of JHA ministers and officials as well as the lesser time available for discussing this issue which made processes of arguing and deliberation difficult, if not impossible.

In comparison with the IGC negotiations in the Representatives Groups, the Convention provided a different scenario. For instance, the negotiating infrastructure facilitated participants to listen to, and reflect upon, each others' views. It induced the development of an 'esprit de corps' and a strong sense of responsibility for a successful outcome in the Plenary and in the Praesidium. In addition, members of the Convention were in a position to act freely and were largely unbound by governmental briefs and bureaucratic (or other domestic) countervailing interests. Moreover, there was also ample time available to lead a sensible debate on the pros and cons of further communitarisation. And finally, the atmosphere, spirit and negotiating structure in the Convention made it very difficult for members to reject something without explanation, or without entering into a reasoned discussion where his or her arguments would become subject to scrutiny. All these factors enabled powerful (structural) arguments to reach negotiators' consideration and thus enter their interest formations much more easily, without being obstructed or hindered by countervailing pressures. Hence, social spillover rationales played a considerable role during the Convention and also activated structural (i.e. functional and exogenous) spillover pressures by inducing greater open-mindedness and disposition for deliberation and learning among actors, which also reinforced the strength of the more actor-based dynamics (especially cultivated spillover). This also shows the importance of social spillover in linking structure and agency.

Overall, despite the tentativeness of my findings, we can conclude from the tracing, analysis and discussion of causal mechanisms and processes in the empirical chapters that the concept of social spillover can be attributed substantial causal relevance within the revised neo-functionalist framework. This point will be further confirmed through my analysis in the section on 'comparison and causality' below.

Recently there has been some renewed and more systemic interest in the role of socialisation processes in EU policy- and decision-making. With few exceptions, recent findings broadly corroborate my revised neofunctionalist account of social spillover. Trondal's study suggests that considerable collegiality has evolved among (Nordic) officials attending EU committees, that an *esprit de corps* tends to develop in Council committees over time and that membership matters in terms of civil servants' construction of role conceptions and attitudes.[21] Beyers and Dierickx have found that communication networks in the Council framework can be largely characterised by supranationalism. For example, intense informal co-operation between national delegates has developed common attitudes to different negotiations partners have been adopted, and the importance of non-state institutional actors has been recognised even by officials from traditionally more Eurosceptic Member States.[22] Egeberg has held that national officials involved in EU decision-making are generally characterised by a substantial degree of collective responsibility which is reflected in the overall willingness to shift and reformulate their positions.[23] The recent scholarship also suggests that the European Union and its institutions are, of course, not the only socialising mechanisms, but that national institutions and the domestic realm, more generally, also provide important, and often prevailing, socialising sources and mechanisms.[24] This ascertainment is not out of keeping with revised neofunctionalism. With the incorporation of countervailing forces and the more explicit accommodation of domestic structures it follows logically that socialisation processes are not unidirectional, as often associated with early neofunctionalism.

While most of the recent studies also implicitly or explicitly accept the claim that duration and intensity of interaction foster socialisation processes[25], some scholars have now also noted that socialisation processes not only depend on the quantity of contact but also on the nature/quality of social interaction. In line with my specification of social

---

[21] See Trondal (2002: esp. 477, 481–4).   [22] Beyers and Dierickx (1998: esp. 313–15).
[23] Cf. Egeberg (1999: esp. 471).
[24] See e.g. Beyers (2002: 23) and Egeberg (1999: 470–1).
[25] Cf. e.g. Trondal (2001, 2002); Lewis (1998b). For a somewhat deviant finding, see Beyers (2002: esp. 17–23).

spillover in Chapter 1, these scholars have incorporated notions of deliberation and persuasion in their accounts of socialisation.[26] Yet, only few scholars have so far tackled the important question of the conditions under which arguing, deliberation and communicative action may be relevant. Checkel's and, outside the EU/European context, Risse's as well as Müller and Risse's work form notable exceptions.[27] This book seeks to contribute to the identification of conditions conducive to arguing and communicative action, but additional and more systematic research is required here.[28] For example, specification is needed as to whether the identified conditions are *conducive*, *necessary* or *sufficient* for the occurrence of communicative action and reasoned preference changes. As scholarship has so far almost exclusively focused on the official level, (more) analysis would be useful, examining the extent to which socialisation processes occur in the Commission or the European Council. The available body of literature suggests that such processes may be taking place,[29] but is generally rather inconclusive on this issue. In addition, the scope of socialisation processes remains unclear. How far into national ministries – and into which ones – do Community negotiating norms spread? Investigation would need to be done into, amongst other things, whether the behaviour 'learned' by civil servants participating in Council working groups or Permanent Representations can be passed on and, in turn, be adopted by officials who are less exposed to the Brussels arena.

Finally, Haas talked about shifting loyalties of national elites to the new European centre which was to be fostered by socialisation and learning processes and particularly the development of national elites looking habitually to the European level for problem-solving. This may be the trickiest and also the most unresolved issue here. There are two ways of approaching this point, both of which however appear unsatisfactory. The first path would be to take the issue seriously. This is problematic, as there is now a large body of literature on identity, struggling with many methodological and definitional problems.[30] Moreover, the resources to be invested in order to arrive at valid causal inferences would be enormous. In short, an adequate investigation would go beyond the scope of this book.

---

[26] See e.g. Checkel (1999, 2001a), Joerges and Neyer (1997), Neyer (2002).

[27] See Checkel (1999, 2001a), Risse (2000), Müller and Risse (2004).

[28] For a more exclusive focus on the conditions for communicative action and arguing (and *not* social spillover more generally), also see Risse (2000), Checkel (2001a), Niemann (2004: 385ff). A detailed debate on this matter would go beyond the scope of this book.

[29] Butler (1986: 9–15); Ross (1994: 514).

[30] Cf. e.g. Morten Egeberg (1998); Aggestam (1999).

Second, the easy way out would be to say that Haas got it wrong and that it was a mistake to talk about changing loyalties and identities. However, this avenue is unsatisfactory because my extensive interviewing with officials in Brussels indicates that there is something to be said in favour of this neofunctionalist hypothesis.[31] This is also somewhat reflected in the literature. While Helen Wallace suggests that national decision-makers working in the Council framework have acquired a 'sense of European identity' or some elements of 'collective identity',[32] Jeffrey Lewis talks about the permanent representatives having developed 'dual personalities', due to the 'continuous tension between home affiliation and the pull of the collective forum'.[33] The development of certain European or EU identities of national officials (participating in EU decision-making) has also been found in the more systematic studies by Trondal and, to a lesser extent, Egeberg.[34]

Two important conclusions can be drawn from the research conducted hitherto on the issue of EU loyalties/identities: first, as already noted in the context of socialisation processes more generally, attitudinal development is no one-way street. Domestic settings and symbols are also important properties in the constitution of actors' identities. Often they seem to be stronger determinants than EU or European-level factors in the construction of identities. As pointed out above, this finding does not disconfirm the revised neofunctionalist version which also accounts for countervailing factors and the domestic realm. Second, the relationship between national and European/EU identities cannot be aptly captured in zero-sum terms. Instead, research suggests that individuals hold multiple loyalties and identities.[35] Contrary to some misleading criticisms of neofunctionalism,[36] Haas, although perhaps going too far in his prediction of the extent to which loyalties shift, already acknowledged the existence of multiple identities.[37] Other more tentative conclusions can be derived from the literature: dual identities, i.e. national and European, as opposed to more exclusively national ones, already seem to foster individuals' willingness to support further European integration.[38] In addition, it is interesting to note that the European Union may have successfully achieved identity hegemony in terms of defining what it means to belong to 'Europe'.[39]

As identities indeed seem to be multiple, the question that has begun to capture scholars' interests is how the relationship between such

---

[31] See also Niemann (1997b: 436f, 1998: 278ff).   [32] H. Wallace (1990: 215–16).
[33] Lewis (1998a: 7).   [34] Trondal (2002); Egeberg (1999).
[35] See e.g.: Cederman (2001), Eder and Giesen (1999), Marcussen *et al.* (1999).
[36] E.g. Marcussen *et al.* (1997).   [37] Haas (1958: 5,9,14).
[38] See Citrin and Sides (2004).   [39] See Laffan (2004).

various allegiances can be conceptualised. Risse has summarised three different models:[40] first, *nested* identities where one is embedded in a larger one which may be nested in yet another, which can also be illustrated by the 'concentric circles' or 'Russian Matruska doll' analogy. Second, the relationship may also be viewed as *cross-cutting*, according to which some members of one identity group are also members of another identity group. Finally, the marble cake model suggests that actors' identities cannot be neatly separated as suggested by the other two conceptualisations.

One way forward in this debate may be Wendt's distinction between (1) personal/corporate, (2) type and (3) role identities.[41] Individuals and groups (and also states) possess certain properties and characteristics – for example, a material base and a consciousness and memory of self – that are prior to interaction. This is what Wendt calls personal or corporate identities. However, individuals and groups only attain actor status relevant identities through interaction with other agents. Here, type and role identity constitute useful concepts. Type identity refers to a social category applied to persons who share some characteristics, such as party affiliation, gender or membership in the same EU committee. Role identity is the positioning of actors/groups to other agents/groups participating in the interaction. In the EU context, identity changes can be explained by drawing on the concepts of type and especially role identity, the realm where socialisation processes can change allegiances and where the development and finalisation of actors' identity constitution takes place. Thus, Wendt's distinction may further specify the concept of social spillover and contribute to our thinking of identity change more generally.

Political Spillover

The role that neofunctionalists attributed to non-governmental elites in the integration process has been substantiated in the recent literature. First, in line with the neofunctionalist hypothesis of interest groups shifting their attention to the European level, authors have emphasised that with the deepening of the integration process (especially through the introduction of QMV and the co-operation and co-decision procedures), lobbying on the European level has become a well-established practice of national pressure groups,[42] that there is a general trend of

---

[40] Risse (2004: 168f).
[41] See Wendt (1999: 224 ff). Thanks to Janina Dill and Nicolas Lamp for drawing my attention to this aspect. Cf. Dill and Lamp (2004).
[42] Armstrong and Bulmer (1996); Eberlie (1993).

national interest groups to become a member of a Brussels-based umbrella organisation,[43] and that more and more lobbying is conducted in a co-ordinated fashion transnationally.[44]

Second, the early neofunctionalists held that interest groups would promote further integration, as they became aware of the benefits of integration.[45] Recently, authors have stated more specifically why interest groups (may) seek supranational solutions. As for (at least partially) integrated sectors, Mazey and Richardson have pointed out that interest groups have realised that the ability of any one state to influence the (EU) policy process is limited. Hence, they argue, it is rational for them to seek supranational solutions.[46] Moreover, Stone Sweet and Sandholtz have pointed out that 'transactors' (e.g. those trading across borders) will always prefer, all other things being equal, to live under one set of rules rather than under fifteen (or twenty-five). If companies operating across national boundaries had to comply with different rules in every Member State, this would impose substantial extra costs. Hence, business interests would generally press for more EU competencies and European legislation.[47] Stone Sweet and Sandholtz thus provide a rationale for political spillover into new sectors.[48] There also seems to be some evidence that interest groups may have undergone certain learning processes leading to more supranational outlooks and more pro-integrative attitudes. It has been pointed out, for instance, that the positive policy experiences at the European level gradually weakened the traditional firm/state relationship and pushed business interests and focus up to the supranational level, much in the way anticipated by Haas.[49] In addition, MacMillan[50] discovered that companies have had to be wary of personnel within their Brussels operations 'going native'.

---

[43] Bindi Calussi (1998: 85) has pointed out that the number of Eurogroups increased from 300 in 1970 to about 3000 in 1992. On this issue also see Rometsch (1996); McLaughlin and Jordan (1993).

[44] Wallace (1984) and George (1996: 54).

[45] However, in the (general) way suggested by Haas, the empirical evidence in terms of such interest-based learning is somewhat doubtful. While farmers are arguably the professional group that has benefited the most from European integration, there is no indication that they per se support (further) supranational solutions. On this point see Risse (2005: 297).

[46] Mazey and Richardson (1997a).

[47] Stone Sweet and Sandholtz (1997: 309).

[48] The other such rationale is when interest groups act upon functional spillover which imply a sector-to-sector logic (cf. e.g. Nye 1970: 804ff).

[49] Cf. Coen (1998: 86).   [50] MacMillan (1991). Also cf. Coen (1997: 91).

Finally, empirical studies have also confirmed the impact of interest groups and political spillover pressures on (integrative) policy outcomes. Sandholtz and Zysman and Green Cowles have pointed to the influence of European business and, especially, the European Round Table of Industrialists on the 1992 programme during the negotiations leading to the SEA.[51] David Cameron has argued that a transnational community of European (central) bankers helped to frame the debate on EMU at Maastricht.[52] O'Reilly and Stone Sweet have found that business and consumer groups played an important role in the transfer of competence to the Community in the field of air transport.[53] Hence, Mazey and Richardson have noted that interest groups are beginning to play a significant role in the process of European integration, much in the way anticipated by neofunctionalists.[54]

All in all, the concept of political spillover (in terms of non-governmental elites) has provided only limited insights for an explanation of the particular outcomes in the three case studies. The PHARE programme did not provoke much attention on the part of organised interest groups. Moreover, most interest group lobbying took place at the level of implementation, which had no impact on the overall design of the programme. In addition, interest groups were weakly organised on the European level, with FEACO, the most prominent actor here, as a rather feeble player. Finally, attempts by organised interest to lobby national governments on the more important decisions concerning the development of the PHARE programme were rather indecisive and had little to no impact.

As for the extension of the Common Commercial Policy at the Amsterdam IGC, interest groups did not effectively further the Commission cause. Although most groups that took up the issue came out in favour of substantial reforms of Article 113, on the whole there was little effective pressure exerted by organised interests. At the Nice IGC political spillover pressures remained at a very modest level. During the Convention political spillover forces slightly grew, but did not surpass a modest to moderate level of pressure.

Throughout the IGC 1996–97 negotiations on the communitarisation of visa, asylum and immigration policy, NGOs asserted only modest pressures on Member States and the central institutions in favour of a more supranational decision-making set-up. However, on the smaller issues of anti-discrimination and rights of third-country nationals,

---

[51] Sandholtz and Zysman (1989: 116ff); Green Cowles (1995: 501ff).
[52] Cameron (1995).   [53] O'Reilly (1997); O'Reilly and Stone Sweet (1998: 451ff).
[54] Mazey and Richardson (1997a).

transnational coalitions of NGOs – also in the form of an advocacy coalition – made a more significant impact on the debate. Pressures stemming from political spillover were very modest during the IGC 2000. Compared to the Nice IGC, NGOs and, to a lesser extent, Think Tanks concerned mainly with issues of migration, refugees and human rights provided a somewhat augmented, albeit not crucial, impetus for Title IV decision rule reform during the last Treaty revision exercise.

A number of conclusions, specifications and refinements concerning the concept of political spillover can be drawn from the three case studies. First, as the two IGC cases have shown, interest groups in the two sectors did not strongly advocate further integration. It has been argued that this was partly because services and intellectual property rights were still perceived as rather new European and international commercial issues and because justice and home affairs was still a relatively novel area of European integration. This corresponds with the neofunctionalist thought. While some have interpreted the theory to hold that all interest groups would undergo a learning process whereby they shift their expectations to the European level,[55] this revised neo-functionalist framework has clarified that Haas was not implying that *all* organised interest would swiftly shift its identity or expectations to the European level, but rather those interest groups that operate within integrated sectors.[56] Hence, an advanced level of (European and/or international) integration of a sector is held to be a factor conducive to (stronger) interest group involvement in that issue area. The slight trend towards an augmentation of political spillover pressures on the above issues may be attributable to the greater integration of these sectors and/or sub-sectors over time, without however being able to establish any firm causality here.

Second, and closely related, the three case studies, and especially those on PHARE and the extension of the CCP, have shown that a lack of transparency and complexity (of GATS/WTO rules and decision-making of the PHARE programme) can severely hinder pressure group formation. Interest groups naturally become less involved when they are not sure of the benefits of supranational governance (especially in the 113 case) or when they are confused about where to start lobbying (as in the case of the PHARE programme). Clear and transparent rules and procedures can be taken as a favourable condition for (effective) interest group involvement.

---

[55] Tranholm-Mikkelsen (1991: 5f).
[56] Cf. Haas (1958: 294). This does not mean, however, that interest groups cannot spur the integration process in new sectors (e.g. Stone Sweet and Sandholtz 1997: 297ff).

Third, on economic and commercial issues, interest groups are less likely to get involved when the potential gains are perceived as moderate or insubstantial. Both in the case of PHARE and even in the case of the extension of the Common Commercial Policy the economic stakes were (perceived as) not that high, certainly when compared with say the SEM, where interest groups played a more critical role.[57]

Although economic interest groups are most likely to get involved in the integration process,[58] the Amsterdam IGC negotiations in the areas of anti-discrimination and the rights of third-country nationals have indicated that other parts of organised interests can make their voice heard successfully. Non-economic interest groups are often held together not by common interests but by common beliefs. In public policy jargon such groups have been referred to as 'advocacy coalitions'.[59] They often consist of actors from a variety of both private and governmental organisations who share a set of policy beliefs and seek to realise them by influencing different spheres of (national and supranational) governance. As their beliefs are less fluid than those of 'material' interest groups, they are less likely to enter into coalitions of convenience. Once their beliefs are well-served on the European arena, advocacy coalitions are not likely to abandon their interest in European solutions, as their beliefs do not easily change. Thus, we can tentatively conclude that they are even more likely than interest groups to become long-term advocates of the integration process.

Two aspects can be highlighted from the analysis of NGO influence on the issues of anti-discrimination and the rights of third-country nationals. First, one important reason why NGOs made an impact on these issues was that they managed to 'frame' the debate by moulding interests from a very early stage. While NGOs had already formulated their demands, governments only began with some preliminary brainstorming in the Reflection Group. Mazey and Richardson have suggested that 'framing' the debate plays a crucial role in the policy process.[60] As Caparoso and Keeler have noted, in relation to the SEA, 'by the time state leaders came to the bargaining table, a substantial amount of work had already been accomplished'.[61] The insights of 'framing' are a valuable specification to the concept of political spillover, pointing to an important condition under which interest groups may provide an impetus to the integration project.

---

[57] Sandholtz and Zysman (1989: 116).   [58] Stone Sweet and Sandholtz (1997).
[59] Sabatier (1988).   [60] Mazey and Richardson (1997b).
[61] Caparoso and Keeler (1995: 45).

Second, although most pressure was exerted at the national level, NGOs managed to build transnational coalitions. Moravcsik's criticism of Sandholtz and Zysman's study of the SEA disputed their findings concerning the role of the ERT by pointing out that it were more its individual members which mattered. However, Moravcsik seems to underestimate the *transnational* organisation of interests and ideas, since those 'networks operate in ways that lead to *co-ordinated* pressure being placed on governments'.[62] The importance of 'transnational organisation of interests' is much in keeping with the neofunctionalist tradition, as Haas emphasised the establishment of (transnational) umbrella organisations.[63]

The revised neofunctionalist framework can accommodate a serious deficiency of the original neofunctionalist approach. As pointed out by Green Cowles,[64] although the 1992 project was driven by organised interests, such as the ERT, interest groups were not so much spurred by an endogenous functional logic as by the exogenous challenge of a globalising world economy and growing international competition. The early neofunctionalists, however, hypothesised that interest groups would be driven rather by functional and technical concerns stemming from the integration process itself. By bringing the concept of exogenous spillover as another structural dynamic into the theory, revised neofunctionalism can account for exogenously motivated interest group agitation. In fact, the (weak) interest group pressure in the Article 113 case was largely due to the lack of concerns of organised interest about the changing world economy and the implications for EU trade policy in the areas of services and IPRs under a shared competence. In addition, it has been pointed out that large firms' and interest groups' preferences, attitudes and behaviour are influenced by domestic factors.[65] This unsurprising finding does not challenge the revised neofunctionalist framework, given the incorporation of domestic constraints and countervailing factors more generally.

Although analysts usually attributed the concept of political spillover (in terms of non-governmental elites) a very important status within neofunctionalism,[66] one should not overemphasise the importance of this dynamic. In fact, Haas himself argued that integration could proceed

---

[62] George (1996: 54, emphasis added).   [63] Haas (1958: ch. 9).

[64] Green Cowles (1995: 521). The importance of exogenous pressures from the formation of interest group interests and attitudes has also been underlined by Bartle (1999: esp. 363–5).

[65] See Coen (1998: 97). For an overview of factors underlying interest organisation and preference formation, see Aspinwall and Greenwood (1998).

[66] C.f. Harrison (1990: 142ff); Cram (1996: 46).

even in the absence of interest group demands for further integration.[67]
My case analysis confirms this. The development of the PHARE programme, the communitarisation of visa, asylum and immigration policy
at the 1996–97 and 2002–04 Treaty revisions and the extension of
Article 133 at the Convention/last IGC could substantially advance
without much support from non-governmental elites, which suggests
that this concept cannot have crucial causal relevance.[68] Having said
that, political spillover in terms of non-governmental elites may still
contribute to the progression of European integration, as recent studies,
pointed out at the beginning of this section, have indicated.

Cultivated Spillover

The combined pressures of the Commission, the Presidency, the European Parliament, the Court of Justice and epistemic communities,
which make up the concept of cultivated spillover, have been of varying
strength throughout my case studies. As for the PHARE programme,
particularly the Commission, but also the EP, the Presidencies and the
role played by an epistemic community in the area of nuclear safety
provided for strong cultivated spillover pressures. In the CCP case, the
integrative impact of the central institutions augmented throughout the
three Treaty revisions. This increase can be attributed to, among other
aspects, the waning distrust of the Commission in trade policy, the
improved scope for the Commission to make use of its greater expertise
on the issue, as well as the gradually more integrative attitude taken by,
and the strengthened role of, the European Parliament (particularly
during the Convention). The case of visa, asylum and immigration
policy saw (medium to) high cultivated spillover pressures except for the
Intergovernmental Conference 2000, during which the Commission
and the EP did not effectively manage to assert themselves and the
French Presidency played a disadvantageous role in terms of achieving
progress on the issue.

On the whole, early neofunctionalism had attributed only secondary
importance to the role of the central institutions.[69] My tracing and
analysis of causal processes and mechanisms in the three empirical
chapters suggest, however, that the concept of cultivated spillover, in its
revised and extended version, has (very) significant causal relevance.
This will be further substantiated in my section on 'comparison and

---

[67] Haas (1958: 297).
[68] See also my section on 'comparison and causality' below in this chapter.
[69] See e.g. Haas (1964a: 78); Haas (1968: preface, esp. xxvii).

causality'. As a result, this pressure can be upgraded in terms of causal significance within the revised neofunctionalist framework, compared with its status in the early neofunctionalist literature.

The Role of the Commission   The European Commission remains the most important element within the concept of cultivated spillover. Those cases which can be characterised by integrative outcomes correlated with active and assertive roles played by the Commission. My tracing of causal mechanisms also suggests that the Commission did indeed contribute to those far-reaching outcomes. The Commission's assertiveness was a vital factor in its clinch of the mandate for co-ordinating the western aid effort leading to the PHARE programme. It was also very influential in the further development of the programme, for instance, in the introduction of co-financing infrastructure from PHARE funds as well as the expansion of the aid volume and more generally the evolution of the programme into a central element within the Union's pre-accession strategy. During the IGC 1996–97 the Commission contributed significantly towards the communitarisation of visa, asylum and immigration policy. In addition throughout the last Treaty revision its role concerning the extension of Article 113 and deepening of Title IV was substantial, even though not decisive. The causal importance of the Commission is also reflected in the fact that in the two instances where it was particularly unfortunate, unskilful or ineffective (the Amsterdam CCP case and the Nice JHA case), this resulted in minimal outcomes, not least due to the absence of the Commission's cultivation of spillover.

A number of potential sources of strengths have been identified which determine the capability of the Commission for effective leadership.[70] First, there is the considerable potential for forging cohesion within the Commission.[71] As seen, for example, in the case of the communitarisation of the third pillar at the 1996–97 IGC and the Commission's quest for the introduction of using PHARE funds for infrastructures at the Copenhagen European Council, the relative cohesion of the Commission allows it to be proactive. In contrast, the Amsterdam IGC negotiations on the modernisation of the Common Commercial Policy have indicated that the Commission's internal divisions compromised its effectiveness and paralysed its efforts at the bargaining table when it mattered.

Second, the Commission usually has a chance to shape the agenda and define national interests, certainly in areas where it has an exclusive

---

[70] Also cf. Beach (2005); Christiansen (2002); Nugent (1995).   [71] Nugent (1995).

right of initiative,[72] but also where such a monopoly is absent. As pointed out in the wider European integration literature[73] Community institutions do matter in shaping the perceptions of national actors and in changing the context of the rational pursuit of interests. This can be done especially in the relatively early stages of the decision-making process,[74] as in the Amsterdam JHA case where the Commission submitted its thorough and comprehensive suggestions on justice and home affairs early on in its report to the Reflection Group. Moreover, as pointed out by Nugent and exemplified in the Amsterdam JHA case study, the Commission can influence the agenda by planting a proposal with another delegation. This way, those delegations that are generally suspicious of the Commission are more likely to be open-minded.[75] In addition, as illustrated in the case of the introduction of PHARE funds for infrastructures, through the timing of its proposals, the Commission can significantly influence and bias the agenda, even at European Councils, if it maintains close ties with the Presidency.

Third, as pointed out by Sandholtz,[76] one of the Commission's leadership functions is to draw potential collaborators into the debate, here referred to as the cultivation of political and social spillover. A number of authors have pointed out that the Commission holds a strategic position and is centrally located within a web of policy networks and relationships. As a result, it can often act as a 'bourse' where problems and interests are traded and through which support for its policies is secured.[77] The strategy of cultivating political spillover has been illustrated, especially in the case studies on the PHARE programme and the communitarisation of visa, asylum and immigration policy. While it was difficult to establish a clear-cut causality between the Commission's cultivation efforts and policy outcomes, the establishment and work of the PHARE information office, the Commission's contacts with EUROCONTROL and its cultivation and utilisation of the epistemic community of nuclear experts suggest that this strategy was effective in the PHARE case. Apart from forging alliances with interest groups and epistemic communities, Lindberg and more recently Ross have pointed to the capacity of the Commission to co-opt governmental elites.[78] For example, the PHARE and Amsterdam JHA cases have underlined this. In the JHA negotiations the contacts and lobbying efforts of

---

[72] E.g. Marks (1993).   [73] E.g. Sandholtz (1993b: 3).   [74] Peterson (1995: 73).
[75] Cf. Nugent (1995: 620).   [76] Sandholtz (1993a).
[77] On this aspect see especially: Mazey and Richardson (1997a); Coen (1997: 105–6); Marks et al. (1996: 359ff).
[78] See Lindberg (1963) and Ross (1994).

Commissioners Oreja and Gradin seem to have played an important role in supporting the Commission strategy.

Fourth, the Commission can build consensus and broker compromises, often while upgrading common interests. This function of Commission policy entrepreneurship which has found significant attention in the literature[79] can be further substantiated by the findings of this study. For example, at the 1996–97 IGC negotiations, the Commission made use of its better overview of national legislations and detached position to find a formula on the communitarisation of asylum and immigration policy which struck a balance between the different national approaches and was eventually acceptable to all delegations.

Fifth, the Commission is often in a position to promote issues and further integration by pointing to functional and exogenous pressures.[80] While this could be witnessed in all of my cases, it has been particularly evident during the IGC 1996–97 negotiations concerning visa, asylum and immigration policy where the Commission went to great pains to suggest that there was an element of inevitability about communitarisation due to the functional internal market and exogenous migration pressures. An interesting variation of this is the Commission's deliberate creation of links, which Héritier has called 'linking-up strategy'.[81] This often involves the creation of an artificial link or overstating the inter-connection of issues. This has certainly been the case, at least to some extent, concerning the Commission's emphasis of the functional logic stemming from the free movement of persons, given the fact that borders have always been permeable and not just since the beginning of the abolition of internal border controls due to the internal market logic.

Sixth, the Commission is in a superior position when it comes to policy implementation, certainly in the more benign advisory and management committees.[82] In that context, it is especially the power of knowledge, which also favours the Commission in many areas on the policy-making level[83] that has put the Commission in a superior position in the PHARE Management Committee. Apart from that, the use of QMV in that committee means that the Commission has been able to be bolder in its approach and that its preferences are not necessarily watered down.[84] Moreover, the fact that the Commission is chairing the meetings ensures its control of the agenda.

---

[79] E.g. Sandholtz (1993a); Nugent (1995: 614). [80] E.g. Sandholtz (1993b: 19).
[81] Héritier (1998: 11). [82] Ludlow (1991: 107). [83] Héritier (1998: 7).
[84] Cf. Nugent (1995: 616).

Finally, having said all the above, the Commission also has to know the limits of its entrepreneurial leadership and has to be careful not to overplay its hand *vis-à-vis* the Member States who are ultimately the ones who decide by unanimity on further Community powers at Intergovernmental Conferences, even if considerable deepening can occur through the day-to-day decision-making.[85] The failure to adequately reform the Common Commercial Policy at the Amsterdam, and (less severely) the Nice IGCs has indicated that a loss of trust in the Commission, stemming from overambitious and intransparent Commission leadership, can seriously impede Member States' willingness to delegate further competencies to the Community, even when such a step may be justified.[86]

While the above analysis suggests that the Commission has considerable capacity for policy entrepreneurship, there are a number of (background) factors affecting its role which are partly/largely beyond the control of the Commission. First, in the absence of (effective) interest groups the Commission is deprived of potential allies and may not succeed in the pursuit of its objectives.[87] A variation of this argument would be that in a newly integrated sector or one where industry has not yet realised the importance of EU policy-making, the Commission would find it hard to mobilise interest groups. Here we have the case of European companies and associations in the services sector which the Commission did not succeed in decisively converting to the idea of extending Article 113, especially during the Amsterdam and Nice IGCs.

Second, as pointed out by George, Commission leadership is most effective when supported by a significant political actor, such as a determined or powerful Member State.[88] Although the Commission may be in a good position to cultivate relations with Member States in order to bring them on board, this is by no means guaranteed. However, the coincidence of a similar policy agenda with other Member States from the very start can give added impetus to Commission leadership. Somewhat more natural allies – and hence perhaps less of a variable – are other Community institutions that are also generally inclined to drive integration forward. Good co-operation between Commission and

---

[85] Cf. Peterson (1995: 72ff).

[86] However, Pollack (2001: 230) has pointed out that where an agent such as the Commission anticipates the reaction of its principles (Member States), and adjusts its behaviour to avoid the costly imposition of sanctions, one cannot speak of autonomous behaviour because agency behaviour is influenced by principles' preferences.

[87] Cf. Nye (1970: 804ff).   [88] George (1996: 44).

other central institutions (such as the Presidency and the EP) provides a fine basis for progressive outcomes.

Third, it has been pointed out that institutions may register the greatest impact on policy outcomes in periods of swiftly changing events, uncertainty and incomplete information[89] and during periods of policy adaptation.[90] Hence, it is acknowledged here that the Commission's quest for the mandate of western aid co-ordination was helped by the fact that events were moving fast and that there was a significant degree of uncertainty about the political and economic stability of Central and Eastern Europe. The reason being that Member States' preferences are less defined in the above circumstances, which makes them more likely to listen to an assertive Commission.

Finally, there are the three factors grouped under the label of 'countervailing forces', namely, sovereignty-consciousness, (anti-)integrationist climate and Member States' domestic constraints (and diversities). When strong countervailing forces are at work, the Commission will find it much more difficult to act as a policy entrepreneur. My analysis – for instance concerning its role at the Copenhagen European Council regarding PHARE and also throughout the Amsterdam IGC negotiations on visa, asylum and immigration policy – has shown that the Commission was able to play such a role and to overcome countervailing pressures. This suggests that supranational institutions and especially the European Commission are more than 'a passive structure, providing a contractual environment conducive to efficient intergovernmental bargaining'.[91]

In line with neofunctionalist theory, a number of recent studies have revealed the Commission's ability to play a proactive and integrative leadership role. This has been indicated by research in the fields of telecommunications,[92] energy,[93] air transport policy,[94] information technology,[95] structural policy,[96] environmental policy[97] and in the launch of the 1992 project,[98] and in paving the way for monetary union.[99]

The Role of the Council Presidency A recurrent theme of this book is that the development of the Community surpassed some elements of neofunctionalist theory. This has certainly happened with regard to the evolution of the Presidency which has taken up some of the

---

[89] Cf. Peterson (1992) and Moravcsik (1995: 616). [90] Cf. Sandholtz (1993a).
[91] Moravcsik (1993: 508). [92] Sandholtz (1993a); Fuchs (1994). [93] Matlary (1997).
[94] O'Reilly (1997). [95] Sandholtz (1992).
[96] E.g. Marks (1992); Marks, *et al.* (1996: 359–60). [97] Sbragia (1993).
[98] Sandholtz and Zysman (1989: 107ff). [99] See Jabko (1999: 475ff).

functions that neofunctionalists had envisaged for the Commission. Most importantly, the Presidency has occupied the role of an institutionalised mediator that also raises common interests and thereby fosters more integrative outcomes. A number of case studies confirm Presidencies' inclination to take on the role of an honest and promotional broker.[100]

The three case studies have illustrated the role played by the Council Presidency for the success or failure of policy outcomes. Generally speaking progressive outcomes were also characterised by Presidencies that performed well in terms of organisation, neutrality, brokerage and leadership. On the other hand, the sub-cases with more meagre results correlated with rather mixed or downbeat Presidency assessments, at least in certain respects or on certain issues. My analysis of causal mechanisms suggests, for example, that the unskilful and biased French Presidency adversely affected the outcomes on CCP and JHA at Nice. The causal relevance of the role of the Presidency could be examined particularly well in Chapter 2 with respect to the 1995–96 negotiations on the TACIS regulation. During the Spanish Presidency negotiations were deadlocked, while the Italian Presidency was able to achieve a satisfactory outcome above the lowest common denominator. Here, we had two units which where nearly homogenous. One of the (very) few factors that changed was the Presidency, from the Spanish one that lacked impartiality and was more concerned with its own interests, to the Italian Presidency that was well organised, neutral and which displayed a considerable degree of leadership.

In view of my empirical analysis, a number of features can be highlighted concerning the role of the Council Presidency. First, in the search for compromises the Presidency often has to sacrifice its own national position. Second, Presidencies are in a position to get to know the problems and positions of the various Member States and are therefore well placed to come up with a formula that all Member States can accept. Third, in order to be successful in their role as 'promotional broker' Presidencies have to be ambitious, but not overambitious. Hence, they have to be on the upper end of realism. Fourth, Presidencies are most likely to be successful when they co-operate well with the Commission, draw on its expertise and sometimes ask the Commission to propose potentially controversial issues in order not to hurt the Presidency's role as 'honest broker'.[101] My empirical analysis has

---

[100] See e.g. Regelsberger and Wessels (1984), Kirchner (1992), Metcalfe (1998), Elgström (2003), Tallberg (2004).
[101] See my analysis IGC 1996/97 JHA case and cf. George (1996: 279).

revealed that in all cases that have led to integrative outcomes (apart from the G7 mandate where the Presidency was not strictly speaking involved) Presidencies collaborated well with the Commission. This further underlines the importance of a well-functioning Presidency–Commission partnership. Finally, when comparing the two case studies examining Treaty revisions, we have noted that the performance and fortune of the same Presidencies can vary across issue areas. This has been particularly evident in terms of the IGC 1996–97.

The Role of the European Parliament   My analysis in the empirical chapters has shown that the European Parliament can make an impact, even though its influence on decision-making has in no way been comparable to that of the Commission. However, we have to distinguish between the study on the PHARE programme, where Parliament was a rather important player, and the IGC cases in which the EP was less influential (although the last Treaty revision has indicated that the EP may be influential on that level, if the Convention method is chosen for preparing an IGC). Hence, one basic and unsurprising conclusion is that the European Parliament can assert itself more on the level of policy-making than on the level of major bargains.

Parliament managed to influence the shape of the PHARE programme, especially through its budgetary powers but also through its more informal powers, including the mobilisation of the media by organising parliamentary hearings and through an informal coalition with the Commission on some issues.

The Amsterdam IGC negotiations on the communitarisation of visa, asylum and immigration policy suggest that, even at an Intergovernmental Conference, Parliament can add a (small) integrative stimulus. Parliament managed to exert some pressure through an informal alliance with the Commission, its cultivation of contacts with national governmental and non-governmental elites and through its participation at the IGC table. Its influence may further increase with the gradually enhanced role granted to the EP at IGCs, which is now (at least formally) on par with the Commission regarding formal participation. As Chapters 3 and 4 have shown, the Convention method further seems to foster Parliament's impact at Treaty revisions, particularly when Convention outcomes have considerable bonding strength.

During the IGC 1996–97 negotiations on the extension of Article 113, Parliament was unable to provide much input. Its contribution, if at all relevant, rather obstructed the Commission's quest as its hesitant *quid pro quo* strategy may have deprived the latter's proposal of a significant element of legitimacy. In the end, both the Commission and the

EP lost out through lack of mutual support. Greater mutual support at the past two Treaty revisions on this issue was beneficial for both the Commission and the EP. The Commission and Parliament have been described as 'natural allies'[102], but informal coalitions between the two institutions have so far received little academic attention and provide a further element which was not recognised in the early neofunctionalist literature.

Finally, due to the fact that the case sample was rather narrow in terms of EP competencies, as it did not include a case of co-operation or co-decision procedure, my conclusions on the role of the EP are inevitably tentative and indeterminate. Elsewhere, however, it has been argued that the European Parliament has used its rights of co-operation and co-decision to build advocacy coalitions.[103] Parliament has also been identified as a 'conditional agenda setter'. Under the co-operation procedure it can make proposals that, if accepted by the Commission, are easier to pass than to overturn.[104] Moreover, under the co-decision procedure which has been used in nearly one quarter of EU legislation considered by the EP since 1996, the European Parliament is now on equal footing with the Council in every state of the procedure.[105] These developments further support the thesis that the European Parliament is becoming an increasingly important agent of spillover.

The Role of the European Court of Justice   Recent case studies, while witnessing a slight recession in the Court's activism, have underlined the integrative role played by the ECJ, for example in the development of the SEM,[106] telecommunications policy,[107] energy policy[108], social policy[109] and environmental policy.[110] Moreover, a number of authors have pointed out that the Court of Justice has increased its institutional powers over the years.[111] Even Moravcsik, one of the foremost sceptics of autonomous action on the part of supranational institutions, has acknowledged that the ECJ developed institutional powers beyond what is 'minimally necessary to perform its functions'.[112]

Chapters 3 and 4 have shown that the Court of Justice can play an important role in the European integration process. In the area of justice and home affairs during the 1996–97 IGC, the ECJ case law seems to

---

[102] Ludlow (1991: 115).   [103] Kohler-Koch (1996).   [104] Tsebelis (1994).
[105] See Maurer (2003b: 230, 234).   [106] Cameron (1992).   [107] Sandholtz (1993a).
[108] Matlary (1997).   [109] Pierson and Leibfried (1995: 438ff).
[110] See Cichowski (1998: 387ff).
[111] See e.g. Rasmussen (1986); Joergesl (1992); Burley and Mattli (1993).
[112] Moravcsik (1993: 513, 1995: 624).

have influenced the debates on immigration, the rights of third-country nationals and especially on anti-discrimination, as reflected in the arguments of NGOs which extensively quoted the case law of the Court. Moreover, the Court of Justice also directly influenced the IGC debate through its report to the Reflection Group which was generally well received and contributed to the debate on the issue of judicial review in the area of JHA. Finally, if one accepts that judicial control is desirable, the ECJ was an almost compelling choice for remedying the deficit of judicial review in the field of justice and home affairs due to the history of its jurisprudence as well as its authority and respectability as an institution.[113]

Perhaps even more influential was the Court's role in the CCP case. However, rather than fostering integration, the ECJ delegitimised some of the Commission's arguments for extending Article 113 in its opinion 1/94. As even the generally activist Court dismissed the Commission's quest, it was clear for many Member States that they would not take such a step (even when the Commission put forward additional arguments during the IGC). The analysis in Chapter 3 of Opinion 1/94, rather than disproving revised neofunctionalism, has provided us with the opportunity to identify some of the conditions delimiting the Court-driven cultivation of spillover. Most importantly, it has been found that high levels of politicisation and the absence of functional inter-dependencies severely limit the basis for Court activism. Moreover, factors such as new judges (who still have to become socialised into the ECJ norms), unsympathetic judge rapporteurs and time pressure can further impair the Court's 'ever-closer union' *leitmotif*. Paying attention to the Court of Justice, as part of the revised neofunctionalist framework, has been beneficial more generally: it has shown that, even when analysing grand bargains, we must take the wider *process* (before and in between IGCs) into consideration.

The Role of Epistemic Communities   The preceding analysis has suggested that epistemic communities may help the integrative process in the short term through their use by the Commission for consultation and backing of its policies and are, therefore, best accommodated within the concept of cultivated spillover. Chapters 1 and 2 have indicated that epistemic communities are not just a variation of interest groups whose instrumental interests will tie them to the European project which may lead to their long-term support of further integration. Instead, epistemic community behaviour is based on a shared knowledge base, common

---

[113] Neuwahl (1995).

ideas and the same causal beliefs. Thus, it is rather unlikely that epistemic communities can take on a similar European vocation as interest groups in the neofunctionalist sense, since continuing support depends on unchanged causal beliefs, the continuation of the problem which drew epistemic communities into the debate as well as unchanged scientific research results.

Although nuclear safety as an area within the PHARE programme was identified as an important and clear-cut case, it is likely that epistemic communities have also had an impact in other areas of PHARE, such as the environment and energy in general. Epistemic communities have not featured in the other two chapters largely due to the nature of the issue areas. In both instances there was less perceived need for decision-makers to rely on specific scientific expert knowledge.[114]

There is more general evidence for epistemic communities fostering integration in Europe (often in co-operation with, or assisting, supranational institutions like the Commission). For example, a number of scholars have pointed to a transnational network of European central bankers who, motivated by principled ideas knowledge, were very influential in promoting the EMU initiative.[115] Similar findings have been made in the areas of competition policy[116] and environmental policy.[117] If Risse-Kappen is right and epistemic communities are likely to flourish with growing regulation of the inter-state relationship by co-operative international institutions,[118] epistemic communities will become more important in the EU policy-making cycle. Moreover, their involvement on the wider European level is likely to increase, as more and more problems can only be solved on grander scales, such as the European.

Exogenous Spillover

The empirical insights of the past decades have indicated the importance of exogenous factors on the integration process in Europe. For example, studies concerning the Cold War origins of the EC,[119] on external competitive pressures inducing the single market programme and increased co-operation in the technology policy,[120] or works on the impact of globalisation pressures on the European integration process[121]

---

[114] Interviews, Brussels, 1997–99.
[115] Cameron (1995: 37ff), Verdun (1999: 308ff) and Kaelberer (2003: 365ff).
[116] See van Waarden (2002: 913ff).
[117] Mazey and Richardson (1997a) and Zito (2001: 585ff).   [118] Risse-Kappen (1995a).
[119] Milward and Sørensen (1993), Neuss (2000).
[120] Sandholtz and Zysman (1989: 103ff).
[121] Rhodes and van Apeldorn (1998: 406–27); Rosamond (2001: 158ff); Hettne (2002: 325ff).

underline that any framework seeking to theorise the (EU) integration should take account of exogenous pressures.

As pointed out in Chapter 1, exogenous spillover, like functional spillover, is largely a structural pressure. In all three case studies, exogenous structures were present which provided a rationale for further integration. However, as with all structures, they are ineffective unless actors find them compelling, feel constrained or pushed by them, i.e. pick up on them.

In the PHARE case the origin of exogenous pressure was the disintegration of the Communist block in Central and Eastern Europe in the late 1980s. Western decision-makers were persuaded to act by the strength of the democratic movements, European defence and security considerations with part of the Warsaw Pact ridding itself of communism, the speed of events in the CEEC and direct appeals by Central and Eastern European elites, such as Walesa and Jaruzelski. Exogenous spillover constituted the main pressure leading to the decision to give the mandate of western aid co-ordination to the Commission. However, for spillover to occur, external pressures needed to be assisted by cultivated spillover pressures and the convergence of domestic preferences of G7 governments.

As for the case of visa, asylum and immigration policy, the substantial exogenous pressures stemmed from high levels of asylum seekers, immigrants and refugees entering the Community and staying there, legally or illegally. European states, confronted with the rise in asylum applications and illegal immigration, adopted ever stricter asylum and immigration regulations. This, however, could not solve the problem, as restrictions in one country only led to more asylum seekers/applications in other countries until those countries adopted similar or even stricter rules. Hence 'solo runs' had become very difficult and decision-makers gradually turned to European solutions. Exogenous pressures are, to some extent, based on functional ones, like the free movement of persons which facilitates the crossing of borders.

In the CCP case, globalisation and changes in the world economy as well as subsequent developments in the multilateral trade regime and the international trade agenda presented clear exogenous pressures, which threatened to erode the Community powers under Article 113/133, as trade in goods has gradually lost in importance. The study of position papers by the Member States and Community institutions as well as interest groups suggests that exogenous spillover constituted the single most important rationale for reform during the IGC 1996–97. External pressures remained considerable (and perhaps further slightly increased) during the subsequent two Treaty revisions. While issues like trade in services, IPRs and investment had been squarely on the table since the Uruguay Round (and the MAI negotiations), after Amsterdam important multilateral negotiations on services and possibly intellectual property, investment and other issues – on which the Community only shared competence with Member States – drew nearer. Hence, the potential disadvantages of mixed competences became somewhat more immediate for the Community and Member States.

A comparison across the different cases also suggests that there are different kinds of exogenous spillover. In the case of the PHARE programme a large part of the external spillover rationale was due to an endogenous logic linking internal and external events. The very fact that a regional integration project got under way and successfully developed common policies induced participants, regardless of their original intentions, to adopt common policies *vis-à-vis* non-participant third countries. As pointed out in Chapter 2, much pressure stemmed from the demands of the extra-Community environment reacting to the successful developments within the Community. This logic has been termed 'externalisation'.[122]

The case of visa, asylum and immigration policy is more grounded in the nature of external problems for which the European level is viewed as a more effective buffer. This is related to the perception that many problems go beyond the governance potential of individual Member States. European democratic nation-states depend on the delivery of economic, social and other well-being to their people. Increasingly, due to regional interdependencies and more global problems, they lose their power to deliver these goods. To circumvent the decrease in influence over their territory, national governments tend to co-operate more closely on the European level.[123] As for the JHA case, it can be argued that EU Member States realised the need to deal jointly with exogenous migratory pressures, as unilateral measures have led to increasingly restrictive national policies, but remained ineffective in solving the problems at hand.

Having incorporated exogenous spillover in the revised neofunctionalist framework also reflects empirical realities more closely. Interest groups and actors falling under the political spillover label more generally tend to form their preferences and identities not merely on the basis of endogenous-functional and domestic structures, but also due to exogenous ones.[124] Also and similarly going beyond early neofunctionalism,

---

[122] Schmitter (1969, 1971).
[123] The latter point has drawn on Wessels' *Ebenendilemma*. See Wessels (1997: 286ff).
[124] Cf. Green Cowles (1995: 522).

the Commission and other supranational actors often not only cultivate functional spillover but also cultivate exogenous spillover pressures. Hence, the introduction of exogenous spillover has allowed us to usefully broaden the structural basis for revised neofunctionalist explanation.

Countervailing Forces and Dialectical Approach

The empirical analysis has revealed the importance of hypothesising for countervailing pressures. Outcomes could not have been (adequately) explained without taking recourse to spillback forces. This certainly goes for the case of visa, asylum and immigration policy at the IGC 1996–97 which is well explained through the interplay of strong dynamics and medium (or medium to strong) countervailing forces which managed to somewhat water down the Title IV provisions in the Treaty of Amsterdam. During the IGC 2000, the weakening dynamics and strengthened countervailing forces provided a persuasive rationale for the rather modest provisions on first pillar JHA issues in the Treaty of Nice. The scenario was reversed during the Convention and last IGC negotiations during which the weak to medium level spillback forces could not significantly curtail the strong spillover pressures.

Also the Common Commercial Policy case could not have been explicated without considering the spillback side of the dialectical equation. Even if the overall pressures exerted during the Amsterdam IGC were moderate, there were still considerable exogenous pressures, which could have suggested a more far-reaching outcome. However, when considering the substantial countervailing pressures, especially stemming from sovereignty-consciousness, the minimal outcome becomes more plausible. Countervailing pressures remained of similar strength during the Nice IGC, but (functional and to a lesser extent cultivated) spillover pressures grew, as a result of which we can reasonably account for the more progressive outcome. The very supranational CCP agreement reached in the Constitutional Treaty, which can be partly explained by even stronger integrational dynamics, only becomes wholly convincing when we look at the weakened countervailing forces.

As for the PHARE case, the absence of strong countervailing pressures, which has been hypothesised as an additional explanatory factor for progressive and integrative outcomes, is an important element in explaining the decision of giving the G7 aid co-ordination mandate for Central Eastern Europe to the Commission. Spillback forces were largely lacking, particularly due to the convergence of domestic constraints and background factors. Moreover, the year 1989 was the height of a positive integrationist climate. In addition, the decision to make PHARE an integral and important part of the Union's pre-accession strategy was facilitated due to only weak countervailing pressures. Despite the moderate (or somewhat more substantial) countervailing forces surrounding the Copenhagen decision to make PHARE funds available for co-financing infrastructure projects, overall the development of the PHARE programme was characterised by only weak spillback pressures.

The analysis of the Intergovernmental Conference 2003/04 has also considered the broader countervailing pressures that threatened overall agreement at the last IGC, since the wider EU context, of course, impacts on individual outcomes. Wider countervailing forces also continue to accompany the ratification process of the Constitutional Treaty. After the referendums in France and in the Netherlands this process has been seriously set back, to the extent that it has become highly questionable whether the Treaty will enter into force.

In many ways the JHA and CCP cases make an interesting comparison. Both cases (and sub-cases) took place at the same time, which holds the negative integrative climate as a countervailing factor largely constant. The rather different outcomes during the 1996–97 IGC across the two areas suggest that this countervailing force cannot have a decisive impact on decision outcomes. This further corroborates my initial hunch that the integrative climate should be regarded as secondary compared to the other hypothesised countervailing forces, domestic constrains and diversities as well as sovereignty-consciousness. The latter pressures provided significantly stronger spillback rationales than the adverse integrative climate.

The inquiry into countervailing pressures has indicated that these forces partly overlap and cannot always be clearly separated from one another. Perhaps most closely intertwined are the countervailing forces of domestic constraints and diversity. In a certain way, diversity among Member States aggravates domestic-level constraints as one government that is restricted on an issue due to the domestic (political) environment may be accommodated within the search for a far-reaching solution. However, substantial domestic constraints in many Member States, which are more likely when countries are politically, economically, culturally or sociologically diverse, tend to considerably obstruct outcomes beyond the lowest common denominator. This also suggests that countervailing pressures, just like dynamics, have a propensity to reinforce each other.

My analysis suggests that strong dynamics can overcome (even) substantial countervailing forces, at least to a certain degree. The Amsterdam JHA case has indicated, for example, that the central institutions (including the Presidency) may skilfully tame spillback pressures as through the Presidency's introduction of the Action Plan on Organised Crime, which kept JHA ministers and officials busy during the IGC. The PHARE case and the Commission's leadership role at the Copenhagen European Council have also shown how moderate (or somewhat more substantial) countervailing pressures can be overcome. It is also interesting to note that even strong countervailing pressures may not completely offset moderate dynamics. Even though the Amsterdam CCP or Nice JHA cases did not bring about any major breakthroughs, they nevertheless provided some, albeit modest, progress. From this finding, as well as my overall empirical analysis, we may derive the informed guess that the odds are in favour of further integration.

The incorporation of countervailing forces and the dialectical nature of the framework have also enabled us to account for more specific aspects of decision outcomes. For instance, the strong spillover pressures during the last IGC concerning Title IV issues suggested the likelihood of full communitarisation. When also considering the countervailing pressures at work, we may be able to estimate that areas, like the right to determine access to the labour market by third country nationals, are excluded from the (immigration policy) provisions. Thus, by analysing both sides of the dialectical equation the specificity of our judgement concerning decision outcomes is (considerably) enhanced.

Another conclusion that can be drawn from my analysis of dynamics and countervailing forces is that these two types of main pressures impact on one another during the (decision-making) interaction and thus already restrain each others' impact. For example, social spillover pressures may be reduced by countervailing forces such as domestic constraints (and sovereignty-consciousness). On the other hand, socialisation and learning processes also, to some extent, soften up sovereignty-consciousness and also curtail domestic constraints and diversities, since national elites are increasingly Europeanised and the European Union (as well as interaction on the European level) contributes to their construction of preferences and identities. On a general level one can also say that different structural pressures inform and constitute decision-makers' interests and attitudes, such as endogenous-functional, exogenous and domestic structures, which suggests that dynamics and countervailing forces check and balance each other on many levels. However, these processes are notoriously difficult to capture empirically.

Closely related to the previous point, spillover pressures and countervailing forces sometimes cannot be neatly separated from one another. For example, during the empirical analysis of the CCP case we have witnessed that the anticipation of functional pressures may be detrimental in the search for far-reaching solutions.[125] In addition, during the same (sub)-case the roles of the Commission and the Council Presidency, which are usually viewed here as essential driving forces, ended up nurturing bureaucratic countervailing pressures due to the distrust of the Commission and the clumsy (e.g. shopping-list) approach of the Dutch Presidency. Conversely, the domestic environment that was here largely viewed as a source of government constraint (and thus as a countervailing pressure) may actually increase the rationale for European solutions. In the PHARE case the significant convergence of domestic policies may have even acted as a spur for giving the mandate for co-ordinating western aid to the Commission. While my overall analysis suggests that my separation into dynamics and countervailing factors makes sense, empirical 'reality' is more complex than any theory, including, needless to say, this revised neofunctionalist framework.

Comparison and Causality

To arrive at causal inferences two main complementary methods are employed in this study: first, my analysis in Chapters 2, 3 and 4 has traced and analysed causal mechanisms and processes. Second and additionally, comparisons can be (and have to some degree already been) made across cases. For a more systematic comparative analysis, my empirical findings are summarised in Table 5.1.

Two variations of the comparative method may be used here for making causal inferences. First, we can identify and isolate the causal processes that lead to different outcomes.[126] One way of advancing this method is to examine whether hypothesised pressures co-vary with outcomes. Changing levels of progressiveness in terms of outcome would corroborate those dynamics changing as hypothesised, and challenge those remaining constant or changing in the direction opposite to the one hypothesised. In other words, higher values on the decision outcome (or on the overall dynamics) would confirm those dynamics that also display higher scores, and challenge the causal relevance of those decreasing or remaining constant. By including countervailing pressures in the revised neofunctionalist framework, an additional layer of complexity has been introduced: spillover pressures may not co-vary

---

[125] A similar argument was made by Lindberg (1966). He held that integration could be a source of stress among states.

[126] Ragin (1987: 47).

Table 5.1. *Summary of hypothesised pressures and outcomes across (sub-)cases*[127]

(Sub-)case / Pressures	PHARE	CCP 1996-97	CCP 2000	CCP 2002-04	JHA 1996-97	JHA 2000	JHA 2002-04
Functional Spillover	Medium to High	Low	Medium	Medium to High	High	Medium	(Medium to) High
Exogenous spillover	Medium to High	Medium to High	(Medium to High)	(Medium to) High	Medium (to High)	Medium (to High)	Medium to High
Social Spillover	Medium to High	Low	Low	Medium to High	Medium	Low	Medium to High
Political spillover	Low	Low	Low	Low (to Medium)	Low to Medium	Low	Low to Medium
Cultivated spillover	High	Low	(Low to Medium)	(Medium to) High	(Medium to) High	Low (to Medium)	(Medium to) High
Dynamics (combined)	Strong ⇨	Weak ⇨	Medium ⇨	Strong ⇨	Strong ⇨	(Weak to) Medium ⇨	Strong ⇨
Countervailing forces (combined)	Weak	Strong	Strong	Weak to Medium	Medium	Strong	Weak to Medium
Outcome (in terms of breadth/depth)	High	Low	Low to Medium	Medium to High	Medium to High	Low (to Medium)	Medium to High

127 Two simplifications of Table 3 shall be briefly highlighted: (1) The PHARE programme has been presented here as one case. Of course, it would be possible to subdivide it into different sub-cases, which is evident from my analysis in chapter II. (2) As for the depiction of countervailing forces: the latter (which may also entail a certain extent of spillback pressure) could have also, alternatively, been expressed through slightly upwards pointing arrows.

with outcomes in a linear fashion due to strong spillback forces. Hence, although the rule still applies, that increased measures of causally relevant dynamics should lead to higher scores on the dependent variable, countervailing forces may lessen or dilute dynamics. Therefore, as a first step, it will be ascertained if spillover pressures co-vary with the values of the combined dynamics (Table 5.1: third row from bottom). And as a second step, I will investigate whether individual dynamics co-vary with the overall outcome of the sub-case in question, while taking the impact of countervailing forces into consideration.

Through closer examination of Table 5.1 we can see that functional, social and cultivated spillover pressures particularly co-vary with the scores determined for the combined dynamics. In those cases where the overall dynamics have been rated as 'strong' (PHARE, CCP 2002–04, JHA 1996–97 and JHA 2002–04), these variables were characterised by values between 'medium' and (more often) 'high', while they have been allocated lesser scores in the cases judged by lower values on the overall dynamics. When looking at final outcomes – while taking account of countervailing forces – this trend is also confirmed.

The causal significance of individual pressures can be ascertained particularly well in those cases where all but a few hypothesised causal variables are constant. Here, it can be seen if the remaining pressures changed in the direction of the combined dynamics/overall outcome. Unfortunately, the distribution of variables across my cases does not give much scope for such an analysis. The first two Common Commercial Policy sub-cases (CCP 1996–97 and CCP 2000) allow for some limited use of this technique. In both units social and political spillover pressures have been ranked as 'low'. Hence, we have 'isolated' functional, exogenous and cultivated spillover pressures to account for the change from a 'weak' to a 'medium' score for the combined dynamics. And in fact, the three pressures do display higher measures on the second case, which substantiates their relevance. The same method can be used for comparing the PHARE case with the CCP 1996–97 sub-case. In both instances, exogenous and political spillover take on the same values. At the same time, functional, social and cultivated spillover displayed substantially lower scores in the second case, thus explaining the change of combined dynamics from 'strong' to 'weak'. However, as indicated the explanatory power of these two findings should not be overemphasised, given the fact that the degree of isolation of these variables was rather limited and could not be backed by more comparisons of this kind.

The most conclusive comparative analysis can be made in terms of countervailing forces given my theoretical framework and the resulting isolation of countervailing forces as a variable. Its causal significance can be measured directly when compared with outcomes in consideration of the values taken by the combined dynamics. In the cases of PHARE, CCP 1996–97, CCP 2000, CCP 2002–04, JHA 2000 and JHA 2002–04, 'weak' (or 'weak to medium') countervailing pressures co-vary with 'high' (or 'medium to high') decision outcomes, while strong countervailing pressures are accompanied by 'minimal' (or 'minimal to medium') decision outcomes. The analysis of these cases becomes even more conclusive when the combined dynamics are taken into account. It indicates that countervailing forces tend to tame dynamics, depending on the values taken by spillback forces. In the CCP 2002–04 and the JHA 2002–04 cases, 'weak to medium' countervailing forces were able to reduce the 'strong' combined dynamics to some extent. Also interesting to note are the CCP 2000 and JHA 2000 cases which indicate that 'medium' and '(weak to) medium' combined dynamics lead to 'low to medium' and 'low (to medium)' outcomes respectively when met by strong countervailing forces. As for the JHA 1996–97 case, here the medium strength countervailing forces somewhat curtailed the strong overall dynamics.

The second variation of the comparative method employed here in the pursuit of causal inferences is Mill's method of agreement.[128] When employing this method, one looks at all cases where the dependent variable takes on the same value. In this way, no positive causality can be established, but irrelevant (or less relevant) variables can be identified. For example, one can identify all cases with strong overall dynamics or far-reaching outcomes. Those dynamics which are (repeatedly) at a low level, according to this logic, are likely to be rather dispensable. As far as political spillover is concerned, we have a constellation of a low value on this pressure in the PHARE case followed by strong overall dynamics and a high score on the overall outcome. Less clear-cut, but going into a similar direction, are the CCP 2002–04, JHA 1996–97 and JHA 2002–04 cases where political spillover has been ranked as low to medium, while the combined dynamics were judged strong and the final outcome medium to high. The method of agreement can also be utilised by looking at cases in which the outcome was close to stalemate or the overall dynamics were weak. Those spillover pressures which are still (repeatedly) displaying high values, following Mill's rationale, cannot have been that important and may overall carry a lesser degree of causal significance. The exogenous spillover dynamic is slightly challenged through this method. In the CCP 1996–97 sub-case 'medium to high' scores still only induced rather modest overall dynamics and the case is also characterised by a minimal outcome. The JHA 2000 sub-case,

---

[128] Mill (1950).

while slightly more ambiguous, goes into the same direction: 'medium (to high)' value for exogenous spillover is correlated with 'weak to medium' overall dynamics and a rather modest outcome. Overall, the CCP and JHA cases have indicated that variation in the strength of exogenous spillover was limited despite relatively diverse outcomes.

What conclusions can be drawn from my comparative analysis? First, the fundamental hypotheses of the revised neofunctionalist framework have clearly been confirmed. The interplay of combined dynamics and countervailing pressures provide us with important insights regarding final decision outcomes. In addition, the hypothesised spillover pressures seem to aptly explain the varying strength of the combined dynamics. Second, of the individual dynamics, functional and cultivated (and to a slightly lesser extent) social spillover pressures have been corroborated the most. For these spillover pressures co-variation with the combined dynamics and the overall outcome was the most evident. In addition, these pressures neither became subject to challenge through the method of difference. Third, the causal relevance of countervailing forces has also been substantiated through my comparisons. Fourth, exogenous spillover pressures have been somewhat challenged, albeit arguably not been 'disconfirmed', through the above analysis. In the two cases accompanied by rather modest values on the combined dynamics and overall outcome, where exogenous spillover pressures displayed substantial strength, other more agency-related pressures' scores were rather low. In line with both my theoretical hypotheses and the empirical process-tracing as well as contextual analysis, structural pressures are more decisively reinforced when they are accompanied by the hypothesised more agency-related pressures of cultivated, political and also social spillover.[129] Hence, the combined dynamics tend to increase especially when structural *and* more actor-based spillover pressures are (substantially) activated. Fifth, of all hypothesised pressures the causal significance of political spillover has been challenged most severely. However, my comparative analysis does not suggest that this pressure has been entirely falsified, given the lack of unambiguous repeated absence in the face of far-reaching outcomes and strong overall dynamics. Although political spillover can tentatively be judged as *not necessary* for the

---

[129] While the recognition of my two structural spillover pressures by (national and other) actors is already part of the determination of their strength, functional and exogenous structural pressures in the EU context may only unfold their full logic when they are pushed by strong pressure on the part of assertive agency, located in their 'core constituencies' of supranational, transnational/organised interests and socialised national actors who find expression in the concepts of cultivated, political and social spillover.

occurrence of progressive decisions, it may – somewhat downgraded – still be regarded as *conducive* in terms of integrative outcomes.

In line with my ontological and epistemological position, causal relations are not viewed as deterministic here, as they are in the natural sciences where causes inextricably connect entities and determine outcomes. Instead, in the social–political world, causes are conditioned and constituted by actors' interests, norms and identities and thus merely provide agents with direction and goals for action, rather than 'determine' their behaviour.[130] On this basis I have built a 'plurality of causes' assumption (elaborated in the methodology section). It was suggested that cause can be defined as any factor conducive or necessary (though itself insufficient) for a conjuncture of conditions that is sufficient for the specified outcome. A cause is thus any factor that is an insufficient but conducive or necessary part of a sufficient but unnecessary condition. It is an unnecessary condition because a combination of other conditions can have the same effect.[131]

This understanding of causality, which allows for multiple causal sequences that unfold independently, is reflected in the empirical parts of this book. In the decisions leading to the PHARE programme becoming an important part of the pre-accession strategy, for instance, functional spillover was a necessary but not a sufficient factor. Similarly, the roles played by the Commission and the Presidency were necessary but in themselves probably not sufficient. However, these factors taken together were sufficient to trigger the decisions making PHARE an integral part in the Union's pre-accession strategy. Moreover, we have seen that progressive and integrative outcomes can be caused by different combinations of factors. For example, while the communitarisation of visa, asylum and immigration policy at the IGC 1996–97 was caused by functional, cultivated and exogenous spillover, assisted by social spillover, the decision on the mandate for the co-ordination of western aid to Poland and Hungary was caused by exogenous and cultivated spillover pressures as well as the convergence of national interests (absence of countervailing forces). Hence, different combinations of dynamics and countervailing forces can be 'sufficient', which implies that no one combination is the 'necessary' one, i.e. that a combination of other conditions can have the same effect.[132] Another

---

[130] For non-deterministic accounts of causality see, for example: Giddens (1984: 345); Adler (1997: 329); Finnemore (1996: 28).

[131] Cf. Dessler (1991: 347).

[132] This may also further the rationale that political spillover pressures, even though they have been relatively absent in my empirical chapters, may still contribute to causing integrative outcomes.

obvious but interesting observation is that all successful and progressive outcomes were caused by significant scores of more than one factor. This further corroborates the thesis that a combination of several spillover pressures – and as mentioned before, particularly the united occurrence of structural and agency-related pressures – is particularly likely to foster outcomes beyond the lowest common denominator.[133]

As has been mentioned at the beginning of this section, two main methods are employed here to arrive at causal inferences. The comparative analysis that has been used throughout this section arguably does not, by itself, carry us much beyond the level of correlation. Hence, in addition it was necessary throughout my empirical analysis to trace, analyse and discuss the various causal mechanisms and processes at play. Causal mechanisms can be viewed as providing the integrative knowledge that is absent at the level of correlations. Hence, by tracing and analysing causal mechanisms and contexts the connection between cause and effect could be elaborated by appealing to the (real) knowledge structures that produce observed phenomena. The results of both types of analysis have very largely been congruent, as my preceding analysis has indicated. A combination of the comparative method with tracing causal mechanisms and processes has thus strengthened the conclusiveness of my findings.

Theoretical Context and Related Debates

The broader theoretical context has already, to some extent, been reflected in the previous chapters. However, some additional points shall be made here through which the revised neofunctionalist framework will be integrated more systematically into the wider theoretical cosmos and related more closely to important disciplinary debates.

It is noticeable from studying the wider literature on European integration theory that some of the more recent approaches bear considerable resemblance to neofunctionalism and that neofunctionalist insights have also informed other theoretical approaches in a number of ways, although few authors have given explicit credit to neofunctionalism. Most plainly drawing on neofunctionalist thought and also most openly acknowledging their neofunctionalist roots – apart from Schmitter (2004) who is also (explicitly) concerned with modifying the original neofunctionalist account[134] – the authors of supranational governance,

---

[133] Future research may specify which of my pressures are *conducive* and which *necessary* (or perhaps even *sufficient*) for integrative outcomes, a task that cannot be accomplished with the data analysed here.

[134] The 'neo-neofunctionalist' account of Philippe Schmitter (2004) shall be briefly contrasted with my revised neofunctionalist framework: Schmitter and I agree for

Stone Sweet and Sandholtz, have emphasised the role of transnational society, EU rules (inducing self-sustaining dynamics) and the importance of supranational institutions.[135]

Multi-level governance – although less a theory of the integration process itself and more an approach that seeks to capture the nature of the European Union that has emerged from that process – also shares many neofunctionalist assumptions, for example, concerning multiple actors, the potentially autonomous role of EU institutions, the possibility of positive-sum games and integration as a process. Some of the conclusions drawn by Marks, Hooghe and other authors working in that tradition thus significantly parallel those of neofunctionalism: national governments are neither in control of supranational institutions, nor of the integration process more generally; and the 'national interest' is neither defined exclusively in the domestic realm nor purely by national governmental actors.[136]

The policy network approach has considerable overlaps with neofunctionalist theory, even though it does not constitute a substantive theory of integration and focuses more on policy than on polity and although it is associated more exclusively with micro- and meso-level decision-making.[137] Similar to neofunctionalism, most of policy network analysis assumes self-interested actors, but also accounts for the influence of politics of expertise. In addition, the approach supposes multiple (private and public) actors, interdependent relationships, the

instance on (1) the importance of the external/exogenous context for the integration process; (2) on the non-automaticity of spillover; (3) the need for taking the European Court of Justice on board for a modified approach; (4) an emphasis on theoretical pluralism; (5) measurement of the dependent variable in terms of scope and level of integration; and (6) the non-specification of a particular end-state (cf. Schmitter 2004: 53–9, 69–70). On other points the two approaches overlap, while accentuating different aspects. For example, Schmitter (2004: 47, 54, 65) alludes to spillback as a (possible) direction of the process, but countervailing forces (as a counter-dynamic to spillover pressures) are made less explicit and treated less systematically. On still other points we seem to somewhat disagree and or hold different views. For instance, Schmitter's ontology seems to lean more towards rational-choice than mine. In addition, his account of learning is more interest-based than the one in my revised framework (Schmitter 2004: 55–7). Finally, in some respect the two approaches have different foci or emphases. While Schmitter (2004: 59) is more concerned with the development of the integration process as a whole, including its different cycles, my framework concentrates more on explaining outcomes within the process (while taking the process and its development into account). Moreover, Schmitter (2004: 54, 60) seems to be more concerned with prediction than I, even though his predictive claims/ elements are presented as probabilistic, a view that we both share.

[135] See Sweet Stone and Sandholtz (1997: esp. 302–9). Also cf. Sandholtz and Stone Sweet (1998).

[136] Cf. Marks, Hooghe and Blank (1996: esp. 347–69); Hooghe and Marks (2001). For an early work see Marks (1993).

[137] On different levels of decision-making see Peterson (1995: 69ff).

tendency to depoliticise issues and the contention that policy outcomes cannot usually be adequately explained by sole recourse to the mediation of member governments' preferences.[138] Given similar ontologies there seems scope for combining the two frameworks. The policy network approach, which does not by itself constitute a theory of European integration, would significantly enhance its explanatory leverage in terms of explaining European integration, including more systemic developments, if it was enriched by neofunctionalist theory. Revised neofunctionalism would benefit, for example, by adding additional micro-foundations to its descriptive and explanatory repertoire.

New institutionalism has developed from general theories of politics and also does not constitute a theory of European integration in and of itself. With neofunctionalism it shares the general dictum that institutions matter in that they affect outcomes.[139] While the merely constraining influence of institutions as conceived by rational-choice institutionalism would seem like underestimating the role of institutions from a neofunctionalist perspective, the thicker institutional understanding of the other institutionalisms is more in keeping with neofunctionalist thought. Much of the rational-choice literature on the European Union arguably neglects a central maxim of early neofunctionalism, namely the conceptualisation of integration of a process. By contrast, the *non*-rational-choice institutionalist versions have embraced this insight of integration as a process. For historical institutionalists,[140] the European integration process unfolds over time and results often from unintended consequences of earlier decisions and restricted time horizons on the part of decision-makers. This is wholly consistent with neofunctionalist assumptions. So is the explanation that autonomously acting European institutions may foster and cement institutional arrangements. However, historical institutionalists go even further in explaining the stickiness and longevity of supranational solutions, and thus provide a more comprehensive account of member governments' constraints. Additional insights provided by historical institutionalism include shifts in governments' preferences, institutional barriers to reform and increased costs of exit. Thus, historical institutionalism and (revised) neofunctionalism seem rather compatible in many respects. They may be supplementary in that neofunctionalism would benefit from drawing on historical institutionalism for specifying

---

[138] On policy network analysis see e.g., Peterson and Bomberg (1999).

[139] Cf. Schneider and Aspinwall (2001a).

[140] This is not to say that historical institutionalists, like Pierson (1996, 1998), do not subscribe to a (not insignificant) number of rational-choice assumptions. Cf. Aspinwall and Schneider (2001a: 11–12).

the conditions of Member State control in response to the effects of unintended consequences. For historical institutionalism – which in itself is not a theory of European integration as the ultimate causes of integration remain exogenous to it – linkage with a wider theory like neofunctionalism would enhance its explanatory leverage for middle-range analyses of the European integration process.

(Revised) neofunctionalism overlaps with sociological institution-alist and (reflexive strands of) governance approaches concerning the emphasis not only on formal by also on informal institutions, which include informal norms and conventions. They also particularly share an understanding concerning the endogenous formation and transform-ability of interests. The many commonalities between sociological institutionalist/constructivist and revised neofunctionalist thought have already been discussed with regard to my ontology and regarding the concept of social spillover and will thus be spared here. The governance approach, of course, does not form a coherent theory and therefore constitutes a difficult item for comparison. However, in terms of the basic research question there tends to be a significant difference from neofunctionalist theory: whereas governance approaches have a pro-pensity to take the EU-polity as the *explanans*, (revised) neofunction-alism – despite feedback-loops and series of decision cycles – is inclined to view the EU-polity as the *explanandum*.[141] Despite essentially dif-ferent research foci, revised neofunctionalism and (certain) threads of the governance approach bear significant resemblance, for example, concerning decision-making processes characterised by incrementalism, depoliticisation and expert deliberation.[142]

The classical intergovernmentalist–neofunctionalist debate is still an important one, albeit not as central as it used to be.[143] As pointed out in my theory chapter, I have taken early neofunctionalism as a starting point but also taken intergovernmentalist elements on board for my theoretical revision. But does this also imply that I am trapped in the supranational–intergovernmental dichotomy? This divide has been described as sterile and unhelpful.[144] Yet, even recent developments of

---

[141] See Jachtenfuchs (2001: 257). However, Jachtenfuchs and Kohler-Koch (2004: 98–9) have spanned the governance approach very broadly to include questions of classical integration theory in which the Euro-polity is the dependent variable.

[142] On the latter aspects cf. e.g. Joerges and Neyer (1997), Joerges (1999), Bogdandy (2003).

[143] Cf. Rosamond (2000: 2); Jachtenfuchs (2001: 255). I have argued in the introduction that approaches falling within this divide focus on the significant question of explaining decision outcomes (while concentrating usually on the polity (and politics) dimension of integration). However, in the past decade scholars have increasing become interested in different research questions (cf. Introduction).

[144] See e.g. Branch and Øhrgaard (1999: esp. 123–4); Risse-Kappen (1996: 56ff).

the original approaches, such as liberal intergovernmentalism (LI) and supranational governance have largely failed to step outside and go beyond it.[145] One major characteristic of this dichotomy is that the two basic theories privilege certain types of actors, either national governments or supranational institutions, dominating decision outcomes and EU integration more generally. By contrast, revised neofunctionalism has integrated both kinds of actors more closely into the framework, not least through the accommodation of countervailing forces (including domestic constraints and diversities). Moreover, although national governments are not expressly hypothesised as a variable on its own, an important part of the estimation of strength regarding my structural pressures (functional and exogenous spillover as well as domestic constraints and diversities) is the extent to which national governmental elites buy into, and act upon, these structural rationales. Another, closely related, point is that my framework also grants the possibility of anticipating spillover pressures, especially functional ones, on the part of national actors, thus further drawing governments into (revised) neofunctionalist theory.

A second and often criticised feature of this dichotomy is that both theories concentrate on different contexts and different parts of empirical reality. My account has arguably managed to avoid this shortcoming by analysing case studies on different levels of decision-making and by combining (in two of my cases) investigations of grand-bargains with analyses of policy-making processes and day-to-day developments.[146] Moreover, my analysis recognised that IGCs are neither purely the result of integration stemming from routine developments, nor the exclusive source of integration. Instead, it has treated grand bargains as both the result of, *and* the cause for, the integration process. Following from the first two criticisms, a third critique has been made, namely that approaches trapped in this dichotomy tend to be unable to explain substantive differences between policy areas. The revised neofunctionalist framework is arguably better equipped than earlier approaches along this divide,[147] through the variation concerning

---

[145] On liberal intergovernmentalism see especially Moravcsik (1993, 1998). On supranational governance see Stone Sweet and Sandholtz (1997) as well as Sandholtz and Stone Sweet (1998). Cf. Branch and Øhrgaard (1999: esp. 123–8, 136–9) for a criticism which suggests that both approaches are still trapped in the intergovernmental–supranational dichotomy.

[146] Within my JHA and CCP IGC cases, meso- and micro-level developments have been considered most thoroughly for the 1996–97 Treaty revision.

[147] One could argue that liberal intergovernmentalism is less prone to such criticism, as variations in the domestic arena shoulder much of this explication. However, Wincott (1995: 601) has pointed to contradictions in Moravcsik's argument. LI asserts that

the distribution (and strength) of spillover pressures and countervailing forces which result from differing policy contexts. The possibilities of accounting for differences between policy areas have increased *vis-à-vis* early neofunctionalist theory by going beyond functional interdependencies as the only real source of structural change. Instead, exogenous and domestic dissimilarities can provide additional causes of transformation (and non-change).[148]

Another criticism of the intergovernmentalist–neofunctionalist debate has been that important dimensions of governance in the EU are ignored, such as the growing inclusion of policy-networks and the not exclusively rational/strategic action orientation on the part of agents.[149] The revised neofunctionalist framework can arguably also address these concerns. By incorporating the concepts of epistemic communities and advocacy coalitions within my framework, important aspects of policy-network analysis have thus been accounted for. Further similarities between the network approach and the revised neofunctionalist framework have been pointed out above. As for the issue of (strategic) action orientation, given the (implicit) reflexive tendencies even within early neofunctionalist theory, this may not in fact be a fair critique. However, the revised framework has broadened the ontological base to include more explicitly a soft constructivist ontology, which is also reflected by integrating concepts such as communicative and normatively regulated action into the framework. Hence, in sum I argue that the revised neofunctionalist framework bridges the old neofunctionalist–intergovernmentalist divide in many ways, while also going beyond this debate.

My concerns with recent intergovernmentalist and supranational theoretical developments, such as liberal intergovernmentalism and supranational governance, are also largely, but not exclusively, related to the above shortcomings. While most arguments are well known, and thus shall not be reiterated here, a number of points are briefly taken up, as they particularly highlight the differences and value-added of the revised neofunctionalist framework. One important criticism of LI (which can also be levelled against rational-choice institutionalism),

---

European integration is a means for states to gain autonomy from domestic pressures, while on the other hand domestic interests are supposed to determine state preferences. Hence, if the Union is a device for member governments to attain autonomy from domestic interests, states may in fact not be constrained by domestic pressures. This also undermines LI's ability to explain differences between policy areas.

[148] These criticisms concerning the one-sidedness of theorising for actors and contexts as well as the inadequacy of explaining variation across sectors have been put forward with regard to supranational governance and liberal intergovernmentalism by Branch and Øhrgaard (1999: esp. 123–8, 136–9).

[149] For this critique see Risse-Kappen (1996: 56f).

partly going beyond the afore-mentioned issues, is that, according to these approaches, preference formation takes place largely exogenously to the integration processes and that the 'national interest' is almost exclusively made up of domestic concerns and constraints. Insights, for example, from constructivist/sociological institutionalist and (multi-level)governance approaches and also from the revised neofunctionalist framework suggest that preference formation is, at least to some extent, an endogenous process, and that EU membership as well as the (formal and informal) institutional environment matter in terms of preference formation and alteration of national governments.[150] These approaches, along with insights from historical and rational-choice institutionalism as well as the empirical findings of this study, also call into question LI's model of intergovernmental bargaining where supranational agents can be strictly controlled by national governments. It can be argued that liberal intergovernmentalism neglects the institutional structure for EU level negotiations and – according to the theoretical perspective taken – ignores the shaping and constituting effects of supranational institutions.[151]

Both liberal intergovernmentalism and supranational governance approaches largely ignore the potential impact of the external realm. In the case of supranational governance, this is specifically peculiar because one of its protagonists, Wayne Sandholtz, had earlier co-authored a well-known article in which the influence of international competitive pressures constituted an important theme.[152] Arguably, LI could relatively easily incorporate the role of the external environment into its analysis, thus upgrading the two-level into a three-level game.[153] However, this begs the question on how many levels we can possibly play. If we added the supranational and the subnational level, the conceptual conciseness and elegance of the Moravcsikian approach would soon give way to a proliferation of variables adding greater complexity and reducing coherence. Although 'an undisciplined proliferation of variables' was found 'unsatisfying' by Moravcsik himself,[154]

---

[150] For constructivist/sociological institutionalist works that implicitly or explicitly call LI's model of preference formation into question see e.g. Marcussen *et al.* (2001: esp. 104, 114); Lewis (1998a); Risse-Kappen (1996). For criticisms of LI on this point from a multi-level governance perspective see e.g. Marks *et al.* (1996: 346).

[151] Cf. Moravcsik (1993, 1998, 1999).

[152] Cf. Sandholtz and Zysman (1989: 103ff).It should be said that Stone Sweet and Sandholtz (1997: esp. 309) do not completely neglect the role of exogenous pressure, as they briefly talk about the role that globalisation may have on supranational governance. However, they do not incorporate this pressure in their actual framework.

[153] This has been done, for example, by Patterson (1997).   [154] Moravcsik (1995: 612).

additional levels would, in my view, justify such sacrifice of theoretical parsimony in light of the complexity of the empirical 'reality'.

The revised neofunctionalist framework and the findings of this study also need to be discussed with regard to another more topical debate: that between rationalist/rational-choice and reflectivist/constructivist approaches. This divide is predominantly about ontology. My work will probably add value and be insightful for those scholars who are more driven by empirical puzzles than by the ontological purity of the argument; revised neofunctionalism has relaxed core assumptions at either end of the rationalist–reflectivist spectrum and combined a soft rational-choice ontology with a soft constructivist one. This way, I was able to take on board the empirical insight that agents tend to be subject to different social logics and rationalities and that they combine several modes of action in their behaviour, such as strategic, norm-regulated and communicative action. A number of scholars have favoured such ontological overlap. Checkel, for instance, argues that the best empirically driven rationalism and constructivism is characterised by ontological tensions and that we should welcome the advent of theoretical models that capture the multiple social dynamics present in everyday EU politics.[155] These scholars may accept the claim that my work, to some extent, contributes to bridging the rationalist-reflectivist divide, or, less ambitiously, to promoting dialogue between the two 'camps'. Other scholars such as Moravcsik seem to attach more importance to ontological purity and would thus deplore the ontological 'tensions' in my work.[156]

As constructivism constitutes an ontology or meta-theory which lacks middle-range hypotheses and which does not make any substantive claims about European integration, it would benefit from closer linkage with other theoretical approaches in order to elicit constructivist insights more concretely for our understanding of the European integration process.[157] The findings of this book suggest that connecting constructivism with (revised) neofunctionalism may be a promising and fruitful undertaking. Constructivist work may gain from this study, as the latter suggests several potentially interesting mid-range propositions that could be further advanced within the constructivist research programme vis-à-vis European integration studies. Concepts such as communicative action and normatively regulated action embedded in

---

[155] See Checkel (2001c: 241). See Schimmelfennig (2001) and Risse et al. (1999) respectively for what Checkel referred to as the best rationalist and constructivist work with ontological tensions. Cf. also Risse (2004: 174–5) arguing the case for an inclusive ontology.

[156] See e.g. Moravcsik (2001a: 226–39).

[157] On this point see Risse (2004: 160–1, 174) and less explicitly Checkel (2001b: 37).

the EU context or the notion of social spillover more generally should provide ample scope in that respect.[158] In addition, my linkage of (functional, exogenous and domestic) structures with (supranational, national and transnational) agents may provide more concrete insights on how structuration can be utilised for generating tangible hypotheses for EU integration. Hence, revised neofunctionalism may provide an appropriate framework for enriching constructivism in order to bring the latter closer to a substantive theory of European integration.

The revised neofunctionalist framework and the empirical findings of this book may also contribute to advancing more rationalist accounts of integration: while my framework accepts the core rational-choice assumption of basically rational and self-interested actors (who under certain conditions follow non-consequentialist action logics), my findings clearly highlight that EU norms and structures as well as supranational institutions and actors, impact on preference formation as a *systemic* (as opposed to exceptional) feature of the EU decision-making process. Hence, exogenously given preferences, which are assumed in liberal intergovernmentalism and rational-choice institutionalism, and to a lesser extent, historical institutionalism, are (once again) called into question. The mounting evidence in that respect should inform scholars working in the rational-choice tradition to modify their assumptions and accounts of preference formation. That embracing a more endogenous understanding of preference formation and alteration may be possible without having to drop core rationalist assumptions (of rational, self-interested actors),[159] has already been indicated by scholars in the early neofunctionalist and supranational governance traditions.[160] This would involve diverging from textbook definitions of rational-choice theory and would imply accepting a certain degree of ontological impurity. If this leads to (rationalist) theory being more closely modelled along empirical reality, then we can certainly endure some ontological 'tensions': after all we specify our assumptions about the nature of

---

[158] How the concept of communicative action may be employed as a more tangible hypothesis in empirical research has been pointed out for international negotiations by Risse (2000: 18–19) and, in the EU context, by Niemann (2004: 384ff).

[159] It has been suggested that the assumption of interest-based egoism and exogenously given preferences are matched. Although they are certainly closely linked, it can be argued that this mainly applies to primary interests such as food, shelter and personal survival, but perhaps to a lesser extent to more secondary or tertiary interests. Cf. Brennan (1997: 96–7). Interestingly, there are now some rational-choice models in which actors change their preference during the interaction (cf. Ferreira *et al.* 1995).

[160] For a *post hoc* specification of early neofunctionalist ontology see Haas (2001: esp. 23–5). The basic assumptions of supranational governance can be ascertained in Stone Sweet and Sandholtz (1997: 302–9).

the world/reality not as an end in itself, but as a means to an end (e.g. explaining European integration).

This study further contributes to another discussion that has gradually developed over recent years: the so-called 'constitutional debate'. The constitutional turn raises different kinds of research questions, depending on the objective, context and perspective from which the issue is assessed. While for many it seems to be primarily a normative[161] or empirical debate, few authors have also emphasised its explanatory theoretical dimension.[162] Arguably, my work has little to offer on normative questions, but analysis of constitutional development requires an account of the underlying dynamics (and countervailing forces), an aspect where the revised neofunctionalist framework has much to offer. In addition, given my empirical focus on Treaty revision, including the materialisation of certain aspects of the Constitutional Treaty, and given my analysis, *inter alia*, of a policy area (JHA) which is very close to the heart of national sovereignty, this book directly contributes to the constitutional debate from a causal theoretical angle.

Another debate is gradually developing in the field of EU integration studies, namely that concerning epistemology.[163] While this theme has been largely ignored for many years by EU integration scholars, lately it has come more to the forefront due to renewed interest concerning this issue in the wider study of international relations.[164] This debate is somewhat related to the rationalist–reflectivist dichotomy, but the dividing lines are less clear-cut than sometimes suggested. For example, there are a number of social constructivists whose work is inspired by more positivist epistemologies. This book has *not* aimed at making a contribution to this emerging debate. However, it may indicate how a certain epistemological middle ground – acknowledging the importance of interpretative and contextual features in establishing causal relationships and generalisations – can be implemented in terms of methodology and research design. Further self-conscious epistemological debate is to be encouraged in the area of EU integration

---

[161] For normative contributions to this debate, see, for example, Schmitter (2000) and Abromeit (1998).

[162] See e.g. Jachtenfuchs and Kohler-Koch (2004: 99) and Wiener and Diez (2004: 245).

[163] See e.g. Smith (2001: 189–98), Moravcsik (2001b: 176–88), Risse and Wiener (2001: 199–205) who all take up the question of epistemology in their articles.

[164] On recent IR literature mainly dealing with epistemology see e.g. Hollis and Smith (1991: ch. 1, 3 and 4), Smith (1996), Nicholson (1996). In many respects the recent epistemological debates in IR are a retake of the behaviouralist–traditionalist divide of the 1960s and 1970s.

studies, both in terms of philosophy of science[165] and, perhaps more importantly, the practical implications concerning research methodology and operationalisation.

As pointed out earlier the revised neofunctionalist framework seeks to explain EU decision-making outcomes. Given this focus and objective, the approach only contributes to certain research questions, namely those related to causal analysis at the nexus of polity and politics, whereas other interesting and topical issues cannot be captured or advanced by the revised framework. Aspects such as the nature of the EU political system, the social and political consequences of the integration process or the normative dimension of European integration remain underexposed or cannot be grasped by it. Other theories have consciously addressed these questions and do a much better job in conceptualising them. My fundamental understanding of the nature of EU theorising shares the mainstream view regarding the appropriateness of theoretical pluralism and diversity. This point has been articulated most prominently by Puchala in his analogy of blind men touching different parts of an elephant (the EU animal) which leads them to draw different conclusions about its appearance (the EU and integration theorising). More recently this point has been reiterated, for example, by Wiener and Diez's characterisation of European integration theory as a 'mosaic'.[166] Hence, following this view, most integration theories are not rivals or substitutes but rather complements due to different foci. Only where research questions and objects of analysis sufficiently overlap may theories be seen as directly competing with each other.

Implicit in the conceptualisation of theoretical pluralism is the rejection of grand theorising, as one single theory tends to fall (well) short of satisfactorily capturing the richness, multiplicity and diversity of the EU polity, politics and policy. Although grand theorising is rejected here, I suggest that the construction of linkages between, and the combination of, concepts and (certain aspects of) theories is permissible and adds value, given the differing theoretical blind-spots and core competencies of individual approaches. This is compatible with a non-competitive view of the theoretical cosmos. Given the inflation of micro-level concepts, such as epistemic communities, advocacy coalition,

---

[165] The question is whether we need to think in terms of philosophy of science and EU integration studies, or whether we should leave this debate to the broader disciplines of political science and international relations. For a good overview concerning philosophy of science and IR see Wight (2002).

[166] See Puchala (1972) and Wiener and Diez (2004: e.g. 238–44). The earliest account I know that advocated theoretical pluralism as regards European integration theory was Schmitter (1971: 264). For example, Checkel (1999: 546), Pollack (2004: 155) and George (1991: 20) also spoke out in favour of it.

policy communities, etc. in the past fifteen years, it may be time to see how such micro-level concepts fit into broader theories. The revised neo-functionalist framework has gone some way in that respect.[167] In addition, linkages have been made between early neofunctionalism and con-structivism, and I have pointed to the possibility of further bridge-building between the revised framework and approaches such as historical insti-tutionalism and policy network analysis. This would further broaden the analytical repertoire of revised neofunctionalism and at the same time enhance the explanatory leverage concerning European integration for these approaches which do not constitute substantive theories of inte-gration. The dangers of bridge-building are two-old. First, there is the risk of ontological impurity, which has been addressed above. Second and perhaps more severely, approaches may become blurred and lose some of their analytical/conceptual sharpness and distinctiveness.

Potential Shortcomings and Final Thoughts

One potential shortcoming is that in some instances my oper-ationalisation of hypothesised pressures could not be entirely imple-mented as set out in Chapter 1. This has already been alluded to in my methodology section. Weaknesses in that respect can be registered particularly concerning social spillover. For example, it was possible, only in few cases, to compare actors and norms *at different times* in order to assess the impact of quantity and duration of interaction/EU exposure on the development of norms and identities. In addition, to ascertain a positive degree of causality concerning the impact of socialisation pro-cesses (and other hypothesised pressures for that matter) on outcomes, ideally alternative explanations for preference changes would have had to be exhausted more fully. Similarly, my operationalisation of com-municative action could not be completely implemented, as for instance the truthfulness of speech acts could not always be satisfactorily verified. Hence, some would criticise that certain issues have remained rather indeterminate and inconclusive. These points have been flagged in the preceding analysis. And, of course, these are common problems in empirical research, particularly when research questions are as empiri-cally demanding as testing a revised neofunctionalist framework. The problem is two-fold: first, it is notoriously difficult to access useful and unbiased data concerning issues such as socialisation processes, which to some degree involves finding out what is going on between agents' earlobes; second, and directly related, the (time) resources to be

---

[167] On this point also see Niemann (1998).

invested for adequate data collection on these questions are very immense. These constraints need to be taken into consideration.

Closely related, from an arch-positivist perspective, the (implementation of my) operationalisation regarding certain hypothesised pressures, especially social spillover, would be unsatisfactory in terms of indication, observation and measurement. However, given my epistemological position, and in view of the complexity of issues analysed, the partial recourse taken to more interpretative and contextual methods should be justified.

A possible criticism that could be levelled against this revised neofunctionalist framework is that it lost much of neofunctionalism's parsimony. Although it is generally desirable to formulate theories that explain as much as possible with as little as possible, it has been pointed out that parsimony is only occasionally appropriate and often constitutes a trade off with 'realism'.[168] While restrictive models are clearer, more elegant and more abstract, they are also less realistic. In contrast, unrestrictive models tend to be detailed, contextual and more realistic, but also less clear and harder to estimate with precision. King et al. have noted that, if a slightly more complicated theory were to explain much more of the world, this would be clearly preferable.[169] This has been the case with revised neofunctionalism which is, without doubt, a more complex and detailed theory, but which can arguably explain a lot more than the original neofunctionalist approach. Moreover, it is believed here that the revised neofunctionalist account is neither too bulky nor too inelegant to apply.

A related but more serious criticism would be to claim that revised neofunctionalism is not falsifiable. Popper's ideas are fundamental for 'reformulating' theories. He holds that we should always design theories that are vulnerable to falsification.[170] Along the same lines, King et al. warn that we must avoid stretching a theory to such an extent that it becomes invulnerable to disconfirmation. Hence, they suggest that one question should be asked of any theory, namely, what evidence would falsify it.[171] Revised neofunctionalism would be falsified, for example, if we arrived at a *status quo*-like outcome, despite the presence of (strong) spillover pressures and weak countervailing forces. This would mean that neofunctionalist dynamics do not really make a difference and do not drive the integration process forward. It would also be falsified, if we were to have an integrative outcome, despite the absence of spillover

---

[168] King et al. (1994: 29f).   [169] King et al. (1994: 99ff).   [170] Popper (1968).
[171] King et al. (1994: 104).

pressures and the presence of strong countervailing forces. This would imply that the integration process is driven by dynamics other than those for which the theory hypothesises. As for the various individual dynamics, a similar falsification test can be conducted through the comparative method, as has been done above. For example, political spillover in terms of (non-governmental elites) has been somewhat challenged, at least as a vital ingredient for integrative outcomes, since it has been largely absent, even when outcomes were progressive.[172]

Some critics may also lament that revised neofunctionalism has lost much of its predictive pretence. This point is taken here, but it needs to be said that political science (including early neofunctionalism) perhaps too often tried to ape the natural sciences in that respect, only to be found wanting. However, it is maintained that the modified approach can make informed judgements – rather than hard prediction – based on a systematic scrutiny of the relevant factors. The incorporation of countervailing factors and the shift from a dynamic to a dialectical account of integration has arguably increased the prognostic leverage of the framework. Hence, while predictive *claims* have been modified, extrapolative *ability* has been increased. The revised neofunctionalist framework stays rather silent on the specific outcome of the integration process.[173] Instead of theorising about the progression of the integration project as a whole, this revised account seeks to provide a model for explaining particular decision-making instances or processes. However, it is supposed here that the process will further continue, both in terms of breadth and depth of integration, as spillback forces will – at least from time to time – not be strong enough to counterbalance the integrational dynamics. In addition, over time diversity among the Member States is likely to diminish and socialisation as well as learning processes are hypothesised to advance – with the European Union increasingly factoring in actors' construction of preferences, norms and identities – although these developments may be offset, to a certain extent, by successive enlargements and (as of now unforeseen) countervailing developments. Hence, overall certain (probably additive) developments (such as learning processes or the evolution of supranational institu-

---

[172] However, as a number of authors have pointed out, this does not imply that a hypothesis has to be outrightly rejected. Deviant cases weaken a hypothesis, but they can only invalidate it if they turn up in sufficient numbers to make the hypothesised relationship disappear altogether (Lijphart 1971; Galtung 1967). For a different view, see Popper (1968).

[173] For some precise thoughts on possible outcomes of the integration process see Schmitter (1996b: 137–8).

tions) feed back into future decision cycles and are likely to provide continued integrative impetus.[174]

Revised neofunctionalism has provided a robust theoretical framework for an analysis of the inception and development of the PHARE programme, the past three Treaty revision negotiations on the reform of the Common Commercial Policy as well as the communitarisation of visa, asylum and immigration policy at the 1996–97, 2000 and 2003–04 IGCs. It has been indicated that revised neofunctionalism can provide useful insights on various levels, ranging from day-to-day policy-making to history-making decisions. Moreover, we have seen that, contrary to earlier predictions,[175] the neofunctionalist dynamics have been able to enter the sphere of high politics and penetrate the very heart of national sovereignty.

The continuing scope for further refinement of the revised neofunctionalist hypotheses, the tentativeness of parts of the preceding analysis (e.g. on social spillover, or the delimitation of spillover pressures), the possibility of greater specification regarding the causal relevance of hypothesised pressures, the existence of potential (other) shortcomings and the absence of further case studies testing the more innovative claims of my work, suggest that there is substantial ground for further research emanating from this study.

---

[174] On the notion of decision cycles and 'additivity' in neofunctionalist thought, see especially Schmitter (1971: 238ff and 2004: 57, 59, 60–1).

[175] Cf. e.g. Hoffmann (1964 [1995]).

References

Abromeit, H. 1998. *Democracy in Europe. How to Legitimize Politics in a Non-State Polity.* New York: Oxford.

Achermann, Alberto 1995. 'Asylum and Immigration Policies: From Co-operation to Harmonisation', in Bieber and Monar (eds), pp. 127–40.

Act4Europe 2003. *IGC: Don't Horsetrade in the Name of National Interest!*, a Campaign of the Civil Society Contact Group. Brussels.

Ad Hoc Group on Immigration 1991. *Report from the Ministers Responsible for Immigration.* Brussels.

Adamantopoulos, Konstantinos (ed.) 1997. *An Anatomy of the World Trade Organisation.* Boston, MA: Hammond Suddards Solicitors, Kluwer Law International.

Adler, Emanuel 1997. 'Seizing the Middle Ground: Constructivism in World Politics', *European Journal of International Relations* 3: 319–63.

Aggestam, Lisbeth 1999. 'Role Conceptions and the Politics of Identity in Foreign Policy', *Arena Working Papers*, http://www.arena.uio.no/publications/wp99_8.htm (last accessed on 3 July 2006)

Alexander, Jeffrey C. 1995. *Fin de Siecle Social Theory. Relativism, Reduction and the Problem of Reason.* London: Verso.

Allison, Graham 1971. *Essence of Decision.* Boston, MA: Little, Brown.

Amato, Giuliano 2003. Statement at the 17th Plenary Session, European Parliament, 'Background Information: Convention 03/04: Area of Freedom, Security and Justice', Brussels, 3 April.

AMCHAM 2000. 'Towards a Wider and More Open Europe: Business calls on EU Leaders to Agree to Significant Reform at Nice', Brussels, 23.11., http://www.eucommittee.be/Press/2000/nov232000.htm (last accessed on 3 July 2006).

Amnesty International, Cimade, ECRE, Finnish Jurists for Human Rights, ILPA, Jura Hominis, JUSTICE, NJCM, OMCT-Europe, Open Society Institute, Statewatch 2003. 'Towards a Constitution for Europe: Justice and Home Affairs – Joint Comments from Non-Governmental Organisations for the IGC', Brussels, 1 October.

Anderson, Malcolm and den Boer, Monica (eds) 1994. *Policing Across National Boundaries.* London: Pinter.

Anderson, Malcolm, den Boer, Monica, Cullen, Peter, Gilmore, William, Raab, Charles and Walker, Neil 1995. *Policing the European Union.* Oxford: Clarendon Press.

Andriessen, Frans 1989. 'Perestroika and the Integration of the European Community', *European Access*, December, pp. 8–9.

Antoniadis, Antonis 2004. 'The Participation of the European Community in the World Trade Organisation: An External Look at the European Union Constitution-Building', in Tridimas and Nebia (eds), *EU Law for the 21st Century: Rethinking the New Legal Order*, Vol I. Oxford: Hart Publishing.

Armstrong, Kenneth 1998. 'Legal Integration: Theorising the Legal Dimension of European Integration', *Journal of Common Market Studies* 36: 155–74.

Armstrong, Kenneth and Bulmer, Simon 1996. 'United Kingdom', in Rometsch and Wessels (eds), pp. 253–90.

Armstrong, Kenneth and Shaw, Jo 1998. 'Integrating Law: An Introduction', *Journal of Common Market Studies* 36: 147–54.

Arnull, Anthony 1996. 'The Scope of the Common Commercial Policy: A Coda on Opinion 1/94', in Emiliou and O'Keeffe (eds), pp. 343–63.

Aspinwall, Mark and Schneider, Gerald 2001. 'Institutional Research on the European Union: Mapping the Field', in Schneider and Aspinwall (eds), pp. 1–18.

Bailey, David and de Propris, Lisa 2004. 'A Bridge Too Phare? EU Pre-Accession Aid and Capacity-Building in the Candidate Countries', *Journal of Common Market Studies* 42: 77–98.

Baker, Kenneth 1993. *The Turbulent Years*. London: Faber and Faber.

Baldwin-Edwards, Martin 1997. 'The Emerging European Immigration Regime', *Journal of Common Market Studies* 35: 497–519.

Baldwin-Edwards, Martin and Schain, Martin 1994. 'The Politics of Immigration: Introduction', *West European Politics* 17: 1–16.

Barber, Lionel 1995. 'The Men Who Run Europe', *Financial Times* 12 March.
  1997. 'World Trade: Brussels Strives to Call the Tune on Trade', *Financial Times* 12 March.

Barnes, James, Carter, Marshall and Skidmore, Max 1980. *The World of Politics*. New York: St. Martin's Press.

Bartle, Ian 1999. 'Transnational Interests in the European Union: Globalization and Changing Organization in Telecommunications and Electricity', *Journal of Common Market Studies* 37: 363–83.

BDA and BDI 2001. *Kernforderungen der deutschen Wirtschaft für eine handlungs- und wettbewerbsfähige Europäische Union*, Positionspapier zur Debatte über die Zukunft Europas. Berlin, 8.

Beach, Derek 2005. *The Dynamics of European Integration: Why and When EU Institutions Matter*. Basingstoke: Palgrave Macmillan.

Belgian Government 1995. *Note de politique du Gouvernement au Parlement concernant la Conférence intergouvernementale de 1996*, October.

Belgian Presidency 2001. 'Evaluation of the Conclusions of the Tampere European Council', Note to the General Affairs Council/European Council, 14926/01, Brussels, 6 December.

Bender, Peter 2002. 'The European Parliament and the WTO: Positions and Initiatives', *European Foreign Affairs Review* 7: 193–208.

Benelux 1996a. *Propositions du Benelux dans le cadre de la Conférence intergouvernementale: coopération policière et judiciaire*, November.

Benelux 1996b. *Mémorandum de la Belgique, des Pays-Bas et du Luxembourg en vue de la CIG.*

Benelux 2000. 'Memorandum from the Benelux', Information Note, CONFER 4787/00, Brussels, 19 October.

Beyers, Jan 2002. 'Multiple Embeddedness and Socialization in Europe: The Case of Council Officials', *Arena Working Papers* WP 02/33.

Beyers, J. and Dierickx, G. 1998. 'The Working Groups of the Council of the European Union: Supranational or Intergovernmental Negotiations?', *Journal of Common Market Studies* **36**: 289–317.

Bieber, Roland 1995. 'The Third Pillar and the 1996 Intergovernmental Conference', in Bieber and Monar (eds), pp. 383–90.

Bieber, Roland and Monar, Jörg (eds) 1995. *Justice and Home Affairs in the European Union: The Development of the Third Pillar.* Brussels: European Interuniversity Press.

Bigo, Didier 1996. 'L'illusoire maîtrise des frontière', *Le Monde Diplomatique*, 10 October: 10.

Bindi Calussi, Federiga 1998. 'The Cost of Staying Out of the European Union: Third States and Foreign Multinational Lobbying', in Cafruny and Peters (eds), pp. 65–91.

Bogdandy, A. 2003. 'Links Between National and Supra-National Institutions. A Legal View of a New Communicative Universe', in Kohler-Koch, Beate (ed.) *Linking EU and National Governance.* Oxford: Oxford University Press, pp. 24–53.

Boone, L. E. and Kurtz, G. L. 1992. *Contemporary Marketing.* Orlando, FL: The Dryden Press.

Börzel, Tanja A. 2005. 'Mind the Gap! European Integration between Level and Scope', *Journal of European Public Policy*, **12**: 217–36.

Bothorel, A. 2000. *The History and Development of the Phare Programme.* Luxembourg: OOPEC.

Bourgeois, Jacques 1995. 'The EC in the WTO and Advisory Opinion 1/94: An Echternach Procession', *Common Market Law Review* **32**: 763–87.

Bourgeois, J., Berrod, F. and Fournier, E. (eds) 1995. *The Uruguay Round Results: A European Layers' Perspective, College of Europe.* Brussels: European Interuniversity Press.

Bouwen, Pieter 2004. 'The Logic of Access to the European Parliament: Business Lobbying in the Committee on Economic and Monetary Affairs', *Journal of Common Market Studies* **42**: 473–95.

Branch, A. P. and Øhrgaard, J. C. 1999. 'Trapped in the Supranational-Intergovernmental Dichotomy: A Response to Stone Sweet and Sandholtz', *Journal of European Public Policy* **6**: 123–43.

Brennan, Geoffrey 1997. 'Rational Choice Political Theory', in Vincent, Andrew (ed.) *Political Theory – Tradition and Diversity.* Cambridge, MA: CUP, pp. 89–111.

Brinkhorst, Laurens Jan 1997. 'Pillar III', in European Policy Centre 1997b, p. 49

Brinkmann, Gisbert 2004. 'The Immigration and Asylum Agenda', *European Law Journal* **10**: 182–99.

Brittan, Leon 1996. 'New Tactics for EU Trade', *Financial Times* 11 November.

Brok, Elmar 1996. 'Perspektiven der Regierungskonferenz für die Europäische Union', *Zentrum für Europäisches Wirtschaftsrecht: Vorträge und Berichte* **78**: 1–21.

Brok, Elmar 1997a. 'The European Parliament', in European Policy Centre 1997b, p. 45.

Brok, Elmar 1997b. 'Kein Papiertiger: der Vertrag von Amsterdam', *Wirtschaftsdienst* **77**: 375–8.

Brok, Elmar 2001. 'Die Ergebnisse von Nizza. Eine Sichtweise aus dem Europäischen Parlament', *Integration* **24**: 86–93.

Brok, Elmar 2002. *What the Constitution of the European Union will Need to Say on "Freedom, Justice and Security"*, CONV 436/02. Brussels.

Brouwer, Evelien 2003. 'Immigration, Asylum and Terrorism: A Changing Dynamic Legal and Practical Developments in the EU in Response to the Terrorist Attacks of 11.09', *European Journal of Migration and Law* **4**: 399–424.

Bulmer, Simon 1994. 'The Governance of the European Union, A New Institutionalist Approach', *Journal of Public Policy* **13**: 351–80.

Bulmer, Simon and Burch, Martin 1998. 'The "Europeanisation" of Central Government: The UK and Germany in Historical Institutionalist Perspective', *Manchester Papers in Politics*, European Policy Research Unit, Paper No. 6/1998.

Bulmer, Simon and Paterson William 1987. *The Federal Republic of Germany and the European Community*. London: Allen & Unwin.

Bundesministerium für Wirtschaft 1996. 'Stellungnahme zu dem Papier der GD I der EG-Kommission Regierungskonferenz – Aussenwirtschaft: Warum muss der Artikel 113 angepasst werden', EA1-110006/23, Bonn 8.10.96.

Burley, Anne-Marie and Mattli, Walter 1993. 'Europe Before the Court: A Political Theory of Legal Integration', *International Organization* **47**: 41–76.

Butler, Sir Michael 1986. *Europe: More than a Continent*. London: Heinemann.

Butt Philip, Alan 1994. 'European Union Immigration Policy: Phantom, Fantasy or Fact?' *West European Politics* **17**: 168–91.

Cafruny, Alan and Peters, Patrick (eds) 1998. *The Union and the World: the Political Economy of a Common European Foreign Policy*. The Hague, Boston, MA: Kluwer Law International.

Cafruny, Alan and Rosenthal, Glenda (eds) 1993. *The State of the European Community: The Maastricht Debates and Beyond*. Boulder, CO: Lynne Rienner.

Callovi, Guiseppe 1992. 'Regulation of Immigration in 1993: Pieces of the European Community Jig-Saw Puzzle', *International Migration Review* **26**: 353–72.

Cameron, David 1992. 'The 1992 Initiative: Causes and Consequences', in Sbragia (ed.), pp. 23–74.

Cameron, David 1995. 'Transnational Relations and the Development of European Economic and Monetary Union', in Risse-Kappen (ed.), pp. 37–78.

Caporaso, James A. 1995. 'Research Design, Falsification, and the Qualitative–Quantitative Divide', *American Political Science Review* **89**: 457–60.

Caporaso, J. and Keeler, J. T. S. 1995. 'The European Union and Regional Integration Theory', in Rhodes and Mazey (ed.), pp. 29–62.

Caporaso, J. and Stone Sweet, Alec 2001. 'Institutional Logics of European Integration', in Stone Sweet, Alec, Fligstein, Neil and Sandholtz, Wayne (eds), *The Institutionalization of Europe*. Oxford: Oxford University Press, pp. 221–39.

Cederman, L.-E. (ed.) 2001. *Constructing Europes Identities: The External Dimension*. Boulder, CO: Lynne Rienner.

Cederschiöld, Charlotte 1996. *Asylum and immigration policy*, Group of European People's Party. Helsinki: Study Days, pp. 115–8.

Chalmers, Damian 1996. 'Legal Base and the External Relations of the European Community', in Emiliou and O'Keeffe (eds), pp. 46–61.

Checkel, Jeffrey T. 1999a. 'Norms, Institutions, and National Identity in Contemporary Europe', *International Studies Quarterly* **43**: 83–114.

Checkel, Jeffrey T. 1999b. 'Social construction and integration', *Journal of European Policy* **6**: 545–60.

Checkel, Jeffrey T. 2001a. 'Why Comply? Social Learning and European Identity Change', *International Organization* **55**: 553–88.

Checkel, Jeffrey T. 2001b. 'Constructing European institutions', in Schneider and Aspinwall (eds), pp. 19–39.

Checkel, Jeffrey T. 2001c. 'From Meta to Substantive Theory? Social Constructivism and the Study of Europe' and 'Constructivism and Integration Theory: Crash Landing or Safe Arrival?', *European Union Politics*, **2**: 2.

Chirac, Jacques 1996. 'Conseil Européen de Dublin – Conférence de Presse du Président de la Republique, M. Jacques Chirac', Ministère des Affaires étrangères.

Christiansen, Thomas 2002. 'The Role of Supranational Actors in EU Treaty Reform', *Journal of European Public Policy*, **9** : 33–53.

Christiansen, Thomas and Jørgensen, Knud Erik 1999. 'The Amsterdam Process: A Structurationist Perspective on EU Treaty Reform' , *European Integration Online Papers*, **3**: 1.

Christiansen, Thomas, Jørgensen, Knud Erik and Wiener, Antje 1999. 'The Social Construction of Europe', *Journal of European Public Policy* **6**: 528–44.

Christiansen, Thomas, Jørgensen, Knud Erik and Wiener, Antje (eds) 2001. *The Social Construction of Europe*. London: Sage.

Churches' Commission for Migrants in Europe 1995. 'Third Country Nationals in the European Union: The Case for Equal Treatment', European Parliament, Audition Publique, *La Conférence intergouvernementale de 1996: le Parlement européene a l'écoute des citoyens*, Volume I, Brussels, 17–18 October.

Cichowski, Rachel A. 1998. 'Integrating the Environment: The European Court and the Construction of Supranational Policy', *Journal of European Public Policy* **5**: 387–405.

Citrin, J. and Sides, J. 2004. 'Is it the Nation, Europe, or the Nation and Europe? Trends in Political Identities at Century's End', in Herrmann, R. K., Risse, T., Brewer, M. (eds.), pp. 161–85.

Clark, Alan 1993. *Diaries/Alan Clark*. London: Weidenfeld and Nicolson.

Cockfield, Lord 1994. *The European Union: Creating the Single Market*. Chichester: Wiley Chancery Law.

Coen, David 1997. 'The Evolution of the Large Firm as a Political Actor in the European Union', *Journal of European Public Policy* 4: 91–108.

Coen, David 1998. 'The European Business Interest and the Nation State: Large-firm Lobbying in the European Union and Member States', *Journal of Public Policy* 18: 75–100.

Coglianese, Cary and Nicolaïdis, Kalypso 1998. 'Securing Subsidiarity: Mechanisms for Allocating Authority in Tiered Regimes', in Woolcock, Stephen (ed.) *Subsidiarity in the Governance of the Global Economy*. Cambridge, MA: Cambridge University Press.

Collier, David 1995. 'Translating Quantitative Methods for Qualitative Researchers: The Case of Selection Bias', *American Political Science Review* **89**: 461–6.

Collinson, Sarah 1993. *Europe and International Migration*. London: Pinter.

Commission of the European Communities 1985. *White Paper on the Internal Market*, COM (85) 331 final.

Commission of the European Communities 1988. *Communication of the Commission on the Abolition of Controls of Persons at Intra-Community Borders*, COM (88) 640 final.

Commission of the European Communities 1989. *Proposal for a Council Regulation (EEC) on Economic aid to the Republic of Hungary and the Polish People's Republic*, COM (89) 536 final.

Commission of the European Communities 1991a. *Communication de la Commission au Conseil et au Parlement européen sur le droit d'asile*, SEC (91) 1857 final.

Commission of the European Communities 1991b. Proposal on the Extension of Article 113, CONF-UP 1742, 28.02.91.

Commission of the European Communities 1992a. *Assistance for Economic Restructuring in the Countries of Central and Eastern Europe: An Operation Guide*. Luxembourg.

Commission of the European Communities 1992b. *Commission Communication to the Council and to Parliament on Abolition of Border Controls*, SEC (92) 877 final.

Commission of the European Communities 1993a. *Towards a Closer Association with the Countries of Central and Eastern Europe*: Communication by the Commission to the Council, SEC (93), 648 final. Brussels.

Commission of the European Communities 1993b. *Conclusions of the Presidency – European Council in Copenhagen, 21–22 June 1993*, SI (93) 500. Brussels.

Commission of the European Communities 1993c. *Communication from the Commission to the Council and the European Parliament: Reinforcing the Effectiveness of the Internal Market*, COM (93) 256 final.

Commission of the European Communities 1993d. *Report to the Council on the Possibility of Applying Article K.9 of the Treaty on European Union to Asylum Policy*, SEC (93) 1687 final.

Commission of the European Communities 1993e. *Communication of the Council and the European Parliament: (I) Proposal for a Decision […] establishing the*

Convention on the crossing of external frontiers of the Member States; (II) Proposal for a regulation [. . .] determining the third countries whose nationals must be in possession of a visa when crossing the external borders of the Member States, COM (93) 684 final.

Commission of the European Communities 1994a. *The Europe Agreements and Beyond: A Strategy to Prepare the Countries of Central and Eastern Europe for Accession*, Communication from the Commission to the Council, COM (94) 320 final. Brussels.

Commission of the European Communities 1994b. *Follow Up to Commission Communication on 'The Europe Agreements and Beyond: A Strategy to Prepare the Countries of Central and Eastern Europe for Accession'*, Communication from the Commission to the Council, COM (94), 361 final. Brussels.

Commission of the European Communities 1994c. *Communication to the Council and the European Parliament on Immigration and Asylum Policy*, COM (94) 23 final.

Commission of the European Communities 1995a. *Presidency Conclusions: Cannes European Council, 26 and 17 June 1995*. Brussels.

Commission of the European Communities 1995b. *Phare 1994: Annual Report*, Phare Information Unit, DG 1A, COM (95), 366 final.

Commission of the European Communities 1995c. 'Proposal for a Directive on the Elimination of Controls on Persons Crossing Internal Frontiers', COM(95) 347 final, *Official Journal*, C 289, 31 October.

Commission of the European Communities 1995d. *Intergovernmental Conference 1996: Commission Report for the Reflection Group*. Brussels, 10 May.

Commission of the European Communities 1996a. *Council Regulation (Euratom, EC) No 1279/96 of 25 June 1996 Concerning the Provision of Assistance to Economic Reform and Recovery in the New Independent States and Mongolia*, OJ, No L165/1–11.

Commission of the European Communities 1996b. *The European Union's nuclear safety programme in Central and Eastern Europe and the New Independent States*, Information Unit – Phare and Tacis, DG 1A.

Commission of the European Communities 1996c. 'Reinforcing Political Union and Preparing for Enlargement', Commission's Opinion on the Convening of an IGC, February 1996, *Intergovernmental Conference on the Revision of the Treaties*, Collected texts. Brussels: General Secretariat of the Council.

Commission of the European Communities 1996d. *Justice and Home Affairs provisions in the EC Treaty – a Possible Location*, Conference of the Representatives of the Governments of the Member States, CONF/ 3912/96. Brussels.

Commission of the European Communities 1996e. *Conférence Intergouvernementale: d'un espace de liberté, securité et de justice*, Note d'information du Secrétariat général diffusé sous l'autorité de M. Oreja, SEC (96) 2004. Brussels.

Commission of the European Communities 1996f. *External Economic Relations*, CONF/3890/96. Brussels.

Commission of the European Communities 1996g. Internal paper of DG I, 'Anmerkungen zur Sellungnahme des BMWi zum dem

Kommissionsvorschlag über die Anpassung des Artikels 113', Brussels, 16.10.96.

Commission of the European Communities 1996h. DG I, Speaking Brief Anpassung des Artikels 113, p. 15 October 1996.

Commission of the European Communities 1997a. *JHA – Free Movement of Persons*, Conference of the Representatives of the Governments of the Member States, CONF/3817/97.

Commission of the European Communities 1997b. 'Article 113 – Possible Fallbacks', note for the file, by F. Perreau de Pinninck, Brussels, 17.03.97.

Commission of the European Communities 1998. *Communication from the Commission to the European Parliament and the Council on the Follow-up to Recommendations of the High-Level Panel on the Free Movement of Persons.* Brussels, 1 July.

Commission of the European Communities 1999. *Adapting the Institutions to Make a Success of Enlargement*, Brussels, 10 November.

Commission of the European Communities 2000a. 'Single Market Scoreboard', Commission Staff Working Paper, May.

Commission of the European Communities 2000b. 'The Reform of Article 133 by the Nice Treaty: The Logic of Parallelism', in Frequently Asked Questions. Intergovernmental Conference discusses Article 133, December, http://europa.eu.int/comm/trade/faqs/rev133_en.htm (last accessed on 15 July 2004).

Commission of the European Communities 2000c. Opinion on the IGC, 26 January 2000, COM (2000).

Commission of the European Communities 2002a. *The Enlargement Process and the Three Pre-accession Instruments*, Enlargement DG, February.

Commission of the European Communities 2002b. *Contribution from Mr Barnier and Mr Vitorino, Members of the Convention: 'The Community Method'*, CONV 231/0. Brussels.

Commission of the European Communities 2002c. *Report from the Commission: General Report on Pre-Accession Assistance (PHARE – ISPA – SAPARD) in 2000*, [SEC (2002) 1418], COM (2002) 781 final. Brussels.

Commission of the European Communities 2002d. *Communication from the Commission to the Convention, 22 May 2002: A Project for the European Union*, CONV 229/02. Brussels.

Commission of the European Communities 2002e. *Biannual Update of the Scoreboard to Review Progress on the Creation of an Area of Freedom, Security and Justice in the European Union – Second Half of 2002*, COM (2002) 738 final. Brussels.

Commission of the European Communities 2002f. *Contribution to a Preliminary Draft Constitution – Feasibility Study (Penelope)*, 4 December.

Commission of the European Communities 2002g. *Communication from the Commission on the Institutional Architecture – For the European Union – Peace, Freedom and Solidarity.* Brussels, 5 December 2002, COM (2002) 728 final.

Commission of the European Communities 2003a. *The Doha Development Agenda (DDA) After Cancun*, Statement by the European Commission, 25 September.

Commission of the European Communities 2003b. *A Constitution for the Union*, Opinion of the Commission. Brussels, 17 September.

Commission of the European Communities 2004. *Report from the Commission: General Report on Pre-Accession Assistance (PHARE – ISPA – SAPARD) in 2002*, [SEC (2003) 1477], COM (2003) 844 final. Brussels.

Consultative Commission on Racism and Xenophobia 1995. *Activities of the Consultative Commission on Racism and Xenophobia – Final Report*, 6906/1/95.

Coombes, David 1970. *Politics and Bureaucracy in the European Communities*. London: Allen & Unwin.

Corporate Europe Observer 2000. 'Intergovernmental Conference 2000: Business and the Amsterdam Leftovers', Issue 6, April.

Council of the European Communities 1989. *Council Regulation (EEC) No 3906/89 of 18 December 1989 on Economic Aid to the Republic of Hungary and the Polish People's Republic*, OJ, No L 375/11–12. Brussels.

Council of the European Union 1994a. *Council Report to the Essen European Council on the Preparation Strategy for the Accession of Associated CEEC*. Brussels.

Council of the European Union 1994b. *Report from the Permanent Representatives Committee to the Council on the Code of Conduct between the Council, the Member States and the Commission on the Post-Uruguay Round Negotiations on Services*, 6948/94. Brussels.

Council of the European Union 1996a. *Draft Compromise Proposal: Council Regulation (Euratom, EC) Concerning the Provision of Assistance to Economic Reform and Recovery in the New Independent States and Mongolia*. Brussels.

Council of the European Union 1996b. 'Presidency Report to the European Council on the Progress of the Conference', *Intergovernmental Conference on the Revision of the Treaties*, Collected Texts. Brussels: General Secretariat of the Council.

Council of the European Union 1996c. 'The European Union Today and Tomorrow', in *Intergovernmental Conference on the Revision of the Treaties: Irish Presidency*, Collected texts, General Secretariat of the Council. Brussels.

Council of the European Union 1997a. *The Amsterdam Treaty as Signed on 2 October 1997*, Conference of the Representatives of the Governments of the Member States, CONF 4007/97. Brussels.

Council of the European Union 1997b. *Consolidated Version of the Treaty on European Union*, Conference of the Representatives of the Governments of the Member States, CONF 4007/97 ADD1. Brussels.

Council of the European Union 1997c. *Consolidated Version of the Treaty Establishing the European Community*, Conference of the Representatives of the Governments of the Member States, CONF 4007/97 ADD2. Brussels.

Council of the European Union 2004a: 'Directive 2004/83/EC of 29 April 2004 on Minimum Standards for the Qualification and Status of Third Country Nationals [. . .]'. *Official Journal* L 304/12, 30.9.2004.

Council of the European Union 2004b. 'Council Decision 2004/927/EC [. . .] Providing for Certain Areas Covered by Title IV [TEC . . .] to be Governed by the Procedure Laid Down in Article 251 of That Treaty', *Official Journal* L 396, 31 December.

Council of the European Union 2005. *Directive on Minimum Standards on Procedures in Member States for Granting and Withdrawing Refugee Status*, 12983/05, 2005/0031 (CNS), 17.11.2005.

Cram, Laura 1996. 'Integration Theory and the Study of the European Policy Process', in Richardson (ed.), pp. 40–58.

Cremona, Marise 2003. 'The Draft Constitutional Treaty: External Relations and External Action', *Common Market Law Review* **40**: 1347–66.

Cuntz, Eckart 2003. 'Ein ausgewogener Gesamtkompromiss: Die Ergebnisse des Konvents aus Sicht der Bundesregierung', *Integration* **26**: 351–6.

De Búrca, Gráinne, 'Rethinking Law in Neofunctionalist Theory', *Journal of European Public Policy* **12**: 310–26.

de Charette, Hervé 1996. 'Conseil Européen de Turin: Intervention Du Ministre des Affaires Etrangères, M. Hervé de Charette', Ministère des Affaires étrangères.

de Lobkowicz, Wenceslas 1994. 'Intergovernmental Co-operation in the Field of Migration – From the Single European Act to Maastricht', in Monar and Morgan (eds), pp. 99–122.

de Swann 1994. *France's Aid Effort to Central and Eastern Europe: A Case Study of a Donor's Interests in Aid-Giving*, Master Dissertation, University of Cambridge.

Dehaene, Jean-Luc 1996. 'Conférence de Jean-Luc Dehaene', Primier Ministre, Brussels, 24 April 1996.

Dehousse, Renaud 1998. *The European Court of Justice*. London: Macmillan.

den Boer, Monica 1994. 'The Quest for European Policing: Rhetoric and Justification in a Disorderly Debate', in Anderson and den Boer (eds), pp. 174–96.

den Boer, Monica 1996. 'Justice and Home Affairs: Co-operation Without Integration', in Wallace and Wallace (eds), pp. 389–409.

den Boer, Monica 1997a. 'Wearing the Inside Out: European Police Co-operation between Internal and External Security', *European Foreign Affairs Review* **2**: 491–508.

den Boer, Monica 1997b. 'Travel Notes on a Bumpy Journey from Schengen via Maastricht to Amsterdam', in den Boer (ed.), pp. 147–54.

Derrida, J. 1992. *[1991]: The Other Heading. Reflections on Today's Europe*. Indiana: Indiana University Press.

Dessler, David 1991. 'Beyond Correlations: Towards a Causal Theory of War', *International Studies Quarterly* **35**: 337–55.

Devuyst, Youri 1992. 'The EC's Common Commercial Policy and the Treaty on European Union – An Overview of the Negotiations', *World Competition – Law and Economics Review* **16**: 67–80.

Devuyst, Youri 1998. 'Treaty Reform in the European Union: The Amsterdam Process', *Journal of European Public Policy* **5**: 615–31.

Diez, Thomas and Wiener, Antje 2004. 'Introducing the Mosaic of Integration Theory', in Wiener and Diez (eds), pp. 1–21.

Dill, Janina and Nicolas Lamp 2004. 'Neofunktionalismus – eine sozialkonstruktivistische Lesart', Term Paper – Seminar on European Integration, University of Dresden.

Dinan, Desmond 1997. 'The Commission and the Reform Process', in Edwards and Pijpers (eds), pp. 188–211.

Dinan, Desmond 2004. 'Governance and Institutions: The Convention and the Intergovernmental Conference', *Journal of Common Market Studies*, Annual Review, **42**: 27–42.

Dinan, Desmond 2005. 'Governance and Institutions: A New Constitution and a New Commission', *Journal of Common Market Studies*, Annual Review, **43**: 37–54.

Docksey, Christopher and Williams, Karen 1994. 'The Commission and the Execution of Community Policy', in Edwards and Spence (eds), pp. 117–44.

Dodd, Tom, Ware, Richard and Weston, Alison 1997. *The European Communities (Amendment) Bill: Implementing the Amsterdam Treaty*, Research Paper No. 1997/112. International Affairs and Defence Section, House of Commons Library.

D'Oliveira, H. 1994. 'Expanding External and Shrinking Internal Borders', in O'Keeffe, D. and Twomey, P. (eds), *Legal Issues of the Maastricht Treaty*, London: Chancery Press, pp. 261–76.

Donner, J. P. H. 1993. 'Abolition of Border Controls', in Schermers *et al.* (eds), pp. 5–26.

Drüke, Luise 1995. 'Harmonisation of Asylum Law and Judicial Control Under the Third Pillar', in Bieber and Monar (eds), pp. 167–87.

Duff, Andrew 1997. *The Amsterdam Treaty: Text and Commentary*, Federal Trust. London: Sweet & Maxwell.

Duff, Andrew 2001. 'From Amsterdam Left-overs to Nice Hangovers', *The International Spectator* **36**: 13–19.

Duff, Andrew 2003. 'Der Beitrag des Europäischen Parlaments zum Konvent: Treibende Kraft für einen Konsens', *Integration* **26**: 3–9.

Durkheim, Emil 1970 [1897]. *Suicide: A Study in Sociology*. London: Routledge & Kegan Paul.

Dutch Presidency 1997a. *Note de la Presidence: Mise en place progressive d'un espace de liberté, securité et de justice*, Conference of the Representatives of the Governments of the Member States, CONF/3823/97. Brussels.

Dutch Presidency 1997b. *Addendum to Dublin II: General Outline for Draft Revision of the Treaties*, Conference of Representatives of the Governments of the Member States, CONF/2500/96 ADD.1. Brussels.

Dutch Presidency 1997c. *Liberté, Securité et justice*, second Dutch text on JHA, Conference of Representatives of the Governments of the Member States, SN 539/97 (C 40). Brussels.

Dutch Presidency 1997d. *Liberté, Securité et justice*, Textes consolides du project de traite, Conference of Representatives of the Governments of the Member States, SN 600/97 (C 101). Brussels.

Dutch Presidency 1997e. *Draft Treaty of Amsterdam*, Conference of Representatives of the Governments of the Member States, CONF/4000/97. Brussels.

Dutch Presidency 1997f. *External Economic Relations*, Conference of Representatives of the Governments of the Member States, SN 456/97. Brussels.

Dyer, Carl, Dyer, Barbara, Hathcote, Jan and Rees, Kathleen 1997. 'Service Markets in the 21st Century: The Impact on the New WTO Regime', Fatemi, Khosrow (ed.), *International Trade in the 21st Century*. Oxford, New York: Pergamon, pp. 213–34.

Eberlie, Richard 1993. 'The Confederation of British Industry and Policy-Making in the European Community', in Mazey and Richardson (eds), pp. 201–12.

Eder, K. and Giessen, B. 1999. *European Citizenship and the National Legacies*. Oxford: Oxford University Press.

Edwards, Geoffrey 1996. 'National Sovereignty vs. Integration? The Council of Ministers', in Richardson (ed.), pp. 127–47.

Edwards, Geoffrey and Pijpers, Alfred (eds) 1997. *The Politics of European Treaty Reform: The 1996 Intergovernmental Conference and Beyond*. London: Pinter.

Edwards, Geoffrey and Spence, David 1994. 'The Commission in Perspective', in Edwards and Spence (eds), pp. 1–23.

Edwards, Geoffrey and Spence, David (eds) 1994. *The European Commission*. London: Longman Group Limited.

Edwards, Geoffrey and Wallace, Helen 1977. *The Council of Ministers of the European Community and the President in Office*. London: Federal Trust.

Eeckhout, Piet 1991. 'The External Dimension of the EC Internal Market – A Portrait', *World Competition – Law and Economics Review* 15: 5–24.

Egeberg, Morten 1998. 'Transcending Intergovernmentalism? Identity and Role Perceptions of National Officials in EU Decision-Making', *Arena Working Papers* WP 24/1998, http://www.arena.uio.no/publications/wp98_24.htm (last accessed on 08 June 2006).

Ehlermann, Claus-Dieter 1984. 'The Scope of Article 113 of the EEC Treaty', in *Etudes de droit des Communautés Européennes: Mélanges offerts à Pierre-Henri Teitgen*. Paris: Pedone, pp. 139–61.

Ehlermann, Claus-Dieter 1989. 'Aid for Poland and Hungary, First Assessment', *European Affairs* 4: 23–7.

El-Agraa, Ali 1994. *The Economics of the European Community*, fourth edition. New York, London: Harvester Wheatsheaf.

Elgström, Ole 2003. '"The Honest Broker"? The Council Presidency as a Mediator', in Elgström, Ole (ed.), *European Union Council Presidencies – A Comparative Analysis*. London: Routledge, pp. 38–54.

Elsig, Manfred 2002. *The EU's Common Commercial Policy: Institutions, Interests and Ideas*, Aldershot: Ashgate.

Emiliou, Nicholas 1996a. 'The Death of Exclusive Competence?', *European Law Review* 21: 294–311.

Emiliou, Nicholas 1996b. 'The Allocation of Competence Between the EC and its Member States in the Sphere of External Relations', in Emiliou and O'Keeffe (eds), pp. 31–45.

Emiliou, Nicholas and O'Keeffe, David (eds) 1996. *The European Union and World Trade Law*. Chichester: John Wiley & Sons.

ERT 1997. *Intergovernmental Conference*, Letter Sent to EU Heads of Government in June 1997, 2 June.

ERT 2002. 'EU Governance: ERT Discussion Paper', Contribution to the Convention on the Future of Europe. Brussels.

Esders, Elke 1995. 'The European Parliament's Committee on Civil Liberties and Internal Affairs – The Committee Responsible for Justice and Home Affairs', in Bieber and Monar (eds), pp. 259–76.

Euro Citizen Action Service 1996. *Giving Substance to Citizens' Europe in a Revised Treaty*. Brussels.

Eurochambres 2003. 'Business Demands a Successful IGC', Press Release. Brussels.

European Council on Refugees and Exiles 1995. 'Position on the Functioning of the Treaty on European Union in Relation to Asylum Policy', European Parliament, Audition Publique, *La Conférence intergouvernementale de 1996: le Parlement européene a l'écoute des citoyens*, I, Brussels, 17–18 October.

European Court of Justice 1995. 'Report of the Court of Justice on Certain Aspects of the Application of the Treaty on European Union'.

European Parliament 1991. 'Resolution on the PHARE Programme', *Official Journal* **C280**: 118–19.

European Parliament 1993a. *Report of the Committee on Civil Liberties and Internal Affairs on Co-operation in the Field of Justice and Internal Affairs under the Treaty on European Union*, rapporteur: Mr Carlos Robles Piquer, EP Doc No. A3-0215/93.

European Parliament 1993b. 'Resolution on European Immigration Policy', *Official Journal* **C 255**, pp. 184–6.

European Parliament 1994a. '1994 General Budget: Resolution on the Draft General Budget of the European Communities for the Financial Year 1994', *Official Journal* **C20**: 161–6.

European Parliament 1994b. 'Resolution on the Conclusions of the Fact-finding Mission by the Committee on Budgetary Control to the Czech Republic on the Management of Appropriations under the PHARE Programme', *Official Journal* **C205**: 84.

European Parliament 1994c. 'Resolution on the General Principles of European Refugee Policy', *Official Journal* **C 44**, pp. 106–9.

European Parliament 1995a. *Relations Between the European Parliament and the Countries of Central and Eastern Europe*, Directorate General for Research, Working Papers, Central and Eastern Europe Series.

European Parliament 1995b. *Resolution on the functioning of the Treaty on European Union with a View to the 1996 Intergovernmental Conference – Implementation and Development of the Union*, rapporteur: Jean-Louis Bourlanges and David Martin, 17 May.

European Parliament 1995c. *Working Document on the Process in the Field of Justice and Home Affairs*, Institutional Affairs Committee, draftsman: Laurens Jan Brinkhorst, A4-0102/95/PART III, PE 212.450/fin./Part III.

European Parliament 1995d. Opinion of the Committee on Civil Liberties and Internal Affairs for the Committee on Institutional Affairs, draftsman: José Barros Moura, A4-0102/95/PART II, PE 212.450/fin./Part II.

European Parliament 1996a. 'Resolution Embodying (i) Parliament's Opinion on the Convening of the Intergovernmental Conference, and (ii) an Evaluation of the Work of the Reflection Group and a Definition of the Political Priorities of the European Parliament with a View to the IGC', *Intergovernmental Conference on the Revision of the Treaties*, Collected texts. Brussels: General Secretariat of the Council.

European Parliament 1996b. Communication by the Committee on Civil Liberties and Internal Affairs, rapporteur: A. Oostlander, A4-0135/96.

European Parliament 1997a. *Opinion for the Committee on Institutional Affairs on the Amsterdam Treaty*, Committee on Civil Liberties and Internal Affairs, draftsman: Claudia Roth, A4-0347/97.

European Parliament 1997b. Report on the Amsterdam Treaty, Committee on Institutional Affairs, co-rapporteurs: Inigo Mendez de Vigo and Dimitris Tsarsos, A4-0347/97, PE 223.314/fin.

European Parliament 2000. 'European Parliament's Proposal for the Intergovernmental Conference', 14094/1999, 13 April 2000.

European Parliament 2003a. Background Information: Convention 03/ 04: Area of Freedom, Security and Justice. Brussels, 3 April.

European Parliament 2003b. 'Resolution on the Draft Treaty Establishing a Constitution for Europe and the European Parliament's Opinion on the Convening of the Intergovernmental Conference', provisional edition, 11047/2003, 24 September.

European Policy Centre 1997a. 'A Threat to Europe's Power to Act in Global Trade', *Occasional Paper*, Brussels, May.

European Policy Centre 1997b. *Making Sense of the Amsterdam Treaty*. Brussels.

European Services Forum 2001. 'ESP Paper on The Temporary Movement of Key Business Personnel', Brussels, 17 September.

European Trade Union Confederation 1995a. *For a Strong, Democratic and Open European Union Built on Solidarity*. Brussels.

European Trade Union Confederation 1995b. 'Three Challenges for the 1996 IGC: Employment, Solidarity, Democracy', *Our Priorities: ETUC Resolutions 1995–1996*. Brussels.

European Union Migrants' Forum 1995. 'Third Country Nationals in the European Union', European Parliament, Audition Publique, *La Conférence intergouvernementale de 1996: le Parlement européene a l'écoute des citoyens*, Volume I. Brussels, October.

Eurostat 2003, 'New Asylum Applications in the EU, 1986 to 2002', Luxemburg, http://europa.eu.int/comm/justice_home/doc_centre/asylum/statistical/docs//asylum_update_1986_2003_en.pdf (last accessed on 15 July 2004).

Eurostat 2004. *EC Economic Data Pocket Book*, Luxemburg, No. 2.

Fearon, James D. 1991. 'Counterfactuals and Hypothesis in Political Science', *World Politics* 43: 169–95.

Feld, Werner and Wildgen, John 1975. 'National Administration Elites and European Integration: Saboteurs at work?', *Journal of Common Market Studies* 13.

Ferreira, J. L., I. Gilboa and M. Maschler 1995. 'Credible Equilibria in Games with Changing Utility', *Games and Economic behavior* **10**: 284–317.

Finnemore, Martha 1996. *National Interests in International Society*. Ithaca, NY: Cornell University Press.

Finnish Government 1996. *Finland's Points of Departure and Objectives at the 1996 Intergovernmental Conference*, Report to the Parliament by the Council of State.

Fischer, Joschka 2003. 'Suggestion for Amendment of Article III-163 (revised)', European Convention Website, http://european-convention.eu.int/ amendments.asp?content=848&lang=DE (last accessed June 2005).

Fletcher, Maria 2003. 'EU Governance Techniques in the Creation of a Common European Policy on Immigration and Asylum', *European Public Law* **9**: 533–62.

Fortescue, John Adrian 1995. 'First Experiences with the Implementation of the Third Pillar Provisions', in Bieber and Monar (eds), pp. 19–28.

French Government 1997. *Etablissement progressif d'un espace de liberté, de securité et de justice*, Conference of the Representatives of the Governments of the Member States, CONF/3824/97.

French Presidency 2000a. 'Extension of Qualified Majority Voting', Presidency Note, CONFER 4753/00, Brussels, 3 July.

French Presidency 2000b. 'Note of the Presidency', September, CONFER 4770/1/00 REV1, p. 1.

French Presidency 2000c. 'Project de Traité de Nice', CONFER 4816/00.

Friederichs, Tania 1995. 'Some Comments on GATS', in Bourgeois, Berrod and Fournier (eds), pp. 395–9.

Fuchs, G. 1994. 'Policy-making in a System of Multi-level Governance – the Commission of the European Community and the Restructuring of the Telecommunications Sector', *Journal of European Public Policy* **1**: 177–94.

Galtung, Johan 1967. *Theory and Methods of Social Research*. Oslo: Universitetsforlaget.

Gans, H. J. 1962. *The Urban Villagers*. New York: Free Press.

Garrett, Geoffrey 1995. 'The Politics of Legal Integration in the European Union', *International Organization* **49**: 171–81.

Geddes, Andrew 1998. 'The Representation of "Migrants' Interests" in the European Union', *Journal of Ethnic and Migration Studies* **24**: 695–714.

Geddes, Andrew 2000a. *Immigration and European Integraton: Towards Fortress Europe?* Manchester: Manchester University Press.

Geddes, Andrew 2000b. 'Lobbying for Migrant Inclusion in the EU: New Opportunities for Transnational Advocacy?', *Journal of European Public Policy* **7**: 632–49.

George, Alexander L. 1979. 'Case Studies and Theory Development: The Method of Structured, Focused Comparison', in Lauren, Paul Gordon (ed.), *Diplomacy: New Approaches in History, Theory, and Policy*. New York: Free Press, pp. 43–68.

George, Alexander and McKeown, Timothy 1985. 'Case Studies and Theories of Organizational Decision Making', *Advances in Information Processing in Organizations* **2**: 21–58.

George, Stephen 1991. *Politics and Policy in the European Community*, second edition. Oxford: Clarendon Press.

George, Stephen 1996. *Politics and Policy in the European Community*, third edition. Oxford: Clarendon Press.

George, Stephen and Bache, Ian 2000. *Politics in the European Union*. Oxford: OUP.

German Government 1996. *Communitarisation of Customs Co-operation*, Conference of the Representatives of the Governments of the Member States, CONF 3938/96. Brussels.

Geurts, C. 2000. 'Programme Implementation – Procedures and the Role of the Parties Involved', Commission, *Overview of the Phare Programme and the New Pre-Accession Funds*. Luxembourg: OOPEC.

Giddens, Anthony 1984. *The Constitution of Society*. Oxford: Polity Press.

Gilsdorf, Peter 1996. 'Die Außenkompetenzen der EG im Wandel: Eine kritische Auseinandersetzung mit Praxis und Rechtsprechung', *Europarecht* **31**: 145–66.

Givens, Terri and Luedtke, Adam 2004. 'The Politics of European Union Immigration Policy: Institutions, Salience, and Harmonization', *The Policy Studies Journal* **32**: 145–65.

Göler, Daniel 2002. 'Der Gipfel von Laeken: Erste Etappe auf dem Weg zu einer europäischen Verfassung?', *Integration* **25**: 99–110.

Göler, Daniel 2003. 'Die Europäische Union vor ihrer Konstitutionalisierung: Eine Bilanz der ersten Verfassungsentwürfe', *Integration* **26**: 17–30.

Göler, Daniel and Marhold, Hartmut 2003. 'Die Konventsmethode', *Integration* **26**: 317–37.

Goode, Walter 1997. *Dictionary of Trade Policy Terms*. Centre for International Economic Studies, University of Adelaide.

Goulard, Sylvie 2003. 'Die Rolle der Kommission im Konvent: Eine Gratwanderung', *Integration* **26**: 371–98.

Grabbe, Heather 2001. 'What comes after Nice', *Centre for European Reform – Policy Brief*, February.

Gray, Mark and Stubb, Alexander 2001. 'Keynote Article: The Treaty of Nice – Negotiating a Poisoned Chalice?', *Journal of Common Market Studies* **39**: 5–23.

Greek Government 1996. *For a Democratic European Union with Political and Social Content*. Hellenic Republic, Ministry of Foreign Affairs.

Green Cowles, Maria 1995. 'Setting the Agenda for a New Europe: "The ERT and EC 1992"', *Journal of Common Market Studies* **33**: 501–26.

Green, Donald P. and Shapiro, Ian 1994. *Pathologies of Rational Choice Theory*. New Haven, CT/London: Yale University Press.

Greens/EFA 2001. 'Towards a Real European Policy on Immigration and Asylum', 4 July 2001. (http://greens-efa.org/en/documents/detail.php?id =56) (last accessed on 19 May 2004).

Grilli, Enzo 1993. *The European Community and the Developing Countries*. Cambridge, MA: Cambridge University Press.

Groom, A. J. R. 1978. 'A Case of Mistaken Identity', *Political Science* **30**: 15–28.

Guild, Elspeth 2003. 'International Terrorism and EU Immigration, Asylum and Borders Policy: The Unexpected Victims of 11 September 2001', *European Foreign Affairs Review* **8**: 331–46.

Guiraudon, Virginie 2003. 'The Constitution of a European Immigration Policy Domain. A Political Sociological Approach', *Journal of European Public Policy* **10**: 263–82.

Guyomarch, Alain 1997. 'Co-operation in the Fields of Policing and Judicial Affairs', in Stavridis, Stelios, Mossialos, Elias, Morgan, Roger and Machin, Howard (eds), *New Challenges to the European Union: Policies and Policy-Making*. Aldershot: Dartmouth Publishing Company, pp. 123–49.

Haas, Ernst 1958. *The Uniting of Europe: Political, Social and Economic Forces, 1950–7*. London: Stevens.

Haas, Ernst 1960. *Consensus Formation in the Council of Europe*. Berkeley, CA: University of California Press.

Haas, Ernst 1961. 'International Integration: The European and Universal Process', *International Organization* **15**: 366–92.

Haas, Ernst 1964a. 'Technocracy, Pluralism and the New Europe', in Graubard, Stephen (ed.), *A New Europe?* Boston, MA: Houghton Mifflin, p. 62–88.

Haas, Ernst 1964b. *Beyond the Nation-State: Functionalism and International Organization*. Stanford, CA: Stanford University Press.

Haas, Ernst 1968. *The Uniting of Europe: Political, Social and Economic Forces, 1950–7*, second edition. Stanford, CA: Stanford University Press.

Haas, Ernst 1970. 'The Study of Regional Integration: Reflections on the Joy and Anguish of Pretheorizing', *International Organization* **24**: 607–44

Haas, Ernst 1976. 'Turbulent Fields and the Theory of Regional Integration', *International Organization* **30**: 173–212.

Haas, Ernst B. 2001. 'Does Constructivism Subsume Neo-functionalism?' in Christiansen, Jørgensen and Wiener (eds), pp. 22–31.

Haas, Ernst B. 2004. 'Introduction: Institutionalism or constructivism?' in *The Uniting of Europe: Politics, Social and Economic Forces, 1950–1957*, third edition, Notre Dame: University of Notre Dame Press, pp. xiii–lvi.

Haas, Ernst and Schmitter, Philippe 1964. 'Economics and Differential Patterns of Political Integration: Projections About Unity in Latin America', *International Organisation*, pp. 705–37.

Haas, Peter 1992. 'Introduction: Epistemic Communities and International Policy Co-ordination', *International Organization* **46**: 1–35.

Habermas, Jürgen 1981a. *Theorie des kommunikativen Handelns. Handlungsrationalität und gesellschaftliche Rationalisierung*, Frankfurt/Main: Suhrkamp.

Habermas, Jürgen 1981b. *Theorie des kommunikativen Handelns. Zur Kritik der funktionalistischen Vernunft*, Frankfurt/Main: Suhrkamp.

Habermas, Jürgen 1986. 'Entgegnung', in Honneth, Axel and Joas, Hans (eds), *Kommunikatives Handeln: 'Theorie des kommunikativen Handelns'*. Frankfurt/Main: Suhrkamp, pp. 327–405.

Habermas, Jürgen 1995. *Vorstudien und Ergänzungen zur Theorie des kommunikativen Handelns*. Frankfurt/Main: Suhrkamp.

Haggard, Stephen and Moravcsik, Andrew 1993. 'The Political Economy of Financial Assistance to Eastern Europe, 1989–1991', in Keohane and Hoffmann (eds) *After the Cold War*. Cambridge, MA: Harvard University Press, pp. 246–85.

Hailbronner, Kay 1992. 'Perspectives of a Harmonisation of the Law of Asylum after the Maastricht Summit', *Common Market Law Review* **29**: 917–39.

Hailbronner, Kay 1994. 'Visa Regulations and Third-Country Nationals in EC Law', *Common Market Law Review* **31**: 969–95.

Hailbronner, Kay 1995. 'Migration Law and Policy within the Third Pillar of the Union Treaty', in Bieber and Monar (eds), pp. 95–126.

Handoll, John 1995. *Free Movement of Persons in the EU*. Chichester: John Wiley & Sons.

Hänsch, Klaus 2001. 'Maximum des Erreichbaren – Minimum des Notwendigen? Die Ergebnisse von Nizza', *Integration* **24**: 94–101.

Hansen, Roger 1973. 'European Integration: Forward March, Parade Rest, or Dismissed?', *International Organization* **27**: 225–54.

Harrison, R. J. 1990. 'Neo-functionalism', in Groom, A. J. R. and Taylor, Paul (eds.), *Framework for International Co-operation*. London: Pinter, pp. 139–50.

Hartley, T. C. 1994. *The Foundations of European Community Law*, third edition. Oxford: Clarendon Press.

Hartwig, Ines 1997. *The Role of the European Parliament in Shaping the EU's Strategy on Central and Eastern Europe*, Paper Prepared for the Second UACES Research Conference. Loughborough.

Hayes-Renshaw, Fiona and Wallace, Helen 1997. *The Council of Ministers*. London: Macmillan.

Heclo, Hugh 1978. 'Issue Networks and the Executive Establishment', in King, Anthony (ed.), *The New American Political System*. Washington, DC: American Enterprise Institute.

Hempel, Carl 1959. 'The Logic of Functional Analysis', in Gross, L. (ed.), *Symposion on Sociological Theory*. New York: Harper.

Héritier, Adrienne 1998. *The European Polity, Deadlock and Development*, Paper Given in EUI Seminar on the Amsterdam Treaty. Florence, March.

Héritier, Adrienne 1999. *Policy-Making and Diversity in Europe*. Cambridge, MA: Cambridge University Press.

Herrmann, Christoph W. 2002. 'Common Commercial Policy after Nice: Sisyphus would have Done a Better Job', *Common Market Law Preview* **39**: 7–29.

Herrmann, R. K. *et al.* (eds) 2004. *Identities in Europe and the Institutions of the European Union*. Lanham, MD: Rowman and Littlefield.

Hettne, Björn 2002. 'The Europeanisation of Europe: Endogenous and Exogenous Dimensions', *Journal of European Integration* **24**: 325–41.

High-Level Panel on the Free Movement of Persons 1997. *Final Report*, C4-0181/97. Brussels.

Hilf, Meinhard 1995. 'The ECJ's Opinion 1/94 on the WTO – No Surprise, but Wise?', *European Journal of International Law* **6**: 245–59.

Hill, Christopher 1993. 'The Capability–Expectations Gap, or Conceptualising Europe's International Role', *Journal of Common Market Studies* **31**: 305–28.

Hirst, P. and Thompson, G. 1996. *Globalisation in Question: The International Economy and the Possibilities of Governance.* Cambridge, MA: Polity Press.

Hix, Simon 1994. 'Approaches to the Study of the EC: The Challenge to Comparative Politics', *West European Politics* **17**: 1–30.

Hix, Simon and Niessen, Jan 1996. *Reconsidering European Migration Policies: The 1996 Intergovernmental Conference and the Reform of the Maastricht Treaty.* Brussels: Migration Policy Group, pp. 1–63.

Hjelm-Wallen, Lena 2002. *Intervention at the Plenary Session of the European Convention held on 21 March.*

Hoekman, Bernard M. and Kostecki, Michel M. (eds) 1995. *The Political Economy of the World Trading System: From GATT to WTO.* Oxford: Oxford University Press.

Hoffmann, Stanley 1964. 'The European Process at Atlantic Crosspurposes', *Journal of Common Market Studies* **3**: 85–101.

Hoffmann, Stanley 1995. 'Obstinate or Obsolete? France, European Integration and the Fate of the Nation-State', in Hoffmann, Stanley (ed.), *The European Sisyphus: Essays on Europe 1964–1994.* Boulder, CO: Westview Press [reprinted from: Hoffmann, S. 1964. *Decline or Renewal? France Since the 1930s,* Viking Penguin].

Holland, Martin 1995. 'Bridging the Capability–Expectations Gap: A Case Study of the CFSP Joint Action on South Africa', *Journal of Common Market Studies* **33**: 555–72.

Holland, S. 1980. *Uncommon Market.* London: Macmillan.

Hollis, Martin and Steve Smith 1991. *Explaining and Understanding International Relations.* Oxford: Clarendon Press.

Hoogenboom, T. 1993. 'Free Movement and Integration of Non-EC Nationals and the Logic of the Internal Market', in Schermers, H., Fliterman, C., Kellermann, A., Haersolte, J., and van de Meent, G. W. (eds), pp. 497–511.

Hooghe, Liesbet 1996. 'Building a Europe with the Regions: The Changing Role of the European Commission', in Hooghe, Liesbet (ed.), *Cohesion Policy and European Integration: Building Multi-Level Governance.* Oxford: Oxford University Press, pp. 89–126.

Hooghe, Liesbet 1999. 'Supranational Activists or Intergovernmental Agents? Explaining Orientations of Senior Commission Officials towards European Integration', *Comparative Political Studies* **32**: 435–463.

Hooghe, Lisbet and Marks Gary 2001. *Multi-Level Governance and European Integration.* New York: Rowman and Littlefield.

Hooghe, Lisbet and Marks, Gary 2005. 'The Neofunctionalists Were (almost) Right: Politicization and European Integration', *Constitutionalism Web-Papers,* ConWEB No. 5/2005.

Hoyer, Werner 1997. 'The German Government', in European Policy Centre 1997b.

Huysmans, Jef 2000. 'The European Union and the Securitization of Migration', *Journal of Common Market Studies* **38**: 751–77.

Iglicka, Krystyna 2002. 'Shaping a Harmonised Migration Policy for an Enlarged Europe', *Perspectives on European Politics and Society* **3**: 325–34.

Immigration Law Practitioners' Association 2001. *Scoreboard on the Proposal for a Council Regulation Establishing the Criteria and Mechanisms for Determining the Member State Responsible for Examining an Asylum Application*. London, http://www.ilpa.org.uk/submissions/dublinIIscoreboard.html (last accessed on 03 July 2006).

Ipsen, Knut 1994. 'Rule of Law in den internationalen Wirtschaftsbeziehungen: Die Welthandelsorganisation', *Recht der Internationalen Wirtschaft* **40**: 717–23.

Ireland, Patrick 1995. 'Migration, Free Movement, and Immigrant Integration in the EU: A Bifurcated Policy Response', in Leibfried and Pierson (eds), 231–66.

Irish Presidency 1996a. *Presidency Note: Minsiterial Meeting on 1 October 1996 (Luxembourg) – Justice and Home Affairs*, Conference of the Representatives of the Governments of the Member States, CONF/3924/96. Brussels.

Irish Presidency 1996b. *Presidency Introductory Note – An Area of Freedom and Security: Introduction of Community Methods and Procedures for Certain Aspects*, Conference of the Representatives of the Governments of the Member States, CONF/3976/96. Brussels.

Irish Presidency 1996c. *Presidency Note: Ministerial Meeting on 28 October 1996 – External Action of the Union*, Conference of the Representatives of the Governments of the Member States, CONF/3956/96. Brussels.

Irish Presidency 2004. 'IGC 2003 – Meeting of Heads of State and Government', Presidency Note to Delegations, CIG 82/04, Brussels, 16 June.

Italian Presidency 1996. *Note de la Présidence*, Conference of the Representatives of the Governments of the Member States, CONF/3850. Brussels.

Italian Presidency 2003. 'Non-institutional Issues, Including Amendments in the Economic and Financial Field' Note to Delegations, CIG 37/03, Brussels, 24 October.

Jabko, Nicolas 1999. 'In the Name of the Market: How the European Commission Paved the Way for Monetary Union', *Journal of European Public Policy* **6**: 475–96.

Jachtenfuchs, Markus 2001. 'The Governance Approach to European Integration', *Journal of Common Market Studies* **39**: 245–64.

Jachtenfuchs, Markus and Kohler-Koch, Beate 2004. 'Governance and Institutional Development', in Wiener and Diez (eds), pp. 97–115.

Jaks, Jaroslav 1993. 'The EC and Central and Eastern Europe', in Andersen, Svein and Eliassen, Kjell (eds), *Making Policy in Europe: the Europeification of National Policy-Making*. London: Sage, pp. 237–54.

Jensen, Carsten S. 2000. 'Neofunctionalist Theories and the Development of European Social and Labour Market Policy', *Journal of Common Market Studies* **38**: 71–92.

Joergesl, C. 1992. *European Economic Law, the Nation-State, and the Maastricht Treaty*. Berlin: Institute of Advanced Study.

Joerges, Christian and Neyer, Jürgen 1997. 'Transforming Strategic Interaction into Deliberative Problem-solving' *European Law Review Journal* **3**: 273–99.

Joly, Danièle 1996. *Haven or Hell?: Asylum Policies and Refugees in Europe.* London: Macmillan Press.

Jørgensen, Knut Eric and Christiansen, Thomas 1998. *The Amsterdam Process: A Structurationist Perspective on EU Treaty Reform*, paper presented at the International Seminar on Theoretical Approaches and Treaty Reform. Brussels.

Julius, DeAnne 1990. *Global Companies and Public Policy.* London: Pinter.

Juppé, Alain 1996. 'Discours de M. Alain Juppé', Premier ministre, Assemblée nationale, 13 March 1996, Ministère des Affaires étrangères.

Justice 1996a. *Human Rights and the 1996–7 Intergovernmental Conference: The Democratic Deficit.* London.

Justice 1996b. *Human Rights and the 1996–7 Intergovernmental Conference – The Union Divided: Race Discrimination and Third Country Nationals in the European Union.* London.

Justus Lipsius 1995. 'The 1996 Intergovernmental Conference', *European Law Review* **20**: 235–67.

Kaelberer, Matthias 2003. 'Knowledge, Power and Monetary Bargaining: Central Bankers and the Creation of Monetary Union in Europe', *Journal of European Public Policy* **10**: 365–80.

Katzenstein, Peter 1996. 'Introduction: Alternative Perspectives on National Security', in Katzenstein, P (ed.), *The Culture of National Security. Norms and Identity in World Politics.* New York: Columbia University Press, pp. 1–32.

Keohane, Robert and Nye, Joseph 1975. 'International Interdependence and Integration', in Greenstein and Polsby (eds), *Handbook of Political Science*, Reading. MA: Addison-Wesley.

Keohane, Robert and Hoffmann, Stanley 1991. 'Institutional Change in Europe in the 1980s', in Keohane and Hoffmann (eds), pp. 1–40.

Keohane, Robert and Hoffmann Stanley 1991 *The New European Community: Decision-making and Institutional Change.* Boulder, CO: Westview Press.

Keohane, Robert and Nye Joseph 1977. *Power and Interdependence: World Politics in Transition.* Boston, MA: Little, Brown.

King, Gary, O. Keohane, Robert and Verba, Sidney 1994. *Designing Social Inquiry.* Princeton, NJ: Princeton University Press.

Kinkel, Klaus 1995. 'Zu Fragen der Regierungskonferenz 1996 ueber die Fortentwicklung und Reform der Strukturen der Europaeischen Union', interview with the Federal Minister for Foreign Affairs, *Stuttgarter Zeitung* 29.03.95.

Kinkel, Klaus and Dini, Lamberto 1997. 'Justiz- und Innenpolitk in der Europaeischen Union: Gemeinsam fuer die Sicherheit der Buerger', *Frankfurter Allgemeine Zeitung* 21.02.1997.

Kirchner, Emil 1992. *Decision-Making in the European Community.* Manchester: Manchester University Press.

Kiso, Jan-Ole 1997. 'COREPER and Political Committee – Damaging for CFSP?', *Cambridge Review of International Affairs* **X**: 222–36.

Kiso, Jan Ole 1999. *Evolving Decision-making Structures of European Foreign Policy and Home Affairs: Leading Towards and Beyond the Fusion Concept*, University of Cambridge, Centre of International Studies.

Kohl, Helmut and Chirac, Jacques 1995. 'Déclaration du chancelier Helmut Kohl et du Président Jacques Chirac au Président du Conseil européen', 6 December 1995.

Kohl, Helmut and Chirac, Jacques 1996. 'Déclaration du chancelier Helmut Kohl et du Président Jacques Chirac au Président du Conseil européen', Bonn and Paris, 9 December 1996.

Kohler-Koch, Beate 1996. 'Catching up with Change: The Transformation of Governance in the European Union', *Journal of European Public Policy* **3**: 359–80.

Koopmans, T. 1986. 'The Role of Law in the Next Stage of European Integration', *International and Comparative Law Quarterly* **35**: 925–31.

Kramer, Heinz 1993. 'The European Community's Response to the New Eastern Europe', *Journal of Common Market Studies* **31**: 213–44.

Kranz, Jerzy 2003. 'Between Nice and Brussels or Life after Death', Warsaw Center for International Relations, Reports and Analyses 03/04/A.

Krause, Axel 1991. *Inside the New Europe*. New York: Harper Collins Publishers.

Kreinin, Mordechai and Schmidt-Levine, Marcella 1997. 'The WTO and the International Trading Environment', in Fatemi, Khosrow (ed.) *International Trade in the 21st Century*. Oxford, New York: Pergamon, pp. 29–48.

Krenzler, Horst-Günter 1996. 'Gemeinsame Handelspolitik: Die EU braucht eine starke Außenvertretung', *EU Magazin* **7–8**: 18–21.

Krenzler, Horst-Günter and da Fonseca-Wollheim, Hermann 1998. 'Die Reichweite der gemeinsamen Handelspolitik nach dem Vertrag von Amsterdam – eine Debatte ohne Ende?', *Europarecht* **33**: 223–41.

Krenzler, Horst Günter and Pitschas, Christian 2001. 'Progress or Stagnation?: The Common Commercial Policy After Nice', *European Foreign Affairs Review* **6**: 291–313.

Krenzler, Horst-Günter and Schneider, Henning 1997. 'The Question of Consistency', in Regelsberger, Elfriede, de Schoutheete de Tervarent, Philippe and Wessels, Wolfgang (eds), *Foreign Policy of the European Union: From EPC to CFSP and Beyond*. London: Lynne Rienner, pp. 133–52.

Kuyper, Pieter-Jan 1995. 'The New WTO Dispute Settlement System: The Impact on the Community', in Bourgeois, Berrod and Fournier (eds), pp. 87–114.

Laffan, B. 2004. 'The European Union and its Institution as "Identity Builders"', in Herrmann, R. K., Risse, T., Brewer, M. (eds).

Lamy, Pascal 2002a. *La politique commerciale et la Convention: un exemple à parfaire*. Brussels: External Action Working Group of the Convention, 15 October.

Lamy, Pascal 2002b. *The Future of Europe: What Global Role For an Enlarged EU?*. Berlin: Institut für Europäische Politik, http://www.europa.eu.int/comm/commissioners/lamy/speeches_articles/spla94_en.htm (last accessed October 2004).

Lamy, Pascal 2002c. 'Convention: l'urgence', in *Le Monde* 13 September, http://europa.eu.int/comm/commissioners/lamy/speeches_articles/in-dexplsub_en.htm#conv

Lamy, Pascal 2003. *The Convention and Trade Policy: Concrete Steps to Enhance the EU's International Profile*. Brussels: European Policy Center, 5 February.

Lavenex, Sandra 2001. 'The Europeanization of Refugee Policies: Normative Challenges and Institutional Legacies', *Journal of Common Market Studies* **39**: 851–74.

Lavenex, Sandra and Uçarer, Emek M. 2002. 'Introduction: The Emergent EU Migration Regime and Its External Impact', Lavenex, Sandra and Uçarer, Emek M. (eds), *Migration and the Externalities of European Integration*, Lanham, MD: Lexingtiion, pp. 1–32.

Leal-Arcas, Rafael 2004. 'The EC in GATT/WTO Negotiations: From Rome to Nice – Have EC Trade Policy Reforms Been Good Enough for a Coherent EC Trade Policy in the WTO?', *European Integration Online Papers (EIoP)* **8**.

Leibfried, Stephan and Pierson, Paul 1995. 'Semisovereign Welfare States: Social Policy in a Multitiered Europe', in Leibfried and Pierson (eds.), pp. 43–77.

Leibfried, Stephan and Pierson, Paul (eds) 1995. *European Social Policy: Between Fragmentation and Integration*. Washington, DC: Brookings Institution.

Lequesne, Christian 2001. 'The French Presidency: The Half Success of Nice', *Journal of Common Market Studies* **39**: 47–50.

Lewis, Jeffrey 1995. *The European Union as a "Multiperspectival Polity"*, Paper Prepared for the Fourth Biennial International Conference of the European Community Studies Association. Charleston, SC. 11–14 May.

Lewis, Jeffrey 1998a. *Wearing a Janus-Face: The Permanent Representatives of the European Union*, Paper for the Eleventh International Conference of Europeanists. Baltimore, MD, 26–28 February.

Lewis, Jeffrey 1998b. 'Is the "Hard Bargaining" Image of the Council Misleading? The Committee of Permanent Representatives and the Local Elections Directive', *Journal of Common Market Studies* **36**: 479–504.

Lewis, Jeffrey 2000. 'The Methods of Community in EU Decision-making and Administrative Rivalry in the Council's Infrastructure', *Journal of European Public Policy* **7**: 261–89.

Libertarians Against Nice 2002. 'Nice and the Corporate Agenda: The Changes to Article 133', press release, http://struggle.ws/ireland/nice/pr/corporate.html (last accessed on 03 July 2004).

Lijphart, Arend 1971. 'Comparative Politics and the Comparative Method', *American Political Science Review* **LXV**: 682–93.

Lijphart, Arend 1975. 'The Comparable-Cases Strategy in Comparative Research', *Comparative Political Studies* **8**: 158–75.

Lindberg Clausen, Charlotte 1998. *The Creation and Development of Schengen: A Case of Neofunctionalist Spill-over?* Master Dissertation. Cambridge, MA: University of Cambridge.

Lindberg, Leon 1963. *The Political Dynamics of European Integration*. Stanford, CA: Princeton University Press.

Lindberg, Leon 1966. 'Integration as a Source of Stress on the European Community System', *International Organization* **20**: 233–65.

Lindberg, Leon and Scheingold, Stuart 1970. *Europe's Would-Be Polity*. Englewood Cliffs, NJ: Prentice Hall.

Lindberg, Leon and Scheingold, Stuart (eds) 1971. *Regional Integration: Theory and Research*. Cambridge, MA: Harvard University Press.

Lindesmith, A. R. 1968. *Addiction and Opiates*. Chicago, IL: Aldine.

Little, Daniel 1991. *Varieties of Social Explanation: An Introduction to the Philosophy of Social Science*. Boulder, CO: Westview Press.

Ludlow, Peter 1991. 'The European Commission', in Keohane and Hoffmann (eds), pp. 85–132.

Ludlow, Peter 1997. 'Institutional Balance', in European Policy Centre 1997b, p. 52.

Luxembourg Government 1995. *Aide-mémoire du Gouvernement luxembourgeois sur la Conférence Intergouvernemental de 1996*.

Luxembourg Presidency 1991. *Draft Treaty*, Document CONF-UP-UEM 2008/91.

MacLeod, I., Hendry, I. and Hyett, Stephen 1996. *The External Relations of the European Communities: A Manual of Law and Practice*. Oxford: Clarendon.

MacMillan, K. 1991. *The Management of European Public Affairs*, Paper Prepared for Presentation to a ECPA/Conference Board Meeting. Brussels, 30–31 May.

Magnette, Paul and Nicolaidis, Kalypso 2004. 'The European Convention: Bargaining in the Shadow of Rhetoric', *West European Politics* **27**: 381–404.

Majone, Giandomenico 1992. 'Market Integration and Regulation: Europe After 1992', *Metroeconomica* **43**: 131–56.

Majone, Giandomenico 1993. 'Deregulation or Re-Regulation? Policy-making in the European Community since the Single Act', *EUI Working Papers in Political and Social Sciences*. Florence: European University Institute.

Majone, Giandomenico 1996. 'A European Regulatory State?', in Richardson (ed.), pp. 264–76.

March, James and Simon Herbert 1958. *Organizations*. New York: John Wiley.

March, James G. and Olsen, Johan P. 1998. 'The Institutional Dynamics of International Political Orders', *International Organization* **52**: 943–69.

Marcussen, Martin and Risse Thomas 1997. *A Europeanisation of Nation-state Identities? Conceptual Considerations and Research Design*, Paper Presented at the Workshop on National Identities. Florence: Robert Schumann Centre, European University Institute, 21–22 November.

Marcussen, M., Risse, T., Engelmann-Martin, D., Knopf, H. J. and Roscher, K. 1999. 'Constructing Europe? The Evolution of French, British and German Nation State Identities', *Journal of European Public Policy* **6**: 614–33.

Maresceau, Marc 1993. 'The Concept of "Common Commercial Policy" and the Difficult Road to Maastricht', in Maresceau, Marc (ed.), *The European Community's Commercial Policy After 1992: The Legal Dimension*, pp. 3–19.

Märker, Alfredo 2001. 'Zuwanderungspolitik in der Europäischen Union: Europäisierte Lösungen oder Politik des kleinsten gemeinsamen Nenners?', *Aus Politik und Zeitgeschichte* 8/2001, pp. 3–10.

Marks, Gary 1992. 'Structural Policy in the European Community', in Sbragia (ed.), pp. 191–224.

Marks, Gary 1993. 'Structural Policy and Multi-Level Governance in the European Community', in Cafruny and Rosenthal (eds), pp. 391–410.

Marks, Gary, Hooghe, Liesbet and Blank, Kermit 1996. 'European Integration from the 1980s: State-Centric v. Multi-level Governance', *Journal of Common Market Studies* **34**: 341–78.

Marks, Scharpf, Schmitter and Streek (eds) 1996. *Governance in the European Union*. London: Sage.

Martikonis, Rytis 2002. Representative of the Lithuanian Government, Intervention at the Plenary Session of the European Convention, Brussels, 6 June 2002. For verbatim reports of the Convention sessions see, http://www.europarl.eu.int/europe2004/index_en.htm (last accessed June 2005).

Martin, Lisa L. 1992. *Coercive Cooperation: Explaining Multilateral Economic Sanctions*. Princeton, NJ: Princeton University Press.

Matlary, Janne Haaland 1994. *The Limits and Limitations of Intergovernmentalism: From De-Constructive to Constructive Criticism*. Lund: Paper Presented within the Master of European Affairs Programme, University of Lund.

Matlary, Janne Haaland 1997. *Energy Policy in the European Union*. London: Macmillan Press.

Mattli, Walter and Slaughter, Anne-Marie 1995. 'Law and Politics in the European Union: A Reply to Garrett', *International Organization* **49**: 183–90.

Mattli, Walter and Slaughter, Anne-Marie 1998. 'Revisiting the European Court of Justice', *International Organization* **52**: 177–211.

Maurer, Andreas 2001. 'Entscheidungseffizienz und Handlungs fähigkeit nach Nizza: die neuen Anwendungsfelder für Mehrheitsentscheidungen', *Integration* **24**: 133–45.

Maurer, Andreas 2003a. 'Die Methode des Konvents – ein Modell deliberativer Demokratie?', *Integration* **26**: 130–51.

Maurer, Andreas, 2003b. 'The Legislative Powers and Impact of the European Parliament', *Journal of Common Market Studies*, **41**: 227–47.

Mayes, David (ed.) 1997. *The Evolution of the Single European Market*. Cheltenham: Edward Elgar Publishing.

Mazey, Sonia (ed.) 2000. 'Women, Power and Public Policy in Europe', *Journal of European Public Policy*, Special Issue, 7, 3 pp. 333–45.

Mazey, Sonia and Richardson, Jeremy (eds) 1993. *Lobbying in the European Community*. Oxford: Oxford University Press.

Mazey, Sonia and Richardson, Jeremy 1993. 'Conclusion: A European Policy Style?', in Mazey and Richardson (eds), pp. 246–58.

Mazey, Sonia and Richardson, Jeremy 1994. 'The Commission and the Lobby', in Edwards, Geoffrey and Spence, David (eds), *The European Commission*. London: Cathermill, pp. 169–87.

Mazey, Sonia and Richardson, Jeremy 1997a. 'The Commission and the Lobby', in Edwards, Geoffrey and Spence, David (eds), *The European Commission*, second edtition. London: Cathermill, pp. 178–98.

Mazey, Sonia and Richardson, Jeremy 1997b. 'Agenda Setting, Lobbying and the 1996 IGC', in Edwards and Pijpers (eds), pp. 226–48.

McDonagh, Bobby 1998. *Original Sin in a Brave New World: An Account of the Negotiation of the Treaty of Amsterdam*. Dublin: Institute of European Affairs.

McLaughlin, Andrew and Jordan, Grant 1993. 'The Rationality of Lobbying in Europe: Why are Euro-Groups so Numerous and so Weak? Some Evidence from the Car Industry', in Mazey and Richardson (eds), pp. 122–61.

McNamara, Kathleen 1993. 'Common Markets, Uncommon Currencies: Systems Effects and European Community', in Snyder, Jack and Jervis,

Robert (eds), *Coping with Complexity in the International System*. Boulder, CO: Westview Press, pp. 303–27.

McNeill, Patrick 1990. *Research Methods*, second edition. London: Routledge.

Mehaignerie, Pierre 1994. 'Internal Security', Group of the European People's Party publication, June/July 1994.

Metcalfe, D. 1998. 'Leadership in European Union Negotiations: The Presidency of the Council', *International Negotiation* 3, pp. 413–34.

Meunier, Sophie and Nicolaïdis, Kalypso 1999. 'Who speaks for Europe? The Delegation of Trade Authority in the EU', *Journal of Common Market Studies* 37: 477–501.

Meunier, Sophie and Nicolaïdis, Kalypso 2000. 'EU Trade Policy: The Exclusive versus Shared Competence Debate', in Green Cowles, Maria and Smith, Michael (eds) *The State of the European Union: Risks, Reform, Resistance, and Revival*, Vol. 5, Oxford: Oxford University Press, pp. 325–46.

Meunier, Sophie and Nicolaïdis, Kalypso 2002. 'EU Trade Policy: The Exclusive versus shared competence Debate', in Green Cowles, Maria amd Smith, Michael (eds), *The State of the European Union: Risks, Reform, Resistance, and Revival*. Oxford: Oxford University Press, pp. 325–46.

Mill, John Stuart 1950. *Philosophy of Scientific Method*. New York: Hafner.

Milward, Alan 1992. *The European Rescue of the Nation-State*. London: Routledge.

Milward, Alan and Sørensen, V. 1993. 'Interdependence or Integration? A National Choice', in Milward, Ranieri, Romero and Sørensen (eds) *The Frontier of National Sovereignty: History and Theory, 1945–1992*. New York: Routledge.

Mitrany, David 1966. *A Working Peace System*. Chicago, IL: Quadrangle Books.

Mitrany, David 1975. *The Functional Theory of Politics*. London: Martin Robertson.

Monar, Jörg 1994. 'The Evolving Role of the Union Institutions in the Framework of the Third Pillar', in Monar and Morgan (eds), pp. 69–83.

Monar, Jörg 1995. 'Democratic Control of Justice and Home Affairs: The European Parliament and the National Parliaments', in Bieber and Monar (eds), pp. 243–58.

Monar, Jörg 1997. 'European Union – Justice and Home Affair: A Balance Sheet and an Agenda for Reform', in Edwards and Pijpers (eds), pp. 326–39.

Monar, Jörg 1998a. 'Justice and Home Affairs', *Journal of Common Market Studies*, Annual Review, 36: 131–42.

Monar, Jörg 1998b. 'Justice and Home Affairs in the Treaty of Amsterdam: Reform at the Price of Fragmentation', *European Law Review* 23: 320–33.

Monar, Jörg 2000. 'Die Entwicklung des "Raumes der Freiheit, der Sicherheit und des Rechts". Perspektiven nach dem Vertrag von Amsterdam und dem Europäischen Rat von Tampere', *Integration* 23: 18–33.

Monar, Jörg 2001a. 'Die Kommission nach dem Vertrag von Nizza. Ein gestärkter Präsident und ein geschwächtes Organ?', *Integration* 24: 114–23.

Monar, Jörg 2001b. 'The Dynamics of Justice and Home Affairs. Laboratories, Driving Factors and Costs', *Journal of Common Market Studies* **39**: 747–64.

Monar, Jörg 2003. 'Der Raum der Freiheit, der Sicherheit und des Rechts im Verfassungsentwurf des Konvents', *Integration* **26**: 536–49.

Monar, Jörg 2004a. 'Justice and Home Affairs', *Journal of Common Market Studies*, Annual Review, **42**: 117–133.

Monar, Jörg 2004b. 'The EU as an International Actor in the Domain of Justice and Home Affairs', *European Foreign Affairs Review* **9**: 395–415.

Monar, Jörg and Morgan, Roger (eds) 1994. *The Third Pillar of the European Union: Co-operation in the Field of Justice and Home Affairs*. Brussels: European Interuniversity Press and College of Europe.

Monti, Mario 1996. *The Single Market and Tomorrow's Europe*. Progress Report from the European Commission, London: Kogan Page.

Moravcsik, Andrew 1991. 'Negotiating the Single European Act: National Interests and Conventional Statecraft in the European Community', *International Organization* **45**: 21–56.

Moravcsik, Andrew 1993. 'Preferences and Power in the European Community: A Liberal Intergovernmentalist Approach', *Journal of Common Market Studies* **31**: 473–524.

Moravcsik, Andrew 1995. 'Liberal Intergovernmentalism and Integration: A Rejoinder', *Journal of Common Market Studies* **33**: 611–28.

Moravcsik, Andrew 1998. *The Choice for Europe. Social Purpose and State Power from Messina to Maastricht*. Ithaca, NY: Cornell University Press.

Moravcsik, Andrew 1999. 'A New Statecraft? Supranational Entrepreneurs and International Cooperation', *International Organization* **53**: 267–306.

Moravcsik, Andrew 2001a. 'Bringing Constructivist Theories of the EU out of the Clouds: Have they Landed Yet?', *European Union Politics* **2** pp. 231–49.

Moravcsik, Andrew 2001b. 'Constructivism and European Integration: A Critique', in Christiansen, Jørgensen and Wiener (eds), pp. 176–188.

Moravcsik, Andrew and Nicolaïdis, Kalypso 1998. 'Keynote Article: Federal Ideals and Constitutional Realities in the Treaty of Amsterdam', *Journal of Common Market Studies* **36**: 13–38.

Moravcsik, Andrew and Nicolaïdis, Kalypso 1999. 'Explaining the Treaty of Amsterdam: Interests, Influence, Institutions', *Journal of Common Market Studies* **37**: 59–85.

Morgan, Roger 1986. 'Communication Between Political Elites', in Morgan and Bray (eds) pp. 120–35.

Morgan, Roger 1994. 'The Third Pillar: An Introduction', in Monar and Morgan (eds), pp. 13–18.

Morgan, Roger and Bray, Caroline (eds) 1986. *Partners and Rivals in Western Europe: Britain, France and Germany*. Aldershot: Gower Publishers.

Müller-Graf, Peter-Christian 1997. 'Justiz und Inneres nach Amsterdam – Die Neuerungen in erster und dritter Säule', *Integration* **20**: 292–304.

Mutimer, David 1989. '1992 and the Political Integration of Europe: Neofunctionalism Reconsidered', *Journal of European Integration* **13**: 75–101.

Myers, Philip 1995. 'The Commission's Approach to the Third Pillar: Political and Organisational Elements', in Bieber and Monar (eds), pp. 277–300.

Nanz, Klaus-Peter 1994. 'The Harmonisation of Asylum and Immigration Legislation Within the Third Pillar of the Union Treaty – A Stocktaking', in Monar and Morgan (eds), pp. 123–33.

Nassauer, Hartmut 1996. *Immigration and Asylum Policy and the Protection of Borders*, Group of European People's Party, Helsinki Study Days, pp. 97–99.

Neuss, Beate 2000. *Geburtshelfer Europas?* Baden-Baden: Nomos.

Neuwahl, Nanette 1995. 'Judicial Control in Matters of Justice and Home Affairs: What Role for the Court of Justice', in Bieber and Monar (eds), pp. 301–20.

Nicholson, M. 1996. 'The Continued Significance of Positivism?', in Smith, S., Booth, K., and Zalewski, M. (eds), pp. 128–48.

Niemann, Arne 1996. *The Concept of Spillover, the European Commission and PHARE*, MPhil dissertation, August. University of Cambridge, Centre of International Studies.

Niemann, Arne 1997a. *Between Fusion and Engrenage: The Formulation and Adaptation of National Trade Policies*, Paper Presented at the UACES Research Conference. Loughborough, 10–12 September.

Niemann, Arne 1997b. 'Europhoria, Friendship and Wine: The Stuff that Built Another Europe', *Cambridge Review of International Affairs* 11: 277–92.

Niemann, Arne 1998. 'The PHARE Programme and the concept of Spillover: Neofunctionalism in the Making', *Journal of European Public Policy* 5: 428–46.

Niemann, Arne 2000. *The Internal and External Dimensions of European Union Decision-Making: Developing and Testing a Revised Neofunctionalist Framework*, PhD Thesis, University of Cambridge.

Niemann, Arne 2004. 'Between Communicative Action and Strategic Action: The Article 113 Committee and the Negotiations on the WTO Basic Telecommunications Services Agreement', *Journal of European Public Policy* 11: 379–407.

Niemann, Arne 2006 forthcoming. 'Beyond Problem-Solving and Bargaining: Genuine Debate in EU External Trade Negotiations', *International Negotiation Journal* 10.

Niemann, Arne and Edwards, Geoffrey 1997. 'Theoretical approaches to the Intergovernmental Conference 1996/97: A Neo-functionalist Approach', 22nd Annual British International Studies Association Conference in Leeds, December.

Nørgaard, Pedersen and Petersen (eds) 1993. *The European Community in World Politics*. London: Pinter.

Nuallain, Colm (ed.) 1985. *The Presidency of the European Council of Ministers*. London: Croom Helm.

Nugent, Neill 1995. 'The Leadership Capacity of the European Commission', *Journal of European Public Policy* 2: 603–23.

Nuttall, Simon 1988. 'Where the European Commission Comes in', in Pijpers, Regelsberger and Wessels (eds), *European Political Co-operation in the 1980s*. Dordrecht: Nijhoff.

Nuttall, Simon 1992. *European Political Co-operation*. Oxford: Clarendon Press.

Nye, Joseph 1970. 'Comparing Common Markets: A Revised Neo-Functionalist Model', *International Organization* 24: 796–835.

Nye, Joseph 1971. *Peace in Parts: Integration and Conflict in Regional Organization*. Boston, MA: Little, Brown.

Nye, Joseph 1987. 'Nuclear Learning and U.S. – Soviet Security Regimes', *International Organization* 41 pp. 371–402.

O'Brien, Conor 2001. ATTAC Ireland, 'Submission to the Forum on Europe, 1st December 2001', http://www.forumoneurope.ie/submission_docs/attac.doc (last accessed on 15 July 2004).

O'Keeffe, David 1995a. 'The Emergence of a European Immigration Policy', *European Law Review* 20: 20–36.

O'Keeffe, David 1995b. 'Recasting the Third Pillar', *Common Market Law Review* 32: 893–920.

O'Keeffe, David 1995c. 'Reforming the Third Pillar: Transparency and Structural Reform in the Long-term Perspective', in Bieber and Monar (eds), pp. 397–422.

O'Keeffe, David 1999. 'Community and Member State Competence in External Relations Agreements of the EU', *European Foreign Affairs Review* 4: 7–36.

O'Reilly, Dolores 1997. *Testing Integration Theories: The Development of A European Air Transport Policy*, Paper Presented to the 2nd UACES Research Conference 1997. Loughborough.

O'Reilly, Dolores and Stone Sweet, Alec 1998. 'The Liberalisation and Reregulation of Air Transport', *Journal of European Public Policy* 5: 447–66.

Oakes, Penelope, Haslam, Alexander and Turner, John 1994. *Stereotyping and Social Reality*. Oxford/Cambridge, M: Blackwell Publishers.

Official Journal of the European Communities 1999. *Action Plan of the Council and the Commission on How Best to Implement the Provisions of the Treaty of Amsterdam on an Area of Freedom, Security and Justice – Text Adopted by the Justice and Home Affairs Council of 3 December 1998* C 19.

Olsen, J. P. 2002. 'The Many Faces of Europeanisation', *Journal of Common Market Studies* 40: 921–52.

Oreja, Marcelino 1997. Newsletter on the Intergovernmental Conference, February 1997, http://europa.eu.int/en/agenda/igc-home/eu-doc/letter/fev97en.htm (last accessed on 15 July 2004).

Padoa-Schioppa, Tommaso 1987. *Efficiency, Stability, and Equity: A Strategy for the Evolution of the Economic System of the European Community: A Report*. Oxford: Oxford University Press.

Paemen, Hugo 1996. 'The EC and the WTO Agenda', in van Dijck, Pitou and Faber, Gerrit (eds). *Challenges to the New World Trade Organisation*. Boston, MA: Kluwer Law International.

Papademetriou, Demetrios 1996. *Coming Together or Pulling Apart: The European Union's Struggle With Immigration and Asylum*. Washington, DC: The Brookings Institution.

Patijn, Michiel 1997. 'The Dutch Presidency', in European Policy Centre 1997b, pp. 38–9.

Patterson, L. A. 1997. 'Agricultural Policy Reform in the European Community: A Three-Level Game Analysis', *International Organization* **51**: 135–65.

Pelkmans, Jacques and Murphy, Anna 1991. 'Catapulted into Leadership: The Community's Trade and Aid Policies *vis-à-vis* Eastern Europe', *Journal of European Integration* **24**: 125–51.

Pescatore, Pierre 1979. 'External Relations in the Case-Law of the Court of Justice of the European Communities', *Common Market Law Review* **16**: 615–45.

Pescatore, Pierre 2001. 'Nice – Aftermath', *Common Market Law Review* **38**: 265–71.

Peters, Guy 1994. 'Agenda-setting in the European Community', *Journal of European Public Policy* **1**: 9–26.

Peterson, John 1991. 'Technology Policy in Europe: Explaining the Framework Programme and Eureka in Theory and Practice', *Journal of Common Market Studies* **29**: 269–90.

Peterson, John 1992. 'The European Technology Community: Policy Networks in a Supranational Setting', in Marsh, David and Rhodes, R. A. W. (eds), *Policy Networks in British Government*. Oxford: Clarendon Press.

Peterson, John 1995. 'Decision-making in the European Union: Towards a Framework for Analysis', *Journal of European Public Policy* **2**: 69–96.

Petersen, Nikolaj 1993. 'The European Union and Foreign and Security Policy', in Nørgaard, Pedersen and Petersen (eds), pp. 9–30.

Peterson, J. and Bomberg, E. 1999. *Decision-making in the European Union*. Basingstoke and New York: Oalgrave.

Petite, Michel 1997. 'The Treaty of Amsterdam: Ambition and Realism', *Revue du Marché Unique Européene* **3**: 17–52.

Petite, Michel 1998a. 'The Treaty of Amsterdam', *Harvard Jean Monnet Chair Working Paper Series* **2**.

Petite, Michel 1998b. 'Amsterdam and European Institutional Balance: A Panel Discussion', *Harvard Jean Monnet Chair Working Paper Series* **14**: 18–29.

Pierson, Paul 1996. 'The Path to European Integration: A Historical Institutionalist Analysis', *Comparative Political Studies* **29**: 123–63.

Pierson, Paul 1998. 'The Path to European Integration: A Historical Institutionalist Analysis', in Sandholtz and Stone Sweet (eds), pp. 27–58.

Pierson, Paul and Leibfried, Stephan 1995. 'The Dynamics of Social Policy Integration', in Leibfried and Pierson (eds), pp. 432–65.

Pinder, John 1986. 'European Community and the Nation State: A Case for Neo-federalism?', *International Affairs* **62**: 41–54.

Pinder, John 1991a. *European Community: The Building of a Union*, second edtition. Oxford: Oxford University Press.

Pinder, John 1991b. *The European Community and Eastern Europe*, The Royal Institute of International Affairs. London: Pinter.

Pollack, Mark A. 2001. 'International Relations Theory and European Integration', *Journal of Common Market Studies* **39**: 221–44.

Pollack, Mark A. 2003. *The Engines of European Integration: Delegation, Agency and Agenda Setting in the European Union*, Oxford: Oxford University Press.

Pollack, Mark A. 2004. 'The New Institutionalisms and European Integration', in Wiener and Diez (eds), Oxford: Oxford University Press, 137–56.

Popper, Karl 1968. *The Logic of Scientific Discovery*. New York: Harper and Row.

Portuguese Presidency 2000a. 'Possible Extension of Qualified Majority Voting – Introductory Note', Presidency Note, CONFER 4705/1/00 REV1, Brussels, 11 February.

Portuguese Presidency 2000b. 'Possible Extension of Qualified Majority Voting', Presidency Note, CONFER 4710/00, Brussels, 22 February.

Praesidium 2003. *Draft Articles on External Action in the Constitutional Treaty*, CONV 685/03, Convention Secretariat. Brussels.

Presidency Conclusions 1999a. *Tampere European Council*, 15–16 October.

Presidency Conclusions 1999b. *Helsinki European Council*, 10–11 December.

Presidency Conclusions 2001. *European Council Meeting in Laeken*, SN 300/1/01 REV 1.

Presidency Conclusions 2002. *Seville European Council*, 21–22 June.

Prevezanos, Klaudia 2001. 'The EU Conference in Nice. More than a Minimum Consensus for Europe and Germany', *At Issue*, American Institute for Contemporary German Studies, John Hopkins University.

Prodi, Romano 2000a. *To Nice and Beyond*, Speech at the European Parliament on the European Council of Nice, Brussels: European Parliament, SPEECH/00/475, 29 November.

Prodi, Romano 2000b. Speech at the European Parliament on the European Council of Nice. Strasbourg: European Parliament, SPEECH/00/499, 12 December.

Puchala, Donald 1972. 'Of Blind Men, Elephants, and European Integration', *Journal of Common Market Studies* 10: 267–84.

Putnam, Robert 1988. 'Diplomacy and Domestic Politics: The Logic of Two-Level Games', *International Organization* 42: 427–60.

Quaglia, Lucia 2004. 'The Italian Presidency', *Journal of Common Market Studies*, Annual Review, 42: 47–50.

Ragin, Charles 1987. *The Comparative Method: Moving Beyond Qualitative and Quantitative Strategies*. Berkley, CA: University of California Press.

Randzio-Plath, Christa 1995. 'Vom GATT zur WTO – fairer Welthandel order Macht des Stärkeren?, *Wirtschaftsdienst* 3: 156–60.

Rasmussen, Hjalte 1986. *On Law and Policy in the European Court of Justice*. Dordrecht/Lancaster, PA/Boston, MA: Nijhoff.

Rasmussen, Hjalte 1988. 'Between Self-Restraint and Activism: A Judicial Policy for the European Court', *European Law Review* 13: 140–58.

Rees, Nicholas 2005. 'The Irish Presidency: A Diplomatic Triumph', *Journal of Common Market Studies*, Annual Review, 43: 55–58.

Reflection Group 1995a. *Reflection Group's Report*. Brussels, 5 December.

Reflection Group 1995b. *Progress Report: From the Chairman of the Reflection Group on the 1996 Intergovernmental Conference*. Madrid, SN 509/1/95 (REFLEX 10) REV 1.

Regelsberger, Elfriede and Wessels, Wolfgang 1984. 'Verwaltungsprozesse Bonner Europapolitik – verwalten statt gestalten?', in Hrbek, Rudolf and Wessels, Wolfgang (eds), *EG-Mitgliedschaft: ein vitales Interesse der Bundesrepublik Deutschland?* Bonn: Europa Verlag.

Rhodes, Martin and van Apeldorn, Bastiaan 1998. 'Capital Unbound? The Transformation of European Corporate Governance', *Journal of European Public Policy* 5: 406–27.

Richardson, Jeremy (ed.) 1982. *Policy Styles in Western Europe*. London: George Allen and Unwin.

Richardson, Jeremy (ed.) 1996. *European Union: Power and Policy-making*. London: Routledge.

Risse, Thomas 2000. "'Let's Argue!'": Communicative Action in World Politics', *International Organization* 54: 1–39.

Risse, Thomas 2004. 'Social Constructivism and European Integration', in Wiener and Diez (eds), pp. 160–76.

Risse, Thomas 2005. 'Neofunctionalism, European Identity, and the Puzzles of European Integration', *Journal of European Public Policy* 12: 291–309.

Risse, Thomas and Wiener, Antje 1999. 'Something Rotten and the Social Construction of Social Constructivism: A Comment on Comments, *Journal of European Public Policy* 6: 775–82.

Risse, Thomas and Wiener, Antje 2001. 'The Social Construction of Social Constructivsm', in Christiansen, Jørgensen and Wiener (eds), pp. 199–205.

Risse-Kappen, Thomas 1995a. 'Bringing Transnational Relations Back In: Introduction', in Risse-Kappen (ed.), pp. 3–33.

Risse-Kappen, Thomas 1995b. 'Structures of Governance and Transnational Relations: What have We Learned?', in Risse-Kappen (ed.), pp. 280–313.

Risse-Kappen, Thomas (ed.) 1995c. *Bringing Transnational Relations Back In: Non-State Actors, Domestic Structures and International Institution*. Cambridge, MA: Cambridge University Press.

Risse-Kappen, Thomas 1996. 'Exploring the Nature of the Beast: International Relations Theory and Comparative Policy Analysis Meet the European Union', *Journal of Common Market Studies* 34: 53–80.

Rollo, Jim and Peter Holmes 2001. 'EU Commercial Policy after Nice', *EUI Briefing Paper*, No. 3, Sussex European Institute.

Rometsch, Dietrich 1996. 'The Federal Republic of Germany', in Rometsch and Wessels (eds), pp. 61–104.

Rometsch, Dietrich and Wessels, Wolfgang (eds) 1996. *The European Union and Member States: Towards Institutional Fusion?* Manchester: Manchester University Press.

Rosamond, Ben 2000. *Theories of European Integration*. London: Macmillan Press Ltd.

Rosamond, Ben 2001. 'Discourses of Globalization and European Identities', in Christiansen, Jørgensen and Wiener (eds), pp. 158–73.

Rosamond, Ben 2005. 'The Uniting of Europe and the Foundation of EU Studies: Revisiting the Neofunctionalism of Ernst B. Haas', *Journal of European Public Policy*, 12: 237–54.

Rosenau, Pauline M. 1992. *Post-Modernism and the Social Sciences. Insights, Inroads, and Intrusions*. Princeton, NJ: Princeton University Press.

Ross, George 1994. 'Inside The Delors Cabinet', *Journal of Common Market Studies* 32: 499–523.

Ross, George 1995. *Jacques Delors and European Integration*. Oxford: Polity Press.

Rupprecht, Reinhard 1997. 'Justiz und Inneres nach dem Amsterdamer Vertrag', *Integration* 20: 264–70.

Russell, Robert 1975. 'L'Engrenage, Collegial Style, and the Crisis Syndrome: Lessons from Monetary Policy in the European Community', *Journal of Common Market Studies* 13: 61–86.

Sabatier, Paul 1988. 'An Advocacy Coalition Framework of Policy Change and the Role of Policy-Oriented Learning Therein', *Policy Sciences* 21: 129–68.

Sabatier, Paul and Jenkins-Smith, Hank C. 1993. 'The Advocacy Coalition Framework: Assessment, Revisions, and Implications for Scholars and Practitioners', in Sabatier and Jenkins-Smith (eds), *Policy Change and Learning: An Advocacy Coalition Approach*. Boulder, CO, Oxford: Westview, pp. 211–45.

Sandholtz, Wayne 1992. *High-Tech Europe: The Politics of International Co-operation*. Berkeley, CA: University of California Press.

Sandholtz, Wayne 1993a. 'Institutions and Collective Action: The New Telecommunications in Western Europe', *World Politics* 45: 242–70.

Sandholtz, Wayne 1993b. 'Choosing Union: Monetary Politics and Maastricht', *International Organization* 47: 1–39.

Sandholtz, W. and Stone Sweet, A. 1998. *European Integration and Supranational Governance*. Oxford: Oxford University Press.

Sandholtz, Wayne and Zysman, John 1989. '1992: Recasting the European Bargain', *World Politics* 41: 95–128.

Santer, Jacques 1995. *Discours du Président Santer devant la Commission Institutionelle du Parlement Européen*. Brussels, 21 March.

Santer, Jacques 1996. *Avis de la Commission sur la CIG: Intervention M. Jacques Santer au Parlement Européen*, Speech/96/53. Brussels.

Sbragia, Alberta (ed.) 1992. *Europolitics: Institutions and Policy-making in the "New" European Community*. Washington, DC: The Brookings Institution.

Sbragia, Alberta 1993. 'EC Environmental Policy: Atypical Ambitions and Typical Problems?', in Cafruny and Rosenthal (eds), pp. 337–52.

Sbragia, Alberta 1994. 'From "Nation-State" to "Member-State": The Evolution of the European Community', in Lützeler, P. (ed.), 1994. *Europe after Maastricht: American and European Perspectives*. Providence: Berghahn Books, pp. 69–87.

Scharpf, Fritz 1988. 'The Joint-Decison Trap: Lessons from German Federalism and European Integration', *Public Administration* 66: 239–78.

Scheingold, Stuart 1965. *The Rule of Law in European Integration*. New Haven, CT: Yale University Press.

Scheinman, Lawrence and Feld, Werner 1972. 'The European Economic Community and National Civil Servants of the Member States', *International Organization* 26: 121–35.

Schelter, Kurt 1996. 'Innenpolitische Zusammenarbeit in Europa zwischen Maastricht und Regierungskonferenz 1996', *Aus Politik und Zeitgeschichte* B 1–2: 19–34.

Schermers, Henry, Fliterman, Cees, Kellermann, Alfred, Haersolte, Johan and van de Meent, Gert-Wim 1993. 'Report of the Conference on Free

Movement of Persons in Europe, 11–12 September 1992', in Schermers *et al.* (eds), pp. 521–46.

Schermers, Henry, Fliterman, Cees, Kellermann, Alfred, Haersolte, Johan and van de Meent, Gert-Wim (eds) 1993. *Free Movement of Persons in Europe: Legal Problems and Experiences*. Dordrecht: Nijhoff.

Scharpf, Fritz 1988. 'The Joint-Decision Trap: Lessons from German Federalism and European Integration', *Public Administration* **66**: 239–78.

Schimmelfennig, Frank 2001. 'The Community Trap: Liberal Norms, Rhetorical Action, and the Eastern Enlargement of the European Union', *International Organization* **55**: 47–80.

Schmitter, Philippe 1969. 'Three Neo-functional Hypotheses About International Integration', *International Organization* **23**: 161–6.

Schmitter, Philippe 1971. 'A Revised Theory of Regional Integration', Lindberg, Leon and Scheingold, Stuat (eds), pp. 232–64.

Schmitter, Philippe 1996a. 'Examining the Present Euro-Polity with the Help of Past Theories', in Marks, Scharpf, Schmitter and Streek (eds) pp. 1–14.

Schmitter, Philippe 1996b. 'Imagining the Future of the Euro-Polity with the Help of New Concepts', in Marks, Scharpf, Schmitter and Streek (eds) pp. 121–50.

Schmitter, Philippe 2000. *How to Democratize the European Union ... and Why Bother?*, London, MD: Roman and Littlefield.

Schmitter, Philippe C. 2004. 'Neo-Neofunctionalism', in Wiener and Diez (eds), 46–74.

Schnappauff, Klaus-Dieter 1998. 'Der Amsterdamer Vertrag – Neuregelungen der Zusammenarbeit im Bereich der Inneren Sicherheit', *Zeitschrift für Innere Sicherheit* **1**: 16–20.

Schneider, Gerald 1994. 'Getting Closer at Different Speed. Strategic Interaction in Widening European Integration', in Allan, P. and Schmidt, C. (eds), *Game Theory and International Relations*. Aldershot: Edward Elgar.

Schneider, Gerald and Aspinwall, Mark 2001a. 'Moving beyond Outworn Debates: A New Institutionalist Research Agenda', in Schneider and Aspinwall (eds), 177–87.

Schneider, Gerald and Aspinwall, Mark (eds) 2001b. *The Rules of Integration: Institutionalist Approaches to the Study of Europe*. Manchester and New York: Manchester University Press.

Schneider, Gerald and Cederman, Lars-Erik 1994. 'The Change of Tide in Political Cooperation: A Limited Information Model of European Integration', *International Organization* **48**: 633–62.

Scott, Dermot 1983. 'Adapting the Machinery of Central Government', in Coombes, David (ed.), *Ireland and the European Communities: Ten Years of Membership*. Dublin: Gill and Macmillan, pp. 68–88.

Searle, John R. 1995. 'The Construction of Social Reality' New York: Free Press.

Sedelmeier, Ulrich and Wallace, Helen 1996. 'Policies towards Central and Eastern Europe', in Wallace, H. and Wallace, W. (eds), pp. 353–87.

Serre, Françoise de la 1991. 'The EC and Central and Eastern Europe', in Hurwitz and Lequesne (eds), *The State of the European Community: Politics,*

Institutions and Debates in the Transition Years. Boulder, CO: Lynne Rienner Publishers, pp. 303–12.

Shaw, Jo 1996. 'European Union Legal Studies in Crisis? Towards a New Dynamic', *Oxford Journal of Legal Studies* 16: 231–53.

Silverman, David 1993. *Interpreting Qualitative Data: Methods for Analysing Talk, Text and Interpretation*. London: Sage.

Smelser, Neil 1995. *Reflections on the Methodology of Comparative Studies*, Paper Given at the European University Institute, SPS Department, Seminar on Comparative Political Institutions, 2 June.

Smith, Karen 1998. 'The Use of Political Conditionality in the EU's Relations with Third Countries: How Effective?' *European Foreign Affairs Review* 3: 253–74.

Smith, Karen 1999. *The Making of EU Foreign Policy: The Case of Eastern Europe*. London: Macmillan Press.

Smith, Michael and Woolcock, Stephen 1999. 'European Commercial Policy: A Leadership Role in the New Millennium?', *European Foreign Affairs Review* 4: 439–62.

Smith, Steve 1996. 'Positivism and Beyond', in Smith, *et al.* (eds), pp. 11–46.

Smith, Steve 2001. 'Social Constructivisms and European Studies', in Christiansen, Jørgensen and Wiener (eds), pp. 189–98.

Smith, Steve and Baylis, John 1997. 'Introduction', in Baylis, John and Smith, Steve (eds), *The Globalisation of World Politics: An Introduction to International Relations*. Oxford: Oxford University Press, pp. 1–12.

Smith, Steve, Booth, Ken and Marysia Zalewski (eds) 1996. *International Relations Theory: Positivism and Beyond*, Cambridge: Cambridge University Press.

Spanish Government 1995. *1996 Intergovernmental Conference – Discussion Document*, SN 1709/95.

Spanish Presidency 1995. *Proposition de la Présidence: Arrangement Entre le Conseil, les États Membres et la Commission sur les Modalitér de Participation aux Travaux de l'OMC*, SN 4697/1/95 REV 1. Brussels.

Spence, David 1993. 'The Role of the National Civil Service in European Lobbying: The British case', in Mazey and Richardson (eds), pp. 47–73.

Standing Committee of Experts on International Immigration, Refugee and Criminal Law 1995. *Proposals for the Amendment of the Treaty on European Union at the IGC in 1996*. Utrecht.

Standing Committee of Experts on International Immigration, Refugee and Criminal Law 1997. *Draft Revision of the EU Treaties : Response on the Dublin II Outline and the Addendum of the Dutch Presidency*. Utrecht.

Standing Committee of Experts on International Immigration, Refugee and Criminal Law, Statewatch, The Immigration Law Practitioners Association and The European Council of Refugees and Exiles 2002. 'Joint Submission to Working Group X', Utrecht and London, 14 November.

Starting Line Group 1994. *The Starting Point: Proposal for Amending the European Community Treaty*. Brussels.

Statewatch 1999. *The Impact of the Amsterdam Treaty on the Third Pillar*. London: draft.

Steunenberg, B., Schmidtchen, D. and Koboldt, C. 1996. 'Policymaking, Comitology and the Balance of Power in the European Union', *International Review of Law and Economics* **16**: 329–44.

Steunenberg, B., Schmidtchen, D. and Koboldt, C. 1997. 'Comitology and the Balance of Power in the European Union: A Game Theoretic Approach', in Dieter Schmidtchen and Robert Cooter (eds), *Constitutional Law and Economics of the European Union*. Cheltenham, Gloucestershire: Edward Elgar, 37–66.

Stone Sweet, Alec and Caporaso, James A. 1998. 'From Free Trade to Supranational Polity: The European Court and Integration,' in Sandholtz and Stone Sweet (eds), pp. 92–133.

Stone Sweet, Alec and Sandholtz, Wayne 1997. 'European Integration and Supranational Governance', *Journal of European Public Policy* **4**: 297–317.

Stuth, Reinhard 2001. 'Der Vertrag von Nizza – eine kritische Analyse', *Zukunftsforum Politik – Konrad-Adenauer-Stiftung* **21**, February.

Sutherland, Peter 1997. 'Has the IGC Succeeded?', in European Policy Centre 1997b, pp. 29–30.

Taifel, Henri and Forgas, Joseph 1981. 'Social Categorisation: Cognitions, Values and Groups', in Forgas, Joseph (ed.) 1981. *Social Cognition*. London: Academic Press, pp. 113–40.

Tallberg, Jonas 2004. 'The Power of the Presidecy: Brokerage, Efficiency and Distribution in EU Negotiations', *Journal of Common Market Studies* **42** pp. 999–1022.

Tarrow, Sidney 1995. 'Bridging the Quantitative–Qualitative Divide in Political Science', *American Political Science Review* **89**: 471–4.

Taylor, Paul 1983. *The Limits of European Integration*. London: Croom Helms.

Taylor, Paul 1989. 'The New Dynamics of EC in the 1980s', in Lodge, J. (ed.), *The European Community and the Challenge of the Future*. New York: St. Martin's Press.

Taylor, Paul 1990. 'Functionalism: The Approach of David Mitrany', in Groom, A. J. R. and Taylor, Paul (eds), Frameworks for International Co-operation. London: Pinter, pp. 125–38.

Tesch, Renata 1990. *Qualitative Research: Analysis Types and Software Tools*. New York: Farmer Press.

The Article 133 Information Group 2002. 'Article 133 and the Nice Treaty', 4 October, http://www.indymedia.ie/article133/ (last accessed on 03 July 2006).

Timmermans, Christiaan 1987. 'Common Commercial Policy (Article 113 EEC) and International Trade in Services', in Caporti, Ehlermann, Frohwein, Jacobs, Koopmans and Kovar (eds), *Du droit international au droit de l'intégration: Liber Amicorum Pierre Pescatore*. Baden-Baden: Nomos, pp. 675–89.

Timmermans, C. W. A. 1993. 'Free Movement of Persons and the Division of Powers between the Community and Its Member States – Why do it the Intergovernmental Way?', in Schermers *et al.* (eds), pp. 352–68.

Tranholm-Mikkelsen, Jeppe 1991. 'Neo-functionalism: Obstinate or Obsolete? A Reappraisal in the Light of the New Dynamism of the EC', *Millenium* **20**: 1–22.

Trans European Policy Studies Association 1996. *Revision of Maastricht: Implementation and Proposals for Reform: A Survey of National Views*, Paper 6.

Trondal, Jarle 2001. 'Is There any Social Constructivist – Institutionalist Divide? Unpacking Social Mechanisms Affecting Representational Roles among EU Decision-makers', *Journal of European Public Policy* **8**: 1–23.

Trondal, Jarle 2002. 'Beyond the EU Membership–Nonmembership Dichotomy? Supranational Identities among National EU Decision-makers', *Journal of European Public Policy* **9**: 468–87.

Tsebelis, George 1994. 'The Power of the European Parliament as a Conditional Agenda Setter', *American Political Science Review* **88**: 128–42.

Tyszkiewicz, Zygmunt 1997. 'Employment and Competitiveness', in European Policy Centre 1997b, p. 52.

Uçarer, Emek, M. 2001. 'Managing Asylum and European Integration: Expanding Spheres of Exclusion?, *Policy and International Studies* **2**: 288–304.

UNICE 1997. 'UNICE Message to the Amsterdam Summit', Brussels, 6 June.

UNICE 2000a. 'Preliminary UNICE Statement in View of the Intergovernmental Conference', Brussels, 3 December.

UNICE 2000b. 'UNICE Position on Extension of Qualified Majority Voting in the Context of the Intergovernmental Conference', Brussels, 11 October, http://www.ciginfo.net/CIGinfo/en/igcdoc/default.htm (last accessed on 15 July 2004).

UNICE 2002. *Convention on the Future of Europe*, position on the EU Convention. Brussels, 17 June.

United Kingdom Government 1996a. *A Partnership of Nations: A British Approach to the European Union Intergovernmental Conference 1996*. London: HMSO.

United Kingdom Government 1996b. *Third Pillar Objectives and Scope of Application*, Conference of the Representatives of the Governments of the Member States, CONF 3918/96. Brussels.

United Nations 1995. *World Investment Report: Transnational Corporations and Competitiveness*. New York: UNCTC.

Van Dijck, Pitou and Faber, Gerrit (eds) 1996. *Challenges to the New World Trade Organisation*. Boston, MA: Kluwer Law International.

Van Outrive, Lode 1995. 'Commentary on the Third Pillar and the 1996 Intergovernmental Conference: What should be on the Agenda?', in Bieber and Monar (eds), pp. 391–6.

Van Schendelen, M. 1996. '"The Council Decides": Does the Council Decide?', *Journal of Common Market Studies* **34**: 531–48.

Van Waarden, Frans and Drahos, Michaela 2002. 'Courts and (Epistemic) Communities in the Convergence of Competition Policies', *Journal of European Public Policy* **9**: 913–34.

Verdun, Amy 1999. 'The Role of the Delors Committee in the Creation of EMU: An Epistemic Community?', *Journal of European Public Policy* **6**: 308–28.

Vitorino, Antonio 2001. 'A la Conférence des Présidents des commissions compéntes en matière d'immigration des parlements de l'UE', Sènate belge, Speech/01/608, Brussels, 4 December 2001.

Vitorino, Antonio 2002. *Renforcer l'espace der liberté, de sécurité et de justice*, Intervention at the European Convention, Speech/02/261. Brussels, 6 June.

Wallace, Helen 1983. 'Negotiation, Conflict, and Compromise: The Elusive Pursuit of Common Policies', in Wallace, H., Wallace, W., and Webb, C. (eds), pp. 43–80.

Wallace, Helen 1985a. 'EC Membership and the Presidency: A Comparative Perspective', in Nuallain (ed.), pp. 261–79.

Wallace, Helen 1985b. *Europe: The Challenge of Diversity*, Chatham House Papers, No. 29. London: Routledge & Kegan Paul for the RIIA.

Wallace, Helen 1986. 'Bilateral, Trilateral and Multilateral Negotiations in the European Community', in Morgan and Bray (eds).

Wallace, Helen 1990. 'Making Multilateral Negotiations Work', in Wallace, W. (ed.), pp. 213–28.

Wallace, Helen and Wallace, William (eds) 1996. *Policy-Making in the European Union*, third edition. Oxford: Oxford University Press.

Wallace, Helen, Wallace, William and Webb, Carole (eds) 1983. *Policy Making in the European Community*, second edition. Chichester: John Wiley & Sons Ltd.

Wallace, William 1990a. 'Introduction: The Dynamics of European Integration', in Wallace, W. (ed.), pp. 1–24.

Wallace, William (ed.) 1990b. *The Dynamics of European Integration*. London: Pinter.

Webb, Carole 1983. 'Theoretical Perspectives and Problems', in Wallace, H. *et al.* (eds), pp. 1–41.

Weber, Max 1949. *The Methodology of the Social Sciences*, New York: Free Press.

Weiler, Joseph 1981. 'The Community System: The Dual Character of Supranationalism' *Yearbook of European Law* 1: 268–306.

Weiler, Joseph 1991. 'The Transformation of Europe', *Yale Law Journal* 100: 2403–83.

Weiler, Joseph 1994. 'Journey to an Unknown Destination: A Retrospective and Prospective of the European Court of Justice in the Area of Political Integration', in Bulmer, Simon and Scott, Andrew,(eds) *Economic and Political Integration in Europe*, pp. 131–60.

Wendt, Alexander E. 1999. *Social Theory of International Politics*. Cambridge, MA: Cambridge University Press.

Wessels, Wolfgang 1994. 'The Third Pillar: Plea for a Single Theoretical Research Agenda', in Monar and Morgan (ed.), pp. 227–36.

Wessels, Wolfgang 1996. 'Institutions of the EU System: Models of explanation', in Rometsch and Wessels (eds), pp. 20–36.

Wessels, Wolfgang 1997. 'An Ever Closer Fusion? A Dynamic Macropolitical View on Integration Processes', *Journal of Common Market Studies* 35: 267–99.

Wessels, Wolfgang 2005. 'Keynote Article: The Constitutional Treaty – Three Readings from a Fusion Perspective', *Journal of Common Market Studies*, Annual Review, **43**: 11–36.

Wessels, Wolfgang and Rometsch, Dietrich 1996. 'Conclusion: European Union and National Institutions', in Rometsch and Wessels (eds), pp. 328–65.

Westlake, Martin 1994a. *A Modern Guide to the European Parliament*. London: Pinter.

Westlake, Martin 1994b. 'The Commission and the Parliament', in Edwards and Spence (eds), pp. 225–48.

Westlake, Martin 1995. *The Council of the European Union*. London: Catermill.

Wiener, Antje and Diez, Thomas (eds) 2004. *European Integration Theory*. Oxford: Oxford University Press.

Wiener, Antje and Diez, Thomas 2004. 'Taking Stock of Integration Theory', in Wiener and Diez (eds), pp. 235–48.

Wight, C. 2002. 'Philosophy of Science and International Relations', in Carlsnaes, W., Risse, T., and Simmons, B. A. (eds) 2002. *Handbook of International Relations*. London: Sage, pp. 23–51.

Wincott, Daniel 1995. 'Institutional Interaction and European Integration: Towards an Everyday Critique of Liberal Intergovernmentalism', *Journal of Common Market Studies* **33**: 597–609.

Woolcock, Stephen and Hodges, Michael 1996. 'EU Policy in the Uruguay Round', in Wallace, H. and Wallace, W. (eds), pp. 301–24.

WTO 2004. 'The Doha Work Programme – Text of the "July package" ', (1 August), http://www.wto.org/english/tratop_e/dda_e/draft_text_gc_dg_31-july04_e.htm (last accessed on 03 July 2006).

Wurzel, Rüdiger 1996. 'The Role of the EU Presidency in the Environmental Field: Does it Make a Difference which Member State runs the Presidency?', *Journal of European Public Policy* **3**: 272–91.

Young, Alasdair R. 2001. 'Extending European Cooperation: The European Union and the 'New' International Trade Agenda', *EUI Working Papers*, RSC No. 2001/12.

Zito, Anthony R. 2001. 'Epistemic Communities, Collective Entrepreneurship and European Integration', *Journal of European Public Policy* **8**: 585–603.

Zypries, Brigitte 2003. 'Der Raum der Freiheit, der Sicherheit und des Rechts in der Verfassung der Europäischen Union', Lecture at the Humboldt University, Berlin, 27 May.

Index